While the First, or 'Great', English Civil War of 1642-6 was largely contested at regional and county level, in often hard-fought and long-lasting local campaigns, historians often still continue to dwell on the well-known major battles, such as Edgehill and Naseby, and the prominent national leaders. To help redress this imbalance, *To Settle The Crown: Waging Civil War in Shropshire, 1642-1648* provides the most detailed bipartisan study published to date of how the war was actually organised and conducted at county level. This book examines the practicalities, the 'nuts and bolts', of contemporary warfare by reconstructing the war effort of Royalists and Parliamentarians in Shropshire, an English county on the borderland of Wales – a region that witnessed widespread fighting. Shropshire was contested during the First Civil War – when it became one of the most heavily garrisoned counties in England and Wales – and experienced renewed conflict during the Second Civil War of 1648.

Based on a Doctoral thesis, and therefore drawing primarily on contemporary sources revealing much new information, *To Settle The Crown* examines key aspects of the military history of the English Civil Wars: allegiance and motivation; leadership and administration; recruitment and the form of armed forces; military finance; logistics; and the nature and conduct of the fighting. Furthermore, while previous studies have tended to concentrate on the Parliamentarians, the comparatively plentiful evidence from Shropshire has allowed the Royalist war effort there to be reconstructed in rare detail. This book reveals for the first time the extent of military activity in Shropshire, describing the sieges, skirmishes and larger engagements, while reflecting on the nature of warfare elsewhere across Civil War England and Wales. In also providing a social context to the military history of the period, it explains how Royalist and Parliamentarian activists set local government on a wartime footing, and how the populace generally became involved in the administrative and material tasks of war effort.

Extensively illustrated, fully referenced to an extensive bibliography, and including a useful review of Civil War historiography, *To Settle The Crown: Waging Civil War in Shropshire, 1642-1648* is a significant fresh approach to the military history of the English Civil Wars.

Dr. Jonathan Worton has a life-long and wide-ranging research and personal interest in all matters historical. In studying for the PhD upon which this book is based, he has in particular researched in depth the military and social history of the mid-seventeenth century English Civil Wars in and around the borderlands of Wales. He has lectured and spoken on aspects of the period on educational programmes and for various bodies and organisations , and has had several articles published. He has acted as an advisor and co-curator on heritage projects, and is currently an independent researcher, writer and educator. Prior to gaining a Masters Degree in Military History – setting him on a fresh career path – Jonathan had spent 20 years in industry as a marketing, publicity and graphic design professional. He lives with his family in Shropshire.

To Settle the Crown

Waging Civil War in Shropshire 1642-1648

Jonathan Worton

Helion & Company Limited

Helion & Company Limited
26 Willow Road
Solihull
West Midlands
B91 1UE
England
Tel. 0121 705 3393
Fax 0121 711 4075
Email: info@helion.co.uk
Website: www.helion.co.uk
Twitter: @helionbooks
Visit our blog http://blog.helion.co.uk/

Published by Helion & Company 2016
Designed and typeset by Farr out Publications, Wokingham, Berkshire
Cover designed by Paul Hewitt, Battlefield Design (www.battlefield-design.co.uk)
Printed by Short Run Press, Exeter, Devon

Front cover: A reconstruction painting depicting Sir William Vaughan leading the all-mounted Royalist force that early on the morning of 5 July 1645 routed the Parliamentarians besieging the garrison of High Ercall Hall. Painting by Peter Dennis © Helion & Company 2016. Rear cover: Moreton Corbet Castle.

ISBN 978-1-910777-98-5

British Library Cataloguing-in-Publication Data.
A catalogue record for this book is available from the British Library.

For details of other military history titles published by Helion & Company
Limited contact the above address, or visit our website: http://www.helion.co.uk.

We always welcome receiving book proposals from prospective authors.

Contents

List of Illustrations

Colour plates

List of Maps

List of Tables

List of Abbreviations

A&O	*Acts and Ordinances of the Interregnum, 1642-1660*, eds. C.H. Firth and R.S. Rait, 3 volumes (London, 1911).
BCHRC	Bishop's Castle Heritage Resource Centre, Bishop's Castle.
BDL	The Bodleian Library, Oxford.
BRL	The British Library, London.
CPCC	*Calendar of the Proceedings of the Committee for Compounding*, ed. M.A. Everett Green, 5 volumes (London, 1889).
CPCM	*Calendar of the Proceedings of the Committee for Advance of Money*, ed. M.A. Everett Green, 3 volumes (London, 1888).
CSPD	*Calendar of State Papers, Domestic Series, of the Reign of Charles I, 1625-1649*, ed. W.D. Hamilton [*et al.*], 23 volumes (London, 1858-97).
HHL	Henry Huntington Library, San Marino, California.
HMC	Historical Manuscripts Commission.
HRO	Herefordshire Record Office, Hereford.
IO List	*A List of Officers Claiming the Sixty Thousand Pounds, &c. Granted by his Majesty for the Relief of His Loyal and Indigent Party Truly* (London, 1663).
JHC	*Journals of the House of Commons*.
JHL	*Journals of the House of Lords*.
LBWB	*The Letter Books of Sir William Brereton*, ed. R.N. Dore, 2 volumes (Gloucester, 1984, 1990).
Mss	Manuscripts.
NAM	The National Army Museum, London.
NLW	The National Library of Wales, Aberystwyth.
NRO	Northamptonshire Record Office, Northampton.
ODNB	*Oxford Dictionary of National Biography*, eds. H.C.G. Matthews and B. Harrison, 40 volumes (Oxford, 2004).
OT List	'A list of the names of the Indigent Officers certified out of the county of Salop by His Majesty's Commissioners appointed by the Act of Parliament for the purpose', in 'Ottleiana: or letters & c. relating to Shropshire chiefly to Sir Francis Ottley, in, Anon., *Collectanea Topographica & Geneaologica* (London, 1841).

'Ottley Papers'	'The Ottley Papers Relating to the Civil War', ed. W. Phillips, in *TSANHS*, 1894, 1895, 1896.
ROP	*The Royalist Ordnance Papers 1642-1646,* ed. I. Roy, 2 parts (Banbury, 1963, 1975).
SA	Shropshire Archives, Shrewsbury.
SRO	Staffordshire Record Office, Stafford.
TNA	The National Archives, London.
TSANHS	*Transactions of the Shropshire Archaeological and Natural History Society.*
TSAS	*Transactions of the Shropshire Archaeological Society.*
WRO	Warwickshire Record Office, Warwick.
WSL	William Salt Library, Stafford.

Acknowledgements

While researching and writing factual history is inevitably a mostly solitary pursuit, I am grateful to others for their help in bringing this work to fruition. First and foremost I wish to thank Professor Peter Gaunt, as the main supervisor of my Doctoral studies at the University of Chester, for both his enthusiastic support and constructive criticism of my work resulting in the PhD thesis from which this book is mostly derived. I am also grateful to Professor Malcolm Wanklyn, for this book is the better for incorporating the minor corrections he recommended should be made to the thesis as a result of his examination. My thanks also to the editorial team at Helion & Company, for their light touch in shaping the thesis into book form with very little lost to the cutting room floor. I am appreciative of Peter Reavill's contribution to the appendix, and also grateful to Keith Pointon and to Shropshire Council/ Shropshire Museums, respectively for taking and for allowing the reproduction of the accompanying photographs. It is customary of authors of historical works to thank the staff of public record offices for performing, what are, after all, their salaried duties, but I would like to single out and thank the staff, past and present, of Shropshire Archives for their help and always courteous service provided in the course of my research. On a more personal note, I am indebted to Barry Oakes, for both his friendship and for so generously providing 'free quarter' during my research visits to London. Last but far from least, I am of course thankful to my family for their forbearance for so long in putting up with the echoes of seventeenth-century military history, and in particular to Beau Boughen, my father-in-law, for stoically proof-reading early drafts of the thesis.

This book is dedicated to my late father Eric John Worton, an able and enthusiastic hobby historian and amateur archaeologist, who instilled in me as a young boy a life-long passion for history.

Explanatory Notes and Conventions

Dates are given according to the Old Style (Julian) Calendar, in use across the British Isles at the time of the Civil Wars. However, the New Year is taken to begin on 1 January, not 25 March as was customary then.

Spellings in contemporary manuscript and printed sources have been modernised to aid readability along with some minimal intervention in punctuation. However, spelling of the titles of contemporary publications has been retained.

Contemporary monetary values have been quoted throughout. Thus 12 pennies (12d) = one shilling (1s); 20 shillings = one pound sterling (£1); £1 = 240d. To put these amounts into some local pre-Civil War context in terms of personal income, in 1640/1 the day rate paid by the corporation of Shrewsbury, Shropshire's county town, to skilled workmen such as carpenters and ordinary masons was 8d including food and drink or 14d without, meanwhile the respective rates for day labourers were 4d and 8d. At the opposite end of the social scale, among the county gentry proposed as suitably wealthy candidates for the shrievalty of Shropshire in 1632 were the future leading Royalists Thomas Wolrych of Dudmaston and John Weld of Willey, whose respective annual incomes were then estimated as £1,200 and £3,000.[1]

Finally, while the author acknowledges the vigorous scholarly debate since the turn of the twentieth century concerned with whether or not the warfare widespread across the archipelago of the British Isles from 1639 into the early 1650s were British civil wars, or, indeed, were wars fought between three kingdoms (or four nations, if Wales is considered as a separate land), because it is concerned with the conflict as if affected an English county this book keeps the traditional convention of classifying the period as the English Civil Wars.

1   M. Reed, 'Early Seventeenth-Century Wage Assessments for the Borough of Shrewsbury', *TSAS*, LV (1954-6), pp. 140-1; HHL, Ellesmere Mss, 7114.

Chronology

Summary of main events in Shropshire during the First and Second English Civil Wars, 1642-8

1642	Summer	King Charles I's supporters gain ascendancy in Shropshire.
	September–October	The King arrives in Shropshire and his field army occupies the county for around three weeks.
1643	January–June	Royalist Shropshire forces engaged in cross-border skirmishing with Cheshire Parliamentarians. Royalists defeated in Shropshire at Whitchurch and Market Drayton.
	September	First Parliamentarian garrison in Shropshire established at Wem. Royalists defeated at Loppington.
	October	Royalist army under Lord Capel defeated in failing to take Wem.
1644	January	Royalists defeated at Ellesmere.
	February–April	Resurgence in Royalist fortunes in Shropshire under Prince Rupert's leadership. Parliamentarians lose several garrisons and in March are defeated in the field at Market Drayton and near Longford/Lilleshall.
	May	Prince Rupert leaves for the north with his partly Shropshire-based field army.
	June–July	Parliamentarians capture Oswestry. Royalists defeated outside Oswestry. Parliamentarian advance attempted against Royalist-held Shrewsbury.
	September	Parliamentarian forces from Shropshire invade neighbouring Montgomeryshire. Royalist regional army, including units from Shropshire, defeated at the battle of Montgomery.
1645	January–March	Royalist military administration disrupted by a rival gentry-led association. Armed civilian activity in south Shropshire by the so-called clubmen. Parliamentarians capture Shrewsbury, the regional Royalist headquarters, on 22 February.
	June–September	Parliamentarian advances result in the widespread reduction of Royalist garrisons. Royalists defeated in the field near Stokesay in July and at Bishop's Castle in August. Parliamentarians

		defeated in early July in Corvedale and at High Ercall during a brief Royalist counter-offensive.
	November	Significant raiding activity by Royalist forces.
1646	March	High Ercall Hall and Bridgnorth, two of three Royalist garrisons remaining in Shropshire, fall to the Parliamentarians. Royalists continue to hold the castle at Bridgnorth.
	April-May	Bridgnorth Castle besieged and surrendered to Parliamentarians. Parliamentarians invest Ludlow, the last Royalist garrison in Shropshire.
	June	With the surrender of Ludlow Castle on 1 June the war in Shropshire ends.
1648	Summer	Royalist uprisings attempted in Shropshire in the name of King Charles and the Scottish Engagement suppressed by the Parliamentary county forces

Maps charting the course of both Civil Wars in Shropshire

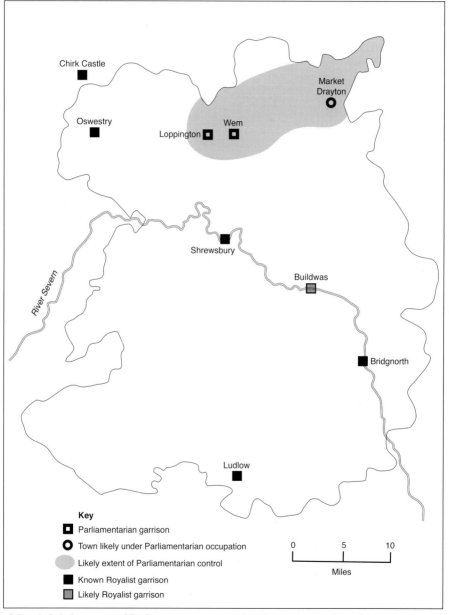

Map 1: Likely extent of Parliamentarian control in Shropshire in later September 1643.

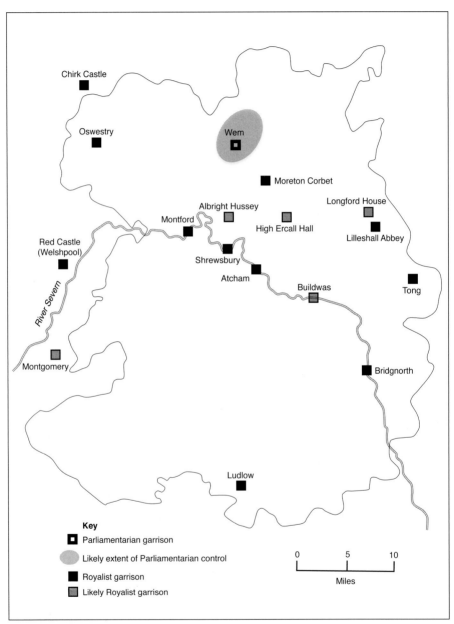

Map 2: Likely extent of Parliamentarian control in Shropshire in April 1644.

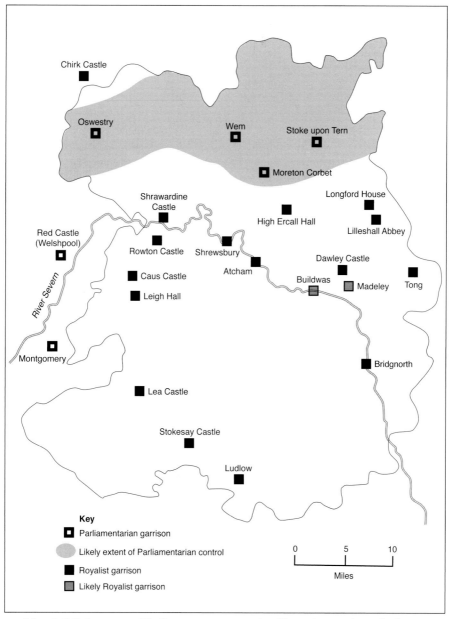

Map 3: Likely extent of Parliamentarian control in Shropshire at the end of 1644.

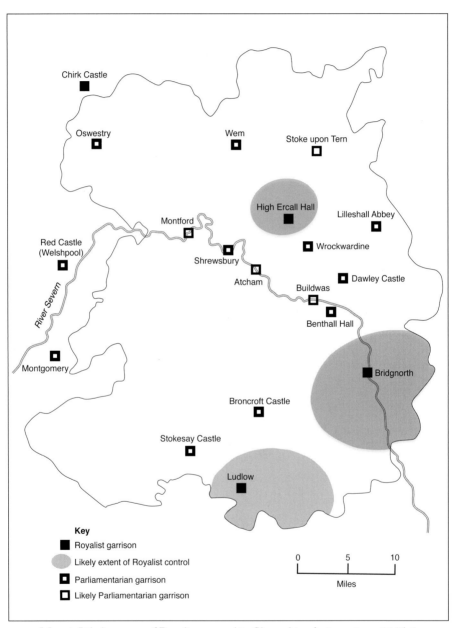

Map 4: Likely extent of Royalist control in Shropshire during winter 1645-6.

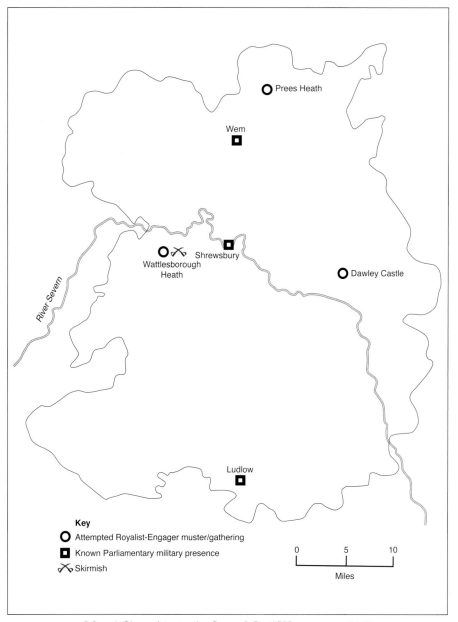

Map 5: Shropshire in the Second Civil War, summer 1648.

Introduction

The King told me that this county put him upon his legs, and if we can settle the Crown upon his head, it will be an honour to us and our posterity.

With these words, a rallying call for further military effort in the cause of King Charles I, on 1 February 1645 Colonel Sir Francis Ottley, the King's high sheriff for the county of Shropshire, concluded an order requiring leading Royalists in the south of the county to enlist 300 local men into the militia.[1]

Ottley alluded to notions of duty and staunch loyalty among the King's followers, for their continued support in order to help defeat Parliament militarily and so settle Charles's crown by restoring his kingship. A primary cause of what would become known to history as the First, or Great, English Civil War had been the actions by Parliament from late 1640 into 1642 to curb and sanction King Charles's prerogative powers. Hence, that the war was being fought to settle the Crown – to challenge or to protect the authority that was traditionally accepted to reside in the monarchy – is a useful metaphor for the motivation of both sides in the conflict. The outcome of the war would also determine the settlement of the form of the established Church, and upholding strongly held views in religious practice was perhaps the main principled reason for taking up arms on both sides. Sir Francis Ottley was one of King Charles's leading supporters in Shropshire. He was on personal terms with the monarch, and had been rewarded with a knighthood for his unswerving loyalty. Ottley's further call to arms after more than two and a half years of civil war alluded to the summer and early autumn of 1642, to the outbreak of hostilities between King and Parliament. Shropshire by becoming a Royalist county had then indeed helped to set the monarch 'upon his legs', when militarily his cause had seemed unsteady.

In August 1642 King Charles had moved south into the English East Midlands from York, the city having become his headquarters after his abandonment of London that January. On 22 August the royal standard was ceremonially raised at Nottingham Castle, an act that can now be seen to have in effect marked the formal declaration of war by Charles I against Parliament and its supporters (although in fact armed clashes between the opposing camps had occurred in several shires since June, and the conflict had already claimed a number of casualties).[2] But in early September

---

1   'Ottley Papers' (1896), p. 272.
2   P. Gaunt, *The English Civil War: A Military History* (London, 2014), pp. 52-65.

1. The way in which King Charles I (1600-1649) was depicted in the contemporary popular press: an illustration printed from a woodcut.

King Charles's position in the East Midlands became insecure, when Parliament's own field army, under the command of its lord general, the Earl of Essex, cautiously advanced into Northamptonshire. With the possibility of being cut off from Wales and its adjoining English shires – where he had strong support, and would gain substantial reinforcements by regiments being raised there on his behalf – and of being defeated by Essex's much larger army, in mid-September the King shifted his position to Shropshire.

He arrived there unopposed as a result of the efforts over the previous seven or so weeks of his active local supporters, notable among them Francis Ottley, then a wealthy but untitled gentleman. The King's party, with relative unanimity among the gentry and a degree of wider popular support, had, as Morrill has put it, engineered a 'solidly Royalist front' in Shropshire that overawed local Parliamentarian dissent.[3] Accordingly, leaving Derby on 13 September and marching via Staffordshire, on 19 September King Charles with his army arrived in Shropshire and paused at Wellington, a small market town.[4] There in a carefully staged address before his army and those of his Shropshire supporters who had made the journey to welcome him, the King read his standing orders of war to the soldiers and then delivered his Protestation, a manifesto stating his war aims that was later widely circulated in print. Charles pledged before God and to 'the utmost of my power' to:

3   J. Morrill, *Revolt in the Provinces: The People of England and the Tragedy of Civil War, 1630-1648* (Harlow, 1994), p. 66.
4   Sir Edward Walker, *Iter Carolinum* (1660), p. 3.

Maintain the true reformed Protestant religion established in the Church of England […] to maintain the just privileges and freedom of Parliament and to govern by the known laws of the land […] and particularly to observe inviolably the laws conferred to me by this Parliament. In the mean while, if this time of war, and the great necessity and straits I am now driven to, beget any violation of those I hope it shall be imputed by God and man to the authors of this war, and not to me who have earnestly laboured for the preservation of the peace of this kingdom.[5]

The next day the King entered Shrewsbury, the county town, which became his headquarters for the next three weeks. Based there he was able to organise, and by receiving the anticipated reinforcements, to considerably increase his army without enemy interference. Charles I marched from Shrewsbury on 12 October, leading from Shropshire the enlarged field army that on more or less equal terms fought the Earl of Essex's army at Edgehill in Warwickshire on 23 October 1642, in the first pitched battle of the English Civil Wars. The King's sojourn in Shropshire had been a vital breathing space, time allowing an effective army to take on Parliament to be gathered and financed. However, other than sometimes acknowledging the importance of the Parliamentarians' capture of Shrewsbury on 22 February 1645 – a damaging loss to the Royalists of an important supply base, and for almost two and a half years their regional headquarters – it is with the end of King Charles's stay in autumn 1642 that Shropshire usually disappears from the pages of general histories of the Civil Wars.

None of the major set-piece battles of the Wars would be fought there. However, Shropshire lay amid a widely fought-over region, encompassing parts of the Principality, and the English shires of the Marches and the western Midlands. King Charles left Shropshire a Royalist county in mid-October 1642, and although Royalist forces there had been engaged with the Cheshire Parliamentarians intermittently since January 1643, the war on Shropshire soil began in earnest that September. For it was then that some of the county's leading Parliamentarians, who had fled upon the Royalist takeover a year before, returned with their own and allied armed forces to plant Parliament's first military foothold in thitherto Royalist territory by occupying and fortifying Wem, an unremarkable northerly market town.

While the military situation in the county thereafter often reflected the ebb and flow of the wider war, there developed in Shropshire a prolonged and often intense local war of attrition. Since the major field armies did not campaign there, the fighting in Shropshire had a distinctly insular nature, characterised – to simplify in the broadest terms a struggle that lasted almost two and three-quarter years – by Royalist defence and counter-attack against intermittent Parliamentarian advances across the county on a generally southerly front. As a result of the progressive military collapse of King Charles's cause across England and Wales, the First Civil War ended in Shropshire on 1 June 1646 with the formal surrender of Ludlow Castle, the last Royalist stronghold in the county. The military operations in Shropshire in summer 1648 during the Second English Civil War were on a far smaller scale, when the ill-coordinated uprisings attempted by local and other regional Royalists were suppressed

5   J. Rushworth, *Historical Collections of Private Passages of State*, 8 vols. (1721), V, p. 21.

by the Parliamentarian county regime.

In introducing his book *The Great Civil War in Shropshire, 1642-1649* – one of two other general histories of the county war published to date – in 1926 Farrow wrote that 'Shropshire epitomised in a peculiar way the struggle of the whole English nation. Within the borders of this one county – better perhaps than anywhere else – can be seen the Great Civil War in miniature'.[6] To present any county as an exemplar or as a microcosm of the First English Civil War is contentious. Many shires were divided in allegiance and witnessed widespread and often heavy fighting. However, Farrow was right to suggest that the eventful and protracted course of the conflict in Shropshire merited further scrutiny.

This book, then, sets out to shed new light on the military history of Civil War Shropshire. It also intends to further understanding of the nature of warfare in England and Wales at this time. However, this is not another straightforward historical narrative of a county war – although from it readers will certainly achieve an understanding of the course of both civil wars in Shropshire. Instead, by six themed chapters forming a series of interlinked but also discrete and self-sustaining essays, this book sets out to present the arguably more varied and interesting story of the nature of war effort during the English Civil Wars by taking Shropshire's experience as an example.

In the mid-seventeenth century the phrase 'war effort' would have been unknown, although its meaning and effects would have been understood only too well. War effort may be defined as the sum of the coordinated actions by which military operations are conducted and sustained in furtherance of the political and military object of war. Given this definition, war effort provides the broad context in which to consider the home front as well as the front line, and vital activities such as leadership and administration, the organisation of armed forces, logistics and finance. Other factors – less distinct, perhaps, than overtly military concerns – such as economics, allegiance, and political and religious motivations may, moreover, be addressed in the wider ambit of war effort.

Turning for a definition to *On War*, the seminal and still outstanding examination of armed conflict, we find that Clausewitz does not conceptualise war effort. But his explanation of 'the art of war in its widest sense', as including 'all activities that exist for the sake of war, such as the creation of fighting forces, their raising, armament, equipment and training' comes close to the meaning of war effort. Furthermore, Clausewitz acknowledged the vital importance of the 'preparations' of 'the fighting forces', in 'such matters as artillery, fortification […] elementary tactics, as well as all the organisation and administration'. Accordingly, this book addresses these and other actions concerned with military effectiveness within the context of war effort.[7]

Most historians of the Civil Wars who have considered war effort in passing or in more detail have, rightly, stressed its social impact, upon daily life and economic activity. Both Tennant and Wroughton, for example, took English regional perspectives to view the effects of war on society and on individuals. Their approach to war effort was to see taxation, recruitment and requisitioning as the cause of much disruption,

6   W.J. Farrow, *The Great Civil War in Shropshire, 1642-49* (Shrewsbury, 1926), preface.
7   C. von Clausewitz, *On War*, (eds.) M. Howard and P. Paret (Princeton, 1989), pp. 127, 131-2.

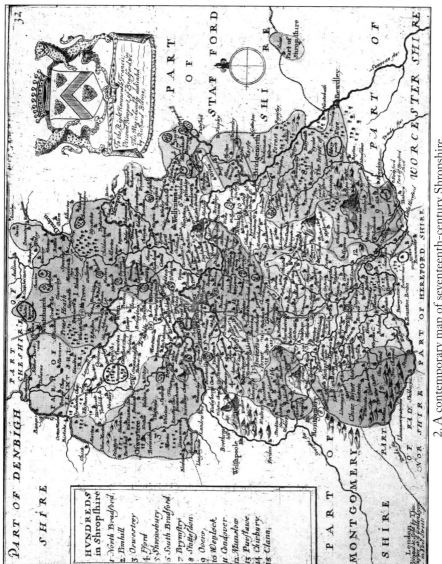

2. A contemporary map of seventeenth-century Shropshire.

suffering and damage. Pennington and also Bennett have viewed civilian hardship at national level in much the same way. Bennett's *The Civil Wars Experienced* drew on widespread anecdotal evidence to illustrate the repercussions of the conflict for the common people of England, Wales, Scotland and Ireland.[8]

This book does not underrate the enormous economic and social dislocation caused by the Civil Wars. Indeed, it often portrays the pervading effects of war effort on the livelihood of the people of Shropshire, in terms of the demands made upon them, and in their interaction with the soldiery. However, this is a military rather than a social history of the period, concerned in particular with the mobilisation of resources for war. Accordingly, it explains the war effort in terms of its military purpose and necessity. In the event, the First Civil War across England and Wales became a lengthy war of attrition because both sides were able to sustain war effort by systematically organising human and economic resources.

Shropshire is viewed here as a case study of what Hutton, in his own wider-ranging regional view of the Royalist war effort, termed the 'collection of tasks' that comprised war effort during the English Civil Wars.[9] The county is considered as a theatre of operations during the First English Civil War of 1642-6, and to a lesser extent during the Second Civil War of 1648. Other than the mopping up by Cromwell's English army and militia forces of those scattered and demoralised Scots-Royalist soldiers who fled northward through easterly Shropshire after the crushing defeat of King Charles II's army at the battle of Worcester on 3 September 1651, the county did not witness any fighting in what is often termed the Third English Civil War.[10] Instead, Shropshire's noteworthy connection with what we may term the Worcester campaign of late summer 1651 lies in those few days in early September when the fugitive King Charles found shelter among Shropshire's Royalist Roman Catholic community after his flight from Worcester; including the day spent evading pursuing Commonwealth soldiers by hiding in an oak tree among the dense woodland that enclosed Boscobel House, near the Shropshire/Staffordshire border.[11]

The main point of geographical reference for this book is of course the modern and historic county of Shropshire (in the seventeenth century and later also concurrently known as Salop), the most westerly of the counties comprising the English Midlands. Seventeenth-century Shropshire was bordered by Cheshire to the north, Staffordshire to the east, Worcestershire to the south-east and Herefordshire to the south. To the west Shropshire adjoined four Welsh counties: Radnorshire to the south-west, then, northwards, Montgomeryshire and Denbighshire, and an enclave of Flintshire bordered northerly Shropshire. Shropshire lay in the northerly central sector of the

---

8   P. Tennant, *Edgehill and Beyond: the People's War in the South Midlands, 1642-45* (Stroud, 1992); J. Wroughton, *An Unhappy Civil War. The Experiences of Ordinary People in Gloucestershire, Somerset and Wiltshire, 1642-1646* (Bath, 1999); D. Pennington, 'The War and the People' in *Reactions to the English Civil War, 1632-1649,* (ed.) J. Morrill (London, 1982), pp. 115-35; M. Bennett, *The Civil Wars Experienced: Britain and Ireland, 1638-1661* (New York, 2000).

9   R. Hutton, *The Royalist War Effort 1642-1646* (2nd edn., London, 2003), p. 94.

10 Historians now tend to see the events of 1651 not as a third civil war, but as a continuation of, what was in effect, an Anglo-Scottish war, begun when the army of the English republic invaded Scotland in July 1650.

11 For a concise readable account of the fugitive King's stay in Shropshire, see T. Bracher and R. Emmett, *Shropshire in the Civil War* (Shrewsbury, 2000), pp. 46-59.

Welsh Marches, the belt of English shires bordering the Principality. In general terms, the topography of Shropshire varies between northerly lowlands and southerly uplands. The River Severn, flowing in a westerly to south-easterly direction, divides the county approximately in half, and its course marks roughly the transition between the north Shropshire plain and the hill and dale country of south Shropshire.

Within this geographical ambit, this book examines English Civil War war effort. Chapter one takes a view of popular allegiance, looking at the reasons that may have determined support for one side or the other. Chapter two is concerned with leadership and structures of command and administration. Beginning by explaining the pre-war hierarchy of officialdom and the nature of county government, it develops to explain how these institutions were shaped to the demands of war effort. The remainder of the chapter examines the tiers of command on both sides at county and regional level. Having thereby introduced the opposing leaderships, chapter three considers the armed forces that campaigned in Shropshire. Here, an order of battle of units engaged in the county war is proposed for the first time. The following two chapters examine the material resources of war. Chapter four is a detailed evaluation of wartime finance – how money, the 'sinew of war', was raised and disbursed. The ad-hoc and more systematic measures to garner funds used by both sides are described and evaluated. This chapter also addresses plundering (sanctioned or indiscriminate looting), and the taking of 'free quarters' (whereby the cost of billeting soldiers was borne by civilians). Both practices indirectly served to subsidise war effort. A wide-ranging chapter five scrutinises logistical matters: in turn, how the means to arm, equip, feed and mount the soldiers were obtained, and how military supplies were shifted to and around the theatre of war. Due attention is given to those facets of Shropshire's economy which contributed to the war effort, in terms of resources, means of production and – such as it was – transport infrastructure. With the first five chapters concerned with the organisation and marshalling of personnel and resources, chapter six explores operational aspects of war effort. While several larger field engagements were fought in Shropshire during the First Civil War, numerous strongholds were established across the county and the subjugation of garrisons became the main concern of military operations. Accordingly, defensive means of fortification and offensive methods of siege-craft are examined in detail here. Intelligence gathering and medical services are also addressed, as important operational aspects of contemporary warfare that historians have tended to overlook until recently.

The historiographical context:
(i)   County and regional studies of the English Civil Wars

Having established the thrust of this book and its geographical remit, furthermore it seems appropriate to locate it within the context of English Civil War research and writing – a huge, wide-ranging and still expanding field of study and publication. The fundamental assertion underlying this work is that the military history of the Civil Wars goes to the heart of the conflict. In particular, that insight into the underlying war effort provides the vital connection between the causes and eventual outcome of events.

However, in 2003 Hutton made the assertion that historians of the English Civil Wars had become overwhelmingly preoccupied with the 'causes and meaning of the war', sensing a decline in academic interest in the military history.[12] Does this still hold true? In studying war effort in Civil War Lancashire, in 2010 Gratton identified a shift away from military topics, that 'nowadays considerable attention is being paid to philosophy, religious and political issues and social and gender issues'.[13] In terms of research published in journals, this appears to remain a trend at the time of completing this present work in 2015. The detailed bibliographical listings compiled by the Cromwell Association, of articles published in 2009-14 concerned with the long period of the Civil Wars and background seventeenth-century British history, reveal that of a total of 670 articles, military (including contemporary naval) history was the subject of just 35, of which only 20 papers (including four archaeological reports) addressed the Civil Wars – just three per cent of the total.[14] Furthermore, of 156 higher-level theses on seventeenth-century British (including Irish) history in progress within UK universities in 2014, only nine, a modest six per cent, were military-focussed studies of the Civil War era.[15] However, over the last decade have been published a number of substantial military histories by academic historians of the period, including narrative and analytical studies of the national scene by Wanklyn and Jones, Donagan and most recently Gaunt (Donagan being more concerned with military culture), a fresh appraisal of Civil War battles and generalship in a brace of books by Wanklyn, and a study by Hopper of military code and conduct, in terms of allegiance and defection.[16]

At the time of writing, then, the field of Civil War studies presents a mixed picture of endeavour. In particular, this book joins a long established and prolific area of the scholarship of the English Civil Wars, the county history. This is a distinct and well-populated genre of long standing, an approach to the history of the period that has never wholly fallen from favour.[17] Accordingly, at this point some justification is necessary for yet another county history.

Many English and Welsh counties now have one or more published histories of the period. The genre has its roots in Victorian curiosity about the Civil Wars. This was stimulated by antiquarian-led interest in the past alongside the growth of county historical societies, and the publication of period histories such as Warburton's 1849

---

12   Hutton, *War Effort*, p. xviii.
13   J.M. Gratton, *The Parliamentarian and Royalist War Effort in Lancashire 1642-1651* (Manchester, 2010), p. xxvii.
14   P. Gaunt, 'Bibliography of Journals' in *Cromwelliana; The Journal of the Cromwell Association*, Series III: 1 (2012), pp. 111-38; 2 (2013), pp. 114-20; 3 (2014), pp. 97-106.
15   'Theses in progress (UK)', listed in *History Online*, the website of the Institute of Historical Research, www.history.ac.uk/history-online.
16   M. Wanklyn and F. Jones, *A Military History of the English Civil War* (Harlow, 2005); B. Donagan, *War In England 1642-1649* (Oxford, 2008); Gaunt, *English Civil War*; M. Wanklyn, *Decisive Battles of the English Civil War* (Barnsley, 2006); M. Wanklyn, *The Warrior Generals: Winning the British Civil Wars, 1642-1652* (London, 2010); A. Hopper, *Turncoats & Renegadoes, Changing Sides During the English Civil Wars* (Oxford, 2012).
17   For a discussion of county histories within a broader examination of Civil War historiography, see R.C. Richardson, *The Debate on the English Revolution* (3rd edn., Manchester, 1998), pp. 162-83.

best-selling three-volume homage to Prince Rupert and Royalism.[18] An early and very good example of a Civil War county history, with a much wider geographical ambit that included Shropshire, was the Webbs' two-volume study of Herefordshire published in 1879.[19] Of an epic 800-page-length, referenced to contemporary sources – a good number of which (some now lost) were incorporated within the narrative – and with a sound chronological grasp of events, the Webbs' work is an outstanding example of Victorian historical scholarship. Kingston's two books, on Hertfordshire (1894) and a broader regional study of East Anglia (1897), followed a path similar to the Webbs. Meanwhile county historians benefitted from the chronology of national Civil War events authoritatively established by Gardiner (1886-91), and by Firth's pioneering examination of military organisation (1902).[20] The early years of the twentieth century saw a fresh crop of county studies, including Willis Bund's study of Worcestershire (1905), while in 1910, with the encouragement of Sir Charles Firth, then a professor of modern history at Oxford, full-length Civil-War histories of Dorset, Sussex and Lancashire were published.[21]

These and the other groundbreaking county histories over the previous 40 years had set out with the laudable straightforward objective of explaining local Civil War events within a coherent narrative. Broxap took a wholly military view of Lancashire, but most other county historians, such as Thomas-Stanford on Sussex, took a broader perspective of the county before the Wars and its rehabilitation thereafter. The view of military affairs was necessarily more narrative than analytical, establishing when, where and how engagements took place, rather than reflecting on the organisation that allowed their occurrence in the first place. But administrative matters were not wholly overlooked. Kingston, for example, addressed recruitment and military taxation as 'effects of the war on public life' in Hertfordshire, and in East Anglia, the financing, provisioning and personnel of Parliament's Eastern Association.

Perhaps in reaction to the experience of the First World War, during the inter-world-war years of the twentieth century there was a discernible trend for county histories to dwell less on military activity, and instead to stress those distinct social, religious and economic factors which had characterised the local struggle (although in fact these had rarely been wholly overlooked by earlier researchers). Books by Coate and Wood, who were both Oxford academics, respectively on Cornwall (1933) and Nottinghamshire (1937), together with Farrow's Shropshire, emphasised distinct county experiences and local reactions to the conflict.[22]

---

18 E. Warburton, *Memoirs of Prince Rupert and the Cavaliers*, 3 vols. (London, 1849).

19 J. Webb and J.T. Webb, *Memorials of the Civil War between King Charles I and The Parliament of England as it affected Herefordshire and The Adjacent Counties*, 2 vols. (London, 1879).

20 A. Kingston: *Hertfordshire During The Great Civil War* (Hertford, 1884); *East Anglia and The Great Civil War* (London, 1897); S.R. Gardiner, *History of The Great Civil War, 1642-1649*, 3 vols. (London, 1886-91; C.H. Firth, *Cromwell's Army: A History of the English Soldier during the Civil Wars, The Commonwealth and The Protectorate* (London, 1902).

21 J.W. Willis Bund, *The Civil War in Worcestershire, 1642-1646; And The Scotch Invasion of 1651* (Birmingham and London, 1905); A.R. Bayley, *The Great Civil War in Dorset* (Taunton, 1910); C. Thomas-Stanford, *Sussex in The Great Civil War and Interregnum, 1642-1649* (London, 1910); E. Broxap, *The Great Civil War in Lancashire* (Manchester, 1910).

22 M. Coate, *Cornwall in the Great Civil War and Interregnum, 1642-1660, A Social and Political Study* (Oxford, 1933); A.C. Wood, *Nottinghamshire in the Civil War* (Oxford, 1937).

The expansion in county record offices after 1945 allowed researchers access to fresh sources of material. This enabled increasing sophistication in county-based work that in the 1960s and 1970s allowed further divergence from the straightforward narrative approach. Everitt's 1966 view of Kent was the first to consider as a model social unit the shire as a somewhat insular community, in which, by taking a long view of the Civil War period up to the Restoration, the social, political, religious and, to some extent, the military aspects of the conflict could be examined in detail.[23] Everitt's approach prompted a lively academic debate on the nature of provincial responses to the conflict. This generated several new county studies, including Norfolk (1969), Somerset (1973), Cheshire (1974), Sussex (1975) and later Warwickshire (1987), which took up and tested the county community thesis.[24] The impact of neutralism and attempted avoidance of the war came to the fore as subjects of growing interest. A feature of these studies, as in the example of Warmington's history of Gloucestershire, was that the years of actual war formed only part of the subject.[25]

Although more concerned with local causations and outcomes, and in particular with the activity of the provincial gentry class, by considering both pre-war and wartime governance these studies began to pay fresh attention to how warfare was actually organised and sustained. In particular, Hughes's view of Warwickshire looked into the problematic development of the Parliamentarian war effort there. Civil War county histories now usually combine socio-political analysis with a military narrative, of which recent examples from Wales and its Marche are John's examination of Pembrokeshire, and Knight's similar approach to Monmouthshire.[26] In reassessing the conflict recent work has revised or supplemented earlier interpretations. Civil War Lancashire, for example, is now well explored – by Broxap's original history, by Bull's largely military narrative, and by Gratton's analysis of war effort.[27] Closer to Shropshire, Atkin's two detailed military histories of Worcestershire have served to supplement (or perhaps supplant) Willis Bund's original effort. On the other hand, Ross's more concise and readable recent study of Herefordshire has not eclipsed the Webbs' original authoritative work.[28] Elsewhere in the Shropshire region, Parker's examination of environmental, social, political and religious contexts and also military events in Radnorshire is an outstanding example of recent county histories.[29]

Distinctively, *Radnorshire from Civil War to Restoration* devoted a short but useful chapter to the local Royalist war effort, considering taxation, military organisation and

23 A. Everitt, *The Community of Kent And The Great Rebellion* (Leicester, 1966).
24 R.W. Ketton-Cremer, *Norfolk in The Civil War: A Portrait of a Society in Conflict* (London, 1969); D. Underdown, *Somerset in the Civil War and Interregnum* (Newton Abbot, 1973); J. Morrill, *Cheshire, 1630-1660: County Government and Society during the 'English Revolution'* (Oxford, 1974); A. Fletcher, *A County Community in Peace and War, Sussex 1600-1660* (London, 1975); A. Hughes, *Politics, Society and Civil War in Warwickshire, 1620-1660* (Cambridge, 1987).
25 A.R. Warmington, *Civil War, Interregnum and Restoration in Gloucestershire, 1640-1672* (Woodbridge, 1997).
26 T. John, *The Civil War in Pembrokeshire* (Almeley, 2008); J. Knight, *Civil War and Restoration in Monmouthshire* (Almeley, 2005).
27 S. Bull, '*A General Plague of Madness': The Civil War in Lancashire, 1640-1660* (Lancaster, 2009).
28 M. Atkin: *The Civil War in Worcestershire* (Stroud, 1995); *Worcestershire Under Arms: An English County During The Civil Wars* (Barnsley, 2004); D. Ross, *Royalist, But … Herefordshire in the English Civil Wars* (Almeley, 2012).
29 K. Parker, *Radnorshire from Civil War to Restoration* (Almeley, 2000).

recruitment. Such a broader view of military affairs at county level is to be welcomed because Royalist activity has left comparatively few traces. Indeed, because of the much greater quantity of surviving records documenting their activity, most detailed work at county level has tended to dwell on the Parliamentarians. Warmington, for example, in looking at Gloucestershire, a county heavily fought over during the First Civil War, paid most attention to the military problems and political infighting that beset the Parliamentarians. Notwithstanding their setbacks, Gloucestershire was seen to have witnessed the resilience of 'Parliamentarian administration at its plodding best'. 'The Royalist party', on the other hand, was summed up as having 'collapsed in the summer of 1644 after some squabbles over authority and a few reverses'.[30] A purpose of this book is to compare the effectiveness of the organisation of the belligerents; whether or not, as Hughes asserted in a keynote article on Royalist and Parliamentarian leadership, the Parliamentarians were adaptable in creating 'a more resilient and broadly based war effort', while organisation in Royalist areas was less robust, less sophisticated and 'more rigid'.[31]

Gratton's commendable recent approach to Civil War Lancashire was to present a more balanced view of both sides. Like Shropshire, Lancashire was a contested county. Gratton's work therefore commands comparison with this book, for having presented a bilateral investigation of personnel, and of administrative, logistical and operational matters at county level. Gratton's *War Effort in Lancashire* and the present study of Shropshire usefully demonstrate how differing, but complementary, approaches may be taken to the examination of Civil War war effort. While Gratton's sources inclined to a meticulous enumeration of personnel (especially in what he termed the 'political direction' of the Lancashire gentry) and of Parliamentarian financing, this view of Shropshire is more concerned with the practicalities of logistical arrangements and of operational conduct. Gratton was also able in detail to enumerate the forces raised by both sides in Lancashire, and similar fresh military analysis of Shropshire is undertaken here. However, due to the terminally weakened condition of the Royalist cause in Lancashire beyond mid-1643 little trace of its activity has survived, so Gratton's work was necessarily slanted to Parliamentarian efforts. This underlines the difficulty in attempting balanced bipartisan analysis of war effort, because the evidence of Royalist activity is usually so sparse. But the comparatively plentiful evidence for the longevity of the King's cause in Shropshire does allow a more balanced appraisal of both sides.

However, the county-centric view of the English Civil Wars has attracted criticism. Despite the stimulating work of the 1960s and early 1970s, by the end of the latter decade, as one noted historian has observed, the county history was tending to be viewed, in academic circles at least, as a somewhat hackneyed field of research. This echoed the reservations expressed 20 years before by Burne and Young, professional soldiers become military historians, that county and regional histories provided an 'unsatisfactory treatment' of the Wars, 'from a military point of view'. 'The treatment by counties', they declared, 'has led to an exaggeration of the view that the war was

---

30 Warmington, *Gloucestershire 1640-1672*, pp. 52-3, 60.
31 A. Hughes, 'The King, the Parliament, and the Localities during the English Civil War', *Journal of British Studies*, 24 (1985), pp. 246, 250.

nothing more than a disconnected series of petty local struggles'.[32]

Having thereby questioned the ongoing viability to Civil War research of the county model, the answer must be that, by often taking a long view of the conflict and by pursuing varied lines of investigation, the county history has been, and remains, a highly productive field of research. Furthermore, the shire was the largest sub-unit of seventeenth-century government and during the conflict the organisational cornerstone upon which both sides footed their war effort. The county was the administrative focus of the commissions of array and of the county committees, the provincial bodies that gave sanction and legal basis to the actions of Royalist and Parliamentarian activists respectively. Most regiments, too, were organised and, at least to begin with, were recruited at county level. While the larger field armies, engaged in often wide-ranging campaigns of march and counter-march, may have had little regard for county boundaries, yet, and as Newman has pointed to, in terms of military organisation and paramilitary administration there were distinct practical differences between shires.[33] Burne and Young's concern to view the First Civil War as a national struggle was correct, but in practice – and in the example of Shropshire in particular – it was, like all civil wars, as much an attritional conflict contested at county and local level.

Broadening the county view, English Civil War studies have also taken the direction of considering regional contexts. 140 years after publication, the noteworthy regional study remains J.R. Phillips's two-part history of the Civil War in Wales and its borderlands. The first volume was a narrative history, the second a still useful compendium bringing together significant manuscript and printed primary sources.[34] Phillips's 1874 landmark work is of course now much dated, and revision and reinterpretation of the conflict in the Principality and its March has been provided by Gaunt's concise narrative account, Tucker's military history of North Wales and by Hutton's impressive study of Royalist war effort across the region.[35] Hutton's approach, which paid considerable attention to Shropshire, had huge merit, and redressed the tendency at the time of its inception for Civil War scholarship to dwell on Parliamentarian organisation. This author freely acknowledges the inspiration of Hutton's *Royalist War Effort*, which, as a narrative history of the war in Wales and its borderlands, as much as an analysis of war effort, necessarily had to skim over the minutiae of Royalist practice that a county study of this kind can address in more detail.

Shifting the regional focus from Wales to the English Midlands, Shropshire featured in Sherwood's geographically wide-ranging narrative of *Civil Strife*, which devoted a chapter to war effort as the 'Extra-Military Consequences of the War'. Further afield – and in geographical terms, and by considering the opposing side, a

---

32 Hutton, *War Effort*, xvi; A.H. Burne and P. Young, *The Great Civil War: A Military History of the First Civil War 1642-1646* (London, 1959, reprinted Moreton-in-Marsh, 1998), pp. xi-xii.

33 P.R. Newman, *The Old Service, Royalist Regimental Colonels and The Civil War, 1642-46* (Manchester, 1993), p. 248.

34 J.R. Phillips, *Memoirs of The Civil War in Wales and the Marches, 1642-1649*, 2 vols. (London, 1874).

35 P. Gaunt, *A Nation Under Siege; The Civil War in Wales 1642-48* (London, 1991); N. Tucker, *North Wales and Chester in the Civil War* (Ashbourne, 2003).

counterpoint to the actions of Hutton's westerly Royalists – the other outstanding scholarly examination of war effort at regional level remains Holmes's analysis of the political and military organisation of the Parliamentarian Eastern Association.[36]

The historiographical context:
(ii) The military history of the English Civil Wars
This book adds to the wider corpus of national Civil War military history. This is a field heavily populated by the writings of academic historians and non-academic researchers alike, and in the number of published works is now a huge genre in its own right. Hence, the following examples have been selected as being representative, or noteworthy for referencing war effort in particular.

General military histories of the period have usually paid some attention to organisation, to a greater or lesser extent.[37] Campaign and battle narratives have also often given due consideration to the importance of resources and logistics to the outcome of events.[38] Histories of particular armies have also addressed their equipping and supply. Gentles's study of the New Model Army, for example, featured recruitment, pay and resources, while Barratt's national overview of the Royalist army looked in some depth at logistical matters.[39] Aspects of supply and finance have also been explored elsewhere. Roy's examination of the papers of the Ordnance Office at Oxford revealed a great deal about central Royalist logistical activity, while pioneering articles by Engberg and Bennett, and a book by Wheeler have addressed the financial organisation of both sides.[40] More recently, Robinson has coupled horse procurement for the Parliamentarian armies to taxation and allegiance in a social and philosophical, more so than a military, discourse on war and society.[41]

However, the scholar who probably has done most to elucidate the activity of Civil War war effort has been Edwards. His research has ranged from arms acquisition at county level, to weapons procurement, logistics, finance and civilian reaction in the wider 'British' context of the Wars.[42] In *Dealing in Death: The Arms Trade and the*

36 R.E. Sherwood, *Civil Strife in the Midlands 1642-1651* (London, 1974), chapter 11, pp. 98-122; C. Holmes, *The Eastern Association in the English Civil War* (Cambridge, 1974).
37 See for example, I. Gentles, *The English Revolution and the Wars in the Three Kingdoms 1638-1652* (Harlow, 2007), 'Building and fuelling the machinery of war', pp. 94-127; M. Braddick, *God's Fury, England's Fire A New History of the Civil Wars* (London, 2008), pp. 397-404.
38 For example by G. Foard in *Naseby, The Decisive Campaign* (2nd edn., Barnsley, 2004), pp. 58-61, 82-3. 172-5.
39 I. Gentles, *The New Model Army in England, Ireland and Scotland, 1645-1653* (Oxford, 1994); J. Barratt, *Cavaliers, The Royalist Army at War, 1642-1646* (Stroud, 2000), chapter six, 'Munitions and Ordnance', and chapter seven, 'Logistics'.
40 I. Roy (ed.), *The Royalist Ordnance Papers 1642-1646*, Parts I and II (Banbury, 1963, 1975); J. Engberg, 'Royalist Finances During the English Civil War 1642-1646', *The Scandinavian Economic History Review*, XIV (1966), pp. 73-96; M. Bennett, 'Contribution and Assessment: Financial Exactions in the English Civil War, 1642-1646', *War & Society*, 4 (1986), pp. 1-11; J.S. Wheeler, *The Making of a World Power: War and The Military Revolution in Seventeenth Century England* (Stroud, 1999).
41 G. Robinson, *Horses, People and Parliament in the English Civil War: Extracting Resources and Constructing Allegiance* (Farnham, 2012).
42 P. Edwards, 'Turning Ploughshares into Swords: The Arms and Equipment Industries in Staffordshire in the First Civil War, 1642-1646, *Midland History*, 27 (2002), pp. 52-79; P. Edwards, 'Logistics and Supply' in *The Civil Wars A Military History of England, Scotland and Ireland 1638-1660*, (eds.) J. Kenyon and J. Ohlmeyer (Oxford, 1998), pp. 234-71.

British Civil Wars, Edwards produced the most wide-ranging study yet of national war effort during the period, addressing activities as diverse as the local acquisition of horses and the international trade in arms. Furthermore, Edwards made the point that hitherto unrecognised evidence for Civil War logistical activity could still be found in the manuscript collections of county record offices.[43] Considerable use has been made in this book of this kind of local detail, which can only serve to broaden our understanding of the nature of war effort in this period.

43   P. Edwards, *Dealing in Death: The Arms Trade and the British Civil Wars, 1638–52* (Stroud, 2001), p. xi.

1

Taking Sides: Popular allegiance in Civil War Shropshire

They are one and all his majesty's good subjects.

The causes and nature of allegiance during the English Civil Wars, especially among the majority population below gentle class, remain problematic. The historic record all too often lacks the sort of quantifiable and comparable evidence that may help historians satisfactorily to explain the actual wartime behaviour of ordinary people. The most obvious reason for this is that few individuals among the commonalty, who as soldiers bore the brunt of the fighting, or as civilians bore the brunt of the war effort, expressed in writing that has survived their motives for taking up arms or for being otherwise active in the cause of King or Parliament. Furthermore, the problem of popular allegiance is made more difficult because support for one side or the other was not always wholly constant; it could waver or shift according to the military situation. Non-alignment and neutrality, as well as active, armed neutralism – notably the sporadic but widespread civilian uprisings by the so-called clubmen in parts of southern and western England in 1645, including south-west Shropshire – further complicates the picture and requires explanation. However, where evidence can be detected and used creatively to support and test ideas, as Stoyle's outstanding work on Devon has shown, the examination of Civil War allegiance at an individual county level can justify a volume in its own right.[1] A single chapter cannot, therefore, provide such a detailed analysis of Shropshire. However, since the effective organisation of war effort depends on the mobilisation of popular support, the reasons for allegiance within the county merit some discussion and this chapter sets out to do that. In particular, to present likely reasons to explain Shropshire's apparent Royalism, which is now a tenet of Civil War historiography.[2]

Contemporaries, too, saw Shropshire as being at least outwardly Royalist. At the close of December 1642, one of the King's officers enthusiastically reported from there, that 'they are one and all his majesty's good subjects'. In early 1643, a young man

---

1   M. Stoyle, *Loyalty and Locality: Popular Allegiance in Devon During the English Civil War* (Exeter, 1994).
2   For Shropshire characterised as a Royalist county, see for example: Morrill, *Revolt*, p. 66; Hutton, *War Effort*, pp. 24-5, 37; Stoyle, *Loyalty and Locality*, pp. 242-3; and A. Fletcher, *The Outbreak of the English Civil War* (London, 1989), p. 298.

who had enlisted for Parliament wrote to his family remaining in Shropshire, that he believed the county's support for the King would soon incur retribution by a vengeful invading Parliamentarian army: 'Our county will be punished sorely', he feared.[3]

Defining the First English Civil War as a class conflict in which allegiance was shaped accordingly, that the commons, propertied or otherwise, tended to support Parliament, while the nobility, titled gentry and clergy and their followers generally supported King Charles, in, in effect, a clash between a rising bourgeoisie and a declining feudal order, is no longer held to be a satisfactory explanation. Instead, historians now accept a more complex situation; that determinates of popular allegiance, like the reasons for the war itself, were multi-causational.[4] While being shaped by current politico-military events, and sometimes emerging in pragmatic response to immediate circumstances, allegiance was moreover influenced by social, economic and, especially, religious factors. Some of these reflected enduring rifts in society and contrasting patterns of long-standing popular behaviour. Furthermore, while division along regional lines can be identified, individual counties could be divided to neighbouring parish level, creating rival areas of Royalist and Parliamentarian allegiance. Similar fissures appeared within individual towns and cities. This sort of local fragmentation in support can be detected in west Shropshire by May 1645. Here, in certain parishes church bells were being rung to alert local men to gather in arms against the King's soldiers when they advanced into the district. The Royalist High Sheriff Sir Francis Ottley angrily threatened that this partisan action would result in 'such town [i.e. in the sense of a township, or settlement] or towns so doing shall be burnt and set on fire'.[5]

Differences in religious outlook and practice that were felt and strongly upheld across all levels of early Stuart society now tend to be seen as the clearest cause of division and allegiance. In particular, the linkage of principled opposition to King Charles I with Puritanism; forms of low-Church, or non-conforming Protestantism, characterised by preaching ministry, unadorned acts of worship and an emphasis on personal study of scripture. There were different shades of Puritan belief, some far more radical than others. While most Puritans before the Civil War probably thought of themselves as members of the Church of England, their theology demanded further reformation – of the elimination of all lingering traces of Roman Catholicism from Anglican practice. Puritan doctrine could also accommodate the substitution of Presbyterianism for the established Episcopalian form of Church government.

Religion was not, however, a detached or compartmentalised aspect of early Stuart culture and thought; rather, it permeated and shaped social and economic life and political attitudes. Some historians therefore have also argued a firmer correlation between religious and socio-economic factors. They have reasoned that among the dispersed communities of pastoral-woodland farming areas, where the established Church and local landowners held less influence, an inclination to Puritan religiosity

---

3   T. Carte (ed.), *A Collection of Original Letters and Papers, Concerning the Affairs of England, from the Year 1641 to 1660. Found among the Duke of Ormonde's Papers* (1739), p. 15; 'Ottley Papers' (1895), p. 261.

4   Useful summaries attempting to explain Civil War allegiance can be found in: Gentles, *English Revolution*, chapter five, 'Popular Allegiance', pp. 128-49; B. Worden, *The English Civil Wars, 1640-1660* (London, 2009), pp. 48-53; and Gaunt, *English Civil War*, pp. 119-22.

5   HRO, CF61/20, ff. 573-4.

encouraged political Parliamentarianism. Predominantly arable or mixed farming districts, with larger, nucleated villages and more structured communities, on the other hand, tended to be Royalist because of the prevalent traditional conservative influences of Anglicanism and of hierarchical social deference.[6]

Such theories, however, when questioned have often been found wanting, and so have not gained widespread acceptance, nor have they been tested in Shropshire. Given that livestock was the mainstay of the farming economy in seventeenth-century Shropshire, and that the north of the county, much as it remains today, was a largely pastoral-woodland landscape, and furthermore that scattered hamlets, rather than nucleated villages, were typical of the pattern of settlement across much of Shropshire, the landed allegiance model would imply more widespread Parliamentarianism than seems to have been the case. But the evidence is equivocal. Pockets of Parliamentarian support in north Shropshire do seem likely – around Market Drayton, Wem and Oswestry, for example. However, in autumn 1643 the Parliamentarians recently based at Wem reported that Whitchurch, the most northerly of Shropshire's market towns, was 'malignant' ('malignancy' being a term used by Parliamentarians to characterise political and religious opposition), while a Cheshire Parliamentarian also remarked that Whitchurch was 'a Cavalier place'.[7] There is also the anecdotal evidence of Richard Gough, who lived through the Wars in a typically woodland-pastoral north Shropshire parish. Although a few very minor gentry and better-off yeomen left the district to serve as Parliamentary officers, the majority of commoners who enlisted fought for the King.[8] Gough's remark that the would-be Parliamentarian officers were 'forced to fly from their houses in the wars, and shelter themselves in garrisons […] to the end they might receive a captain's pay to maintain them', does not suggest that there was much support for Parliament in his neighbourhood. On the other hand, Royalist support in and around Bridgnorth, in east Shropshire, where arable farming was probably more widespread, was encouraged by the actions of four local landowners in particular, the leading Royalists John Weld, Sir Thomas Wolyrche, Edward Acton and Francis Billinglsey. Richard Baxter, a Shropshire-born minister of Puritan character, who had left the county before the war but returned for a while as a chaplain to Parliament's forces in Shropshire, acknowledged the role played by the local Royalist gentry in Bridgnorth becoming a Royalist town: 'When the war was begun, the town (being against the Parliament) was a garrison for the King, kept by the neighbour gentlemen of the country'.[9]

John Weld, one of the county's wealthiest men and the high sheriff of Shropshire

6   This theory was developed by D. Underdown in 'The Chalk and the Cheese: Contrasts among the English Clubmen', *Past and Present*, 85 (1979), pp. 25-48, in the context of three south-western English counties – Somerset, Dorset and Wiltshire. See also Underdown's, *Revel, Riot and Rebellion: Popular Politics and Culture in England, 1603-1660* (Oxford, 1985), and Hughes, *Warwickshire*, chapter four.
7   HMC, *Thirteenth Report, Appendix Part I*, p. 141; T. Malbon, 'Memorials of the Civil War in Cheshire and the Adjacent Counties by Thomas Malbon of Nantwich, Gent.', (ed.) J. Hall, *The Record Society for the Publication of Original Documents relating to Lancashire and Cheshire*, XIX (1889), p. 84.
8   R. Gough, *Antiquityes and Memoyres of the Parish of Myddle*, (ed.) D. Hey as *The History of Myddle* (Harmondsworth, 1981) pp. 32, 62, 71-2, 116, 226-7.
9   R. Baxter, *Reliquiae Baxterianae: Or Mr. Richard Baxter's Narrative of The Most Memorable Passages of His Life and Times* (1696), p. 20.

3. Richard Baxter (1615-1691), a Shropshire-born minister and theologian who sided with Parliament. Baxter's autobiography offers a revealing insight into the reasons for allegiance in the First Civil War.

in 1642, is a good example of the influential landed gentry who by their actions could shape popular allegiance. On 29 August 1642, Weld wrote to his fellow Royalist Francis Ottley of having 'given his best advice to Bridgnorth', and that he thought the townspeople 'will follow it'; advice that Weld furthered by repeatedly visiting the town, by ensuring that the King's proclamations were read publicly at the market cross in the town centre, and by courting the aldermen of Bridgnorth, supplying them cuts of venison from the deer in the park around his home estate at nearby Willey.[10]

Unlike Weld, however, Sir Richard Newport of High Ercall, another very wealthy gentleman, with the largest land holdings in Shropshire outside the peerage, at first adopted a neutral stance. He attempted to avert an armed confrontation by mediating between the rival activists in Shropshire. However, by mid-August 1642 Newport had aligned with the King's party and brought his influence to bear accordingly. As a local Parliamentarian later wrote, when Newport was seen in public wearing in his hat Francis Ottley's emblem (Ottley then being a captain of Royalist volunteers):

> The country [i.e. those who until then had backed the local Parliamentary activists] taking notice of […] grew discouraged […] which was for the greatest pity, and fell off, looking upon Sir Richard as a man of vast estate, having many tenants, allied to many gentlemen of quality in the county by marriage […] After this the said Sir Richard was

10 'Ottley Papers' (1894), p. 37; SA, BB/D/1/2/1/52.

one of the forwardest of the commission of array.[11]

The capacity of notable individuals like Newport to influence allegiance and to mobilise support in a hierarchical society was clearly recognised and accepted by contemporaries. What motivated Newport and his fellow gentlemen to actively side with the King is less clear, but familial and other ties of kinship can be detected in the correspondence between Francis Ottley and other Royalists among the county gentry. The most plausible explanation, argued by Newman, is that militant Royalists of gentry class – in wealth and status a very broad social group indeed – were united by genuine motives of personal loyalty, obligation and a sense of duty and obedience to the King. Furthermore, they shared conservative values: that 'Royalism in arms was the pure expression of a traditional and learned commitment to patriarchal government on the part of a very large number of Englishmen and Welshmen'.[12] On the other hand, many moderate Parliamentarians, who wished to see the King returned, albeit chastened, to the centre of governance, would have shared some common ground in that respect.

Sir Richard Newport, as a Shropshire magnate, and John Weld, as the King's high sheriff, were notable authoritarian and influential figures. However, historians now recognise that deference and unthinking obedience to their social superiors by the commonalty can no longer be seen as wholly convincing reasons to account for popular allegiance. Individual conscience and circumstance often dictated the stance of ordinary people, who usually had some reasoned understanding of the events and issues at stake. By the information made available to them, it seems that many of the inhabitants of the town of Ludlow, for example, would have been reasonably well informed about the national political crisis as it unfolded during 1642. From January, the town council ensured that the printed declarations and counter declarations issued by King or Parliament they received were duly proclaimed at the market place, meanwhile the aldermen regularly purchased copies of the newsbooks – the contemporary newspapers – published in London.[13]

Ludlow may also provide a further example of allegiance being a pragmatic or emotive response to local factors: as seen in Derbyshire, for instance, where the King gained support from lead mining districts by offering the miners tax breaks and his support in their disputes with local landowners; and in the Forest of Dean, in westerly Gloucestershire, where the pre-existing hostility that certain mining communities felt against the area's leading land owner, who was a notable Royalist, animated them to support Parliament.[14] In Ludlow's case, the town since the reign of King Henry VIII had been the seat and usual meeting place of the Council in the Marches of Wales, a body which combined the duties of a high court of law under the royal prerogative with the regional administration of the Principality and the English Marcher counties. The Council was an obvious symbol of regional royal authority, and, from late 1640, along with other extraordinary bodies under the royal prerogative, came under intense

11 W. Phillips (ed.), 'Sequestration Papers of Sir Richard, First Baron Newport and Francis, his son', *TSANHS*, 2nd Series, XII (1900), pp. 4-5.
12 Newman, *The Old Service*, chapter one, 'The Concept of Obligation', esp. pp. 20-21.
13 SA, LB8/1/162, f. 6.
14 Gaunt, *English Civil War*, p. 120.

4. Ludlow castle in the 1630s remained the seat and usual meeting place of the Council in the Marches of Wales. The buildings of the inner ward, pictured, provided comfortable apartments and administrative accommodation for the Council's staff. Ludlow was held as an important Royalist stronghold throughout the First Civil War and the castle was the garrison's citadel.

Parliamentary scrutiny. As a result, its jurisdiction was abolished in July 1641. The Council as a civil court limped on until the outbreak of the war, but its authority and purpose was greatly diminished.

By the residency of its staff and through the spending power of its attendees and visitors, the Council had been a major, and perhaps the main, source of Ludlow's prosperity. In April 1642 the town petitioned Parliament, that the Council's demise had caused a local economic crisis: 'whereby many families are already much decayed in their estates, and the greatest part of the inhabitants will in short time grow so poor, that they will not be able to provide maintenance for their families'. That Ludlow's townsfolk feared a result of Parliament's actions would be to cause 'great poverty and misery, and will be the utter undoing of thousand poor souls', was probably the main reason why by June 1642 in Ludlow and nearby areas of south Shropshire individuals who seemed religiously or politically inclined to Parliament were being subjected to verbal and physical abuse. In Ludlow itself, the townsfolk 'set up a Maypole and a thing like a head upon it, and so they did at Croft [Croft Castle in northern Herefordshire], and gathered a great many around it, and shot at it in the derision of Roundheads'.[15]

15 *Two Petitions. The One, Presented to the Honourable House of Commons, from the Countie of Hereford, May the*

5. The interior and still mostly early Jacobean furnishings of the manorial chapel at Langley together represent a remarkable survival of the unadorned pre-Laudian arrangement of Shropshire churches in the early seventeenth century. The communion table is unceremoniously located, and the two pulpits reflect the importance of preaching ministry - an important facet of Puritan doctrine.

The local focus of this enmity, which linked Puritanism with radical Parliamentarianism, and in which antipathy to both coalesced, were the Harley family and their associates. Headed by the religiously zealous Long Parliament MP Sir Robert Harley, the Puritan Harley's had made their home at Brampton Bryan Castle, in far north-west Herefordshire, just a couple of miles from the south-Shropshire border, a focus for Godly worship in the central Marches. By mid-July 1642 hostility against the Harley's and their fraternity had grown to the extent that Sir Robert's wife Brilliana reported how 'every Thursday [a market day] some of Ludlow, as they go through the town [meaning the village of Brampton Bryan, which lay on a trading route into neighbouring Radnorshire] wish all the Puritans of Brampton Bryan hanged'.[16] In time the Harley's made Brampton Bryan a Parliamentary stronghold. When the castle was surrendered in April 1644, after Royalists had determinedly laid siege to it for a second time, the garrison and the non-combatants from among the

fourth, 1642. *The Other, To his Majestie, and the Parliament, From the Towne of Ludlow in the Countie of Salop* (London, 1642), pp. 6-8; J. Eales, *Puritans and Roundheads: The Harleys of Brampton Bryan and the Outbreak of The English Civil War* (Cambridge, 1990), p. 143.

16 Eales, *Puritans and Roundheads*, p. 144.

families of the Harley's associates sheltering there found as they went into captivity that popular hostility against them was undiminished. As one of their officers later remarked, 'The inhabitants of Ludlow baited us like bears and demanded where our God was'.[17]

This serves to demonstrate how antipathy to militant Puritan-Parliamentarianism was a strong motivating force for popular Royalism. Yet allegiance across south Shropshire as a whole was not perhaps so clear-cut. Parts of the border area straddling Herefordshire and south-westerly Shropshire became, as suggested above, a focus for Puritanism under the local influence of Sir Robert Harley and a geographically wider-ranging body of associated groups and individuals, among them the More family of Linley near Bishop's Castle in south Shropshire. Richard More, one of the two Long Parliament MPs for Bishop's Castle, and his eldest son Samuel, who were both active wartime Parliamentarians, were numbered among Harley's Puritan gentry intimates. However, the religious influence of the 'Harley Circle' was socially more diverse. Reverend Peter Studley, the minister of St. Chad's church in Shrewsbury and a high-Church Anglican, who embraced King Charles's religious reforms, in the mid-1630s had noted with disdain that there was a community of commoner 'Puritans about Bishop's Castle'. It may have been as a result of their presence coupled with the More's local familial influence that by mid-1645 both sides seem to have regarded Bishop's Castle as a Parliamentarian town.[18]

Elsewhere, support for Parliament was strong in places where popular Puritanism had gained general favour, often in centres of manufacturing and trade, including certain ports, and the cloth and clothing towns of Essex, Suffolk, Somerset, Lancashire and the West Riding of Yorkshire, for example. The lack of such commercial centres in Shropshire – with the notable exception of Shrewsbury, a marketplace and finishing manufactory for the trade in Welsh woollen textiles – may have made it more difficult for Parliamentarian support to coalesce. Pre-war Shrewsbury, however, had a significant non-conforming community, and during the war the town, although more than ostensibly Royalist, was of uncertain allegiance.

Shrewsbury's Puritans in the mid-1630s were characterised by reverend Studley, whose intense distrust and dislike for Shropshire's scattered Puritan fraternity compelled him to monitor their activity, as:

> A generation of men strongly addicted to hear no other ministers, but those of their own character and print, and such men […] they extol and advance up to the clouds in raptures of admiration […] in the meantime neglecting the ministry of […] learned and Godly men.

Studley also remarked that those devoted to such extemporising preaching ministry included not only men and women of gentle and mercantile class, but also labouring commoners: 'mechanical fellows of many artifices and professions, masons, carpenters, brick layers, courvoisers [leather workers], weavers, stone-gravers'; in fact, the kind of

---

17   HMC, *Manuscripts of the Marquis of Bath,* I, p. 33.
18   Eales, *Puritans and Roundheads,* p. 59; P. Studley, *The Looking-Glasse of Schisme* (London, 1635), pp. 100-3.

urban trades from which Parliament often drew much wartime support.[19]

Political disagreement, shaped by differences in religious outlook, had affected Shrewsbury's elders and governing corporation during the 1630s. Accordingly, in April 1637 Shropshire's high sheriff, Sir Paul Harris, a future Royalist, wrote in frustration to the Privy Council about the desultory efforts of Shrewsbury's aldermen in levying ship money. Harris found that because there was so 'much division and factions between them about a preacher, that they mind nothing else'. Two rival parties dominating town politics coalesced around the two bailiffs, the chief aldermen, one of them, Thomas Nicolls, heading the Puritan-dominated 'religious party'.[20] Nicolls would become one of Shropshire's leading Parliamentarians, and his notable wartime associates Humphrey Mackworth, Thomas Hunt and Thomas Mytton, along with other aldermen, in 1642 seem to have based their opposition to the King on religious grounds, derived from their involvement or association with Shrewsbury's Puritans.[21]

In 1642, once a neutral common front among the aldermen, intended to maintain law and order and the security of the town, was overtaken by events, factionalism came to the fore in determining Shrewsbury's allegiance. Nicolls, Hunt, Mackworth and their compatriots were drawn into opposition to a Royalist party including the mayor, Richard Gibbons, and gentry from the rural hinterland, among them Francis Ottley and Sir Paul Harris. Eventually, and bloodlessly, the Royalist party prevailed, and on 30 August the corporation agreed that 'if the King's majesty come to this town that he shall have free access […] and the town do make the best entertainment these troublesome times afford'.[22] The royal army's arrival there three weeks later and Shrewsbury's occupation as a Royalist garrison thereafter determined the outward appearance of the town's allegiance.

Shrewsbury's situation is an example of how a military presence, and especially a long-standing garrison, would influence allegiance. This depended on whether the military was accepted as a friendly force, or resented as an occupying power; more often they were probably seen as being one and the same. The military could hearten and sustain existing support, although its demands would sooner or later take its toll on civilian goodwill. A sustained show of force would of course suppress and discourage opposition. An anonymous Parliamentarian supporter reporting from Bridgnorth in early October 1642 described how by the occupation of the royal army, 'our county of Shropshire is very much awed, and many well-affected persons withdraw themselves'. Indicating that the 'well-affected' supporters of Parliament, although overpowered, were not an insignificant movement in the county, he added 'for all the reports you have heard […] Shropshire is not altogether so malignant as it is reported. Fear makes us yield to many things'.[23]

Once the King and his army had left Shropshire in mid-October 1642, the Royalist

19   Studley, *Looking–Glasse of Schisme*, pp. 181, 185.
20   *CSPD, 1637*, pp. 13, 194.
21   See esp. B. Coulton, *Regime and Religion, Shrewsbury 1400-1700* (Almeley, 2010), chapter four, 'Puritans and Laudians', pp. 69-90.
22   SA, 6001/290, f. 133.
23   *A True and exact Relation of the Proceedings of His Majesties Army in Cheshire, Shropshire and Worcestershire* (1642), p. 4.

leadership at Shrewsbury continued to detain or closely monitor known or suspected Parliamentarian activists. They also proposed an amnesty of sorts for Parliamentarian sympathisers and neutrals alike, providing that they renounced their support for the enemy: 'That all the gentry, of what quality [what]soever, that have showed themselves disaffected, or neutral, may give in caution, that if any enemy come they may find no party to assist them'.[24]

Despite such measures, however, doubts would remain among Royalist leaders about the county town's loyalty to their cause. In November 1643, a prominent North-Walian Royalist reported that recent military defeats under his leadership meant that Lord Capel, the Royalist regional commander, feared to leave Shrewsbury, his headquarters, in case of revolt, the townsmen allegedly having 'not only a mean but a malignant estimation of his lordship'. This probably exaggerated the actual situation, but towards the end of January 1644 Sir Gilbert Gerrard, the governor of Royalist Worcester, did not have confidence in Shrewsbury's loyalty. He based his decision to redirect from Worcester a munitions convoy from Oxford bound for Shrewsbury to Ludlow instead not only on hearsay, that Shrewsbury was 'so ill affected', but on the firmer grounds of orders from one of Prince Rupert's aides, that 'he holds not Shrewsbury a place of security'.[25]

On the other hand, Parliamentarian commanders, too, felt unsure of the town's allegiance. They doubted the actual strength and influence of 'a party in Shrewsbury', as the Earl of Denbigh termed them, when he briefly campaigned in Shropshire in summer 1644, 'who would upon any advantage declare themselves in our favour'.[26] When the Shropshire Parliamentarians eventually captured Shrewsbury in February 1645, they worryingly found there was no widespread or determined show of support for them. Disturbed at this outcome, on the 23rd they reported to Sir William Brereton: 'Did you know the condition of this place, the disaffection of most and how poor and faint the spirits and resolution of such as seem to wish well to the cause, you might well conceive what our fears and dangers are'.[27]

It may be over simplistic to suggest that indicators to Civil War allegiance may be seen in the ways in which counties or urban centres responded to aspects of royal policy during the eleven years of the so-called 'Personal Rule', when, from 1629, King Charles I ruled without calling a parliament. Nonetheless, many of the MPs who, from November 1640, sat in what became the Long Parliament expressed a litany of grievances from their home shires that were a hangover from the Personal Rule. These grievances coalesced and gave impetus to the Parliamentary reforms during 1641, removing many of the instruments of King Charles's period of sole governance. These actions in turn contributed to the breakdown in political relations between the King and his Parliamentary opponents in early 1642, precipitating open civil war. It does seem appropriate, therefore, to briefly consider Shropshire's reaction to the Personal Rule.

24 SA, 6000/13291.
25 Phillips, *Civil War in Wales*, II, p. 94; BDL, Firth Mss C6, f. 51.
26 *CSPD, 1644*, p. 338.
27 *LBWB*, I, p. 45.

6. With its seventeenth-century communion rail enclosing the table
like an altar at the east end, the layout of the originally eleventh-century
chapel at Heath evokes the Laudian order adopted in Shropshire churches
during the 1630s. Contemporary churchwardens' accounts record how this
arrangement was adorned with elaborate altar cloths, and with carpets
and kneeling cushions - as reflected in the modern setting at Heath.

Four aspects of royal policy during the 1630s are considered here as indicators:
local government reform; military affairs – both the national policy to 'perfect' an
'exact' militia, and Shropshire's response to the demands of the Bishops' Wars of 1639
and 1640; taxation, taking the example of ship money, the most significant fiscal
policy of the Personal Rule; and the attempted changes to the established Church –
King Charles's policy, in concert with William Laud, the Archbishop of Canterbury
appointed by Charles in 1633, to foster high-Church Anglicanism.

Promulgated by directives in the Privy Council's regulatory 'Book of Orders'
published in 1630, King Charles's policy to reform and standardise local government
required county justices of peace to prepare quarterly reports of their activity, as part of
a hierarchical reporting procedure informing the Privy Council. Here, it is interesting
to note that Shropshire presents the third highest number of certificated justice reports
extant from the 1630s, from among 44 shires. This may represent a misleadingly high
chance survival or records, but it may also indicate that Shropshire's JPs undertook
their duties with a good will to royal policy.[28]

28   H. Langelüddecke, "Patchy and Spasmodic"? The response of Justices of the Peace to Charles I's Book of

King Charles's policy to improve the training and equipment of the national militia, the trained bands, gained momentum during the limited Anglo-French and Anglo-Spanish wars of 1625-9, but the pace of reform lessened with the restoration of peace. There is, however, good evidence that reasonable effort to maintain military preparedness in Shropshire was maintained throughout the 1630s and until the eve of civil war. This extended to the training and re-equipping of the trained bands, including musters of the county force.[29] In 1642, therefore, the Shropshire Trained Bands seem to have remained a reasonably coherent force that on the whole readily came under Royalist authority.

In both Bishops' Wars Shropshire appears to have provided its quota of recruits for the King's armies: 300 foot and 35 horse in 1639, and 500 foot soldiers in 1640. This was not, however, a straightforward process, especially the raising of 'coat and conduct' money, levied at their home county's expense to clothe the recruits and provide for their subsistence, until they were formally enlisted by the King's regimental officers. In mid-May 1640 Shropshire's deputy lieutenants, entrusted with what was largely a process of conscription, reported that the recruits had so far been well provided for. However, the deputies were increasingly encountering difficulties in raising the money needed to maintain the levies and to recruit others. Concerned about 'their weak interests in the opinion of the county', they declared a conflict of loyalty to the sovereign and to their locality: 'betwixt whom we labour to pass by equal numbers'. As their patron and immediate superior as lord lieutenant, the Earl of Bridgewater sympathised. On 22 May he reported that while 500 recruits were made ready in Shropshire, coat and conduct money was coming in far short of expectation, and that some districts were disinclined to pay on administrative grounds.[30] However, notwithstanding the practical and personal difficulties that they encountered in their duties during 1639-40, it was the case that the same deputy lieutenants, perhaps bar one, became active Royalists in 1642.

The difficulties that officials in Shropshire and elsewhere across the Kingdom of England and Wales experienced during 1640 in providing forces to take on the Scots Covenanter regime were compounded by the concomitant requirement to raise ship money. From 1635 the tax had been levied upon inland as well as coastal counties in order to finance the Royal Navy. Ship money was seen by many contemporaries, and by historians since, as the most contentious of the policies of the Personal Rule prior to military intervention against the Covenanters in 1639. Yet until it became a universal fiscal crisis at county level during 1640, the tax was a remarkable success. Indeed, in strictly financial terms Shropshire's contribution appears to have been exemplary. Apart from the final writ, or levy, for 1639, extending into 1640, which collapsed administratively in Shropshire, as elsewhere in the kingdom, with just two and a half per cent of the county levy of £4,500 paid, cumulatively the four previous writs from 1635 had achieved a remarkably high collection rate in Shropshire of around 96

Orders', *The English Historical Review*, 113 (1998), esp. pp. 1236-8.

29 See the author's 'Ludlow's Trained Band: A Study of Militiamen in Early Stuart England', *Journal of the Society for Army Historical Research*, 99 (2013), pp. 4-23.

30 *CSPD, 1640*, pp. 173, 204-5.

per cent.[31] This impressive headline figure does, however, obscure the administrative difficulties and protracted rating disputes, some of which may have masked more principled or politicised opposition to the tax, that a succession of incumbent high sheriffs, charged with collecting ship money, encountered annually and which are well-documented in the calendared state papers.

The wartime Parliamentarian allegiance of two Shropshire MPs in particular seems explainable in political terms, to have been grounded in their objection to the policies of the Personal Rule. William Pierrepont's own experience as a ship money sheriff for Shropshire in 1637/38 could well have shaped his later opposition to King Charles as a Long Parliament MP and then as a leading Westminster-based Parliamentarian. Sir John Corbet's long-standing record of principled opposition to King Charles's policies certainly made him a political, and later a would-be military opponent of the King. In 1635 he had been imprisoned in London for six months pending trial for publicly disputing in Shropshire the crown's right to enforce military charges.[32] Corbet's return to the Long Parliament as one of two knights of the shire for Shropshire – MPs representing broader county interests, rather than individual borough towns – was probably because he had gained a reputation as a libertarian. His election suggests some backing from like-minded individuals politicised by the Personal Rule. Corbet's political supporters may in turn have been inclined to support Parliament during the war.

However, it would be wrong to suggest that grievances resulting from aspects of Charles I's policy necessarily set individuals on a path that eventually led to their taking up arms against the King. John Weld, for example, petitioned the Privy Council in objection to his personal assessment to pay ship money, yet he was as staunch supporter of the King in 1642.[33]

Beyond certain individual cases – with Sir John Corbet being the notable example – there does not seem to be a great deal of evidence of widespread principled or concerted resistance to royal policy in Shropshire in the 1620s and 1630s. This may help to account for the relative lack of support for Parliament there in 1642. Shropshire instead appears to have shared similarities with neighbouring Wales, which was almost wholly Royalist in 1642. Popular Royalism within the Principality seems to have sprung mostly from a prevailing conservative culture of conformism and compliance. These attitudes were shaped within a predominantly rural and traditionalised economy and a deferential society, where the aristocracy and the gentry remained particularly influential. Moreover, the majority of Welsh men and women had a deep attachment to ritualised Protestantism in the form of the Church of England. They generally remained unresponsive to non-conformist activism, and Puritanism had made few inroads into the Principality.[34]

Shropshire was certainly economically more prosperous than neighbouring Welsh shires. However, in religion it seems to have shared the Principality's majority

---

31 H. Langelüddecke, "I finde all men & my officers all soe unwilling": The Collection of Ship Money, 1635-1640', *The Journal of British Studies*, 46 (2007), esp. the tabular information on pp. 534, 536, 538-9, 541.

32 *ODNB*, 13, p. 389.

33 *CSPD, 1636–1637*, p. 20.

34 L. Bowen, *The Politics of the Principality – Wales, c. 1603–1642* (Cardiff, 2007), esp. pp. 231-4, 254-61,

commitment to established Anglicanism. Furthermore, the reforms to the established Church that Charles I sought to introduce in the 1630s, reforms that were intended to promote religious conformity and ceremonial public worship, appear to have found acceptance in Shropshire.

The King and Archbishop Laud set out to reinvigorate the actual and spiritual authority of the Church of England, as the traditional pillar of state alongside the monarchy. This policy, now popularly known as the 'Laudian reforms', stressed the ceremonial aspects of public worship, requiring the clergy and laity alike strictly to observe the liturgy in the form of the Book of Common Prayer. Respect for the Church and its authority was required by obedience to ecclesiastical canon law. In its most visible form, the Caroline-Laudian rectification of Anglicanism sought to exalt the holy beauty inherent in churches as the house of God, by expressing this beauty in the adornment and repair of the buildings.

Investment that is indicative of Laudian reform is recorded in churchwardens' accounts for the period from across Shropshire. New vestments, bibles, prayer books and sacramental objects were purchased. The churchwardens of St. Alkmunds, Whitchurch, for example, in 1635/6 purchased a 'flagon bought off London, of the best making, for the communion table', and in 1637/8 spent more than £8 on a new communion cup and an elaborate case in which to keep it.[35] The fabric of many churches was renovated, including re-plastering and re-glazing. Their roofs were repaired or expensively replaced. At Chetton and also at Myddle the tower of the parish church was rebuilt or extensively repaired, in 1632/3 and 1634 respectively. Bell lofts were overhauled, and in some parishes new bells were cast at considerable expense. New porches and lych gates were erected, church grounds were cleared and landscaped, and the enclosing walls or fences were put in good order. New pulpits were installed and existing ones often decoratively refurbished. Communion tables were positioned like an altar at the church's east end, enclosed by decorative timber rails or ballustrades. At St. Peter's, Myddle, for example, in addition to the new pulpit and pews, 'there was a new communion table made, a very good one, and also the new communion rails, which were placed square on three sides of the communion table'.[36] This railing-in of communion tables, now interpreted as a characteristic feature of Laudian church interiors, reinforced the sacerdotal role of the minister, who alone could approach God's table. Post-reformation church interiors had been uniformly whitewashed, but a number of Shropshire churches were now painted in an exuberant fashion reminiscent of the decoration of medieval churches. At St. Mary's, Shrewsbury, in 1634/5 the arches and pillars were coloured and decorated and extracts of scripture painted on the walls, while across town at the church of the Holy Cross, in 1636/7 a painter was paid the large sum of almost £12 for his work in 'adorning and beautifying the church'.[37]

Parishioners funded this widespread expenditure, and some of the wealthier of them may have been significant benefactors. It represented a considerable investment in the

---

35   SA, P303/B/1/1/2, unfoliated.
36   Gough, *Myddle*, p. 78-9.
37   For a summary of this activity, see the author's 'Beautifying Shropshire's Churches', *The Salopian Recorder*, 74 (2012), pp. 2-4.

religious life of the county, and seems to indicate an enthusiasm for the sort of religion favoured by the King and Archbishop Laud. Shropshire lay part within the diocese of Coventry and Lichfield, part within the diocese of Hereford, but neither Robert Wright, bishop of Coventry and Lichfield from 1632, nor the four bishops who, due to death in office, in quick succession held the bishopric of Hereford during the 1630s – Francis Godwin, from 1617 to 1633, Augustine Lindsell, in 1634, Theophilus Field, from 1635 to 1636, and George Cook, from 1636 – while upholding the policy, were not especially dogmatic or zealous Laudian reformers. It is likely, therefore, that the revision of public worship and the refurbishment of Shropshire churches proceeded with the general acceptance of the laity, and perhaps often with their enthusiastic support. Shropshire's experience is not easily explained as being just a result of compulsion by the bishops or their archdeacons during their annual tours of inspection, known as visitations, or by enforcement in the diocesan consistory courts. The inhabitants of Kenley, who in June 1637 agreed 'by the consent of the most part of the parish being present' to pay to repave the floor of their parish church, St. John the Baptist, may well have reflected the prevailing goodwill for Church reform in Shropshire.[38]

To further the regulation of religious practice, King Charles promoted the re-publication in 1633 of the Book of Sports. Introduced by his father King James I, this royal declaration gave sanction to participation in accustomed pastimes after church attendance on Sunday and on certain feast days. While the Book of Sports posed a direct challenge to Puritan sabbatarianism, the strict observance of Sunday as a day of rest and of religious devotion, it appealed to a cultural attachment to festivity and merry-making. Richard Baxter alluded to the fondness for traditional communal recreation in early seventeenth-century Shropshire. He remembered how as a boy, growing up in a 'country [county] that had but little preaching at all', after Sunday worship the inhabitants of Eaton Constantine, Baxter's home village, often spent the day 'in dancing under a May pole and a great tree […] where all the town did meet together'; and so 'we could not read the scripture in our family without the great disturbance of the tabor and pipe and noise in the street'. When Baxter heard his boisterous neighbours 'call my father Puritan, it did much to […] alienate me from them'. Before the Civil War Baxter was for a short time employed as a preacher at Bridgnorth, but found that the locals, other than 'a small company of converts, who were humble, Godly and of good conversations', were wholly unresponsive to his form of Puritan ministry: 'An ignorant, rude and revelling people for the greater part, who had need of preaching'.[39]

The inhabitants of the parish of Berrington in central Shropshire were also fond of their traditional revelry. During the 1630s they still upheld the ancient custom of the 'love feast', a communal dinner and accompanying festivities held at Easter in the parish church attended by the whole community and by local worthies. It was also customary for the feast to be paid for by the incumbent rector. When in 1639 the new rector objected to the feast and intended to cancel it, the parishioners quickly gained the support of Sir Richard Lee, a prominent local landowner who was also the

38 SA, 2310/1.
39 Baxter, *Reliquiae Baxterianae*, pp. 2, 20.

incumbent high sheriff of Shropshire (and three years later a prominent Royalist). Lee appealed on behalf of the villagers to the bishop of Coventry and Lichfield, Robert Wright, to uphold the feast. Pragmatically Wright agreed to the continuation of the feast elsewhere than the church, and that the rector should still foot the bill.[40]

It is argued here, then, that the religion of the majority of people in Shropshire in the 1630s was closer to that of King Charles and Archbishop Laud than it was to the Harleys, the Mores and Shrewsbury's Puritan fraternity. On the whole, Shropshire seems to have accepted, and many people may have embraced, the form of high-church Anglicanism favoured by the King, which could also accommodate popular communal recreation and traditional merriment.

This may go further to explain the county's Royalism in 1642. The increasingly sweeping religious 'root and branch' reforms promoted in Parliament by Puritan-leaning radicals and reformers throughout 1641 and into 1642 were intended to overturn Charles's policy of the 1630s. However, they went further and deeper in challenging Episcopal authority, and such established tenets of religious practice as the Book of Common Prayer itself, along with the Book of Sports (formally prohibited by Parliament in 1643). Parliament came to represent religious change that was anathema to many, and reaction against it in Shropshire coalesced in support for the King. The argument that Charles was able effectively to promote during 1642, that only he could be trusted to maintain a 'true' reformed form of Protestantism, as established in the Church of England, would engage support in conforming and religiously conservative places, as most of Shropshire may have been.

A vocal and influential body within the county clergy were important in promoting Charles's cause. As will be seen, in summer 1642 they endorsed the efforts of the gentry-led Royalist party in Shropshire, and the county's churchmen would continue to engage support for the King. In the case of Pontesbury, for example, a village seven miles south-west of Shrewsbury, in October 1643 a Parliamentarian military dispatch remarked that it was 'a parish most envenomed by reason of their malignant ministers against the Parliament'.[41] The wartime sermons delivered by Isaac Martin, the rector of Great Bolas, were later described as being 'stuffed up with bitter invective against the professors of religion [in other words, the Godly, Puritan-leaning sort], branding them with the name of Puritans, Precisians, Scismatics and factious people'. During 1644 Martin urged his parishioners to assist Prince Rupert's war effort, allegedly 'saying that the King had such a Prince for him, that he never drew his sword in battle but he prevailed', and in 1645 directed them to actually dismantle part of the village church in order to prevent it being occupied by Parliamentarian troops as a garrison.[42] In mid-1644 Parliament officially granted powers to the county committee for Shropshire to drive out such ministers to put an end to their influence. As a result, according to the Reverend Samuel Garbet, who as an eighteenth-century antiquarian wrote the history of Wem, one Doctor Medcalf was driven from the rectory of Wem itself, and elsewhere in north Shropshire John Arnway was evicted from the rectory of

40 A. Thursby-Pelham (ed.), 'The Berrington Love Feast', *TSANHS*, 2nd Series, VII (1895), pp. 203-6.
41 WRO, C2017/C10, f. 60.
42 SA, 811/87, Martin's sequestration papers, transcribed by F.S. Acton.

Hodnet, 'and James Fleetwood from the vicarage of Prees'. Farrow reckoned that for having actively supporting the King almost one third of the incumbent ministers in Shropshire were ejected from office by Parliament during the latter part of the First Civil War and afterwards.[43]

Churchmen who were inclined to Parliament could also find themselves removed from their ministry in Royalist territory, either by compulsion or as a result of their own conscience. Mr Gilbert Waldron, for example, in July 1641 had been appointed as the public preacher to the town of Bridgnorth, a post previously held by Richard Baxter. But in Easter 1644 Waldron fled the Royalist garrison, reportedly having 'vanished and gone out of the said town and hath departed his place'. His replacement was the chaplain to the military governor of Bridgnorth, Sir Lewis Kirke.[44]

Active Parliamentarianism in Shropshire probably had a largely religious basis, as a militant reaction to Laudian Anglicanism. A result of the policy was to encourage the polarisation of religious opinion and to weaken the middle ground, an important factor in causing warring factions to coalesce in 1642. Those whose religious outlook compelled them to become Royalists or Parliamentarians were equally able to present their opponents as divisive schismatics, responsible for promoting dangerous 'innovations' in religious practice that threatened to ruin the established Church and to destabilise society.

Sir William Brereton, who during the First Civil War would play an influential role in the fighting in Shropshire as commander-in-chief of Parliament's Cheshire Forces, as a tourist visited Shrewsbury in August 1635. Brereton, a Puritan, briefly visited St. Chad's church, where the Laudian Peter Studley was minister, which he was disturbed to find adorned with religious paintings and texts. Brereton noted with disgust how: 'This church is of late gaudily painted, wherein you may find many idle, ridiculous, vain and absurd pictures, representations and stories, the like whereunto I never saw in England'.[45]

Brereton's reaction was an example of how many individuals inclined to simplicity in religious practice, not just Puritans, but also many mainstream Anglicans, found the Laudian changes so profoundly disturbing – especially when expressed in such an ostentatious way as the adornment of St. Chad's. This appeared to mark an unwelcome shift under King Charles of the established Church from its Protestant post-reformation form – Elizabeth I's compromise settlement, held together under the religious pragmatism of James I – in a direction that was appearing to resemble Roman Catholicism. The practice of Catholicism was despised, and its religious and political influence feared, in equal measure, by the majority of English people at that time. These pent up fears had open expression from November 1640 by the sitting of the Long Parliament. It encouraged more radical opinion: that King Charles, who had a French Catholic queen, and who seemed to favour Catholic courtiers, intended to re-introduce Catholicism through the back door, and with it Papal interference in

43 Garbet, *History of Wem*, p. 223; Farrow, *Civil War*, p. 26.
44 SA, BB/C/1/1/1, unfoliated.
45 E.W. Hawkins (ed.), *Travels in Holland, The United Provinces, England, Scotland and Ireland, M.DC.XXXIV-M.DC.XXXV By Sir William Brereton, Bart.* (London, 1864), p. 187.

English affairs.

The uprising of the Irish Catholics begun in October 1641, and the stories of the atrocities they inflicted on Protestants – some of which were true, some of which were imagined or grossly exaggerated – provoked widespread alarm and fear across England and Wales of a similar uprising by native Catholics, or even of an invasion by the rebel Irish. Such a scare swept across Shropshire in November 1641. At Bridgnorth, on the night of the 19th the aldermen and townsmen kept an armed vigil, or 'Great Watch', across the town, 'upon information of a sudden insurrection and rising of the Papists that night in the Kingdom […] although God be praised it was not so'.[46] The Irish uprising brought into question the King's attitude to Catholicism, and among more radical opinion in Parliament, whether in fact he could be trusted with the army that would urgently have to be raised in England and Wales in order to crush the rebellion.

As the political crisis extending to the control of the Kingdom's armed forces unfolded into 1642, support for Parliament began to coalesce among those prepared to believe that the King was attracting a dangerous malignant following. This is reflected in a petition from Shropshire, said to have been subscribed by 10,000 of the county's inhabitants, which was presented and read in Parliament on 7 March 1642 and published soon after.[47] The true number of subscribers cannot be verified and the promoters of the petition are unknown, but Sir John Corbet, MP, seems a likely leading candidate. The petition was stated to represent the county's 'well-affected', and in tone was politically and religiously inclined to Parliament. It stressed the destabilising political and economic ill effects of:

> Mischievous plots, whereby the Popish malignant party daily attempt to keep us […] in deep and desperate dangers […] they have much retarded the proceedings of Parliament and by an un-exampled way, attempted the violation of the privileges, yea, the very being of Parliament; by reason whereof the rebels in Ireland have been encouraged to go on in their barbarous, and bloody designs […] and besides the kingdom may be exposed to foreign invasion, and your petitioners to the mercy of the Popish party.

Parliamentarian support could increasingly be motivated in the belief that the King's followers were dangerous Papists. High-Church Anglicans who had favoured King Charles's religious policy could easily be aggressively stereotyped and targeted as crypto-Catholics.

It seems likely, then, that the main reason for taking up arms in Shropshire against the King, as in fighting for him, was over religion.

To conclude this discussion, it is appropriate to return to Richard Baxter, a local man who as a contemporary theologian remarked at length on the reasons for allegiance in the First Civil War. Inspired as a young man by aspects of Puritan ideology, as a minister Baxter's religion inclined him to Presbyterianism. Baxter supported Parliament in the Civil War, and so was not a neutral observer of events. However,

---

46   SA, BB/D/1/2/1/51.
47   *The Petition of Knights, Justices of Peace, Ministers, Gentlemen, Free-holders and others, Inhabitants of the County of Salop, to the number of 10,000.* (London, March 1642).

the thoughtful reflection in his autobiography on motivation and allegiance merits quotation at length.[48]

Interestingly, Baxter first pointed to social division and the war as a class conflict – ideas that historians have more recently tended to question. 'A very great part of the knights and gentlemen of England in the several counties (who were not Parliament men [i.e. not MPs]) adhered to the King', reckoned Baxter:

> And most of the tenants of these gentlemen, and also most of the poorest of the people, whom the other side called the rabble, did follow the gentry, and were for the King. On the Parliament's side were (besides themselves [i.e. the Parliamentarian lords and MPs]) the smaller part (as some thought) of the gentry in most counties, and the greatest part of the tradesmen and free-holders, and the middle sort of men; especially in those corporations [i.e. towns] and countries which depended on clothing and such manufactures.

Baxter continued to develop his main point and argument, that religion, above all, was vital in determining allegiance and in sustaining motivation:

> But though it must be confessed, that the public safety and liberty wrought very much with most, especially with the nobility and gentry who adhered to the Parliament, yet it was principally the differences about religious matters that filled up the Parliament's armies, and put the resolution and valour into their soldiers, which carried them on in another manner than mercenary soldier are carried on. Not that the matter of bishops or no bishops was the main thing (for thousands that withheld for good bishops were on the Parliament's side) […] but the generality of the people through the land (I say not all, or every one) who were then called Puritans, Precisions, religious persons, that used to talk of God, and heaven, and scripture and holiness, and to follow sermons, and read books of devotion, and pray in their families, and spend the Lord's day in religious exercises, and plead for mortification, and serious devotion, and strict obedience to God, and spoke against swearing, cursing, drunkenness, prophaneness [and suchlike] I say, the main body of this sort of men, both preachers and people, adhered to the Parliament.
>
> And on the other side, the gentry that were not so precise and strict against an oath, or gaming, or plays, or drinking, nor troubled themselves so much about the matters of God and the world to come, and the ministers and people that were for the King's book of dancing and recreations on the Lord's day; and those that made not so great a matter or sin, but went to church and heard common prayer, and were glad to hear a sermon which lashed the Puritans, and which ordinarily spoke against this strictness and preciseness in religion, and this strict observation of the Lord's day, and following sermons, and praying extempore, and talking so much of scripture and the matters of salvation, and those that hated and derided them that take these courses, the main body of these were against the Parliament.
>
> Not that some such for money, or a landlord's pleasure, served them [i.e. either side]; as some of the stricter sort were against them, or not for them (being neuters): but I speak of the notable division through the land.

---

48 Baxter, *Reliquiae Baxterianae*, p. 31.

2

Leaders and Administrators: Organising the war effort

That honest and valiant committee in Shropshire.

In 1642 the first task of war effort was to create hierarchies of command and control. Both sides managed this at county level by grouping their chief supporters into similar rival bodies – the Royalist commissions of array and the Parliamentarian county committees. These were paramilitary organisations with civil and military authority, whose membership acted as civilian officials and/or army officers to direct the war effort in their shire. By exercising new martial powers and manipulating the traditional structures of county government, while asserting their local standing and influence, the commissioners and committeemen fashioned wartime administrations of varying effectiveness. Meanwhile, as the First Civil War intensified both King and Parliament attempted to direct the wider war effort by organising adjacent counties into regional commands, or associations. This was intended to facilitate the pooling of warlike resources for effective collaborative military action, but in practice concerns for local defence often prevailed over the pursuit of regional or wider strategic objectives. On both sides the regional commanders were usually peers of the realm, appointed for their social standing rather than their military experience.[1]

This chapter examines the vital organisational structures underpinning the opposing war efforts in Shropshire. First to be considered are the offices and mechanisms of local government that the belligerents would attempt to harness.

---

1 Set against events in the English East Midlands, an appraisal of the commissions of array and county committees is provided by M. Bennett in 'Between Scylla and Charybdis, The Creation of Rival Administrations at the beginning of The English Civil War' in *The English Civil War: The Essential Readings,* (ed.) P. Gaunt (Oxford, 2000), pp. 167-83. The commissions of array are further explored by Morrill, in *Revolt*, pp. 59-62, and by Hutton, in *War Effort*, pp. 5-7, 86-90, while on pp. 49-83 Hutton considered Royalist attempts to establish regional commands in Wales and the Marches during 1643. The most thorough studies of a Parliamentary county committee and of a regional association remain D.H. Pennington and I.A. Roots (eds.), *The Committee at Stafford, 1643-1645* (Manchester, 1957), and Holmes's *Eastern Association.*

Pre-war county governance and administration

Local government in Shropshire before the Civil War followed the general pattern throughout the shires of early Stuart England.[2] The will of central government, of the king and his executive Privy Council, and also the administration of local affairs was exercised by a hierarchical body of mostly part-time and unsalaried officials: the lord lieutenant and his deputies; the high sheriff; the justices of peace; the office-bearers of the corporate towns; the high constables of the county hundreds; and the numerous parochial officers – the petty constables, churchwardens, the overseers of the poor and the overseers of the highways. When Parliament sat Shropshire sent 12 MPs to Westminster – two knights of the shire and ten burgess, or borough, MPs, two each for the towns of Shrewsbury, Much Wenlock, Bridgnorth, Ludlow and Bishop's Castle.

At the apex of county officialdom was the lord lieutenancy, a sought-after appointment exercising great influence and considerable authority. For the ten years preceding the Civil War the lord lieutenant of Shropshire was John Egerton, first Earl of Bridgewater, a privy councillor. Bridgewater was also Lord President of the Council in the Marches of Wales, holding residency at Ludlow Castle.[3] By virtue of his presidency by 1640 Bridgewater was not only lord lieutenant of Shropshire, but also of Worcestershire, Herefordshire, Monmouthshire and the 12 shires of Wales. Bridgewater's chief responsibility was ensuring the military preparedness of these counties. In each shire arrangements for home defence, and especially the organisation of the practised militia, or trained bands, were delegated to notable gentry appointed as the lord lieutenant's deputies. In early 1642 there were eight deputy lieutenants for Shropshire: Sir Richard Lee, MP; Sir Richard Newport; Sir Gilbert Cornwall; Henry Bromley; Thomas Screven; Sir Thomas Wolrych; Sir Vincent Corbet; and Richard Herbert, the MP for Montgomery in neighbouring Montgomeryshire. All of them became active Royalists. Three deputy lieutenants, Screven, Wolrych and Corbet, together with Pelham Corbet, another future Royalist, also captained the four companies of Shropshire's Trained Bands, with Cornwall captain of the county Troop of Horse.[4]

By the early seventeenth century the office of high sheriff had declined in importance as the crown's chief executive in a shire. In particular, the traditional powers of the shrievalty in military affairs had largely devolved to the lord lieutenancy. But the office regained authority during the 1630s, when the high sheriff had to levy and personally account for his shire's annual rate for ship money. However, the high sheriff and his under-sheriff deputy were more routinely involved in administering law and order,

2   This section draws on: A. Fletcher, *Reform in the Provinces, The Government of Stuart England* (London, 1986); R. Lockyer, *The Early Stuarts – A Political History of England, 1603-1642* (Harlow, 1999); L.M. Hill, 'County Government in Caroline England, 1625-1640' in *The Origins of the English Civil War*, (ed.) C. Russell (London, 1973), pp. 66-90; D.C. Cox, 'County Government, 1603-1714' in *A History of Shropshire Volume III*, (ed.) G.C. Baugh (Oxford, 1979), pp. 90-114; R. Lloyd Kenyon (ed.), *Orders of the Shropshire Quarter Sessions, Volume I, 1638-1708* (Shrewsbury, undated); and H. Langelüddecke "The Pooreste and Sympleste Sorte of People"? The Selection of Parish Officers During the Personal Rule of Charles I', *Historical Research*, 80 (2007), pp. 225-60.
3   *ODNB*, 27, pp. 996-7.
4   HHL, Ellesmere Mss, 7443, 'A list of the deputy lieutenants and captains in the Principality and the Marches of Wales, 1637, revised and amended 1642'.

including hosting their county's six most important annual judicial and administrative events and social gatherings – the four seasonal courts of session and the bi-annual courts of assize.

Although virtually no records from them survive, Shropshire's pre-war quarter sessions were usually held for up to three days at Shrewsbury. The sessions were the quarterly main gatherings of the justices of the county magistracy, or commission of the peace. In 1642 Shropshire had around 50 justices of peace, appointed by the King from among the ranks of the gentry. At quarter sessions the JPs addressed legal matters, adjudicating on civil and lesser criminal cases, and also administrative affairs, such as local trade regulation and the county rates. The JPs in their work were assisted by a grand jury empanelled by the high sheriff, a body of 15 or more respectable men of middling rank but generally lower social status than the magistracy. The grand jury was itself an important and respected institution. As well as being trial jurors the grand jurymen were a sort of quasi-supervisory body, representing in various issues the informed opinion of the wider county community. The sessions were also attended by the high constables of the county hundreds, who acted as intermediaries between the JPs and lesser local officials. Weighty criminal cases and contentious administrative matters were referred to the assize courts presided over by visiting higher court judges sitting with a local grand jury. The assizes also gave the Privy Council an indirect opportunity to exercise higher policy and to intervene in county affairs. In 1639, for example, the Council instructed the circuit judges at the assizes to resolve long-standing rating problems affecting parts of Shropshire.[5] The assizes were held at Bridgnorth in March, at Lent, and in high summer at Shrewsbury. Shropshire formed part of the wide-ranging Oxford assize circuit encompassing also Oxfordshire, Berkshire, Gloucestershire, Monmouthshire, Herefordshire, Worcestershire and Staffordshire.

While the gentry served as chief agents of higher local government, the day-to-day practice and enforcement of policy depended on the many lesser officials – who were typically artisans, yeomen and better-off husbandmen – voluntarily serving their elective part-time annual tenure as petty constables and churchwardens, or as overseers of the poor and of the highways. Petty constables had most responsibilities in their often-conflicting roles as royal officer and also village headman. They were charged with upholding law and order in their parish, and administrative tasks such as ensuring that the local militiamen of the trained bands attended musters and were properly paid and equipped. Petty constables assessed and collected most local rates and central taxes. They were expected meanwhile to report on their work and any pressing local matters by making regular 'presentments' to the justices and high constables. Churchwardens, as lay superintendents of the parish church, set and collected rates for its upkeep and, together with the overseers of the poor, disbursed relief to the local needy. Finally, the overseers of the highways were responsible for their parish's statutory duty to maintain public roads in the district.

Braddick has pointed out that local government in Caroline England was 'densely populated with officeholders', and this would have been the case in Shropshire.[6]

5   Lloyd Kenyon, *Sessions*, I, p. 1; *CSPD*, 1639, p. 252.
6   Braddick, *God's Fury*, p. 59.

Most parishes had two petty constables, but some townships also had their own; John Bowland, for example, was in 1638 the petty constable of Woodcote and Lynn, a scattered hamlet within Lilleshall parish. Constables also enlisted the occasional paid help of deputies such as John Marshall of Worfield, who sometime in 1640 assisted the parish officers in punishing vagrants.[7] Shropshire parishes typically had two churchwardens and several overseers. Condover, for example, into the 1640s had two churchwardens and four sidemen, several overseers of the poor and up to seven overseers of the highways. In addition, the parish's lay governing body of eight vestrymen audited the churchwardens' annual accounts.[8] The contemporary geographer John Speed identified 170 parishes in Jacobean Shropshire.[9] Therefore, in 1642 there were probably around 2,000 incumbent parochial officials, besides their deputies and other bodies of overseeing lay folk, all having some practical experience of local administrative affairs.

The officers of Shopshire's largely self-governing corporate towns provided another tier of local government. Shrewsbury, Much Wenlock, Bridgnorth, Ludlow and Bishop's Castle, which, as borough towns, elected ten of the county's 12 MPs, were each administered by an elective body of aldermen headed by one or two bailiffs. Shrewsbury differed from 1638 in having a mayor, replacing the two bailiffs under a revised royal charter issued that June. The mayor headed a corporation of 23 other aldermen, who appointed 48 lesser town officials known as assistants. Bishop's Castle, meanwhile, was governed by 15 'headburgesses', from whom one was elected bailiff. This assembly appointed the town's standing executive officials, some of whom were also headburgesses. They were the two sergeants at mace and two constables, whose main duties were law and order, and three clerical officers – two chamberlains and the town clerk.[10]

Town officials found themselves drawn into the war effort. Thomas Crowther, for example, as the senior, or high bailiff of Ludlow during 1645 played an effective role in gathering Royalist military taxes. But near Ludlow one night in October 1645 he was captured by a Parliamentarian patrol. Major Hungerford, the governor of Stokesay Castle, the nearest Parliamentary garrison to Ludlow, reckoned that Crowther's removal would certainly hamper Royalist tax-collection: 'So you may think they [now] get it with much difficulty', he remarked in a dispatch to headquarters at Shrewsbury.[11]

The officials of county governance in seventeenth-century Shropshire acted within a framework of administrative districts, the largest being the 15 hundreds (Map 6). Three main towns, Shrewsbury, Much Wenlock and Ludlow, with their immediate environs, or liberties, each counted as a hundred. From west to east Shropshire's northerly hundreds were Oswestry, Pimhill and then Bradford, the largest hundred, with northerly and southerly divisions. In an approximately central belt lay the westerly hundred of Chirbury, Ford hundred, the town and liberties of Shrewsbury, Condover

7   SA, P161/M1, ff. 8-9, constables' accounts, 1638-40; P314/M/1, f. 38.
8   SA, P81/Fiche 115-28.
9   Speed, *Great Britaine*, pp. 71-2.
10   J.B. Blakeway and H. Owen, *A History of Shrewsbury*, 2 vols. (London, 1825) I, p. 406-7; BCHRC, First Minute Book, f. 202v.
11   *LBWB*, II, p. 134.

hundred, the town and liberties of Much Wenlock (the Wenlock Franchise) and the easterly hundred of Brimstree. The most westerly of the southerly hundreds was Clun, then Purslow, Munslow and Overs, the latter incorporating the town and liberties of Ludlow. Finally, Stottesdon hundred lay in the south-east and included the town and liberties of Bridgnorth.[12]

The administrative importance of the hundreds increased during the 1630s as the focus of Charles I's policy to systematise local government, in such matters as poor relief, alehouse licensing, highway maintenance and countering vagrancy. This required the magistracy to superintend monthly supervisory meetings of the parochial officers within each hundred. An example of these so-called 'petty sessions' in Shropshire was that for Condover hundred held at Acton Burnell in October 1632, when the local justices met with the high and petty constables, the churchwardens and the overseers.[13] The county militia was also ordered on the basis of the hundreds. In 1642, of Shropshire's four companies of Trained Band infantry, the men of Captain Vincent Corbet's company were recruited from Bradford hundred and the town and liberties of Shrewsbury, while the soldiers of Captain Thomas Screven's company were more widely drawn from the hundreds of Condover, Clun, Purslow, Overs, Munslow and Ludlow. Regulatory inspections of the trained bandsmen and their maintainers (those officials or wealthier individuals accountable for providing the soldiers' equipment and pay) were also held according to hundreds. In November 1634, for example, Edward Burton – the county muster master, and as such Shropshire's sole full-time stipendiary military officer – reported to the Earl of Bridgewater that musters had taken place in seven hundreds and were planned in the remaining eight.[14]

Since the 1590s county rates and national taxes had been apportioned in Shropshire according to the subdivision of the 15 hundreds into 100 areas of approximately equal wealth known as allotments. Their relative size is now difficult to characterise, but a town, or a grouping of rural constablewicks, could be counted similarly as one allotment. Allotments also overlaid the boundaries of parishes such as Myddle, split between the allotment of Myddle and Loppington and the liberties of Shrewsbury. Chirbury hundred was divided into three allotments, the Wenlock Franchise counted as seven.[15] Shrewsbury and its liberties together comprised six and a half allotments, hence the county town paid one-fifteenth and a half part of county rates.[16] Dividing a rate by 100 and charging all allotments equally was normal procedure. During the 1630s this applied, for example, to the muster-master's annual salary of £50, charged at 10s per allotment, and also to purveyance – the customary annual obligation to provide the royal household with provisions or cash in kind. Accordingly, in 1639 each allotment paid 52s towards Shropshire's £260 charge for this 'provision money'.[17] From its introduction in Shropshire in August 1635 the annual levy for ship money was apportioned by allotments, but the unprecedentedly large sums required changes

12 SA, 3365/225, f. 10, a list of Shropshire's hundreds, c. 1642.
13 *CSPD, 1631-1633*, p. 421.
14 HHL, Ellesmere Mss, 7443, 7625.
15 Gough, *Myddle*, p. 29; *CSPD, 1637-1638*, p. 312; *CSPD, 1636-1637*, p. 20.
16 SA, 6001/290, f. 115; *CSPD, 1635*, pp. 516.
17 HHL, Ellesmere Mss, 7625; SA, BB/D/1/2/1/49.

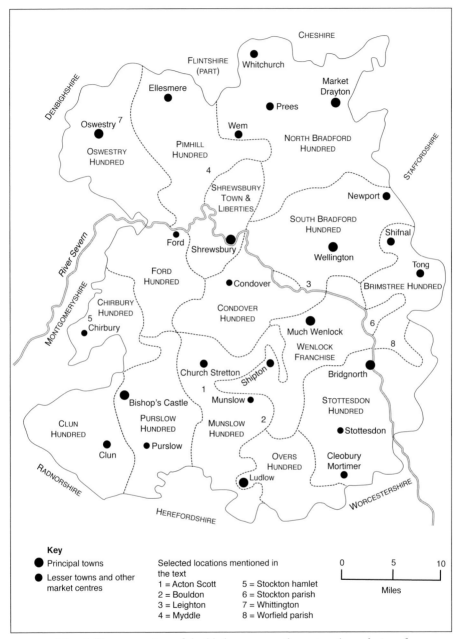

Map 6: Reconstruction of the likely seventeenth-century boundaries of the Shropshire hundreds (modern county boundary shown). (Sources: the mapping by John Speed in *The Theatre of the Empire of Great Britaine* (1611), unpaginated, and by Robert Blome in *Britannia: Or, A Geographical Description of the Kingdom of England, Scotland and Ireland* (1673), unpaginated.)

to the traditional uniform assessment. The resultant wrangling over variable valuation and rating hampered not only the collection of ship money, but in 1640 also the levying of coat and conduct money during the Second Bishops' War.[18] Nonetheless, levies would be imposed according to allotments during the Civil Wars.

Petty constables and churchwardens administered the charges upon the hundreds and allotments by setting parish rates, known in Shropshire as lewns. These were levied annually but also on an ad-hoc basis as need arose. In 1639/40, for example, from two lewns levied by their constables the parishioners of Kenley contributed to the nearest workhouse, or 'house of correction', to purveyance, to the muster-master's stipend, and to cover the expense of conscripting three local men as soldiers during the Bishops' Wars.[19] Land value was the predominant measure of assessment, calculated at a variable rate according to a unit of acreage known as yard land. For instance, in 1638 the churchwardens of Lydbury North set two lewns for church maintenance and two for the parish poor, respectively at the rate of 2s and 18s 'the yard land'. More than two thirds of one lewn levied during 1634/5 by the constables of Worfield – 'after the rate of every yard land, 16 pence' – paid for military charges, for the parish trained bandsmen and towards the muster master's salary. The proceeds of lewns were usually paid to coincide with the quarter sessions, like the churchwardens of Donnington who during the 1630s gave their 'quarter pay' in installments to the high constable to deposit at the sessions.[20]

The adaptation of county governance to Civil War

In organising war effort at county level it was to be expected that the combatants would appropriate the machinery of local government, which, as has been seen, was in many respects already geared to taxation and procuring military resources. The use of familiar administrative structures gave the abnormal demands of wartime a legitimate veneer. Moreover, it made good sense to engage local officials who were familiar with implementing financial or material impositions, while higher officials who became activists could exercise their influence in support of the cause.

In 1642 the powers of the lord lieutenancy would elude both sides in Shropshire. As lord president Bridgewater had dutifully and diligently served Charles I. However, the difficulties of the later years of the Personal Rule and the consequent censure he experienced from the Long Parliament, which entailed the abolition of the Council at Ludlow, sapped Bridgewater's support for the monarch. On 5 March 1642 Parliament finally enacted the national militia ordinance in order to lever military authority away from the King, thereby placing under its authority the militia and the lieutenancy and instigating a purge of the lords lieutenant across England and Wales. This included Bridgewater's presidency, and it was reported in the Lords on 24 March that he would 'with all convenient speed' relinquish his lieutenancies, 'for he doth willingly submit unto their lordships' order'.[21] Although King Charles in summer 1642 and into spring

---

18   Lloyd Kenyon, *Sessions*, I, p. 1; *CSPD*, 1639, p. 252; *CSPD, 1640*, pp. 173, 180.
19   SA, SRO 2310/1.
20   SA, P177/B/2/1, unfoliated; SA, P314/M/1/1, ff. 36-7; SA, P94/B/1/1, unfoliated.
21   *A&O*, I, pp. 1-5; *JHL*, IV, p. 666.

1643 hopefully appointed Bridgewater the titular head of commissions of array in Shropshire and other shires of his former presidency, he played little part and later neutrally sat out the war at his Hertfordshire estate.

By the militia ordinance Parliament replaced Bridgewater as lord lieutenant of Shropshire with the county-born Edward, Lord Littleton, Lord Keeper of the Great Seal. The politically ambivalent Littleton was an unfortunate choice, however, for in May he defected to King Charles's court at York. In the Commons on 3 June 1642 it was therefore gloomily reported of Shropshire, that 'there is no lord lieutenant to appoint the execution of the militia [ordinance]'. On 5 September following Parliament formally ejected Littleton from his post, making the Earl of Essex, the Lord General of Parliament's field army, the lord lieutenant of Shropshire; in the event a titular appointment that had no practical influence on the outcome of events there.[22] King Charles more credibly revived the office in 1644, when on 3 April he made Prince Rupert Lord President of Wales and the Marches and thereby the *ex officio* lord lieutenant of Shropshire.[23]

Following Littleton's appointment as lord lieutenant, on 18 March 1642 Parliament approved several new deputy lieutenants for Shropshire, of whom two at least – Sir William Whitmore, MP for Bridgnorth, and John Weld junior, son of the high sheriff – would become Royalists. Accordingly, on 6 September following Parliament 'discharged' them both of their deputyship, along with Sir Vincent Corbet and Sir Thomas Wolrych. Parliament's replacement deputies appointed the same day were Walter Barker of Haughmond, Humphrey Walcot of Walcot, Sir Gilbert Cornwall, Thomas Hunt of Shrewsbury and Walter Long (a Wiltshire MP with landed interests in Shropshire). They had mixed loyalties, and of the local men only Hunt, and Barker to some extent, became active Parliamentarians.[24] For the purposes of the Parliamentarian war effort in Shropshire the lieutenancy therefore became a dead letter. However, the Royalist deputies, including those discharged by Parliament, exercised the authority of the office into 1643 at least.[25]

The collection of ship money generated a revival in the powers of the shrievalty that continued into the Civil War. During summer 1642, in each shire Charles I called upon the high sheriff to coordinate a commission of array, reviving in both of these originally medieval institutions military powers lapsed since the Tudor creation of the lord lieutenancy. As the incumbent High Sheriff John Weld of Willey adroitly headed Shropshire's commission of array, and at the summer assizes held on 8 August (at Bridgnorth, within Weld's sphere of local influence, instead of Shrewsbury) with the connivance of the circuit judge, Baron Edward Henden, he engineered a packed grand jury under the commissioners' sway that proclaimed its support for the King.[26] On 14 September the Commons ordered Weld's impeachment, but he was well beyond their

22 *JHC*, II, pp. 602, 752.
23 NRO, Finch-Hatton Mss 133, unfoliated.
24 *JHC*, II, pp. 485, 755.
25 A meeting of deputy lieutenants took place at Bridgnorth in January 1643, for example: SA, BB/D/1/2/1/53.
26 'Ottley Papers' (1894), pp. 33, 37, (1895), pp. 241-4; W. Yonge, *Walter Yonge's Diary of Proceedings in the House of Commons, 1642-1645*, I, (ed.) C. Thompson (Wivenhoe, 1986), p. 5.

reach and from 21 September the high sheriff sat on King Charles's council of war at Shrewsbury and issued warrants to summon the militia, to enlist volunteers and to solicit arms donations.[27] Weld's successors as the King's high sheriff, Henry Bromley in 1642/3, Thomas Edwards in 1643/4 and, from later 1644 until he surrendered in April 1646, Sir Francis Ottley, were active in the Royalist war effort. Henry Bromley, for example, in April 1643 invoked in south Shropshire the sheriff's traditional power to summon the posse comitatus – a general, usually county-wide, call to arms of most physically able men aged 16 to 60 – and in November, when superintending tax collection, ordered the town bailiffs of Ludlow to pay arrears.[28] Shropshire had concurrent opposing high sheriffs from December 1643, when Parliament created a rival shrievalty by the appointment of Colonel Thomas Mytton who was Parliament's high sheriff into 1646.[29]

Given their social and political status a number of justices of peace inevitably took sides. Of 17 Shropshire JPs gathered at Shrewsbury in January 1642, during the First Civil War ten were active as Royalists and five as Parliamentarians. For the first year of the conflict at least, it was acceptable for magistrates to authorise warlike activity. The Royalists Edward Cressett and Edward Acton, MP, for example, in May 1643 directed military affairs at Bridgnorth in their capacity as local JPs rather than as commissioners of array.[30]

There is little extant evidence of the wartime activity of the justices' immediate under officers, the high constables. But they seem to have remained the important intermediaries between higher authority and lesser officials. In June 1648, for instance, Shropshire's governing Parliamentary committee gave orders for Richard Holland, a high constable of Stottesdon hundred, to instruct the town bailiffs of Bridgnorth to make arrangements for the militia.[31]

The quarter sessions and courts of assize were the assemblies in which JPs, grand jurymen, the sheriff and other officials and interested parties had managed county affairs. When war came, with King Charles's endorsement attempts were made in Royalist areas to ensure that the body politic kept at least an ostensible say in taxation and other aspects of war effort, voiced via the continuation in some form of sessions and assizes, or by public gatherings of gentry and freeholders. In Worcestershire, for example, the grand jury became in effect a county assembly.[32] Meanwhile, the Oxford assize circuit remained operational into summer 1643 at least.[33] There is vestigial evidence of the survival of the formal courts in Shropshire, of the Lent and summer assizes in 1643, and of a grand jury sitting in late summer 1644.[34] But there is more evidence that Royalist policy was disseminated and approved by public gatherings. Mass meetings of gentry and freeholders, convened by the high sheriff and held at

27   *JHC*, II, p. 766; SA, LB7/2317, LB7/2233, warrants directed to the town of Ludlow.
28   SA, LB7/2235; SA, LB7/1932.
29   *JHC*, III, p. 354; *JHL*, VIII, p. 41.
30   SA, LB7/2315; SA, BB/C/1/1/1, unfoliated.
31   SA, BB/C/8/1/6.
32   Braddick, *God's Fury*, p. 285; Morrill, *Revolt*, pp. 78, 112, 116; Hutton, *War Effort*, pp. 37, 135.
33   BDL, Dugdale Mss 19 [first part], f. 123.
34   'Ottley Papers' (1895), pp. 269-70; SA, 3365/587, f. 11; SA, 3365/588, f. 19.

7. Thomas Edwards, King Charles's high sheriff of Shropshire during 1643/4.

Shrewsbury, are known to have taken place, on 22 November 1642; upon Prince Rupert's arrival in February 1644; and in 1645, on 7 January and again on 5 February, the latter gathering held before Prince Maurice.[35] Furthermore, references to Royalist meetings attended jointly by commissioners of array and other gentry demonstrate more widespread participation in the direction of the Royalist war effort.[36] For their part, the Parliamentarians in Shropshire, as generally elsewhere during the First Civil War, do not appear to have made any use of rival courts or public meetings.

The responsibilities and duties of parochial officers had increased considerably during the years of the Personal Rule, and for most their workload intensified during the First Civil War when both sides engaged their services. Higher civil and military officers usually sought to act with the authority of warrants when demanding material support for the war effort. In early October 1643, for example, the Parliamentarians served warrants from their base at Wem, ordering petty constables in north Bradford hundred to provide horses, arms and provisions.[37] Royalist soldiers felt justified in enlisting the support of civilian officials who held their office in the King's name. A Royalist transport officer posted to Shropshire in February 1644 carried Prince Rupert's warrant, to enlist the support of 'all mayors, sheriffs, justices of peace, bailiffs, high constables, constables, headboroughs, tithing men [the latter two being titles

35 SA, BB/D/1/2/1/52; WSL, SMS 551/2; HRO, CF61/20, f. 569; BDL, Firth Mss C6, f. 303.
36 For example, BRL, Additional Mss 18981, f. 19.
37 The warrant was reproduced on pp. 650-1 of the Royalist journal *Mercurius Aulicus* for the week ending 19 Nov. 1643. Although published with propagandist intent, there seems little reason to doubt the transcript's accuracy.

synonymous as petty constables or their deputies], post masters, all other of his majesty's officers […] but more especially to the constables'.[38]

Their wartime duties made petty constables especially active. For example, during 1644 and 1645 the constables of Stockton performed many assignments for the Royalist garrison at Bridgnorth, five miles south of their parish. Among other tasks, they assessed and collected military taxes, impressed local conscripts and gathered provisions. Later in 1645 the constables also executed warrants served by the nearby Parliamentarian garrison across the River Severn at Benthall.[39] Petty constables were especially hard tasked, but other local officials were also drawn into the war effort. Before the Civil War the churchwardens of the Shrewsbury parish of the Holy Cross had levied funds to maintain the parish's two trained bandsmen, and they continued to do so from 1642 to 1644 when their soldiers were in Royalist service. After Shrewsbury fell to the Parliamentarians, from 1645 the churchwardens in turn assessed and collected Parliamentary military taxes. At Ludlow, both bailiffs acted as chief assessors of Royalist taxation whilst deputising collection to two under-officers, the chamberlains and high constables of the town. Meanwhile at Bridgnorth the 24 aldermen forming the town council met periodically during the First Civil War. Under the oversight of the military governor and some commissioners of array, the aldermen addressed matters relating to the garrison and the town defences.[40]

Some officials found that their wartime duties imposed an intolerable burden. The troubles of John Acton, a glover by trade and in 1644 one of the petty constables of Ludlow, illustrate the point. For failing to adequately fulfill warrants issued by the town's military governor Sir Michael Woodhouse, Acton was repeatedly committed to the provost martial's cell, and one market day he was arrested and forced out of his shop by Woodhouse's musketeers. On another occasion the governor angrily struck Acton and threw a stone at him.[41] Constable Acton may have been incompetent, obstructive or just plain unfortunate. But local officials often adapted to circumstances for their own or their neighbours' sake, and in so doing performed satisfactorily for either King or Parliament. This sort of pragmatism can be detected in the hinterland of Shrewsbury into 1646, where among 27 of the petty constables serving under the Parliamentarian regime, 40 per cent had acted for the Royalists as parish officers or local tax officials.[42] At Bridgnorth, John Lawrence capably assisted both sides as the Beadle, or general factotum to the town council. Having previously executed many warrants for the Royalists, Lawrence remained in office into 1647 when he implemented orders from the Parliamentarian county committee for the demolition of Bridgnorth Castle, formerly a Royalist strong point.[43]

Something remains to be said of the involvement in the First Civil War of the Shropshire MPs elected to sit from November 1640 in the Long Parliament.[44] Four

---

38   SA, LB7/2249.
39   SA, P270/B/1/1, ff. 55-8.
40   SA, P250/325-8; SA, LB7/1932; SA, BB/C/1/1/1, unfoliated.
41   SA, LB7/2108, Acton's petition of grievances, dated 20 Jan. 1645.
42   Individuals named in: SA, 3365/589, ff. 1-3; SA, 3365/1267, ff. 91-148, *passim*; SA, 3365/2711, f. 23.
43   SA, BB/D/1/2/1/57.
44   D. Brunton and D.H. Pennington, *Members of the Long Parliament* (London, 1954), pp. 10-13.

of them opposed King Charles. Listed in descending order of their likely importance to the Parliamentarian cause, they were: William Pierrepont, a burgess MP for Much Wenlock; Sir John Corbet, a knight of the shire; and Richard More and William Spurstowe, respectively burgesses for Bishop's Castle and Shrewsbury. Shropshire's remaining eight MPs were more or less active as Royalists. Sir Richard Lee of Langley and Sir Robert Howard of Clun, respectively the second knight for the shire and burgess for Bishop's Castle, were commissioners of array and early active supporters of King Charles. Consequently, on 6 September 1642 they were both 'disabled', or formally ejected from the Commons.[45] In 1644 Lee and Howard attended the Royalist parliament sitting at Oxford from 22 January into April together with the six other Shropshire MPs, whose presence there confirmed their allegiance beyond any further doubt. Accordingly, also on 22 January the Westminster Parliament disabled Francis Newport, the second burgess for Shrewsbury, for 'being in the King's quarters, and adhering to that party', and in a final round of ejections for the same reasons on the following 5 February disabled Thomas Littleton, the second burgess for Much Wenlock, Sir Edward Acton and Sir Thomas Whitmore, the burgesses for Bridgnorth, along with both burgesses for Ludlow, Charles Baldwin and Ralph Goodwyn.[46]

Royalist leadership and administration in Shropshire
The commission of array, 1642-6

The means by which King Charles I sought to engage widespread military support during summer 1642 was by instituting for each county a commission of array, the name given to the body itself and also to the impressive charter, written in Latin and bearing the royal seal, that brought it into being. Later medieval English kings had issued commissions of array to the high sheriffs and leading magnates in the shires to raise men for war, but as a military device it had long been superseded by the powers of the Tudor lord lieutenancy. However, the commission of array remained on the statute book and King Charles had issued them in 1640 at the time of the Second Bishops' War, including to the Earl of Bridgewater in mid-September instructing him to raise forces within the Presidency of Wales and its Marche.[47]

King Charles constituted the first 28-man commission of array for Shropshire at his court at York on 22 June 1642 (Table 1), where the same day his secretary Sir Edward Nicholas wrote justifying the commissions generally, as 'issued by his majesty for disposing of the militia into the hands of the estated [i.e. landed] sober men, in the ancient and approved way'.[48] Shropshire's commissioners therefore had a deliberately narrow military remit, to conduct the trained bands and ensure that they were adequately trained and equipped under loyal local officers, and to tax Recusants (individuals who refused to attend Anglican services but who were allowed to avert persecution by paying an annual fine) in order to provide arms in the anticipated event of a wider call up of the untrained militia, the posse comitatus. Accordingly, trained

45   *JHC*, II, p. 755.
46   Rushworth, *Historical Collections*, V, pp. 573-5; *JHC*, III, pp. 374, 389.
47   HHL, Ellesmere Mss, 7684.
48   *CSPD, 1641-1643*, pp. 344-5.

bandsmen were being mustered in the Shrewsbury area by 2 July.[49] The value of the commission of array to King Charles was that it enabled him, with some legitimacy, to circumvent Parliament's militia ordinance, and, if necessary, bypass the lieutenancy, in order to muster military support by the royal prerogative in time-honoured fashion.

The commission of array in each shire was a cross-section of notable or otherwise influential gentry entrusted by Charles to raise support, esquires as well as titled gentlemen, under the purported leadership of a leavening of peers of the realm with local interests. Hence, under the titular headship of the 12-year old Charles, Prince of Wales, the commission for Shropshire was headed by five peers with estates in the county but who never or only rarely resided there: Robert, Viscount Kilmorey; Thomas Howard, Earl of Arundel; William, Lord Craven; Edward Herbert, Lord of Cherbury; and the Earl of Bridgewater. Other than Kilmorey, who was active mostly in Cheshire, none of these noblemen as figureheads appear to have done much to uphold the King's cause in Shropshire in 1642 or later: both Howard and Craven voluntarily went into Continental exile; Herbert was infirm and his Royalism was lukewarm, and, retired to his fastness at Montgomery Castle, he hoped to distance himself from the conflict; while Bridgewater shunned commitment, as has already been seen.[50]

To all intents and purposes, then, in Shropshire it was the local gentry who rallied to King Charles and who served as commissioners of array, including the trained band captains, and, except for Sir Richard Newport and Sir Gilbert Cornwall, the deputy lieutenants holding office in earlier 1642. As has been seen, Sir Richard Newport was at first ambivalent in his allegiance, appointed to the first commission of array of 22 June, but dropped from the second a month later. So it was a vital moment for the Shropshire Royalists when, probably in mid-August, Sir Richard committed his support and considerable local influence to the King. In the meantime, at York on 18 July Charles had re-constituted a second commission of array for Shropshire (Table 1) intending to bring more active men to the fore by dropping seven original commissioners and appointing 14 newcomers, making a total of 33. Spurred into renewed activity, by warrants issued on 26 July the commissioners mustered the Trained Bands in the Shrewsbury area on 2 August. The commissioners meanwhile gathered at the county town on 28 July, where, leading a body of followers armed militia-like with improvised weapons, several angrily confronted the local Parliamentarian MPs on 1 August.[51] This belligerent activity was headed by the commissioners Sir Paul Harris, Edward Cressett, Sir Vincent Corbet, Richard Lloyd, High Sheriff John Weld, the Mayor of Shrewsbury Richard Gibbons, and notably by Francis Ottley of Pitchford, who in 1646 was still characterised in the London press as 'the first man that acted the commission of array in Shropshire'.[52]

As has been seen, at the assizes on 8 August the commission of array secured a declaration professing lawful obedience to the King, by 'putting the country [Shropshire]

49 'Ottley Papers' (1894), pp. 33-4; SA, P250/Fiche 325.
50 *ODNB*: 40, p. 323; 28, p. 445; 14, p. 65; 26, p. 667.
51 *JHL*, V, pp. 269-70.
52 *Perfect Occurrences of Both Houses of Parliament and Martiall Affairs*, w/e 10 Apr. 1646, unpaginated.

in a posture of arms for the defence of his majesty and the peace of the kingdom'. Furthermore, at Much Wenlock on 16 August the sheriff and 17 other commissioners issued another declaration, threatening to confront any opposition as enemies of the King and summoning the gentry to back the assizes declaration. From then on, with a firm grip on the Shropshire Trained Bands, but it seems without using actual force, by public proclamation, by lobbying groups and individuals in correspondence and private meetings, and with the backing by a declaration on 24 August of a sizeable and voluble Royalist faction among the county clergy, the commission of array gradually gained support and a momentum that dissuaded many from supporting Parliament.[53] This movement expressed a degree of commitment to the King that was more than a show of local unanimity meant to keep the peace and avert public disorder. More than outwardly, then, the commission of array secured Shropshire for King Charles, who, by visits from Shropshire Royalists as the court moved into the East Midlands in later August and into September, was kept well informed of developments there before he entered the county on 19 September 1642. Charles rewarded several commissioners with knighthoods, including Francis Ottley who assumed, de facto, a leading role as governor of Shrewsbury, an appointment the King confirmed in January 1643.[54]

The commission of array, in cooperation with a succession of regional Royalist commanders and their officers, would remain the executive of the Royalist war effort in Shropshire throughout the First Civil War, a number of commissioners also serving as military officers. The 63 known Shropshire commissioners are listed in Table 1. With 36 apparently active during 1642 and 1643 and 37 during 1644, the number of effective commissioners during the first two years of the war exceeded the commission of 33 re-appointed in July 1642. This was not, however, a monolithic bloc of Royalist support, for, excluding the peers and Sir Sampson Eure, an outsider, and allowing for the deaths of Francis Charleton and Thomas Screven, of 33 men appointed to either or both of the commissions in summer 1642, only 22, two-thirds, appear to have remained active into 1644 (although we probably lack evidence for others). On the other hand, newcomers who may have been more committed joined the commission from time to time. As the only extant full listings of the commission of array for Shropshire are from summer 1642, Table 1 inevitably makes assumptions about the involvement of certain individuals. Sir Richard Prince, for example, when making settlement with the Parliamentarians claimed that he had joined the commission of array only reluctantly, but in fact seems to have been an active participant.[55] On the other hand, given the fragmentary nature of the evidence of their activity some commissioners may remain unidentified, perhaps including John Newton of Heightley who reportedly was involved in conscription.[56] Simon Weston, a Shrewsbury draper and the influential Master of the Drapers' Company in 1644, is similarly unrecorded as a commissioner, but during 1643 and 1644 he was a senior Royalist financial official and most likely the county treasurer for military taxation.[57]

53 Yonge, *Diary,* pp. 3-5; 'Ottley Papers' (1894), pp. 34, 35-8, (1895), pp. 244-5.
54 'Ottley Papers' (1894), pp. 37-8, 41, 45-6, 56, 59; Blakeway and Owen, *Shrewsbury,* I, p. 423.
55 *CPCC,* II, p. 1609.
56 Ibid., p. 1045.
57 SA, 1831/1/4/17, f. 61; SA, LB7/2235; SA, P270/B/1/1, f. 55.

Whereas the duties of the several Parliamentarian committees for Shropshire are made clear in the respective ordinances of Parliament, we lack similar detail on the division of responsibilities within the commission of array. However, the list of tasks demanded of the commissioners in Shropshire and elsewhere in Prince Rupert's regional command embraced all aspects of war effort and were made clear when he took over in January 1644. The Prince's commissioners, as they were now titled, had to see to the recruitment of new and existing military units; provide the soldiers with provisions and clothing; procure artillery, weaponry and ammunition; of course raise money; and generally attend to all other 'habiliments [in this sense, the activity] of war'.[58] This list neatly summarises the greatly expanded role of Royalist commissioners from their deliberately restrained remit of summer 1642. Meanwhile Prince Rupert had authority to dismiss and appoint commissioners, and so several from Shropshire identified in Table 1 were most likely his appointees, including Edward Baldwin, Lawrence Benthall, Thomas Ireland and James Lacon.

Like the Parliamentarian county committees, the commissions of array were concerned with military finance. Chapter four will show that in Shropshire there were Royalist sub-commissions for sequestration and for the excise, while references from 1644 to (unnamed) 'commissioners for the levying of contributions' show that some were responsible for supervising the main Royalist military tax.[59] Furthermore, in June 1644 a regulatory accounting commission for Shropshire was appointed headed by Sir Robert Howard and Sir William Whitmore.[60] Although probably much of their administrative work was done at Shrewsbury, the Royalist headquarters, groups of commissioners, perhaps those from the locality, appear to have also attended regular organisational meetings in quorum, of several days' duration, held at the other main Royalist strongholds of Ludlow and Bridgnorth.[61] A minimum quorum of three commissioners was necessary to authorise warrants; for example the order to levy conscripts in the Ludlow area subscribed by Sir Paul Harris, Thomas Ireland and High Sheriff Thomas Edwards on 25 April 1644.[62]

Table 1 shows a marked decline in the number of commissioners during 1645 and into 1646. However, because evidence from that time is so sparse, there were probably more than the 13 commissioners identified here. The commission of array suffered a damaging blow on 22 February 1645 when Shrewsbury fell to the Parliamentarians, when 12 commissioners, including the stalwarts from 1642 Sir John Weld and Sir Richard Lee, were captured there. All were later transferred to Nantwich and dispersed further afield to Stafford and Manchester, held as captives or given restricted parole.[63] Furthermore, a few days before Shrewsbury fell the Parliamentarians in a daring, long-distance raid on Sir William Whitmore's house at Apley near Bridgnorth appear to have captured several commissioners, including Sir Francis Ottley (who either soon

---

58 BDL, Dugdale Mss 19 [second part], f. 75.
59 BL, Additional Mss 18981, f. 225; BL, Harleian Mss 6802, f. 227; BDL, Firth Mss C7, f. 229.
60 BDL, Dugdale Mss 19 [second part], ff. 11-12.
61 Evidence from 1644 is found in SA, P270/B/1/1, ff. 55-6, and SA, LB/8/3/75, respectively for commissioner meetings at Bridgnorth and Ludlow.
62 SA, LB7/2236.
63 *LBWB*, I, pp. 40-3; Malbon, 'Memorials', pp. 166-7.

Individual and status in early 1642. Where no title is given the individual was then known as an esquire or a gentleman. Wartime knighthoods shown in brackets.	Likely Resident Hundred (Residency elsewhere than Shropshire is italicised).	Status as a Commissioner of Array (COA)				
		Made COA June 1642	Made COA July 1642	Active COA 1642-3	Active COA 1644	Active COA 1645-6
Acton, Edward, MP (later Bart.)	Stottesdon	✗	✗	?	✓	✓
Baldwin, Charles, MP	Munslow	✗	✗	?	?	✓
Baldwin, Edward	Munslow	✗	✗	?	✓	✓
Benthall, Lawrence	Wenlock	✗	✗	?	✓	✓
Betton, Robert	Shrewsbury	✗	✗	✗	✓	?
Billingsley, Francis, Snr. (later Knt.)	Stottesdon	✗	✗	✓	✓	✓
Briggs, Morton	Brimstree	✗	✗	✓	Killed	-
Bromley, Henry	Pimhill	✗	✓	✓	✓	?
Charleton, Francis	S. Bradford	✓	✓	Died	-	-
Corbet, Pelham	Shrews. Lib.	✓	✓	?	✓	✗
Corbet, Robert	Brimstree	✓	✗	?	?	?
Corbet, Sir Vincent, Knt. & Bart.	N. Bradford	✓	✓	✓	✓	✓
Cornwall, Sir Gilbert, Knt.	Overs	✓	✗	✓	✓	?
Craven, William, Earl of Craven	London	✓	✓	✗	✗	✗
Cressett, Edward	Condover	✗	✓	✓	✓	✓
Edwards, Thomas (later Knt.)	Overs	✗	✓	✓	✓	✓
Egerton, John, Earl of Bridgewater	Herts.	✓	✓	?	✗	✗
Eure, Sir Sampson, Knt.	Hereford.	✓	✗	✗	✗	✗
Eyton, Robert	Oswestry	✗	✗	✓	?	✗
Eyton, Sir Robert, Knt.	Oswestry	✗	✓	✓	✗	✗
Eyton, Thomas (later Knt.)	S. Bradford	✗	✓	✓	✓	✓
Fox, Somerset, Snr.	Overs	✓	✗	?	?	?
Fox, Somerset, Jnr.	Overs	✗	✗	?	✓	?
Gibbons, Richard (later Knt.)	Shrewsbury	✗	✓	✓	?	✗
Harris, Sir Paul, Knt. & Bart.	Oswestry	✗	✓	✓	✓	Died
Herbert, Edward, Lord of Cherbury	Montgom.	✓	✓	?	?	✗
Herbert, Richard, MP	Montgom.	✗	✓	✓	✓	?
Howard, Sir Robert, MP, Knt. & Bart.	Clun	✓	✓	✓	✓	✓
Howard, Thomas, Earl of Arundel	Antwerp	✓	✓	✗	✗	✗
Ireland, Thomas	Shrewsbury	✗	✗	?	✓	✗
Kynaston, Edward	Pimhill	✗	✗	✓	✓	✗
Kynaston, Sir Francis, Knt.	S. Bradford	✓	✓	✓	?	?
Lacon, James	Pimhill	✗	✗	?	✓	?
Lee, Sir Richard, MP, Knt. & Bart.	Condover	✓	✓	✓	✓	✗
Leveson, Sir Richard, MP, Knt. & Bart.	S. Bradford	✓	✓	✓	✓	✗
Littleton, Thomas, MP	Wenlock Fr.	✓	✗	?	?	?
Littleton, Timothy	Overs?	✗	✗	?	?	✓
Lloyd, Andrew	Oswestry	✓	✗	✗	✗	✗
Lloyd, Richard	Oswestry	✗	✓	✓	✓	?

Table 1: Alphabetical listing of Royalist commissioners of array, 1642-6.

Individual and status in early 1642 Where no title is given the individual was then known as an esquire or a gentleman. Wartime knighthoods shown in brackets.	Likely Resident Hundred (Residency elsewhere than Shropshire is italicised).	Status as a Commissioner of Array (COA)				
		Made COA June 1642	Made COA July 1642	Active COA 1642-3	Active COA 1644	Active COA 1645-6
Mainwaring, Sir Arthur, Knt.	N. Bradford	✓	✓	?	?	✗
Needham, Robert, Viscount Kilmorey	N. Bradford	✓	✓	✓	?	?
Newport, Francis, MP (later Knt.)	S. Bradford	✗	✓	✓	✓	✗
Newport, Sir Richard (later Peer)	S. Bradford	✓	✗	✓	✓	✓
Oakeley, Richard	Purslow	✗	✗	✓	?	?
Ottley, Francis (later Knt.)	Condover	✓	✓	✓	✓	✓
Owen, Richard	Shrewsbury	✗	✗	✓	?	✗
Owen, Roger	Shrewsbury	✗	✗	✓	✓	✗
Owen, Thomas	Shrewsbury	✗	✓	✓	✓	✗
Owen, Sir William, Knt.	Condover	✓	✓	✓	?	✗
Prince, Sir Richard, Knt.	Shrewsbury	✗	✗	✓	✓	✗
Sandford, Francis	N. Bradford	✗	✗	✓	✓	✗
Screven, Thomas (later Knt.)	Condover	✓	✓	✓	Died	-
Smith, Francis	Wenlock Fr.	✗	✗	✓	✓	✗
Studeley, Richard	Shrewsbury	✗	✗	?	✓	✗
Talbot, Sherrington	*Worcs.*	✓	✗	?	?	✗
Thornes, Francis	Oswestry	✗	✓	?	✓	✗
Treves [Trevor, Trevys?], Richard	Oswestry?	✗	✗	?	✓	✗
Vernon, Henry	N. Bradford	✓	✗	?	?	?
Waring, Walter	Purslow	✗	✓	✓	✓	?
Weld, John, Snr. (later Knt.)	Wenlock Fr.	✓	✓	✓	✓	✗
Whitmore, Sir Thomas, Knt., MP	Brimstree	✗	✗	?	✓	✗
Whitmore, Sir William, Knt.	Brimstree	✗	✓	✓	✓	✗
Wolryche, Sir Thomas, Knt.	Stottesdon	✓	✓	✓	?	✗

Table 1 (part 2): Alphabetical listing of Royalist commissioners of array, 1642-6.

Sources for Table 1: The only extant full listings of commissions of array for Shropshire are for the first, constituted by King Charles at York on 22 June 1642, and for the second commission re-constituted at York the following 18 July. Both are listed here from the NRO, Finch Hattton Mss 133, unfoliated. Otherwise, Table 1 is a composite of information derived from several less uniform sources. References to Shropshire commissioners are scattered throughout the 'Ottley Papers', in the volumes of the *CPCC* and *CPCM*, and also the *CSPD*. Dugdale Mss 19 and Firth Mss C7, f. 211, both in the BDL, mention Shropshire commissioners in 1644. There is evidence of commissioner activity in the manuscript collections of Shropshire Archives, for example in: BB/C/1/1/1; LB7/2234 and LB7/2236; 3365/2711, ff. 22, 25-6, mentioning commissioners at Shrewsbury in spring 1644; and especially 5460/8/2/2, a petition from early 1644 subscribed by 20 commissioners. Some commissioners in 1642 are named in the Sutherland Papers, D868/2/35, 37-8, 41, at the SRO. The Parliamentary *Journals,* of the Lords, Vol. V, and the Commons, Vol. II, both mention Shropshire commissioners of array that Parliament found especially troublesome in autumn 1642. Much genealogical and topographical information on these individuals came from G. Grazebrook and J.P. Rylands (eds.), *The Visitation of Shropshire Taken in the Year 1623*, 2 vols. (London, 1889).

escaped or was inadvisably exchanged, because by May he was once again active as Royalist high sheriff).[64] During the remainder of 1645 and into 1646 the remaining commissioners were based at Bridgnorth. Besieged in Bridgnorth Castle, the last active group of them, Sir Francis Ottley, Sir Robert Howard, Sir Vincent Corbet and Sir Edward Acton, Royalist die-hards described by their local opponents in the county committee as 'the commissioners of array […] embittered against the Parliament', surrendered to the Parliamentarians on 27 April 1646.[65]

Royalist associations and regional commanders

By mid-August 1642 the commissions of array in Shropshire, Cheshire, North Wales and Staffordshire were maintaining contact with each other, developing a spirit of informal regional cooperation among the King's supporters that by September had resulted in weekly meetings being held at Whitchurch, Shropshire, attended by commissioners from Shropshire, Cheshire, Denbighshire and Flintshire.[66] Meeting on 2 September, including the Shropshire representatives Francis Ottley, John Weld, Paul Harris and Sir Richard Lee, MP, they agreed a seven-point declaration in support of King Charles to create a regional association army of trained bandsmen and volunteers, 'for the necessary defence of our counties and preservation of ourselves'. This 'confederacy', as it was known in London by 20 September, was a platform of support that held King Charles in good stead while he remained in and around Shropshire building an army.[67] However, once the King had left the region active cooperation among the region's Royalists faltered into the winter. Opinion in Staffordshire in September had favoured neutrality and a fresh attempt to avoid conflict in the county began in November. In Cheshire neutralists engineered a cease-fire in December that was detrimental to the county Royalists.[68] These developments were also disadvantageous to the Shropshire Royalists. Recognising that their county could become a frontline in defence of regional Royalism, they had expected a tangible expression of inter-county association:

> That North Wales, Cheshire & Lancashire, since Shropshire is their guard from the Parliament […] it is desired they should contribute somewhat to our charge through these whole counties, so that […] we are able to defend ourselves on our own strength that is now to be raised & our Train[ed] Bands.[69]

In spring 1643 King Charles created provincial military commands headed by trusted peers of regional standing. In early April the Principality and its Marche was divided between three deputy or lieutenant-generals, holding command under the

---

64 *LBWB*, I, p. 43; J. Vicars, *The Burning-Bush Not Consumed Or The Fourth and Last Part of the Parliamentarie-Chronicle* (1646), pp. 115-16.

65 Quotation from BDL, Tanner Mss 59, ff. 28-9; I. Carr and I. Atherton (eds.), *The Civil War in Staffordshire in the Spring of 1646: Sir William Brereton's Letter Book, April-May 1646* (Bristol, 2007), pp. 171, 175.

66 HMC, *Thirteenth Report, Appendix Part I*, pp. 51-2; SRO, D868/2/37-8.

67 SRO, D868/2/41; Yonge, *Diary*, p. 3.

68 Morrill, *Revolt*, p. 55.

69 SA, 6000/13291 .

teenage Charles Prince of Wales as titular captain-general: Richard Vaughan, Earl of Carberry in command of south-west Wales; Edward Somerset, Lord Herbert, in command of south-east Wales and Herefordshire; and Arthur, Lord Capel, given charge of Shropshire, Worcestershire, Cheshire and the six counties comprising North Wales – Anglesey, Caernarvonshire, Denbighshire, Flintshire, Merionethshire and Montgomeryshire.[70] Unlike the indigenous leaders Carberry and Herbert, Capel was a trusted and committed outsider, a Hertfordshire peer appointed to command a region that lacked an obvious or outstanding native figure to take charge. Capel was later handicapped by this distinction: as one of his former officers reminisced many years later, Capel came to be seen by the local Royalists as 'a stranger not fit to govern them, as one whose lands and interest lies among them'.[71]

Lord Capel's lieutenant-generalship was confirmed on 4 April 1643, when he had already held two councils of war at Shrewsbury as his headquarters, having arrived in Shropshire at Bridgnorth on 25 March.[72] Capel had no military experience beyond that acquired in leading his regiment of horse in the war so far, but he was accompanied by two experienced professionals, Lieutenant Colonel Sir John Mennes, a cavalry officer in the Second Bishops' War and later captain of the King's ship *Victory* until discharged by Parliament in July 1642, and Major Michael Woodhouse, a senior regimental officer returned from Ireland. Respectively, they were Capel's general of ordnance (a logistical role) and sergeant-major-general of foot. Furthermore, in May Sir Richard Willys arrived from Oxford as Capel's major-general of horse.[73] Capel also relied on local leaders, Mennes sharing responsibility for the defence of Shrewsbury with Sir Thomas Screven, colonel of the Trained Bands, and the governor Sir Francis Ottley, while Sir Thomas Wolryche and Thomas Fisher governed Bridgnorth and Ludlow respectively.[74]

Energetically Capel set about putting his command on a heightened war footing, expecting his subordinates to adopt a collective approach to military operations in place of local self-interest. Accordingly, when in April 1643 the Denbighshire commissioners failed to supply their county soldiers serving in Shropshire with his field army, Capel angrily chided them, that 'in the defence of these parts and offence of the rebels here lies your preservation'. Responding in July to complaints by the Flintshire gentry about Royalist cavalry billeted there, Capel retorted that 'if [the Royalist controlled city of] Chester be precious to them they will conclude a necessity of quartering of horse near it', and stubbornly kept the horsemen in place.[75] However, Capel also sought to foster greater unity of purpose across the region by proposing a consultative assembly comprising three representatives from each county under his command. The assembly would meet at Shrewsbury, and afterwards a commissioner from each shire would remain in a standing council of war. The assembly met around

70   BDL, Dugdale Mss 19 [first part], ff. 99-100.
71   HMC, *Twelfth Report, Appendix Part IX*, p. 42.
72   'Ottley Papers' (1895), p. 303; SA, BB/D/1/2/1/53.
73   *CSPD, 1641-1643*, pp. 21, 93, 350, for Mennes's appointments; 'Ottley Papers' (1895), pp. 301-3; HMC, *Twelfth Report, Appendix Part IX*, p. 40.
74   'Ottley Papers' (1895), pp. 321-3; BB/C/1/1/1, unfoliated; SA, LB/Fiche 1816.
75   NLW, Crosse of Shaw Hill Correspondence, 1099; WRO, CR2017/C9, f. 22.

3 July 1643 and it engendered some enthusiasm among its delegates, but we lack evidence for it and the council thereafter.[76]

Capel's approach did not sit well with a localist outlook. Discontent engendered by his demands may account for a London newsbook in May 1643 reporting that Capel had violently argued with Sir Thomas Screven, and that several Shropshire Royalists had petitioned the King to replace him with Lord Newport, 'their own country man'. The report cannot otherwise be substantiated, however, and in July Capel favourably contrasted the cooperative 'gentlemen of Shropshire' with the apathetic commissioners in Caernarvonshire.[77]

Lord Capel was an active field commander, but he came off worst against his chief opponent, Sir William Brereton, the commander-in-chief of Parliamentarian forces in Cheshire throughout the First Civil War, who during 1643 kept control of much of Cheshire. In abortive attacks, in May and again in August, Capel signally failed to capture Brereton's headquarters at Nantwich.[78] This left the way open for the Parliamentarians to establish themselves in Shropshire at Wem in September 1643, which Capel did not prevent. The attempts on 17-18 October by Capel's army to storm Wem were beaten off. This encouraged Brereton, together with allied forces, to launch three weeks later a campaign into north-east Wales that threatened Chester. This was a worsening military situation reflected upon by a well-informed North-Walian Royalist in mid-November, at the height of the Parliamentarian offensive, who saw Capel as a hesitant and 'unfortunate commander' lacking support and respect, especially in Shropshire.[79]

On 21 November, John, Lord Byron, an experienced regimental and brigade commander and now ostensibly Capel's field marshal and deputy, left the royal headquarters at Oxford to go to his help with 1,300 horse and foot. Byron quickly arrived at Shrewsbury on the 28th to find the military situation had shifted in the Royalists' favour.[80] Two thousand foot soldiers repatriated from the English Army in Leinster and landed on the Flintshire coast a week or so earlier had joined with Capel's forces and caused the Parliamentarians hastily to retreat from North Wales.[81] During November and December it appeared likely that Capel's replacement would be the Marquis of Ormond, the King's commander-in-chief in Ireland, who in September had settled the ceasefire in the concurrent war with the Catholic Irish Confederacy that was allowing detachments of the so-called 'English-Irish' forces to be transferred to the Royalists in England.[82] But in the event Ormond remained in Ireland, promoted to lord lieutenant, while Byron, whose commission confirmed at Oxford on 29 November presupposed that he would become Ormond's deputy, based himself at Chester as field-marshal-general (under the Prince of Wales) of Shropshire,

76 NLW, Llanfair-Brynodol Letters, 54-5; NLW, Crosse of Shaw Hill Correspondence, 1102, 1123.
77 *Certaine Informations from Severall Parts of the Kingdom*, 22-29 May 1643, p. 151; NLW, Llanfair-Brynodol Letters, 55.
78 Malbon, *Memorials*, pp. 55-6, 67-9.
79 T. Carte, *The Life of James Duke of Ormond*, 6 vols. (Oxford, 1851), V, pp. 507, 515.
80 Ibid., pp. 521, 527; SA, 3365/588, f. 26.
81 Carte, *Ormond*, V, pp. 510, 526.
82 Ibid., pp. 510-13, 529-32, 539.

Worcestershire, Cheshire and the six counties of North Wales. Capel meanwhile was respectfully recalled to Oxford, arriving there on 19 December 1643.[83]

Left, de facto, as regional commander-in-chief and engaged during December and into the New Year in a winter campaign in Cheshire, Byron paid little heed to affairs in Shropshire. Writing to Prince Rupert in mid-January 1644, he dismissed Shrewsbury as a 'disaffected town' and Sir Francis Ottley as an 'old, doting fool'.[84] After Byron's damaging defeat at Nantwich on 25 January 1644 even less was heard from him at Shrewsbury, which within days of the battle was unsettled after the failure of a plot by Parliamentarian fifth-columnists to overpower the town, and by the subsequent arrival of Sir Michael Woodhouse with 300 of his regiment to restore martial law.[85] From Shrewsbury on 2 February 1644 Sir John Mennes wrote to Prince Rupert of being excluded from the meetings of the local Royalists: 'these insulting people who now tell us their power and that three of the commissioners of array may question the best of us, from which power good Lord deliver me'. Complaining further of cross-purposes in command, on 9 February Mennes wrote hopefully that Prince Rupert would 'put better rules unto us', because on 6 January 1644 instead of the Marquis of Ormond, King Charles had appointed his nephew, in the Prince of Wales's stead, as captain-general of Shropshire, Worcestershire, Cheshire, Lancashire and North Wales.[86] Byron would remain at Chester as field marshal and Rupert's deputy.

Arriving there from Oxford late on 18 February, the next day Prince Rupert was formally welcomed by Shrewsbury's aldermen and made the town his headquarters.[87] Although his duties often took him elsewhere, especially during most of March on the long-distance Newark campaign, until embarking in mid-May to the relief of York Prince Rupert spent about eight weeks based in Shropshire, when his forces successively confined the Parliamentarians to a small enclave around Wem.[88] Like Capel before him but with greater military and political authority and administrative ability, by reforms and making greater demands Prince Rupert set about reinvigorating the Royalist war effort in Shropshire and elsewhere under his command. His appointment on 3 April as lord president coupled with promotion on 8 May to captain-general of the remainder of Wales and of Herefordshire, Monmouthshire and Gloucestershire made the Prince in effect (for he remained, on paper, a subordinate of the Prince of Wales) the overlord of the Principality and its Marche.[89] Rupert also revived Capel's idea of a regional council, but although it probably met at Shrewsbury soon after his arrival there, we lack evidence of it thereafter.[90]

The local military governors in Shropshire were replaced by Prince Rupert with professional soldiers, the senior English regimental officers returned from the army in

---

83   BDL, Dugdale Mss 19 [first part], f. 164; W. Hamper, *The Life, Diary and Correspondence of Sir William Dugdale, Knight* (London, 1827), p. 48.
84   BRL, Additional Mss 18981, f. 8.
85   Ibid., ff. 23, 25, 27; BDL, Firth Mss C6, f. 71.
86   BRL, Additional Mss 18981, ff. 25, 28; Ibid., f. 28; BDL, Dugdale Mss 19 [first part], ff. 172-3.
87   SA, 3365/588, f. 24.
88   C.H. Firth (ed.), 'The Journal of Prince Rupert's Marches, 5 September 1642 to 4 July 1646', *The English Historical Review*, 13 (1898), pp. 735-6.
89   NRO, Finch-Hatton Mss 133, unfoliated.
90   WSL, SMS 551/2.

8. Sir Michael Ernle (1599-1645), Royalist major-general of Shropshire
from August 1644 and from later that September also governor
of Shrewsbury. (By courtesy of Roy Precious Fine Art)

Ireland he favoured, the Prince, according to one of his aides, being 'mightily in love with the Irish'.[91] Accordingly, before arriving in Shropshire Rupert made Sir Michael Woodhouse governor of Ludlow in place of Richard Herbert. Sir Lewis Kirke and Sir Abraham Shipman were put in charge of Bridgnorth and Oswestry respectively, but it took longer to lever the governorship of Shrewsbury from Sir Francis Ottley. Although on 12 March King Charles had acceded to Rupert's requests to replace him, Ottley meanwhile journeyed to Oxford seeking the King's approbation, and returned to Shrewsbury on 29 March apparently having done so. Nonetheless, probably in late April Ottley was replaced by Sir Fulke Hunckes, another veteran from Ireland.[92] By July, in the wake of recent local successes by the enemy Hunckes was quarrelling with the commissioners of array, questioning their commitment and condemning them as 'so many caterpillars' for their apparent inactivity.[93] In early August Prince Rupert made two further senior appointments in Shropshire, replacing Hunckes with Colonel

91 Quotation from Carte, *Ormond*, VI, p. 87. The senior officers who later served in Shropshire are listed under their respective regiments in Ireland in 1642 in *A List of the Old and New Regiments of Horse and Foot under the command of the Honourable Robert Sidney, Earl of Leicester* (1642), unpaginated.
92 WSL, SMS 551/2; W.A. Day (ed.), *The Pythouse Papers: Correspondence Concerning the Civil War, the Popish Plot and a Contested Election in 1680* (London, 1879), p. 4; WSL, SMS 478/13/36, SMS 537.
93 *CSPD, 1644*, p. 332.

Robert Broughton as governor of Shrewsbury to placate the local Royalists, and putting Sir Michael Ernle in overall command, probably as brevet major-general.[94] Again, both officers had previously served in Ireland.

After being defeated at Marston Moor on 2 July Prince Rupert had returned to Chester on the 25th, and was based there for a few weeks unsuccessfully attempting to rebuild his army. However, on 20 August he left Chester for Bristol as a new headquarters, arriving on the 26th.[95] In November Prince Rupert was given overall command of all Royalist forces as captain-general. Thereafter he would return to Shropshire only in March 1645, in support of his younger brother Prince Maurice who then was regional commander.

Within a month of Prince Rupert's departure, on 18 September the regional Royalist field army numbering around 4,500 men led by Lord Byron, once again the effective area commander-in-chief, was beaten in battle and routed by a smaller Parliamentarian army at Montgomery, just over the Shropshire border in Montgomeryshire.[96] This major defeat coupled with growing war weariness had a profoundly depressing effect on Royalist morale, expressed during October by a marked decline in both popular support for and local cooperation with the garrisons in Shropshire. Sir Michael Ernle, now governor of Shrewsbury after Colonel Broughton was captured at Montgomery, reported to Prince Rupert on 2 October how in particular, 'the edge of the gentry is very much abated, so that they are all at a stand and move but heavily to advance this service'.[97]

The situation encouraged a gathering of gentry, clergy and freeholders on 7 November to agree a declaration calling on Parliament to engage fully in peace negotiations, whilst expressing stolid support for the King and encouraging other counties to act likewise.[98] The self-professed war-weary Shropshire men had followed the example of a declaration by the gentry of Somerset a month earlier, a peace initiative that nonetheless aligned them to the King rather than Parliament, which had accrued some wider support in the West Country.[99] In turn, the Worcestershire grand jury on 6 December proposed that an inter-county association would carry greater sway with Parliament, especially if expressing more belligerent support for the King. Accordingly, meeting at Ludlow around 9-11 January 1645 representatives from Shropshire, Herefordshire, Worcestershire and Staffordshire agreed to a military association, which as a result of an exchange of proposals with Oxford came into effect in mid-February with King Charles's tacit support. This so-called Marcher Association (a descriptive modern term not used at the time) would recruit for its defence 2,000 militiamen (600 of them from Shropshire) as levies from the posse comitatus, which would serve as a general reserve of manpower. As well as control over recruitment,

94 BL, Additional Mss 18981, f. 233; BDL, Firth Mss C7, f. 150.
95 Firth, 'Rupert's Marches', p. 737.
96 *JHL*, VI, pp. 712-16.
97 BL, Additional Mss 18981, ff. 284, 299; BDL, Firth Mss C7, f. 191.
98 Anon., *Collections Historical and Archaeological relating to Montgomeryshire and its Borders*, XX (1886), pp. 23-4.
99 E. Hyde, Earl of Clarendon, *The History of the Rebellion and Civil Wars in England*, 7 vols. (Oxford, 1859), III, pp. 525-6; Sir Edward Walker, *Historical Discourses upon Several Occasions* (1705), pp. 100-3.

the commissioners of the Association would inherit from the commissions of array full powers to raise military taxes, much of which would be diverted to finance the Association forces.[100] Shortly after consenting to the Association, on 26 February King Charles issued a regulatory proclamation intending to 'ensure a fair carriage' between the Association and the regular 'soldiers in pay', because to its proponents the Association was a means to keep the military in check and to control the behaviour of the garrisons. This had become an especially pressing matter in south Shropshire, where depredations by Royalist soldiers had caused civilians to arm themselves and band together in self-defence; these were the so-called clubmen reportedly active in the southerly hundreds of Clun and Purslow from December 1645 into the New Year.[101]

Understandably the regular officers in Shropshire viewed the Marcher Association with undisguised suspicion, as a rival organisation intending to divert resources from their own forces and generating confusion to the detriment of the war effort, whilst doubting – correctly, as matters turned out – that it could deliver the promised manpower.[102] This was the situation that Prince Maurice inherited in Shropshire when he arrived at Shrewsbury on 4 February 1645 as the new lieutenant-general of the region in Prince Rupert's stead, having left Oxford for Worcester on 14 January.[103] At Worcester in later January Maurice had met with commissioners of the Association. Afterwards he wrote to his brother expressing suspicion of the 'cunning men among them', and that 'the Association tends much to the destruction of military power and discipline'.[104] Maurice attended a freeholder gathering at Shrewsbury, but he left there on 13 February, marching to the relief of Lord Byron's stronghold at Chester with forces including the best part of the Shrewsbury garrison and other detachments from Shropshire. This left Shrewsbury weakened and it fell relatively easily to the Parliamentarians by surprise attack nine days later.[105] From then on we know little about Prince Maurice's involvement in the war effort in Shropshire, although during March he joined forces with his brother Rupert in north Shropshire and relieved Parliamentarian pressure on Chester. Thereafter Maurice made Worcester his centre of operations until, together with Prince Rupert, he lost command and the King's favour in autumn 1645.

What effect did the Marcher Association movement have on the Royalist war effort in Shropshire? From its formation the Association never fully functioned as a regional organisation, although it was revived to some extent at county level, in Staffordshire

---

100 'Ottley Papers' (1896), pp. 268-9; H. Townsend, *The Diary of Henry Townsend of Elmley Lovett, 1640–1663*, (ed.) J.W. Willis Bund, 3 vols. (London, 1920), III, pp. 189-99; BDL, Dugdale Mss 19 [second part], ff. 105-6

101 *The Perfect Occurrences of Parliament And Chief Collections of Letters*, 20-27 Dec. 1644, unpaginated; *Mercurius Britannicus*, 6-13 Jan. 1645, unpaginated.

102 BDL, Firth Mss C6, ff. 303, 332; 'Ottley Papers' (1896), pp. 270-1.

103 SA, 3365/591, f.8; Hamper, *Sir William Dugdale*, p. 77.

104 WSL, SMS 556; BRL, Additional Mss 18982, f. 27, Maurice to Prince Rupert, 29 Jan. 1645.

105 R. Williams (ed.), 'An Account of the Civil War in North Wales, Transcribed from the MS. Notebook of William Maurice, esq., Preserved in the Wynnstay Library', *Archaeologica Cambrensis*, I (1846), p. 38; BDL, Firth Mss C6, ff. 332, 342; Clarendon, *History*, III, p. 512.

in spring 1645, and in Shropshire that summer.[106] Moreover, in Shropshire it appears that the county commission of Association did not in fact become active in February, so that in August King Charles attempted to re-appoint and revive it.[107] The Association was an overly ambitious plan that in Shropshire was overtaken by events, by the loss of Shrewsbury. Many local leaders were lost to the Royalist cause, together with the meeting place of the gentry-led gatherings that had driven the Association movement – a further meeting at Shrewsbury planned for later February had to be abandoned.[108] Furthermore, it remains unclear to what extent the commissioners of array embraced the Association. Some, like Sir Francis Ottley and Sir Robert Howard, were enthusiastic proponents. However, the appointment in August 1645 by King Charles of otherwise previously active commissioners of array, such as Sir Vincent Corbet and Sir Thomas Eyton, as 'additional commissioners' suggests they previously had not fully supported the Association, or indeed may have opposed it. In reporting the activity in Shropshire in January 1645, one of Prince Rupert's aides had warned of the Association replacing 'former commissioners', which would cause the commission of array to be 'quite spoiled and the effect will be nothing but distraction'.[109]

While Prince Maurice would remain commander-in-chief of Shropshire for much of 1645, the effective operational commander was Sir William Vaughan, a veteran cavalryman returned from Ireland. According to the Royalist soldier and diarist Richard Symonds, sometime in 1644 Vaughan became 'general of Shropshire'.[110] However, Symonds's inexact dating cannot be corroborated, and while Vaughan had been based in Shropshire since spring 1644 it is difficult to see him as being in command there until after Sir Michael Ernle was captured at Shrewsbury in February 1645. No records of Vaughan as an administrator appear to survive. But he was certainly an active and often successful field commander of mobile forces, including his own regiment of horse. Vaughan spent most of May to September 1645 away from Shropshire attached to the King's forces.[111] Marching from his headquarters at Shrawardine Castle in mid-May 1645 to join the main Royalist field army, on the 16th or 17th Vaughan with his regiment routed a body of Parliamentary horse at Much Wenlock.[112] Returning briefly to Shropshire after the battle of Naseby, Vaughan twice heavily defeated the local Parliamentarians, in Corvedale on 4 July and at High Ercall the next day. Vaughan led a brigade of horse in the Royalist defeat at Rowton Heath outside Chester on 24 September, and in October returned to Shropshire with King Charles's commission as General of Horse for Wales, Shropshire, Worcestershire, Staffordshire and Herefordshire. Leading from Shropshire a task force of detachments numbering around 1,200 men intending to disrupt enemy operations around Chester,

106 WSL, SMS 502, 'A new commission of Association for Staffordshire', dated Lichfield 5 May 1645; for Shropshire, *CSPD, 1645-1647*, pp. 143-4.
107 *CSPD, 1645-1647*, pp. 80-1.
108 BRL, Additional Mss 18982, f. 36.
109 *CSPD, 1645-1647*, pp. 80-1; BRL, Additional Mss 18982, f. 15.
110 R. Symonds, *Diary of The Marches of the Royal Army During the Great Civil War kept by Richard Symonds,* (ed.) C.E. Long (London, 1859), p. 256.
111 Ibid., pp. 181, 218, 225, 231, 242, 256.
112 Rushworth, *Historical Collections*, VI, p. 29.

9. Sir Jacob Astley, first Baron Astley of Reading (1579-
1652), Royalist regional commander in charge of Shropshire
during winter 1645/6. (© Philip Mould and Company)

on 1 November Vaughan was defeated near Denbigh (Denbighshire).[113] Over winter
1645-6 Vaughan's operations increasingly took the form of raids against ostensibly
Parliamentarian territory, in Shropshire and as far afield as Radnorshire. Lacking a
permanent base and hence regular contribution, Vaughan's mobile forces increasingly
lived off the land and acquired a reputation for looting. As a result, in December 1645,
Vaughan's horsemen were not allowed to enter Royalist Ludlow for fear of the harm
they might cause.[114]

The last Royalist regional commander-in-chief over Shropshire during the First
Civil War was Jacob, Lord Astley, the King's veteran general of infantry. At Oxford
on 5 December 1645 Astley was commissioned lieutenant-general of the Marcher
Association counties of Shropshire, Herefordshire, Worcestershire and Staffordshire.
His orders were to recruit new forces and also to re-establish order and governance in
the region, where the Royalist war effort was in disarray and coming under increasing
enemy pressure.[115] Acknowledging that his immediate task was to restore 'a posture
of defence and compose the differences occasioned among the governors and those
who relate to the garrisons', Astley arrived at Worcester on 23 December and made
the city his headquarters.[116] Over the winter Astley generally restored order across his

113 Symonds, *Diary*, pp. 242-3, 256, 258-9; Walker, *Discourses*, p. 135.
114 *The Citties Weekly Post*, 10-17 Feb. 1646, pp. 4-5; Symonds, *Diary*, p. 276.
115 BDL, Dugdale Mss 19 [second part], f. 128.
116 'Ottley Papers' (1896), p. 294; Symonds, *Diary*, p. 277.

command, overcoming the obstructiveness of several governors including Sir Lewis Kirke at Bridgnorth and Sir Michael Woodhouse at Ludlow. Ill-discipline among the soldiers and disputes between Kirke and the commissioners had disrupted the garrison at Bridgnorth. Informed by Sir Francis Ottley of the unrest there, in reply on 10 January 1646 Astley confided that 'I can meet with no garrisons free from such distempers', but soon after he saw to it that Kirke was replaced as governor by the local man Colonel Sir Robert Howard.[117] Apart from reorganisation, Astley's main strategic concern was to maintain communications with Lord Byron's increasingly beleaguered garrison at Chester. But his efforts together with Sir William Vaughan to muster at Bridgnorth by the end of January a relief army around 3,000 strong came to nothing. News arrived of the defeat and retreat of a Royalist force in north-east Wales that was to have provided support and that in any case Byron had entered negotiations to surrender – Sir William Brereton's forces occupied Chester on 3 February 1646.[118] In early March, Astley again gathered near Bridgnorth a small field army of detachments from several Midland garrisons including Bridgnorth and Ludlow. Marching for Oxford, on 21 March in what was the last battle of the First Civil War Astley's army was intercepted, defeated and broken near Stow on the Wold by a Parliamentarian army partly commanded by Sir William Brereton. Astley was taken prisoner at Stow, although Sir William Vaughan managed to evade capture.[119]

Parliamentarian leadership and administration in Shropshire
Wartime committees, 1642-5
Because the Long Parliament had conducted much of its own business by committee, the Parliamentarian war effort came to be directed by numerous national and provincial committees, each acting under the authority of an ordinance of Parliament – a statute enacted without royal assent. Many committees were primarily concerned with executing fiscal ordinances. Typically, six of the seven committees created for Shropshire affairs during 1643 and 1644 were responsible for military finance. The seventh and most important Shropshire committee was the controlling county committee.

This originated in July 1642, when on the 23rd Parliament instructed the MPs Sir John Corbet, William Pierrepont and Richard More to return to Shropshire. Their objectives were to solicit for contributions for Parliament's cause and to promote the militia ordinance – by opposing the commission of array and securing the county magazine and the support of the Trained Bands. Arriving at Shrewsbury on 29 July, over the next five days the MPs addressed public gatherings, confronted several Royalist commissioners in the near riot in the market square, and inspected a body of armed local volunteers led by the alderman Thomas Hunt. On 3 August the MPs left Shrewsbury to garner support elsewhere but could not prevent the commissioners of array from dominating the assizes five days later, or, it seems,

---

117 Walker, *Discourses*, p. 150; Day, *Pythouse Papers*, p. 21; quotation from the 'Ottley Papers' (1896), pp. 293-4.
118 *CSPD, 1645-1649*, p. 330; 'Ottley Papers' (1896), pp. 295-6; BDL, Tanner Mss 60, f. 386; Phillips, *Civil War in Wales*, II, pp. 292-6.
119 *The Moderate Intelligencer*, 5-12 Mar. 1646, p. 328; Walker, *Discourses*, p. 152; *A True Relation By Colonell Morgan In a letter of the totall Routing of the Lord Astley, by him and Sir William Brereton at Stow* (1646).

10. Thomas Mytton (1596/7-1656), one of the leading Shropshire
Parliamentarians and de facto commander of the county forces for much of
the First Civil War. (By courtesy of Shropshire Archives, ref. PR/1/744)

counter their bellicose declaration from Much Wenlock on the 16th. By the time
Charles I entered Shrewsbury on 20 September, More, Corbet and Pierrepont had
returned to London.[120] Meanwhile, on 29 August this tripartite Westminster-based
'Committee of Shropshire' had been augmented by John Blakiston, John Wylde,
Lawrence Whitaker and William Wheeler, respectively MPs for Newcastle-on-
Tyne, Worcestershire, Okehampton and Westbury, Wiltshire.[121] All became effective
Westminster committeemen, whose involvement as outsiders in Shropshire affairs
reflected the situation that two thirds of the shire's MPs supported the King. William
Spurstowe, Shropshire's fourth Parliamentarian MP, played little part in these events
and later was appointed to just one Shropshire committee.

For their part Spurstowe's Parliamentary colleagues continued actively to support
the cause in Shropshire. Richard More sat on all Shropshire committees up to his
death in December 1643, as did William Pierrepont into 1648. A respected member
of the Long Parliament and an advocate of Parliamentary powers, 'Wise William' was
one of ten members of the Committee of Safety, formed in July 1642 as the directing
council of the Parliamentarian cause, and was in turn a prominent member of its
replacement as a national military executive from February 1644, the Committee of

120 *JHL*, V, pp. 233, 269-70; *JHC*, II, p. 774.
121 *JHC*, II, p. 741.

Individual and status. Where no title is given the individual was known as an esquire or a gentleman.	Likely Resident Hundred (Residency elsewhere than Shropshire is italicised).	Committee Membership					
		AC Feb. and Aug. 1643	SC Mar. 1643	CC Apr. 1643	5&20 May 1643	SCS June 1644	IC Oct. 1644
Ashurst, William, MP	Lancashire	✗	✗	✗	✗	✓	✗
Barclay, William	London	✗	✗	✗	✗	✓	✗
Barker, Walter	S. Bradford	✓	✗	✗	✓	✗	✓
Bradshaw, John	Cheshire	✗	✗	✗	✗	✓	✗
Brereton, Sir William, MP, Knt. & Bart.	Cheshire	✗	✗	✗	✗	✓	✗
Briggs, Sir Morton, Knt. & Bart	Brimstree	✗	✗	✓	✗	✗	✗
Charleton, Robert	S. Bradford	✗	✗	✗	✗	✓	✗
Clive, Robert	N. Bradford	✗	✗	✗	✗	✓	✗
Corbet, John	Ford	✗	✓	✗	✗	✓	✓
Corbet, Sir John, MP, Knt. & Bart.	N. Bradford	✓	✓	✓	✓	✓	✓
Corbet, Robert	Pimhill	✓	✗	✓	✓	✗	✓
Cornwall, Sir Gilbert, Knt.	Overs	✗	✗	✓	✗	✗	✗
Edwards, Humphrey	Shrewsbury	✗	✗	✗	✗	✓	✗
Heylyn, John	Shrews. Lib.	✗	✗	✗	✗	✓	✗
Hunt, Thomas	Shrews. Lib.	✗	✓	✓	✗	✓	✓
Kinaston, Samuel	Oswestry?	✗	✗	✗	✗	✓	✗
Knight, Thomas	Shrewsbury	✗	✗	✓	✗	✗	✗
Kynnersley, Hercules	Stottesdon	✗	✗	✓	✗	✗	✗
Kynnersley, Thomas	Stottesdon?	✗	✗	✓	✗	✗	✗
Lee, Lancelot	Stottesdon	✓	✓	✓	✓	✗	✓
Leighton, Harcourt	Munslow	✗	✗	✗	✗	✓	✗
Lloyd, Andrew	Oswestry	✓	✓	✓	✓	✓	✓
Lloyd, John	Shrews. Lib.	✗	✗	✓	✗	✗	✗
Long, Walter, MP	Wiltshire.	✗	✗	✗	✗	✓	✗
Mackworth, Humphrey	Condover	✓	✓	✓	✓	✓	✓
Meredith, Christopher	?	✗	✗	✗	✗	✓	✗
More, Richard, MP	Purslow	✓	✓	✓	✓	Died	
More, Samuel	Purslow	✗	✗	✓	✗	✓	✗
More, Thomas	Munslow?	✗	✗	✗	✗	✓	✗
Myddelton, Sir Thomas, MP, Knt.	Denbighshire	✗	✗	✗	✗	✓	✗
Mytton, Thomas	Oswestry	✓	✓	✓	✓	✓	✓
Nicolls, Thomas	Ford	✓	✓	✓	✓	✓	✓
Owen, Leighton	Ford	✗	✗	✗	✗	✓	✗
Pierrepont, William, MP	Brimstree	✓	✓	✓	✓	✓	✓
Proud, John	Shrewsbury	✗	✗	✓	✗	✗	✗
Rowley, William	Shrewsbury	✗	✗	✓	✗	✗	✗
Shute, Francis	London?	✗	✗	✗	✗	✓	✗
Spurstowe, William, MP	Cheshire	✗	✗	✗	✗	✓	✗
Talbot, Robert	Brimstree	✗	✗	✓	✗	✗	✗
Wallop, Robert, MP	Hampshire	✗	✗	✗	✗	✓	✗
Ward, Arthur	Shrews. Lib.	✗	✗	✗	✗	✓	✗

Table 2: Alphabetical listing of Parliamentarian committeemen, 1643-4.

Key to Table 2: AC = the committee appointed by the national ordinance of 24 February 1643 for raising the weekly assessment, re-appointed on 3 August following (*A&O*, I, pp. 85-100, 223-241); SC = committee appointed by the national ordinance of 27 March 1643 authorising sequestration (*A&O*, I, pp 106-17); CC = the standing county committee appointed by the ordinance of 10 April 1643 (*A&O*, I, pp. 124-7); 5&20 = the committee appointed by the national ordinance of 7 May 1643 'for taxing such as have not at all contributed or lent, or not according to their estates and abilities', known as The Fifth and Twentieth Part (*A&O*, I, pp. 145-55); SCS = the sequestration committee for Shropshire appointed under the ordinance of 13 June 1644 (*JHL*, VI, p. 586-7); IC = the committee appointed by the national ordinance of 18 October 1644 for raising a 12-month weekly assessment for the Parliamentary forces in Ireland (*A&O*, I, pp. 531-553).

Both Kingdoms.[122] Thereby Pierrepont was advantageously placed to secure resources for Shropshire. Alluding to the MP's supportive background role, in July 1644 Colonel Thomas Mytton wrote from Shropshire to his wife in London, to 'present my services unto Mr Pierrepont and desire him that ammunition and ordnance may be hastened to me'.[123] Sir John Corbet of Stoke and Adderley had consistently opposed King Charles's policies. Accordingly, Corbet assumed the leadership of the Shropshire Parliamentarians, and on 10 April 1643 was appointed, as colonel-general, commander of the county forces. However, discord among his compatriots in the meantime caused the Commons on 4 July following to instruct Corbet to put aside his commission and instead attend to Westminster business.[124] Rejected as a military leader, nonetheless Corbet was appointed to all Shropshire committees into 1648 and, like Pierrepont, his London-based contribution to the war effort was in securing fiscal and military resources.

On 3 August 1642, More, Pierrepont and Corbet in jointly reporting to Parliament had acknowledged the support of 'many gentlemen of great quality in this county', including several Shrewsbury aldermen.[125] The identity of several of these active Shropshire Parliamentarians becomes clearer given their situation in the wake of the Royalist take-over there. Foremost among them were the Shrewsbury aldermen Humphrey Mackworth of Betton Strange, Thomas Nicolls of Boycott and Thomas Hunt, all of whom in mid-October King Charles had charged with high treason.[126] But Mackworth was in London before Charles entered Shropshire; meanwhile both Walter Barker of Haughmond and Robert Charleton of Apley after fund-raising for Parliament were believed to have fled with others to Bristol. Gathered on 8 October at Worcester under the protection of the Earl of Essex's Army, 17 leading Parliamentarian activists from Shropshire, Worcestershire, Herefordshire and Gloucestershire signed a declaration of mutual support. Representing Shropshire were the MPs Corbet and More, the brothers Thomas and Hercules Kynnersley of Stottesdon hundred and, notably, Thomas Mytton of Halston, near Oswestry.[127]

On 24 February 1643, by the ordinance to levy a national weekly tax, or assessment, to finance its forces, Parliament appointed the ten members of the first fiscal committee for Shropshire: Corbet, More, Pierrepont, Mackworth, Nicolls, Barker and Mytton were joined by Andrew Lloyd of Aston Hall, Lancelot Lee of Alveley and Robert Corbet of Stanwardine. All were reappointed when the assessment ordinance was re-enacted on 3 August 1643. In the meantime, Shropshire committees were created on 27 March and 7 May for two other national fiscal ordinances, respectively for the sequestration of enemy assets and to enforce subscriptions. Given the membership of these committees listed in Table 2, it seems that Mackworth, Myttton, Nicolls, Lloyd, Lee and the three MPs jointly provided leadership in Shropshire affairs.

122 *ODNB*, 44, p. 265.
123 NLW, Sweeney Hall Mss A1, f. 20.
124 *A&O*, I, pp. 124-7; *JHC*, III, pp. 152, 155.
125 *JHL*, V, p. 270.
126 W.G. Clark Maxwell (ed.), 'King Charles I's Proclamation of October 14th 1642', *TSANHS*, 4th Series, X (1925-6), pp. xxv-vi.
127 HMC, *Fifth Report, Part I*, p. 49; HMC, *Fourteenth Report, Appendix Part II*, p. 100.

They were also the coterie at the heart of the enlarged committee of Shropshire, instituted on 10 April 1643 by the ordinance associating the county militarily with Staffordshire and Warwickshire. Headed by Sir John Corbet, the county committee could act in quorum to raise revenue – three, including Corbet, to accept loans, four together to sequestrate assets. Among the 20 county committeemen (identified in Table 2) were Thomas Hunt and Richard More's eldest son Samuel, who both became active soldiers. On the other hand, Thomas Knight, Robert Talbot, William Rowley, John Proud and the Kynnersley brothers were not on any other committee, although the Shrewsbury men Proud, a draper, and Rowley, a brewer, as notable dissidents had been detained by the Royalists in 1642.[128] Proud and Hercules Kynnersley were both active in the post-First Civil War Parliamentarian county administration. While the wartime activity of some committeemen remains uncertain, only one of them was certainly ill chosen, the Royalist or side-shifter Sir Gilbert Cornwall. However, this remained a committee in exile until it gained a foothold in Shropshire by the occupation of Wem in September 1643.

By February 1644 Westminster was considering ways to set the Parliamentarian war effort in Shropshire on a firmer financial footing.[129] On the following 13 June this resulted in an ordinance that endorsed and augmented the financial powers of the committee of Shropshire and appointed the 22-member committee for sequestrations named in Table 2. Further, the ordinance empowered the county committee to eject 'scandalous' ministers and schoolmasters and to appoint 'able, godly' replacements. There was a purge of (unnamed) ineffectual committeemen, replaced by five newcomers – Robert Clive of Stych Hall near Market Drayton, Harcourt Leighton of Plaish, Leighton Owen of Braggington and Humphrey Edwards of Shrewsbury, together with Robert Charlton who had been active in 1642. The ordnance of June 1644 confirmed the county committee's fiscal powers for the remainder of the war, although it could not levy duties in Shropshire according to the national excise ordinance enacted on 22 July 1643 until the passing of a further enabling ordinance on 8 January 1646.[130] Additionally, in October 1644 an eleven-man Shropshire committee was appointed to execute the national ordinance to finance Parliamentary forces in Ireland (Table 2).[131]

By mid-1644 Thomas Mytton, Humphrey Mackworth, Thomas Hunt, Andrew Lloyd, Samuel More, Robert Clive and Leighton Owen – who were then, or later became, commissioned officers – were, in effect, a committee within a committee, operating in the front line from their headquarters at Wem. This committee at Wem acted semi-autonomously from their colleagues elsewhere, since a Commons order on 10 May 1644 had given any five of them power to act in committee.[132] Table 3 shows how by 1645 executive military authority was held by just eight committeemen based at Shrewsbury after its capture on 22 February. Five days later the Commons gave them authority to appoint a governor for Shrewsbury. Accordingly, on 26 March his colleagues there nominated Humphrey Mackworth, but for reasons that remain

128 SA, 6000/13291-2.
129 *JHC*, III, p. 394.
130 *JHL*, VIII, pp. 91-2; *A&O*, I, 202-14.
131 *A&O*, I, p. 542.
132 *JHC*, III, p. 488.

uncertain it was not until 6 June 1646 that Mackworth's appointment was finally confirmed. The committeemen had, however, prevented Colonel Thomas Mytton from becoming Shrewsbury's governor, who was by then estranged from his erstwhile colleagues and disliked by them.[133]

Report from Shrewsbury, 23.2.45[1]	Captain Farrington's commission, 1.3.45[2]	Report to Speaker Lenthall, 3.4.45[3]	Captain Brett's accounts, 20.5.45[4]	Authorisation for Captain King to collect assessment, 31.7.45[5]	Report to Sir William Brereton, 23.12.45[6]	Report to Speaker Lenthall, 26.3.46[7]
Charlton	-	Charlton	Charlton	Charlton	Charlton	Charlton
Clive	Clive	-	-	Clive	Clive	-
Hunt	Hunt	Hunt	Hunt	Hunt	-	-
Lloyd	Lloyd	Lloyd	Lloyd	Lloyd	Lloyd	Lloyd
-	Mackworth	Mackworth	Mackworth	Mackworth	Mackworth	Mackworth
More	-	More	-	-	-	More
-	-	-	Nicolls	-	-	Nicolls
Owen	Owen	Owen	-	Owen	Owen	Owen

1 LBWB, I, p. 46.
2 TNA, SP28/174 Part 1, Farrington's account book.
3 BDL, Tanner Mss 60, f. 52.
4 TNA, SP28/34 Part 4, f. 470.
5 TNA, SP28/242 Part 2, King's account book.
6 LBWB, II, p. 421.
7 BDL, Tanner Mss 59, f. 5.

Table 3: Sample of documents signed by the committee at Shrewsbury during 1645.

Mytton's absence from the committee's meetings at Shrewsbury during 1645 is apparent from Table 3. Since mid-1643 he had been the leading soldier in the committee of Shropshire. By autumn 1644, however, the disputation of military command (for reasons to be explored more fully here and in chapter three) had divided the Shropshire forces between rival headquarters, Mytton's base at Oswestry and the committee's stronghold at Wem. In February 1645 the committee at Wem had attempted to sideline Mytton during the operation to capture Shrewsbury. Furthermore, they encouraged their patron Sir William Brereton in his reports to Parliament to downplay Mytton's role. The committee had instead given overall command of the Shrewsbury operation to their military expert, the Dutch or German mercenary Lieutenant-Colonel Wilhelm (anglice William) Reinking, who as a professional soldier challenged Mytton's military leadership.[134] Consequently, the following May their rivalry spilled into the London press in pamphlet form. Reinking's *Relation* presented Mytton as playing a peripheral role in the capture of Shrewsbury, to

133 *JHL*, VIII, p. 360; BDL, Tanner Mss 60, f. 11; *LBWB*, I, pp. 33, 52.
134 *LBWB*, I, pp. 51-2; NLW, Sweeney Hall Mss A1, f. 24.

which Mytton, styling himself 'the ancientest [i.e. most senior] colonel in that county', responded in his *Reply* by questioning Reinking's fitness to command.[135]

Essentially both pamphlets were vehicles of self-advancement. Reinking, with a glowing reference from the committee at Shrewsbury dated 17 April, had gone to London seeking reward from the Committee of Both Kingdoms. Mytton was in the capital by the end of March furthering his candidacy for the governorship of Shrewsbury, when he may well have engineered the blocking of Mackworth's appointment.[136] The surviving draft of a public petition, calling on Parliament to grant Mytton 'the commanding place in chief of the town and county of Salop', shows that he pursued a broader military-politico agenda, and on 12 May 1645 Parliament appointed him to succeed his brother-in-law Sir Thomas Myddelton as commander-in-chief for North Wales.[137] Notwithstanding this infighting, their military achievements won the committee of Shropshire plaudits in the London Press. In early July 1645 the *Moderate Intelligencer* praised the

> brave proceedings of that honest and valiant committee in Shropshire. It were good if there were more of them. They go forth into the field by turn in arms: A fighting committee, that's good. They have almost cleared their country, began last and will have done first.

In mid-March 1646 the *Kingdomes Weekly Intelligencer* similarly commended 'that most exemplary and active committee', for its 'soldier[l]y' and 'politic' acts.[138] The committeemen, and especially the self-reliant and closely-knit group holding power at Shrewsbury in 1645, were not, however, representative of Shropshire's leading landed families. Andrew Lloyd, Leighton Owen and Robert Clive were lesser gentry with modest estates, while Robert Charleton was a landless lawyer. Shropshire's leading Parliamentarians have been characterised as being from the less affluent middling and lower sort of the county gentry.[139] This is supported by the example of 32 of Shropshire's wealthiest men listed in November 1632 as candidates for the shrievalty. While 11 of them or their sons became commissioners of array, just three, Sir Morton Briggs, Richard More and Thomas Hunt's father Richard, were fathers of or were themselves committeemen.[140] While the committee of Shropshire lacked wealthy landowners, it included men who in 1642 were otherwise influential in commerce or politics. Andrew Lloyd was a JP and sufficiently noteworthy to have been appointed to King Charles's first commission of array for Shropshire. Thomas Mytton, a mid-ranking landowner, was also a JP and an alderman of Shrewsbury. Thomas Nicolls was

---

135 *A More Exact And Particular Relation of the taking of Shrewsbury, than hath hitherto been published, With the manner and performance thereof by Lieutenant Collonel William Reinking* (1645); *Colonell Mitton's Reply to Lieutenant Collonell Reinking's Relation of The taking of Shrewsbury* (1645).

136 *The Kingdomes Weekly Intelligencer*, 6-13 May 1645, pp. 796-7; *The Weekly Account*, 26 Mar.-2 Apr. 1645, unpaginated.

137 NLW, Sweeney Hall Mss A1, unfoliated; *JHC*, IV, p. 139.

138 *The Moderate Intelligencer*, 3-10 July 1645, p. 151; *The Kingdomes Weekly Intelligencer*, 10-17 Mar. 1646, p. 45.

139 M. Wanklyn, 'Landed Society & Allegiance in Cheshire and Shropshire in the First Civil War' (Manchester, unpublished PhD thesis, 1976), pp. 152, 264-5, 515-6.

140 HHL, Ellesmere Mss, 7114.

a JP and had been high sheriff in 1640/1.[141] Thomas Hunt was a wealthy Shrewsbury draper, while the lawyer Humphrey Mackworth was an alderman of Shrewsbury and since the early 1630s had been the recorder to the town corporation, its influential legal expert and 'learned counsel'.[142]

The Parliamentary county administration, 1646-8

Parliament's military victory in 1646 left the English shires controlled by the county committees. They supplanted much of the traditional powers of the lieutenancy and magistracy for defence and taxation, and were responsible for the financial punishment of Royalists. The committee of Shropshire assumed the title of committee for safety of the county, but executive power remained in the hands of the foremost wartime committeemen. Authority to sequestrate local Royalists and other 'delinquents', for example, was distilled from the overblown 22-man committee of 1644 to the six-man group sitting at Shrewsbury in February 1646, comprising Humphrey Mackworth, Robert Clive, Thomas Nicolls, Andrew Lloyd, Robert Charleton and Leighton Owen.[143] Colonels Mackworth and Lloyd together with Captain Owen oversaw security measures in mid-1647, and just over a year later Mackworth, Clive, Nicolls and Owen collectively appointed their colleague Andrew Lloyd to the colonelcy of the county militia.[144] In spring 1648 collection of the monthly assessment was demanded by warrants subscribed by Mackworth, Nicolls and Samuel More.[145]

The committeemen also occupied senior military and political posts. In 1646 Lloyd was made governor of Bridgnorth and More governor of Ludlow, in April and June respectively, while in July More was appointed deputy commander of the county forces.[146] Thomas Nicolls, meanwhile, was the mayor of Shrewsbury in 1645/6.[147] In the so-called 'recruiter' Parliamentary by-elections held in 1645-6 to replace Shropshire's ousted Royalist MPs, Thomas Hunt was elected for Shrewsbury; Robert Charleton and Robert Clive for Bridgnorth; the prominent committeeman (and cousin of Samuel More) John Corbet for Bishop's Castle; while Humphrey Mackworth's son Thomas was elected for Ludlow.[148] The ever-present Mackworth senior emerges now, if not before, as the first amongst equals in the county committee – in effect as Shropshire's county boss, like Sir William Brereton in Cheshire and William Purefoy in Warwickshire. Accordingly, Parliament made Mackworth commander-in-chief of the county forces in July 1646 and renewed his governorship of Shrewsbury in March 1647.[149]

The county committee for safety delegated administration to reliable local officials

---

141 *JHL,* IV, p. 531; SA, LB7/2315.

142 Wanklyn, 'Landed Society & Allegiance', p. 248; SA, 6001/290, f. 104.

143 W.G.D. Fletcher (ed.), 'The Sequestration Papers of Thomas Pigott of Chetwynd', *TSANHS*, 4th Series, IV (1914), p. 83.

144 NLW, Aston Hall Estate Records: Correspondence, C2; D1 Manuscripts, 2468.

145 SA, LB7/1933.

146 Carr and Atherton, *Civil War in Staffordshire,* p. 175; *JHL*, VIII, p. 360; *JHC,* IV, p. 614.

147 SA, 3365/592, f. 2.

148 The second Recruiter MP for Shrewsbury was William Masham, an outsider from Essex. Brunton and Pennington, *Long Parliament*, pp. 211, 229, 234, 236; *ODNB*, 13, p. 390.

149 *JHC*, IV, p. 614; *JHC*, V, p. 122.

whom it could trust. A small Parliamentarian commission of the peace with what would have been very localised powers appears to have been instituted during the winter of 1644-5, and a county magistracy much reduced from its pre-war size to number just 20-28 JPs was in place into 1648, its membership subject to intervention by the rival Presbyterian and Independent factions at Westminster.[150] It was of course politic for the county committee for safety, who were also JPs, to act with the sanction of the wider magistracy; hence warrants issued by committeemen during the emergency of mid-1648 were subscribed 'with the consent of the justices of peace'.[151] But the Parliamentarian regime included a larger number of local officials. During 1647 and 1648 Parliament nationally appointed new county commissions for taxation and the militia, in adjunct to the county committees. The membership of these commissions for Shropshire are listed in Table 4, as follows: a commission of 55 in June 1647 for the monthly assessment; a commission of 58 in February 1648 for the army in Ireland tax (the same commissioners would also oversee the assessment re-enacted in March 1648); and the 32 men nominated in December 1648 to reappoint the county commission for the militia. Table 4 also lists a fourth administrative body, concerned with religious conformity, the appointees to the six 'classical presbyteries' promulgated in April 1647 to bring Presbyterianism to the parishes of Shropshire. Notwithstanding the actual extent of Presbyterian ministry in Shropshire being limited, the inclusion of 42 (of a total of 79) presbyters, or elders, who as men of local standing were also committeemen or commissioners, allows a broader view of the Parliamentarian regime.

Table 4 shows that the leading committeemen from the First Civil War were appointed to all four bodies. However, other individuals who hitherto seem to have been less active in the Parliamentary cause now came to the fore. Sir Humphrey Briggs, son of the county committeeman Sir Morton, joined William Pierrepont as the recruiter MP and second burgess for Much Wenlock, while the recruiter MPs Thomas More for Ludlow – brother of the soldier Samuel – and Humphrey Edwards (replacing the Royalist Sir Richard Lee as the second knight for the shire) had previously sat only on the 1644 sequestration committee.[152] Hercules Kynnerlsey and John Proud became important financial officials. By 1646 they were chief members of the six-man accounting committee sitting at Shrewsbury as Shropshire's agency of the London-based Committee for Taking Accounts of the Whole Kingdom.[153] In 1647 Kynnerlsey was a leading commissioner for the assessment, and in 1648 treasurer of the army tax for Ireland. Meanwhile Proud became the county Treasurer at War.[154] Another important financial officer was John Browne, a presbyter and in 1647/8 the county Solicitor for Sequestrations.[155]

However, putting aside the three MPs, Myddelton, Wallop and Long, who were outsiders with landed interests in Shropshire, of the remaining 59 local officials

---

150 Cox, 'County Government', p. 91.
151 SA, LB7/1936.
152 Brunton and Pennington, *Long Parliament*, pp. 13, 211, 228, 231, 237.
153 TNA SP28/242 Part 1, Captain King's accounts, f. 54.
154 TNA, SP28/50 Part 3, f. 310.
155 W.G.D. Fletcher (ed.), 'The Sequestration Papers of Sir Thomas Whitmore Knight and Baronet of Apley', *TSANHS*, 4th Series, IV (1914), pp. 312-13.

Individual and status. Where no title is given the individual was known as an esquire or a gentleman.	Likely Resident Hundred (Residency elsewhere than Shropshire is italicised).	Membership of administrative bodies					
		CC 1642-1645	CP Apr. 1647	AC June 1647	IC Feb. 1648	AC Mar. 1648	MC Dec. 1648
Aston, John	Munslow	✗	✓	✗	✓	✓	✗
Baker, Thomas	Oswestry	✗	✓	✓	✓	✓	✓
Briggs, Sir Humphrey, MP	Brimstree	✗	✓	✓	✓	✓	✓
Chambers, Arthur	Pimhill	✗	✓	✓	✓	✓	✓
Charleton, Robert	S. Bradford	✓	✓	✓	✓	✓	✓
Child, Dr. William	Stottesdon?	✗	✗	✓	✓	✓	✗
Clive, Robert, MP	N. Bradford	✓	✓	✓	✓	✓	✓
Clive, Thomas	Pimhill	✗	✓	✓	✗	✗	✗
Corbet, Sir John, MP	N. Bradford	✓	✓	✓	✓	✓	✓
Corbet, John, MP	Ford	✓	✓	✓	✓	✓	✓
Corbet, Robert	Pimhill	✓	✓	✓	✓	✓	✓
Cotton, William	N. Bradford	✗	✓	✓	✓	✓	✓
Cresset, Edward	Munslow	✗	✓	✓	✓	✓	✓
Edwards, Humphrey, MP	Shrewsbury	✓	✗	✓	✓	✓	✓
Forester, Francis	Munslow	✗	✓	✓	✓	✓	✓
Gardner, Thomas	Shrews.	✗	✗	✗	✓	✓	✗
George, Owen	Shrews.	✗	✗	✗	✓	✓	✗
Harris, Francis	Purslow?	✗	✓	✓	✓	✓	✗
Harris, Richard	Chirbury	✗	✓	✓	✓	✓	✗
Hill, Rowland	N. Bradford	✗	✓	✓	✓	✓	✗
Hunt, Rowland	Shrewsbury	✗	✓	✓	✓	✓	✓
Hunt, Thomas, MP	Shrews. Lib.	✓	✓	✓	✓	✓	✓
Jones, William	Stottesdon	✗	✓	✗	✓	✓	✓
Kettleby, Thomas	Overs	✗	✓	✓	✓	✓	✓
Knight, Thomas	Shrewsbury	✗	✓	✓	✗	✗	✗
Kynnersley, Hercules	Stottesdon	✓	✓	✓	✓	✓	✗
Lee, Lancelot	Stottesdon	✓	✓	✓	✓	✓	✗
Leighton, Harcourt	Munslow	✓	✓	✓	✓	✓	✓
Littleton, William	Purslow	✗	✓	✓	✓	✓	✓
Llewellin, Richard	Shrewsbury	✗	✗	✗	✓	✓	✗
Lloyd, Andrew	Oswestry	✓	✓	✓	✓	✓	✓
Lock[y]er, Thomas	?	✗	✗	✓	✗	✗	✗
Long, Walter	Wiltshire	✓	✗	✓	✓	✓	✗
Mackworth, Humphrey	Condover	✓	✓	✓	✓	✓	✓
Mackworth, Thomas, MP	Condover	✗	✗	✓	✓	✓	✓
More, Samuel	Purslow	✓	✓	✓	✓	✓	✓
More, Thomas, MP	Munslow?	✓	✗	✓	✓	✓	✓
Myddelton, Sir Thomas, MP	Denbighshire	✓	✗	✓	✓	✓	✗

Table 4: Alphabetical listing of officials of the Parliamentarian administration in Shropshire, 1646-8.

Individual and status Where no title is given the individual was known as an esquire or a gentleman.	Likely Resident Hundred (Residency elsewhere than Shropshire is italicised).	Membership of administrative bodies					
		CC 1642-1645	CP Apr. 1647	AC June 1647	IC Feb. 1648	AC Mar. 1648	MC Dec. 1648
Mytton, Thomas	Oswestry	✓	✓	✓	✓	✓	✓
Nicolls, Thomas	Ford	✓	✓	✓	✓	✓	✓
Owen, Leighton	Ford	✓	✓	✓	✓	✓	✓
Pierrepont, William, MP	Brimstree	✓	✓	✓	✓	✓	✓
Powell, Henry	Clun	✗	✓	✓	✓	✓	✗
Powell, Jeremiah	Clun	✗	✗	✓	✓	✓	✗
Powell, Robert	Oswestry	✗	✓	✓	✓	✓	✓
Proud, John	Shrewsbury	✓	✓	✓	✓	✓	✓
Rowley, Roger	Chirbury	✗	✓	✓	✓	✓	✗
Sandford, Samuel	Bradford	✗	✓	✓	✓	✓	✗
Shepherd, Isaac	Munslow	✗	✓	✓	✓	✓	✗
Sone [Stone?], William,	?	✗	✗	✓	✗	✗	✗
Stevens, Michael	Munslow	✗	✓	✓	✓	✓	✗
Steventon, William	Pimhill	✗	✓	✓	✓	✓	✗
Taylor, Creswell	N. Bradford	✗	✓	✓	✓	✓	✗
Thomas, Esau, MP	Purslow	✗	✓	✓	✓	✓	✓
Thyne, John	Munslow?	✗	✗	✓	✓	✓	✓
Towers, Samuel	?	✗	✗	✓	✗	✗	✗
Wallop, Robert, MP	*Hampshire*	✓	✗	✓	✓	✓	✓
Ward, Arthur	Shrews. Lib.	✓	✗	✓	✓	✓	✗
Whichcott, Edward	Overs	✗	✓	✓	✓	✓	✗
Whitehall, Richard,	?	✗	✗	✓	✓	✓	✗
Wright, Nathaniel	Shrewsbury?	✗	✗	✗	✗	✗	✓
Wyburnbury, John	?	✗	✗	✓	✓	✓	✗

Table 4 (part 2): Alphabetical listing of officials of the Parliamentarian administration in Shropshire, 1646-8.

Key to Table 4: CC = First Civil War Shropshire committees; CP = *The Several Divisions And Persons For Classical Presbyteries In The County of Salop*, dated 29 April 1647; AC = commission for the monthly assessment, appointed by ordinance of 23 June 1647 (*A&O*, I, pp. 958-84), re-enacted on 20 March 1648 (*JHL*, X, pp. 121-4); IC = commission for 'raising £20,000 a month for the relief of Ireland', appointed by ordinance of 16 February 1648 (*A&O*, I, pp. 1072-1105). MC = commission for 'settling the militia […] within the kingdom', appointed by ordinance of 2 December 1648 (*A&O*, I, pp. 1233-51).

identified in Table 4, 34 (58 per cent) were neither First Civil War committeemen, nor, it seems, army officers, apart from Colonel Robert Powell, high sheriff in 1646/7, and Thomas Kettleby, an officer of the Stokesay garrison in 1646. Some may otherwise have upheld the Parliamentarian cause, but the political *arrivistes* whose wartime role now appears indiscernible included William Cotton and Thomas Baker, high sheriff in 1647/8 and 1648/9 respectively, and Esau Thomas, the town clerk of Bishop's Castle elected as its second recruiter MP in 1646.[156] The appointment of an individual as a commissioner or a presbyter does not, of course, prove his active participation. However, given the comparative data in Table 4 it seems that governance by the post-First Civil War Parliamentarian regime in Shropshire from 1646 to 1648 resided with around 40 officials, while executive power was retained by the core membership of the county committee for safety.

Parliamentarian associations and regional commanders

The formation of inter-county regional associations was a progressive development of the Parliamentarian war effort. Parliament soon recognised the importance of collaborative action by its supporters in curbing Royalist activity, and on 4 July 1642 the Commons sanctioned military intervention by adjacent counties in a neighbouring shire. Parliament towards the end of August instructed it supporters in Kent, for example, to ally themselves with adjoining counties, while on 18 November, in furtherance of widespread inter-county collaboration, Parliament ambitiously instituted an association of 12 northerly English shires.[157]

Given that Shropshire turned Royalist, Parliamentarian attempts to associate the county were intended to secure military intervention there. This encouraged the declaration of support between Shropshire, Worcestershire, Herefordshire and Gloucestershire Parliamentarians agreed at Worcester on 8 October 1642, when Parliament's field army was occupying the city and a detachment commanded by the Earl of Stamford had secured Hereford. But in the event Essex's main body left Worcester on 20 October and by mid-November Parliamentarian troops had evacuated Worcestershire. Remaining meanwhile at Hereford, Stamford was considered by Parliament advantageously placed to be the regional commander, and accordingly on 13 December was appointed commander-in-chief of Shropshire, Worcestershire, Herefordshire and Gloucestershire.[158] This was of course unbeknown to Stamford, who the next day abandoned his isolated outpost at Hereford to the local Royalists, withdrawing his forces, via Gloucester, to join Parliamentarians in the West Country.[159] Shropshire was next attached to a far-flung Western Association also including Worcestershire, Gloucestershire, Somerset and Wiltshire, created by Parliament on 11 February 1643 under the command of Sergeant-Major-General Sir William Waller, Stamford's immediate superior.[160] Five days later, however, the Commons debated a draft ordinance to join Shropshire instead with Staffordshire and

156 R.D. Davies, *The Sheriffs of Shropshire* (Shropshire, 2013), p. 61; BCHRC, First Minute Book, ff. 209-09v.
157 *JHC,* II, p. 649; *JHL,* V, pp. 331, 451.
158 Yonge, *Diary,* p. 143; *JHC,* II, p. 886.
159 Ross, *Royalist, But ..,* p. 52.
160 *A&O,* I, pp. 79-80.

11. Basil Feilding, second Earl of Denbigh (c.1608-1675). During 1643 and 1644 Denbigh was general of the Parliamentarian regional command including Shropshire.

Warwickshire, associated since 31 December 1642 under the command of Parliament's lord lieutenant for Warwickshire, Robert Greville, Second Baron Brooke.[161] Eventually on 10 April 1643 Shropshire joined this more geographically cohesive association, under the same ordinance that formally constituted the county committee. But this new West Midland Association (a descriptively convenient modern term not used at the time) was leaderless since the killing on 2 March of the energetic and capable Brooke, shot dead whilst besieging Royalist Lichfield.

While Shropshire remained within the West Midland Association, cooperative 'mutual association' with North Wales was encouraged by the ordinance of 12 June 1643 making Sir Thomas Myddelton sergeant-major-general and Parliament's commander-in-chief of the six shires – albeit a paper command of then entirely Royalist territory.[162] Sir Thomas was an anglicised Welshman, a wealthy landowner and the MP for Denbighshire, whose home estate there at Chirk Castle had been seized by Royalists early in 1643. Because of their shared strategic objectives – a Parliamentarian recovery in Shropshire could allow Myddelton to springboard operations into Wales – Myddelton cooperated with the Shropshire Parliamentarians as an active ally until the Self-Denying Ordinance brought his generalship to an end in June 1645. This was a generally collaborative relationship that benefitted from Myddelton's friendship with his brother-in-law Thomas Mytton. Their mutual interests in the region also resulted in collaborative military operations between Myddelton and Sir William Brereton in command of Cheshire.

161 Yonge, *Diary*, p. 313; *A&O*, I, pp. 53-5.
162 *JHL*, VI, pp. 90-2.

On 12 June 1643 Parliament also ended the three-month hiatus in the leadership of the West Midland Association by making Basil Feilding, Second Earl of Denbigh general and commander-in-chief and also the lord lieutenant of his native Warwickshire. Worcestershire was also attached to the Association.[163] With both Worcestershire and Shropshire under Royalist control, however, Denbigh would have to secure support from the county committees of Staffordshire and Warwickshire. The committee at Stafford was only recently established, but the committee based at Coventry was gaining a firm hold on Warwickshire, Parliament's most secure county in the central Midlands largely as a result of Lord Brooke's actions and leadership there in 1642. However, since Brooke's death both committees had abandoned formal cooperation and instead had looked inwardly to their own defence.[164]

Denbigh's operational command began inauspiciously in late August 1643, when after leaving London for the Midlands with some small forces, he was summarily recalled because intercepted correspondence from Oxford had raised suspicions about his loyalty to the Parliamentarian cause.[165] Denbigh was swiftly exonerated, but further delayed in October over fresh uncertainty about his fidelity, doubts that his background tended to encourage.[166] Whereas Lord Brooke had been a determinedly radical Parliamentarian, Denbigh was a moderate, an ex-courtier of Royalist parentage. In 1642 father and son had fought on the opposing sides at Edgehill, the First Earl as a volunteer in the King's Lifeguard and Basil, then Lord Feilding, as a colonel of Parliamentary horse leading his own troop and a regiment. The Earl died in April 1643 of wounds sustained in taking part in Prince Rupert's notorious raid on Birmingham, leaving Lady Feilding, his widow and Basil's mother, as a close companion of Queen Henrietta Maria.[167]

Eventually fully absolved by Parliament, the Committee of Both Kingdoms and by the Earl of Essex, in mid-November Denbigh finally established his headquarters at Coventry. There he became entrenched in a pre-existing quarrel with the politically and religiously radically minded associates and appointees of Lord Brooke who dominated the county committee of Warwickshire. As will be seen in chapter four, what began as a dispute over military resources deepened when the committee rejected Denbigh's authority to take the Warwickshire forces, probably the best resourced and well-recruited units in the Association, into Shropshire.[168] From Coventry on 1 December, Denbigh wrote to Westminster of being 'hindered from carrying the forces of this county to the relief of our friends [at Wem]'.[169]

Those 'friends' had written increasingly urgently for Denbigh to come to their assistance and in November to support Sir Thomas Myddelton and Sir William Brereton's advance into Royalist north-east Wales. In their petitioning elsewhere, including to the Lord General, the Parliamentarians holding out at Wem became

163 Ibid., p. 92.
164 Hughes, *Warwickshire*, pp. 181-2
165 *A Perfect Diurnall of some passages in Parliament,* 28 Aug.-4 Sept. 1643, p. 54.
166 Hughes, *Warwickshire*, pp. 224-5; *JHL*, VI, pp. 202, 218, 255, 261.
167 Hughes, *Warwickshire*, pp. 221-3.
168 Ibid., pp. 221-5; *JHL*, VI, pp. 325-6.
169 BDL, Tanner Mss 62, f. 402.

increasingly critical of the Earl's apparent inactivity.[170] Still short of military resources and moreover hamstrung by the committee at Coventry, Denbigh returned to London by Christmas to pursue his case against them in Parliament.[171] In the New Year Denbigh remained in London until mid-February. He probably returned to Warwickshire around the same time that Prince Rupert arrived in Shropshire.[172]

With his relations with the county committee showing little improvement and still obstructed by them, Denbigh in spring 1644 built up his own regiments of horse and foot and accumulated military supplies for the Association.[173] In the meantime Shropshire, and in particular the relief of Wem, remained a priority with the Committee of Both Kingdoms, but its attempts in early March and again in mid-April to orchestrate ambitious plans to send Denbigh into Shropshire leading an army around 4,000 strong – of units from the West Midland Association and detached from adjacent county forces – foundered on both occasions. The main reason for this was that units allocated to Denbigh instead remained in their native counties or else were unavoidably deployed elsewhere, while in March Prince Rupert's bold advance across the Midlands to relieve Newark and his victory there on the 21st threw the Parliamentarians into disarray.

Eventually, in early May 1644 the Earl of Denbigh cautiously advanced into south Staffordshire with an army of around 2,500 men, with Shropshire as his objective. Denbigh's manoeuvres and his subsequent campaigning into July – in southerly Staffordshire, Shropshire and then briefly into Cheshire – were mostly determined by enemy activity and by the often overambitious instructions of the Committee of Both Kingdoms in response; by Prince Rupert's march into Lancashire after leaving Shropshire in mid-May; and by a sudden advance by the King from Oxford into Worcestershire in early to mid-June, which on the 11th forced Denbigh's army to fight a successful defensive engagement at Tipton Green, near Dudley in south Staffordshire. Denbigh afterwards resupplied Wem and, while under pressure from the Committee of Both Kingdoms to march north to reinforce Parliamentarian forces allied against Prince Rupert, seized the opportunity of helping Colonel Mytton take Oswestry on 22/23 June. On 4 July his forces also threatened Shrewsbury. Capturing Oswestry was an important regional success, but while Denbigh's first campaign into Shropshire and Staffordshire had been useful, it would also be his last. In mid-July he returned to London, ostensibly to seek greater powers over his Association but actually abandoning his command to lick his wounds. Eventually, on 20 November 1644, after a series of motions and votes of confidence concerned with his conduct, the Commons decided that rather than return to command his Association Denbigh would do better as a negotiator of terms for peace with King Charles.[174] Thereby, to all military intents and purposes, the West Midland Association came to an end.

What can be said about the Earl of Denbigh's relationship with the committee of Shropshire? Clearly, relations became increasingly fractured and disrespectful over

---

170 HMC, *Thirteenth Report, Appendix Part I*, pp. 158-61.
171 *JHL*, VI, pp. 336, 354.
172 Assumed from Denbigh's attendance in the House of Lords, recorded in the *Journals*.
173 This summary of Denbigh's operations draws on *CSPD, 1644*, pp. 34-355, *passim*.
174 *JHC*, III, pp. 700-1.

Denbigh taking so long to intervene in Shropshire. By July 1644 the committee at Wem was not only openly demanding that Parliament replace him, but also alleged that Denbigh's officers had threatened and abused them.[175] In turn, as a peer of the realm with a heightened sense of status Denbigh would have found discourtesy unpalatable.[176] The Earl's relations with the leading committeemen Humphrey Mackworth and Thomas Mytton served to divide the committee. Mackworth had attached himself to the committee of Warwickshire, and, with their backing, in February 1644 presumed to prod Denbigh into action by proposing a plan for the relief of Wem. Further, on 27 March Mackworth, exasperated, penned an insubordinate ultimatum, presenting the 'bleeding condition of Shropshire' and demanding 'that your Lordship would plainly declare what you intend to do, whether you will go on to their relief or not'; otherwise Mackworth would advise his colleagues to evacuate Wem.[177] This evidence of Mackworth's disrespect for the Earl helps explain the testimony of some Warwickshire Parliamentarians in 1649, that in an angry meeting sometime five years earlier Denbigh had insulted Mackworth and threatened to kill him, and on another occasion had demanded Mackworth's dismissal along with several of his colleagues at Wem.[178]

On the other hand, Denbigh had an amicable relationship with Mytton as a senior colonel of the Association, while Mytton welcomed the Earl's patronage. Returning from a stay in London in April 1644, in May Mytton attached himself to Denbigh's staff and so attended councils of war held at Tamworth (Staffordshire), on 12 May, and at Stourbridge (Worcestershire), on 15 June.[179] After the action at Tipton Green, on 13 June Mytton wrote to his wife applauding Denbigh's gallant conduct, and that 'the Earl hath engaged me not to leave him and promised to do me right, which I doubt not while he is there'.[180] Mytton's loyalty was duly rewarded on 23 June at Oswestry, when, during a council of war and without consulting the committee at Wem, Denbigh appointed him governor.[181] It may have been with a sense of abandonment, then, that on 16 July Mytton wrote after him that the Earl's departure from Shropshire would be 'exceedingly ill taken'. However, from London on 27 October Denbigh wrote to Mytton expressing common cause against vitriol directed against them: 'I will not trouble you with [relating] the injuries that are offered to you and myself by the committee of Wem'.[182] Notwithstanding their animosity, in January 1645 the committeemen grudgingly and somewhat sheepishly acknowledged Denbigh's recent help – perhaps some logistical support – which they were surprised to have received.[183]

Once it seemed unlikely that Denbigh would return, Sir William Brereton sought to extend his influence as de facto regional commander of Shropshire and Staffordshire.

175 HMC, *Sixth Report, Part I*, pp. 19-20; *CSPD, 1649-1650*, p. 444.
176 Hughes, *Warwickshire*, p. 227.
177 WRO, CR2017/C9, ff. 46, 72.
178 *CSPD, 1649-1650*, pp. 444-5.
179 WRO, CR2017/C9, f. 98a; *CSPD, 1644*, p. 236.
180 NLW, Sweeney Hall Mss A1, f. 22.
181 *Two Great Victories: On[e] Obtained by the Earle of Denbigh at Oswestry […] The Other by Colonel Mitton* (1644), unpaginated.
182 WRO, CR2017/C10, f. 16; NAM, 8812-63, f. 5.
183 *LBWB*, I, p. 33.

In October 1644 an officer of the Oswestry garrison informed the Earl of Denbigh about an unsuccessful coup attempted there in Colonel Mytton's absence, when certain committeemen had encouraged the soldiers 'to elect Sir William Brereton general over this county'.[184] There the matter seems to have ended, leaving Brereton as patron to the committee at Wem. However, in a successful *coup d'état* at Stafford in December 1644, Brereton, with the backing of the Committee of Both Kingdoms, purged the county committee of Denbigh's adherents, notably the leading Colonels Chadwick and Rugeley.[185] Brereton thereby gained effective control of the Staffordshire forces, which he deployed in February 1645 to enable the committee at Wem to capture Shrewsbury. But once the committee at Shrewsbury had strengthened their own forces, during 1645 they gradually shifted the terms of their relationship with Brereton, from one of semi-dependence to being instead reliable but sometimes questioning allies.[186]

Conclusions

During the First English Civil both sides adopted similar approaches, by organising their leading supporters into politico-military executive bodies, respectively the Royalist commission of array and the Parliamentarian county committee, and by placing Shropshire within a regional command structure by means of inter-county association. Both sides also attempted to channel the gathering of warlike resources through the pre-existing structures of county government. This led to their active participation in the war effort, voluntarily or otherwise, of numerous individuals holding varying degrees of authority and responsibility. This is seen most clearly on the Royalist side by their involvement as commissioners of array of MPs, deputy lieutenants, JPs, militia officers, senior aldermen and the incumbent high sheriffs. All told, the means to organise and direct war effort in Shropshire were much the same as elsewhere in the shires of England and Wales. This chapter has also shown how the Parliamentarian regime holding power in Shropshire during the renewed hostilities of 1648 came to be organised.

War effort in Shropshire from 1642 to 1646 was directed by in all around 60 Royalist commissioners and 40 Parliamentarian committeemen drawn from the middling and higher ranks of the county gentry. Considering the scale of their task this was a modest number of activists, particularly as among them were some outsiders and local men whose involvement was peripheral. Furthermore, even among the 'activists' the degree and duration of personal commitment varied from individual to individual. This resulted in effective authority being devolved to a smaller number of highly committed chief men, shown by the Parliamentarian example of the eight-man committee at Shrewsbury during 1645 and 1646. Looking even more selectively, within both sides was a nucleus of determined leaders who remained at the forefront of events from 1642 into 1646, notably the Royalists Sir Francis Ottley, Sir Vincent Corbet and Sir Thomas Eyton, and the Parliamentarians Humphrey Mackworth,

---

184 WRO, CR2017/C10, f. 38.
185 *CSPD, 1644-1645*, pp. 69-70, 80, 84, 91.
186 In November 1645, for example, the committee tetchily badgered Brereton to repay £100 he owed them: BL Additional Mss. 11332, f. 111.

Thomas Hunt and Thomas Mytton.

Shropshire was attached to several regional associations, but for both sides these were never wholly stable blocs of territory, being often under partial enemy occupation or else threatened by hostile incursion from adjacent counties that in turn were contested. For these reasons Parliament's West Midland Association in particular was unworkable, without the recovery by a substantial army under a skilful commander of swathes of territory in Shropshire, Staffordshire and Worcestershire. A sufficient army never came together, and although, as explored further in chapter four, the Earl of Denbigh laboured without effective powers against localism and as a result lacked military resources, he was a pedestrian soldier and an uncharismatic leader probably temperamentally unsuited to high command. Consequently, he remained unable to overcome the military and political difficulties that bedevilled his Association. Shropshire of course fell more easily within Royalist boundaries of association, which, apart from contested Cheshire, until autumn 1643 generally remained secure. The military high commands of Lord Capel and Prince Rupert were far more successful in organising the regional war effort than the gentry-led associations of 1642 and 1645, which looked inwardly in attempting to secure political cohesion to achieve limited objectives of provincial self-defence and security. However, both generals only enjoyed reasonable success for a period of around six months, respectively in 1643 and 1644, before military events caused destabilisation – Parliamentarian inroads into Capel's territory in autumn 1643, and, indirectly, Prince Rupert's defeat at Marston Moor in July 1644.

The ultimate purpose of wartime leadership is of course to further the creation, support and direction of armed forces. With the *dramatis personae* of the Civil War in Shropshire having been identified, chapter three will turn to military organisation.

3

Of Officers and Men: The armed forces

I have not yet beaten my drums but shall this week,
And in honour Shropshire must assist in their contributions.

War effort of course demands the mobilisation and organisation of large and sustainable numbers of soldiers. Throughout the history of sustained armed conflict the primary purpose of any war effort has been to create and deploy military forces, with all other organisational tasks of war being directed to that end. Accordingly, this chapter looks at the recruitment, nature and number of the Royalist and Parliamentarian armed forces that campaigned in Shropshire from 1642 to 1648.

Much has been written on military organisation during the English Civil Wars, and the following is a brief summary of what is generally accepted to have been the organisational norms across all armies of the period. The contemporary theoretical size and structure of units was straightforward, and both sides followed the same practice. Apart from the pre-existing county militias, the trained bands, the issuing of commissions for colonelcies and captaincies, respectively for the recruitment of regiments and of troops or companies, enabled new units to be raised. Accordingly, the cavalry, generally referred to in contemporary sources as the horse, were grouped into regiments of 400-500, subdivided into troops of around 60 or 70 of all ranks, while the nominal strength of a regiment of infantry, termed the foot, was 1,300 men, in companies of 100 or so. Dragoons, being mounted infantry, were also organised into companies and regiments. There were also some semi-independent unregimented companies and troops. Artillery, or ordnance, was organised on a more ad hoc basis, grouped at army level into artillery trains, but at the tactical level operating in batteries of two or more cannon or mortars, or sometimes just as single pieces.

Because of ongoing attrition, by combat, sickness and desertion, and the difficulties of recruitment, most units were actually well below their theoretical establishment. The Warwickshire Parliamentarian units Colonel Barker's Regiment of Foot and Colonel Purefoy's Regiment of Horse, as the chief regiments of that county and probably the largest units within the West Midland Association, can be seen by muster rolls dating from January 1644 to have been by First Civil War standards very strong regional regiments, with all ranks numbering 797 foot soldiers and 428 cavalry and dragoons respectively.[1]

In the absence of informative military records (such as muster rolls), many Shropshire units remain very shadowy bodies indeed. For example, the Royalist MP for Bridgnorth Sir Edward Acton was a colonel by 1645, but of his 'regiment' there is evidence of just a diminished troop of ten horsemen at Bridgnorth that October.[2] This example cautions against attributing full regimental status to units that may never have been larger than a troop or a company or two. Determining the size of the units and formations that campaigned in Shropshire is also problematic, because contemporary accounts of military events were often given at second or third hand, and for that reason hearsay and misinformation readily passed as fact. In February 1644, Humphrey Mackworth advised the Earl of Denbigh to use the tendency to exaggerate troop numbers to his advantage, for by marching to the relief of Wem with an army of 2,000 men, 'these in reputation', as Mackworth pointed out, 'will be [considered] 3,000 at least'.[3] Senior officers, who, for reasons of security or special pleading, or out of laxity, were vague in their reporting, also obscured the actual number of soldiers available. Sir Thomas Myddelton, for example, later declared that in early September 1644 he had no more than 650 men, yet at the time his most senior cavalry officer had numbered Myddelton's brigade as around 800.[4] Furthermore, determining the size of units and formations is made more difficult by contemporary sources often being unclear whether or not their numbering included officers as well as rank and file, indeed Myddelton's discrepancy may be an example of this. Given that musicians as well as commissioned and non-commissioned ranks were counted among the proportionately high number of Civil War officers, their omission from a written account would mean the size of a force being significantly understated.[5]

With these limitations in mind, this chapter examines in turn the various ways of recruitment, the variety and character of Royalist units in Shropshire, and the expansion and eventual disbandment of the Parliamentary county forces. While Royalist units are generally named here, as in contemporary usage, after their commanding officer, the term Shropshire forces has, as at the time, been used to describe those units raised and commanded by the committee of Shropshire. Similarly, the use of the term brigade to describe Sir Thomas Myddelton's mixed Parliamentary force of foot, horse, dragoons and gunners follows contemporary usage.

Recruitment

The rank and file of the armies of the First Civil War consisted of volunteers, especially among the cavalry, or conscripts (or impressed men), who increasingly came to predominate in the infantry as the war progressed.

While many reluctant conscripts took to soldiering and not all volunteers became effective soldiers, most commanders would probably have accepted the maxim

1 WRO, CR2017/C9, ff. 39-40.
2 SA, P270/B/1/1, ff. 57-8; Symonds, *Diary*, p. 252.
3 WRO, CR2017/C9, f. 46.
4 *CSPD, 1644-1645*, p. 34; NLW, Herbert Mss and Papers, Series II, Vol. IX, E6/1/3.
5 The problem of establishing troop numbers was acknowledged by Burne and Young, in *Great Civil War*, p. 13, and considered in depth by Foard, in *Naseby*, pp. 202-3, 206-7.

propounded in a London newsbook in 1644, that, being generally more committed and reliable, 'none but volunteers do the work on both sides'.[6] If the 20 men from the parish of Myddle who enlisted were representative of the shire, then many Shropshire men served ostensibly as volunteers. Richard Gough, whose portrayal of the soldiers from Myddle was written within living memory of the Wars, described a typical Royalist recruitment drive in the parish during winter 1642-3. Responding to warrants issued by a local commissioner of array, men from Pimhill hundred gathered at a landmark hilltop to listen to a recruiting agent calling for volunteers for the King with the enticement of generous pay.[7] Voluntarism had different shades. Some were motivated on grounds that were more or less ideological, if sometimes parochial. Ralph Griffiths, for example, a freeman of Shrewsbury's guild of clothiers, when in 1646 applying to become a free burgess of the town professed that he had 'ventured his life' as a Parliamentarian soldier, until Shrewsbury 'was fully settled under the command of Parliament'. Veterans of Continental wars returned to soldiering, such as Sergeant William Preece of Newton on the Hill. After campaigning in the Low Countries, on his return to Shropshire Preece had joined the Trained Bands and later served in the Royalist army.[8] With the accepted minimum age for liability to military service being 16 years, the reputedly adventurous life of a soldier attracted young men whose own living was mundane. Consequently, 'many young boys' were seen enlisting in the King's army at Shrewsbury in 1642. Thomas Formeston of Marton was a similarly eager young recruit. Unfortunately, he was also most likely the one and the same Thomas Formestone buried at St. Michael's Church, Munslow, on 5 July 1645, a Parliamentarian trooper and fatal casualty of the cavalry action fought nearby at Broncroft the day before.[9] The prospect of regular pay and occasional plunder attracted volunteers driven by pressing economic reasons such as unemployment and indebtedness. In the example of Myddle parish, a group of itinerant quarrymen and a local jobbing tailor of no fixed abode left uncertain employment and enlisted at Shrewsbury in 1642. Another parishioner, Thomas Ash, an otherwise respectable tenant farmer, had fallen into debt and to escape his creditors joined the Royalist army.[10] If voluntarism often masked economic coercion, then social coercion in a hierarchical society also played a part. In September 1642 High Sheriff John Weld wrote to the town bailiffs of Ludlow that if they encouraged volunteering, 'his majesty will take it as an expression of your affection to his person'. Landowners too could stimulate voluntarism, by exerting local influence over tenants, dependants and others. Accordingly, in August 1644 the committee at Wem hoped to engage the neutralist Earl of Bridgewater and the side-shifting Sir Arthur Mainwaring to foster Parliamentarian recruitment in their north Shropshire estates.[11]

Would-be commissioned officers enjoyed greater latitude when volunteering

6   *A True and Perfect Journal of the Civill Warres in England*, 30 Apr. 1644, p. 12.
7   Gough, *Myddle*, pp. 71-2, 116.
8   SA, 3365/2263, unfoliated; Gough, *Myddle*, p. 32.
9   *A Continuation of the late proceedings of His Majesty's Army at Shrewsbury, Bridge North and Manchester* (1642), p. 6; Gough, *Myddle*, p. 71; SA, P200/Fiche 24.
10 Gough, *Myddle*, pp. 62, 71, 226-7.
11 SA, LB7/2233; NLW, Sweeney Hall Mss A1, f. 21.

their services. The more adventurous of them sought employment with renowned commanders, such as the gentleman seeking a commission from Colonel Thomas Mytton in 1645 who earnestly declared, 'Sir, I am resolved to do you service or no man'. Common soldiers were also attracted to serve a respected or charismatic leader, like the committeeman Thomas Hunt who, according to his associate Richard Baxter, was 'entirely beloved and trusted by the soldiers for his honesty'.[12] In February 1644 Colonel Mytton feared that with his arrival in Shropshire Prince Rupert's renown would boost Royalist recruitment, 'in regard of the reputation of the man, whose name sounds loud in the ears of the country people'. Given reinforcements, Mytton hoped to inflict an early defeat on the Prince, thereby making him 'so contemptible to the country that he would be altogether disabled […] to raise and levy in these parts'.[13] In an often very localised war, recruitment was influenced by victories and by a strong military presence in an area, especially an established garrison. In later October 1643, when their foothold at Wem remained uncertain, the Shropshire Parliamentarians complained that not a single recruit had joined them. However, a month later they optimistically reported increased popular support, a 'strong body' that might provide 1,000 recruits if they could be armed. In November 1644 the governors of the Parliamentarian garrisons at Moreton Corbet and Stoke upon Tern enthusiastically set about recruiting in their localities, the Royalist defeat at the battle of Montgomery in September having left 'the enemy in these parts […] altogether disheartened'.[14]

The Parliamentarians at first appear to have recruited largely in the London area because local recruiting grounds were under enemy control, but by an ordinance enacted on 10 August 1643 county committees further afield had been empowered to impress recruits.[15] However, the committee of Shropshire would have found it awkward to do so, not only because their recruiting areas were limited, but also on the grounds that they thought of themselves as liberating the shire from Royalist military oppression.

The Parliamentarian press was quick to condemn Royalist conscription in Shropshire. In April 1643 the newsbook *Certaine Informations from Severall Parts of the Kingdom* reported that Lord Capel 'presseth and enforceth men to serve him because few or none there offer themselves as volunteers for his service'.[16] Capel did not introduce conscription to Shropshire – the local authorities were already impressing men in early 1643.[17] That spring, however, Royalist conscription increased under Capel's leadership, when Shropshire was bound to find 600 recruits for the Prince of Wales's Lifeguard of Foot. Each allotment was to find ten likely recruits, of whom six would be enlisted.[18] A year later Royalist conscription intensified in Shropshire to provide recruits for Prince Rupert's forces and for King Charles's Oxford-based army. During the second week of March 1644 warrants were sent from Oxford to the sheriffs of 30 shires instructing

12   NAM, 8812-63, f. 6; Baxter, *Reliquiae Baxterianae,* p. 45.
13   WSL, SMS 557.
14   HMC, *Thirteenth Report, Appendix Part I,* pp. 160-1; WRO, CR2017/10, f. 41.
15   *A&O,* I, pp. 241-2.
16   Edition for 10-17 Apr. 1643, pp. 101-2.
17   SA, BB/D/1/2/1/53, dragoons raised by warrant in the Bridgnorth area, 16 Feb. 1643.
18   'Ottley Papers' (1895), pp. 313-4, 329, 337.

them to impress recruits, including 200 men from Shropshire. Consequently, from Shrewsbury on 26 March Sir John Mennes wrote to Prince Rupert that High Sheriff Thomas Edwards's instructions, for the 'seizing of pressed men for recruiting his majesty's army', would restrict Rupert's own recruitment drive. Towards the end of May, another order from Oxford demanded the unfeasibly large number of a further 800 Shropshire conscripts.[19]

The civic records of the Royalist garrison towns provide evidence of widespread impressment at this time. During April 1644 petty constables at Ludlow 'pressed soldiers several times', and on the 25th the bailiffs were ordered to send more conscripts for enlistment at Shrewsbury on 2 May. Meanwhile the under-officers of the county town were also gathering conscripts.[20] Warrants to impress in and around Bridgnorth were issued monthly from April to August 1644. On 4 April John Law, a Bridgnorth constable, was given £2 10s in expenses to escort 'soldiers to Shrewsbury which were impressed within this town for his majesty's service'.[21] As the Royalists' regional recruiting centre Shrewsbury also drew in conscripts from further afield, including 100 pressed men from Denbighshire captured en route by the Parliamentarians at Montford bridge in May 1644.[22]

In addition to the influx of fresh recruits, troop numbers were sustained by the repatriation of prisoners of war in accordance with the laws of war. These customary practices regulated conduct in such matters as the surrender of a stronghold and the treatment of captives, eventualities that allowed soldiers to return to their own side. A garrison who had conducted their defence honourably, but not in an unduly prolonged or unnecessary way, could be granted favourable terms allowing them to fight another day. Thus the Royalists left isolated in Shrewsbury Castle after the town fell in February 1645 promptly capitulated and were allowed safe conduct to Ludlow.[23] It was common practice for captive commissioned officers of equivalent status to be exchanged, as in the case of Parliamentarian Captain Samuel More in 1644. Captured at Hopton Castle in March, by mid-May More was paroled and contemplating the completion of his negotiated exchange: 'I am delivered out of the prison of Ludlow', he wrote from Upton Cresset Hall, a family home of his Royalist counterpart, 'into the hands of Mr Francis Cressett with promise to remain with him till his father Edward Cressett shall be set at liberty'.[24] Common soldiers, however, were detained in much less hospitable circumstances. In April 1644 Colonel Lewis Chadwick, the Parliamentarian governor of Stafford, wrote to his Royalist counterpart at Shrewsbury, Sir Francis Ottley, complaining of 'the ill usage of our prisoners in not having straw, sweet water, [and] without remedy, or necessary food or liberty', abuses that Chadwick threatened 'must be answered here of necessity by us'.[25]

But there was also much interchange of rank and file prisoners of war, because few

19   BDL, Dugdale Mss 19 [second part], ff. 29-33, 71; BL, Additional Mss 18981, f. 62.
20   SA, LB8/1/164, f. 6; SA, LB7/2236; SA, 3365/588, ff. 38, 42-3.
21   SA, BB/D/1/2/1/54.
22   Williams, 'Notebook of William Maurice', p. 37.
23   *Relation […] by […] William Reinking*, p. 6.
24   WRO, CR2017/C9, f. 98.
25   WSL, SMS 493.

buildings other than churches or some castles were large or secure enough to hold them in numbers, while feeding and providing for them was expensive and problematic. Hence deals were negotiated like that agreed in July 1644 between Sir Fulke Hunckes, as governor of Shrewsbury, and Colonel Mytton, as governor of Wem, for the exchange between their respective garrisons of 100 Royalist soldiers for the same number of Parliamentarians. The switch was conducted with due protocol by the despatch and reception of drummers, acting as the traditional emissaries between opposing forces. Back in April, in spite of his ire over the ill treatment of his men, Colonel Chadwick had remained hopeful of concluding a similar interchange of prisoners with Hunckes's predecessor Sir Francis Ottley. Chadwick professed his willingness, to 'exchange all fitting courtesies which will be both honourable and charitable for both parties'.[26]

Although desertion was rife during the First Civil War the habit tended to sustain the armies, for deserters not only joined the enemy but also shifted amongst their own side seeking preferential conditions. Captain Hannay, for example, an officer in Sir Thomas Myddelton's brigade, found upon his return from Royalist captivity that his troop of 40 horsemen had shrunk to just 12, 'the rest being run to other brigades which hath better pay'. A fellow officer Captain Simon Farmer calculated that of the 22 troopers and officers missing from his originally 50-strong troop, just three were lost in action – two killed and one captured in the fighting for Oswestry on 2 July 1644 – while 19 had deserted, 13 of them to the enemy.[27] The published articles of war regulating the armies condemned desertion as a capital offence, and during the First Civil War both sides customarily hanged individuals and small groups of deserters as an exemplary disciplinary measure. A particularly notorious case in Shropshire was the hanging ordered by Prince Rupert at Whitchurch on 19 March 1645 of 13 Royalist deserters captured in Parliamentarian service. This was moreover a reprisal, for the summary execution ordered by the county committee of 13 Irish Royalist soldiers taken prisoner when Shrewsbury fell; an act deemed permissible after an ordnance of October 1644 instructed that all Irishmen (deemed to be all Catholics and thus Papists) captured in arms against Parliament should be put to death.[28] However, endemic side changing also came to be accepted as a fact of war and both sides encouraged desertion by defection. Once characterised as 'the vagabond privates who shifted about […] under temptation of richer spoil or higher pay', recent scholarship has attributed wider, sometimes ideological, motives to the likely thousands of side-changing soldiers.[29] The practice is now seen to have had a significant effect on the nature of Civil War armies: in Donagan's opinion, large-scale rank and file defection was 'a major form of troop attrition and acquisition'.[30]

Side changing permeated the war in and around Shropshire. In October 1645, for instance, officers at Montgomery Castle were prepared to accept the return to the

---

26   NLW, Sweeney Hall Mss A1, f. 23; WSL, SMS 493.
27   TNA, SP28/41 Part 4, f. 483, Hannay's accounts; TNA, SP28/37 Part 1, f. 89, Farmer's certificate.
28   *LBWB*, I, pp. 141, 227; *JHL*, VII, pp. 305-6.
29   Quotation from Webb and Webb, *Civil War […] as it affected Herefordshire*, II, p. 94. For the revisionist view of side changing, see B. Donagan, *War in England 1642-1649* (Oxford, 2008), pp. 275-8, and Hopper, *Turncoats & Renegadoes*, especially pp. 78-99.
30   Donagan, *War in England*, p. 275.

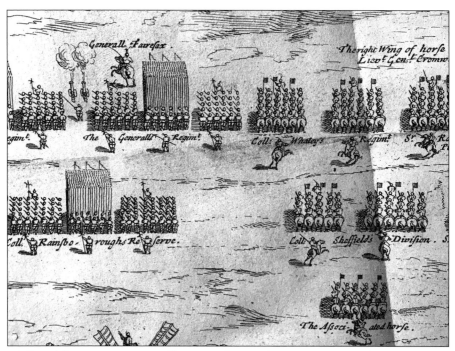

12. Detail from a contemporary illustration showing the opposing armies drawn up before the battle of Naseby (14 June 1645), which usefully depicts the fighting arms of Civil War armies: the horse (pictured here of the right wing of the Parliamentary New Model Army); the musket and pike blocks of the foot; and the ordnance, with cannon shown interspersed along the infantry front line. (Courtesy of Helion & Company Limited)

Parliamentarian fold of three troopers who since deserting had served as Royalists. At Shrewsbury six months earlier the committeemen had become wary of their ex-Royalist rank and file, and so placed reliable chosen men under Colonel Hunt's direct command to garrison Shrewsbury Castle.[31] Defeat and disaffection encouraged side changing. During August 1644 refugee Royalist horsemen, from the Northern army and of Prince Rupert's regiments defeated at Marston Moor and elsewhere since, were reported to 'come in daily to the Parliament's garrisons of Oswestry and Wem'.[32] By far the largest instance of side changing in the region was the defection of many of the 1,500 or so Royalist soldiers recently repatriated from Ireland taken prisoner after the battle of Nantwich on 25 January 1644. Hundreds reenlisted and some were sent to reinforce the Parliamentarians in Shropshire, where for many their new allegiance was short-lived. Several had deserted Wem for Shrewsbury already by late February, and when the Royalists took Apley Castle on 24 March they offered re-employment to the turncoats among the Parliamentarian garrison.[33] The 60 men of Captain Wood's

31 *LBWB*, II, p. 135; *LBWB*, I, p. 343.
32 *Mercurius Civicus*, 8-15 Aug. 1644, p. 612.
33 HMC, *Thirteenth Report, Appendix Part I*, pp 170-1; 'Ottley Papers' (1896), p. 231.

company of the Parliamentarian garrison at Longford House were mostly ex-Royalists enlisted at Nantwich, and when the garrison surrendered to Prince Rupert in April 1644 almost to a man they re-enlisted for the King.[34]

In addition to their regular forces both sides had the occasional support of irregular militias. Under the auspices of the Marcher Association, as Royalist high sheriff in 1645 Sir Francis Ottley periodically summoned the posse comitatus. On 1 February, for instance, Ottley issued warrants to mobilise 300 militiamen from Munslow hundred. Similarly, the several hundred countrymen gathered near Morville in early June who reportedly confronted, fired upon, and were then dispersed by a party of Parliamentarian horsemen had probably responded to a widespread call to readiness at arms circulated by Ottley towards the end of May. Again in July, Ottley and the sheriffs of Worcestershire and Herefordshire were ordered to raise the posse comitatus against the threatened advance of Lord Leven's Scots Covenanter army.[35]

Also in 1645 both sides endeavoured to benefit from the militancy of the south Shropshire clubmen. In late March the county committee intended to send soldiers into the area in alliance with the clubmen, who were again hostile to the King's men after a punitive raid on the Bishop's Castle district by Royalist forces out of Montgomeryshire. A month later, however, a clergyman and other local worthies were reportedly attempting to enlist clubmen for the Royalist cause.[36] The combatants also encouraged militia activity elsewhere. In late April 1645, the committeemen reported that countrymen in the contested territory between Shrewsbury and Bridgnorth had 'promised to rise with us, and we intend to put them to it'.[37] Parliamentarian efforts to secure local alliances of this sort came to fruition in south Shropshire that summer. In early August, men from the hundreds of Clun, Purslow and Munslow twice attended armed gatherings near Bishop's Castle under the direction of local man Colonel Samuel More, and on the 30th a body of townsmen and countrymen joined with around 200 regular Parliamentarian soldiers to defeat a Royalist force from Ludlow near Bishop's Castle.[38]

Before turning from this general review of military organisation to consider in detail the particular composition of the opposing forces, it should be explained that both sides maintained a corps of artillerymen to operate their garrison, siege and, on occasion, field artillery; at the battle fought near Stokesay on 8 June 1645, for instance, the Royalists deployed at least two cannon.[39] In later 1644 Sir Thomas Myddelton's brigade included a unit of at least ten gunners and their matrosses, or assistants, while a party of Royalist 'cannoneers' was based at Shrewsbury.[40]

---

34 *CSPD, 1645-1647*, p. 298; Mercurius *Aulicus*, w/e 6 Apr. 1644, p. 921.
35 'Ottley Papers' (1896), p. 272; *Mercurius Veridicus*, 7-14 June 1645, p. 72; *The Weekly Account*, 4-11 June 1645, unpaginated; HRO, CF61/20, ff. 573-4; BRL, Harleian Mss 6852, f. 276.
36 H.G. Tibbutt (ed.), *The Letter Books of Sir Samuel Luke, 1644-45* (London, 1963), p. 490; *LBWB*, I, p. 277.
37 *LBWB*, I, p. 291.
38 *Heads of Some Notes of The Citie Scout*, 19 Aug. 1645, p. 4; *The Kingdome's Weekly Intelligencer*, 2-9 Sept. 1645, p. 934; HMC, *Thirteenth Report, Appendix Part I*, pp. 95-6.
39 *Perfect Passages of Each Dayes Proceedings in Parliament*, 11-18 June 1645, p. 267.
40 NLW, Chirk Castle Mss 1/Biii, 93, unfoliated; SA, 3365/588, f. 45

Royalist forces in Shropshire
Local units under local commanders

During the First Civil War Royalist leadership and manpower was divided between the twin priorities of local defence and prosecuting the wider war. Like the Staffordshire gentleman who on 9 October 1642 wrote excitedly how he had enlisted at Shrewsbury and next day would march with the King's cavalry, many militarily active Royalists felt duty-bound to serve in propinquity to Charles I.[41] The royal army that left Shropshire in October 1642 comprised marching regiments raised to campaign beyond their locality. Thereafter, the tendency to gravitate to the Royalist centre – to the forces based around Oxford – and to celebrated units was detrimental to the King's supporters locked in provincial struggles. In the case of Lancashire, for example, from mid-1643 the Royalist cause was left moribund after the departure of the most enterprising officers and a number of units.[42] Although it did not haemorrhage in the way of Lancashire, the Royalist war effort in Shropshire also suffered by the diminution of officers and rank and file. Of some 133 Shropshire men named in post-Restoration *Indigent Officer* lists who claimed to have held the King's commission, 40% purportedly served in regiments that never or only fleetingly campaigned in Shropshire.[43] Furthermore, the more or less temporary withdrawal of units and the posting of others further afield had a detrimental effect on the Royalist military situation in Shropshire. During 1645, for example, the detachment in February of much of the Shrewsbury garrison to Prince Maurice's mobile force, and in May of Shropshire-based units to the main field army, contributed respectively to the loss of Shrewsbury and to the local Parliamentarian successes during June.[44] Captain Edward Lloyd of Llanvorda raised locally a troop for Lord Capel's Horse in 1643 and campaigned with the regiment (later Trevor's Horse) in Shropshire, the Marches and further afield during 1644. But the regiment including Lloyd's Troop was later posted to the West Country, and Lloyd eventually surrendered at Truro in Cornwall in March 1646.[45]

In 1642 three locally-led Royalist regiments were recruited in Shropshire, and they performed provincial and wider strategic roles. Two served as marching regiments (although neither was ready to accompany the King when he left Shropshire), while the third was raised and operated as a local defence force. Probably the first to be raised was Sir Robert Howard's Regiment of Dragoons, who local Royalists expected would defend Shropshire alongside the Trained Bands. However, by January 1643 Howard had taken his dragoons to Oxford (although a company was still being recruited in south Shropshire in March).[46] Two companies fought at Prince Rupert's storming of Bristol in July, and after the battle of Newbury in September Howard's Dragoons went into garrison at Donnington Castle in Berkshire.[47] By mid-1644 Howard had returned to Shropshire, perhaps accompanied by the remaining dragoons of his regiment.

---

41   SRO, D868/2/43.
42   Gratton, *Lancashire*, pp. 258, 260, 267.
43   *IO List, OT List.*
44   Clarendon, *History*, III, p. 511; *LBWB*, I, p. 393.
45   NLW, Sweeney Hall Mss A4 (Vol. II), f. 93.
46   SA, SRRU Deeds, 6000/13288, 13291; *ROP*, II, p. 463; 'Ottley Papers' (1895), pp. 286-7.
47   Warburton, *Prince Rupert*, II, pp. 237, 314.

The second regiment was of infantry. On 3 September 1642 King Charles issued a colonelcy to Richard Herbert, MP, to raise 1,200 foot. Although Herbert came from Montgomeryshire, as an active member of Shropshire's commission of array he intended to recruit there. Accordingly, on 13 September he wrote informing Francis Ottley that 'I have not yet beaten my drums but shall this week, and in honour Shropshire must assist in their contributions'.[48] Furthermore, on 17 October Herbert was commissioned to raise some horse and also appointed governor of Bridgnorth, where his recruits would muster.[49] Herbert's Regiment and Troop joined the Oxford army in mid-January 1643 where they remained during the spring and summer, the infantry participating in the capture of Bristol.[50] On 28 September Herbert was appointed governor of Ludlow, and his regiment arrived there from Oxford soon afterwards.[51] Herbert's Foot remained in the central Marches into 1644, garrisoning Montgomery in February and at the siege of Brampton Bryan Castle in northern Herefordshire in April, but its whereabouts thereafter are uncertain.[52]

The third regiment was Sir Vincent Corbet's Dragoons. In late 1642 High Sheriff Henry Bromley and certain gentry sought the King's approval of their resolution to recruit 'up to a thousand or at least 600 dragoons'. Accordingly, at Oxford on 9 December the regiment and Corbet's colonelcy was given royal assent, 'for the defence of his majesty and that county'. Sir Vincent's commission also to raise a body of horse was authorised soon after.[53] All ten known mounted officers who served under Corbet were Shropshire men, including dragoon company Captains Thomas Pigott, Edward Baldwin, Robert Sandford and (probably) Edward Owen, and Captain of Horse John Young.[54] Baldwin, for example, obtained recruits in south Shropshire including 26 men from Ludlow.[55] Under strength and inexperienced, Corbet's Dragoons were worsted in early engagements against Sir William Brereton's forces; the Cheshire Royalist Sir Thomas Aston described them at Whitchurch on 17 March 1643 as 'those few dragoons in fear of daily surprise'.[56] Early the following May, Brereton's forces beat Corbet's 300 dragoons again at their base at Market Drayton, and a London newsbook reporting the action claimed that the entire regiment had been routed.[57] Corbet's Dragoons thereafter appear to have served in detachments; for example, 40 men of Captain Baldwin's company were in garrison at Ludlow in mid-1643, and in February 1644 a detachment briefly occupied Hopton Castle.[58] For much of 1644 Corbet was governor of Moreton Corbet Castle and his dragoons probably operated from there, while the regiment later became synonymous with the garrison at High

48 'Ottley Papers' (1894) pp. 41-42.
49 NLW, Powys Castle Records 3(A), D24/1/16-17A; SA, BB/C/8/1/11, 14-3, billeting bill.
50 *Mercurius Aulicus*, w/e 14 Jan. 1643, p. 17; *ROP*, II, pp. 164, 236-9; Warburton, *Prince Rupert*, II, pp. 237, 251.
51 NLW, Powys Castle Records 3(A), D24/1/17b; TNA, WO55/459/Part 3, ff. 477-9, 481.
52 BRL, Additional Mss 18981, ff. 67, 152.
53 SA, SRRU Deeds, 6000/13291; BRL, Harleian Mss 6851, ff. 236, 248.
54 *IO List*, p. 31; *OT List*, pp. 318-9; 'Ottley Papers' (1894), p. 73.
55 'Ottley Papers' (1895), pp. 259-60; SA, LB7/2015.
56 Phillips, *Civil War in Wales*, II, p. 60.
57 Malbon, *Memorials*, p. 53; 'Ottley Papers' (1895), p. 338; *Mercurius Civicus*, 4-11 May 1643, unpaginated.
58 SA, LB7/2015; J. Lewis (ed.), *Fire and Sword along the Marches: The Notebook of Sir William Maurice and the Memoranda of Captain Francis Sandford* (Newtown, 1996), p. 70.

Ercall, Corbet's base in 1645; on 1 November a detachment of the 'Arcall Dragoons' were with Sir William Vaughan's task force at the battle of Denbigh.[59]

From the onset of hostilities Shropshire's trained militia, the Trained Bands and the county Troop of Horse, served Charles I's cause. Colonel Francis Billingsley, commanding the foot in mid-1644, acknowledged that: 'The regiment of Trained Bands did suppress the militia [ordinance] and kept this county for his majesty'.[60] As has been seen, the four company captains of the Trained Bands in 1642 were Royalists and they would have influenced the loyalty of the 600 rank and file, who had numbered 341 musketeers and 259 pikemen in 1638.[61] By mid-1643 Thomas Screven was colonel of this not wholly reliable regiment of part-time soldiers, who reportedly tended to neglect Lord Capel's orders 'in performing their watches or other military services'.[62] Demoralised that October after their defeat against Wem when Screven received an ultimately fatal wound, in February 1644 the Trained Bands were found to be in 'great disorder' after his recent death.[63] Capel was frustrated by the parochial-mindedness of the Trained Bands – because, as Richard Herbert observed, they 'refuse to go out of their own country' – but he accepted their limitations as 'soldiers of the place', unsuited 'to be built upon for service out of their proper county'.[64] Accordingly, the Shropshire Trained Bands were most usefully deployed in reserve guarding strategic points: a role they performed into winter 1642-3 defending Shrewsbury, the Royalist headquarters; in spring 1643 at Capel's forward base at Whitchurch; and in May 1644 at Bridgnorth, stationed to guard the easterly approaches to Shropshire after the departure of Prince Rupert's field army. Evidence of these and other deployments – from the activity of soldiers from Ludlow, Shrewsbury and Bridgnorth – shows that the Trained Bands were regularly called to arms from summer 1642 until autumn 1644.[65] That November, however, Colonel Billingsley found that lack of pay and higher administrative neglect had caused his regiment mostly to disband, and some trained bandsmen to join the Parliamentarians. Nonetheless, in autumn 1645 there remained a Trained Band company under Billingsley's command at Bridgnorth.[66]

There is little evidence of the wartime service of the nominally 100-strong County Troop, other than the difficulty of calling it to arms in later 1642, and that it was commanded by Captain-lieutenant Edward Stanley of Knockin, who was captured by the enemy at Shrewsbury in February 1645.[67]

59 Symonds, *Diary*, p. 259.
60 BRL, Harleian Mss 6802, f. 227, Billingsley to Lord Digby, 15 June 1644.
61 HHL, Ellesmere Mss, 7443; TNA, SP16/381, f. 66, 'The Trained Bands of the Several Counties'.
62 *Certaine Informations from Severall Parts of the Kingdome*, 12-19 June 1643, pp. 169-70.
63 HMC, *Twelfth Report, Appendix Part IX*, p. 41; WRO, CR2017/C10, f. 60; BRL, Additional Mss 18981, f. 25.
64 BRL, Additional Mss 18980, f. 90; HMC, *Seventy-Eighth Report*, p. 99.
65 SA, LB7/2015; SA, BB/C/1/1/1; SA, BB/D/1/2/1/52-4; SA, P250/325-6.
66 BDL, Firth Mss C7, f. 229; Symonds, *Diary*, p. 252.
67 SA, LB7/2234, warrant concerning absence from musters; *CPCC*, III; *LBWB*, I, p. 41.

Units of Horse and Dragoons	Units of Foot
The County Horse Troop (extant in 1642)	The County Regiment of Trained Band Foot (extant in 1642)
Colonel Sir Vincent Corbet's Regiment of Dragoons (1642)	Colonel Richard Herbert's Regiment of Foot (1642)
Colonel Sir Vincent Corbet's Horse (1642)	Sir Francis Ottley's Regiment of Foot (1642)
Colonel Sir Robert Howard's Regiment of Dragoons (1642)	Colonel Henry Bromley's Foot (1643)
Sir Francis Ottley's Dragoons (1642)	Colonel Sir Vincent Corbet's Foot (1643)
Sir Richard Leveson's Horse (1643?)	Sir Richard Leveson's Foot (1643?)
Colonel Sir Edward Acton's Horse (1644?)	Colonel John Corbet's Foot (1644?)
Colonel Francis Billingsley's Horse or Dragoons (1644)	
Colonel John Corbet's Horse (1644?)	
Colonel Somerset Fox's Horse (1644)	
Colonel Sir Francis Ottley's Horse (1644?)	
Sir Thomas Whitmore's Horse (1644?)	

Table 5: Royalist units raised by local commanders (with date).

Other local Royalist units are known only from a very limited number of sources (Table 5). Sir Thomas Whitmore's horsemen, for example, although active in spring 1644 are otherwise known only from the name of their quartermaster. Similarly, the purchases they made at local horse fairs seem the only trace of the horse soldiers under Francis Billingsley's command at Bridgnorth.[68] Furthermore, although Henry Bromley, as high sheriff, and Sir Vincent Corbet were both granted commissions to raise regiments of foot in 1643, in March and July respectively, it remains unknown to what extent these units became operational.[69] More definitely, we know that John Corbet of Childs Ercall led a unit of horse by spring 1644, was a colonel in the garrison at High Ercall in April 1645, and had a company of foot at Bridgnorth that October.[70] In February 1644, Somerset Fox, of Caynham near Ludlow, was only a junior officer in Prince Rupert's Horse, but a year later his own cavalry regiment was quartered near Shrewsbury under the deputy command of a relative, Major Richard Fox, while four other local officers of the unit are known.[71] Sir Richard Leveson meanwhile based his own horse and foot as a garrison at Lilleshall Abbey. A troop and a company of Leveson's fought at nearby Longford in March 1644, and in May 1645 the garrison was 160 strong. Six of seven of Leveson's known officers came from Shropshire.[72]

Sir Francis Ottley also became an active commander. He captained a militia company by early August 1642 – reported as 'new volunteers by the King's commission to him' – and from mid-September raised a further 200 foot.[73] They were the nucleus of a permanent garrison and town militia regiment at Shrewsbury under Ottley's

68   *Mercurius Aulicus*, w/e 30 Mar. 1644; *IO List*, p. 151; SA, BB/C/1-6.
69   BDL, Dugdale Mss 19 [first part], ff. 97, 123.
70   *Mercurius Aulicus*, w/e 30 Mar. 1644, p. 909; 'Ottley Papers' (1895), p. 297; *Mercurius Aulicus*, w/e 20 Apr. 1645, p. 1571; Symonds, *Diary*, p. 252.
71   *ROP,* II, pp. 239-40; BRL, Additional Mss 18981, f. 40; *IO List*, 'errata' and p. 51; *OT List*, pp. 317-18.
72   *Mercurius Aulicus*, w/e 30 Mar. 1644, p. 909; Symonds, *Diary*, p. 172; *IO List*, pp. 84, 153; *OT List*, pp. 317-18.
73   Flintshire Record Office, D/G/3275/f. 84, Samuel Wood to Sir John Trevor, 6 Aug. 1642; 'Ottley Papers' (1894), pp. 39-40.

governorship. In 1644 the corporation reported that 'the inhabitants of the town were all soldiers, or maintained soldiers under them (if they did not do their duty in their own persons)'.[74] That January, however, Lord Byron had disparagingly characterised Shrewsbury's militiamen as 'a garrison of burghers [burgesses]', lacking discipline and of suspect loyalty.[75] On paper, Ottley's Foot had five companies numbering around 600 townsmen, subdivided into 26 localised squadrons or corporalships. Six at least of its ten known commissioned officers came from Shropshire.[76] From late December 1642 a company of dragoons was also raised in and around Shrewsbury under Ottley's governorship, and captained successively by Ottley and two local men, Roger Owen and John Allen, it was active into 1644.[77] By that autumn Ottley was also colonel of a regiment of horse, which was then operating from Ludlow. A troop of Ottley's Horse was at Bridgnorth in October 1645, and some of the regiment fought at Denbigh that November.[78]

Besides Ottley's regiment at Shrewsbury, local militias were established at the other Royalist garrison towns of the First Civil War. A night watch was on duty at Bridgnorth from January 1643, and the training of volunteers – 'for the defence of the town and thereabouts' – began that May.[79] At Oswestry, 'eighty townsmen in arms' were reported to have readily surrendered to the Parliamentarians in June 1644.[80] Armed townsmen guarded Ludlow by keeping watch at night and ward by day. One of them, Edward Steple, complained of being forcibly disciplined by regular officers of the garrison, he 'being no soldier under their command'.[81] Notwithstanding such friction, in February 1645 Sir Michael Woodhouse intended to deploy up to 600 well-equipped militiamen in defence of Ludlow.[82]

Royalist military organisation in Shropshire in 1648 during the Second Civil War remains shadowy. Forces were necessarily raised clandestinely and their role was short-lived. Nonetheless, in early August the Parliamentarian Humphrey Mackworth found 'the whole party of the King's in this county being engaged, directly or indirectly, in this business'.[83] Lord Byron returned in spring 1648 to command the region he had often been responsible for during 1644-6, but later was reticent about the extent of the military support in Shropshire provided by 'friends' and 'some gentlemen of quality and interest'.[84] Byron issued commissions to raise forces in Shropshire, including colonelcies to Edward Lloyd – as an experienced cavalry officer from the First Civil War – to raise a regiment of horse, and to Sir Francis Ottley to command

74   'Ottley Papers' (1896), p. 240.
75   BRL, Additional Mss 18981, f. 8.
76   SA, 3365/2571, ff. 9-12; SA, SRRU Deeds, 6000/13288, 13291; *IO List*, p. 101; *OT List*, pp. 315, 319.
77   'Ottley Papers' (1895) pp. 266, 311, 355-6.
78   'Ottley Papers' (1896), pp. 252-3, 272-3; SA, LB7/2064; Symonds, *Diary*, p. 252; *LBWB*, II, p. 197.
79   SA, BB/C/1/1/1, unfoliated; SA, BB/D/1/2/1/53.
80   *The Kingdome's Weekly Intelligencer*, 25 June-2 July 1644, p. 490.
81   SA, LB7/2319, unfoliated; SA, LB7/2125.
82   BDL, Firth Mss C6, f. 332.
83   *JHL*, X, pp. 425.
84   J. Barratt, 'The Letters of the First Baron Byron of Rochdale (1600-1652), *Journal of the Society for Army Historical Research*, 49 (1971), pp. 132-3.

in chief in the county.[85] The officers and men who took up arms in Shropshire for King Charles and the Engagement were, however, dissipated in the uncoordinated uprisings attempted across the region that summer. Seven commissioned officers from Shropshire who joined Sir John Owen's insurrection in North Wales were captured when Major-General Mytton's Parliamentarians routed Owen's small force at Y Dalar Hir on the north Caernarvonshire coast on 5 June 1648.[86] In Shropshire a month later, at Dawley Castle a covert gathering of would-be Royalist officers was surprised and captured by a Parliamentarian detachment from Shrewsbury. The abortive 'general rendezvous for Shropshire' attempted at Wattlesborough Heath on the night of 1/2 August attracted 50-100 Royalist horsemen in two troops. Of a third mounted party who dispersed from Prees Heath in north Shropshire, 30 or so joined the reportedly 300-strong body of horsemen with which Byron withdrew into North Wales.[87] Several Shropshire Royalists also appear to have joined Sir Henry Lingen's force that Parliamentarians defeated near Llanidloes in Montgomeryshire on 18 August, putting an end to Lingen's uprising that had begun in Herefordshire.[88]

Units of Horse and Dragoons	Units of Foot
Lord Capel's Regiment of Horse, later Colonel Marcus Trevor's Regiment (1643-4)	Colonel Sir Francis Beaumont's Regiment of Foot (1643)
Colonel Henry Crowe's Regiment of Dragoons (1643)	Colonel Sir William Russell's Regiment of Foot (1643)
Colonel Sir Richard Willys's Regiment of Horse (1643-4)	Colonel Sir William Wynne's Regiment of Foot (1643)
Colonel Sir John Hurry's Regiment of Horse (1644)	The Prince of Wales's Lifeguard of Foot (1643-6)
Prince Rupert's Regiment and Lifeguard of Horse (1644)	Colonel Robert Ellice's Regiment of Foot (1644)
Major Sacheverall's Horse (1644)	Prince Rupert's Regiment of Foot (1644)
Colonel Johan Van Geyrish's Horse (1644)	Colonel Robert Broughton's Regiment of Foot (1644-5)
Colonel Giovanni Devillier's Regiment of Horse (1644-6)	Colonel Richard Gibson's Regiment of Foot (1644-5)
Sir Lewis Kirke's Horse or Dragoons (1644-6)	Colonel Sir Fulke Hunckes's Regiment of Foot (1644-5)
Sir William Vaughan's Regiment of Horse (1644-6)	Colonel Henry Tillier's Regiment of Foot (1644-5)
	Colonel Henry Warren's Regiment of Foot (1644-5)
	Sir Michael Ernle's Regiment of Foot (1644-6)
	Sir Lewis Kirke's Foot (1644-6)
	Colonel Sir Charles Lloyd's Regiment of Foot (1645-6)
	Prince Rupert's Regiment of Firelocks (1645)

Table 6: Royalist outsider units and units led by outsider commanders serving in Shropshire (with service date).

85 NLW, Sweeney Hall Mss A4 (Vol. II), f. 93; *A New Rising by divers Knights, Colonels, Gentlemen, and others for the King. To Associate the foure Counties of Stafford, Worcester, Hereford, and Shropshire* (1648), pp. 1-3.
86 *A Narrative, Together with Letters Presented by Captaine Taylor To the Honourable House of Commons, Concerning the late success obtained by the Parliament forces in Carnarvonshire* (1648), pp. 5, 10-11.
87 *A New Rising*, p. 4; *JHL*, X, pp. 425; *The Moderate*, 1-8 Aug. 1648, unpaginated.
88 *JHC*, V, p. 679; *Perfect Occurrences of Every Daies Journall in Parliament*, 18-25 Aug. 1648, on p. 422 lists the captured officers.

Outsider units and units led by outsider commanders

A credible Parliamentarian report of the campaign to capture Wem in October 1643 described how Lord Capel's army included units from Shropshire and garrisons further afield, including from Chester, Dudley and Worcester.[89] This reflected the situation throughout the First Civil War, that the local Royalist forces were reinforced by units from outside Shropshire, posted there for specific operations or stationed for longer periods (Table 6).

Lord Capel arrived in Shropshire in March 1643 with just his own depleted regiment of 80 horsemen. By mid-summer, however, the regiment had been recruited to 400 and participated in actions such as the defeat of Brereton's horsemen at Hanmer (Flintshire) in June. Remaining in Shropshire after his departure in December, Capel's Horse declined in numbers and morale, and after being defeated at Ellesmere on 12/13 January 1644 was reduced to few more than a troop. The regiment was re-formed under the command of Prince Rupert's appointee Colonel Marcus Trevor, and in March the troop of local Captain Lawrence Benthall was reported in action near Wem. The 400 men of Trevor's Horse later fought as part of Prince Rupert's army at Marston Moor.[90] In May 1643 Sir Richard Willys's Regiment of Horse arrived from Oxford to reinforce Lord Capel and was billeted in and around Shrewsbury. Willys's was often brigaded with Capel's Horse and so shared in the victory at Hanmer, but was also beaten at Ellesmere whereafter it withdrew from the region.[91] Colonel Henry Crowe's Dragoons were also stationed in Shropshire during 1643. Crowe was based at Ludlow by May, and his men were also billeted around Shrewsbury.[92] Detachments from two regiments of Worcestershire Foot also joined Capel in Shropshire. Sir Francis Beaumont's Foot were at Ludlow during 1643, while the 80 'well armed' men and 70 clubmen sent from Worcester in early October fell disappointingly short of the expected 400 well-equipped soldiers of Sir William Russell's Regiment.[93] Meanwhile Sir William Wynne's Denbighshire-raised Regiment of Foot also served in Shropshire under Capel. Described by their opponents as 'their chiefest [foot] in all that part of Wales', Wynne's 700 men fought in the Wem campaign.[94]

The Prince of Wales's Lifeguard of Foot was raised in March 1643 as a planned 1,500-strong marching regiment under the command of Sergeant-Major Michael Woodhouse. The Lifeguard was recruited from the counties under Capel's command, and included, as has been seen, Shropshire conscripts. On 30 May the regiment was blooded in Brereton's attack on Capel's base at Whitchurch – where it reportedly fought as a stubborn rear guard – but later joined the Oxford army, and numbering around 700 men fought at Newbury in September.[95] Returning to Shropshire in early October, the Lifeguard fought in the Wem campaign.[96] From December 1643 until

89 WRO, CR2017/C10, f. 60.
90 HMC, *Twelfth Report, Appendix Part IX*, p. 39-42; Malbon, *Memorials*, pp. 62-3; *Mercurius Aulicus*, w/e 30 Mar. 1644, p. 890.
91 TNA, WO55/459/1, f. 160; SA, 3365/2566, unfoliated; HMC, *Twelfth Report, Appendix Part IX*, pp. 40-1.
92 SA, LB8/1/163, f. 4; SA, LB7/2320; SA, 3355/2566; 'Ottley Papers' (1895), pp. 327, 345-6.
93 SA, LB7/2015; Townsend, *Diary*, II, pp. 134, 140, 146, 156.
94 HMC, *Twelfth Report, Appendix Part IX*, pp. 39, 41; HMC, *Thirteenth Report, Appendix Part I*, p. 143.
95 HMC, *Twelfth Report, Appendix Part IX*, p. 40; Day, *Pythouse Papers*, p. 16.
96 HMC, *Twelfth Report, Appendix Part IX*, p. 41; WRO, CR2017/C10, f. 60.

the close of the First Civil War Woodhouse's regiment was the mainstay of his garrison at Ludlow, its long-standing occupation attested by the billeting bills of soldiers from several companies.[97] There it assumed an increasingly local character. Of 11 known commissioned officers, 9 were Shropshire men. Some of the ten Ludlow townsmen who were Royalist officers of foot probably served in the Lifeguard.[98]

Prince Rupert's appointment as regional commander-in-chief in place of Capel brought a fresh influx of outsider units and officers to Shropshire. Rupert led 600 or more horsemen of his own Regiment and Lifeguard to Shrewsbury in February 1644, and the Prince's Regiment of Foot arrived from Bristol in March.[99] Sir John Hurry's Regiment of Horse was also in Shropshire by March, along with Colonel Robert Ellice's Foot, a Denbighshire regiment re-embodied for the third time after defeats during 1643.[100] On 24 March 1644 Ellice led his regiment in the successful assault upon the recently established Parliamentarian garrison at Apley Castle.[101] Sir Lewis Kirke as governor of Bridgnorth recruited new or reinforced his existing units. One of Kirke's horsemen purchased a remount at the town's livestock fair in July 1644, and at least two of his officers of foot hailed from Shropshire. In October 1645 a 60-strong troop and a 50-man company under Kirke's command were at Bridgnorth.[102] The Florentine mercenary Giovanni (anglice John) Devillier recruited a regiment of horse in Shropshire in which four local officers are known to have served. As Symonds noted in 1645, Devillier 'took his troop to Ludlow and is now colonel'.[103] Devillier was in fact a colonel at Ludlow by September 1644, and in 1645 led the force defeated outside Bishop's Castle on 30 August. Eighty of his troopers fought at Denbigh that November.[104]

Units repatriated from the English Army in Ireland made a significant contribution to the Royalist war effort in Shropshire. Devillier captained one of the four troops of Sir William Vaughan's Horse, a regiment from the army in Leinster around 300 strong, which landed in North Wales and arrived in Shropshire during February 1644. From autumn 1644 the regiment was stationed in the garrisons at Shrawardine, Caus, High Ercall, Lilleshall and Dawley, where Vaughan's troop captains were made governors. As has been seen, Vaughan's Horse often served further afield – 'drawn out according to the several designs', as Symonds noted – including at Marston Moor and Naseby (where it was 400 strong), but the regiment also campaigned in Shropshire and the Marches into 1646, and was regarded by Sir William Brereton 'as good as any horse' in the Royalist army.[105] Vaughan's regiment seems also to have included a company of dragoons. Dragoons commanded by one Captain Johnson operated from Shrawardine

97   SA, LB7/2015, and, for example, SA, LB7/2067, 2069.
98   *OT List*, pp. 315, 318; *IO List*, 144; *CPCC*, II, pp. 1544, 1484.
99   Lewis, *Fire and Sword*, p. 70; Warburton, *Prince Rupert*, II, p. 380.
100 *Mercurius Aulicus*, w/e 23 Mar. 1644, p. 894; BRL, Additional Mss 18981, ff. 62, 103; Tucker, *North Wales and Chester*, p. 178.
101 *Mercurius Aulicus*, w/e 30 Mar 1644, pp. 905-6.
102 SA, BBC/C/6/1-6, unfoliated; *IO List*, p. 79; Symonds, *Diary*, p. 252.
103 *IO List*, p. 37; *OT List*, pp. 315, 317; Symonds, *Diary*, p. 255.
104 'Ottley Papers' (1895), p. 252; HMC, *Thirteenth Report, Appendix Part I*, p. 264; Symonds, *Diary*, p. 259.
105 HMC, *Fourteenth Report, Appendix Part VII*, pp. 145-6; BDL, Firth Mss C6, f. 74; Symonds, *Diary*, pp. 181, 255-6; *LBWB*, I, pp. 130-1.

Castle, Vaughan's headquarters until May 1645, while Johnson appears to have served in Shropshire with Vaughan into 1646.[106] However, little is known of a unit of horse in Shropshire during 1644 under the command of another veteran of the Irish war, one Major Sacheverall, who in October 1643 was lieutenant of a disbanding troop at Dublin.[107]

Regiments of the Anglo-Irish Foot that arrived in the region from late 1643 also campaigned in Shropshire. The 1,200 or more men of the regiments of Colonels Robert Broughton and Henry Tillier arrived in Shropshire from Ireland at around the same time as Vaughan's Horse. They joined Sir Fulke Hunckes's Regiment, survivors of the defeat at Nantwich in January, and detachments from these regiments participated in Prince Rupert's relief of Newark in March 1644.[108] In April, the regiments of Sir Michael Ernle and Colonels Richard Gibson and Henry Warren, reformed after the defeat at Nantwich and together numbering around 1,000 men, appear to have been transferred from Chester to Shropshire.[109] In September 1644 Broughton's, Tillier's, Warren's, Hunckes's and Ernle's, or detachments from them, fought at the battle of Montgomery. By then these regiments would have been largely re-recruited, apart from Hunckes's all having served in the campaign for the relief of York and subsequent battle of Marston Moor.[110] Drawn together as the Shrewsbury Foot, what remained of the Anglo-Irish regiments in 1645 fought as a division of the Royalist infantry at the battle of Naseby and were lost or captured in the defeat, although in October a company of Ernle's Foot remained at Bridgnorth.[111]

Two other Royalist units serving in Shropshire in later 1645 arrived after defeats in the West Country during September. Having surrendered at Devizes, a company of Sir Charles Lloyd's Regiment of Foot was in garrison at Bridgnorth by October, while Prince Rupert's capitulation of Bristol resulted in around 200 redcoats of the Prince's Regiment of Firelocks joining Sir William Vaughan's forces in Shropshire.[112]

The number of Royalist soldiers stationed in Shropshire at a given time cannot be determined accurately. In late 1644 Prince Rupert fixed the county establishment at 1,500 foot and 240 horse (plus officers), divided between the main bases at Shrewsbury, Bridgnorth and Ludlow; however, in January 1645, as Sir Michael Ernle reported, the number of Royalist soldiers then in Shropshire was somewhat higher, including many supernumerary officers.[113] Contemporary estimations of the size of forces engaged in the larger actions provide an indication of Royalist military capability in Shropshire. For example, the previously mentioned Parliamentarian dispatch numbered Lord Capel's army in the campaign for Wem in October 1643 as 3,000 men.[114] Two Royalist

---

106 *CPCC*, III, p. 1816.
107 HMC, *Fourteenth Report, Appendix Part VII*, p. 144; SA, 3365/2566; WRO, CR2017/C9, f. 131.
108 BDL, Firth Mss C6, ff. 11, 74; *Mercurius Aulicus*, w/e 23 Mar. 1644, p. 894.
109 BDL, Firth Mss C7, f. 24.
110 P. Young, *Marston Moor 1644 – The Campaign and the Battle* (Moreton-in-Marsh, 1997), p. 13; Carte, *Original Letters*, p. 65; *JHL*, VI, p. 714.
111 Warburton, *Prince Rupert*, III, unpaginated; Rushworth, *Historical Collections*, VI, p. 48; Symonds, *Diary*, p. 249
112 Symonds, *Diary*, p. 252; *LBWB*, II, pp. 394, 441-2.
113 BDL, Firth Mss C6, f. 303.
114 WRO, CR2017/C10, f. 60.

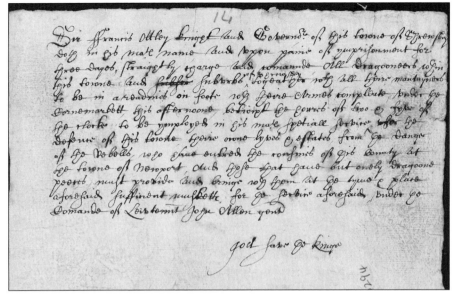

13. Warrant issued in Sir Francis Ottley's name sometime in 1643 to muster
the town dragoons at Shrewsbury under the command of Lieutenant
John Allen. (Courtesy of Shropshire Archives, ref. 6001/13294)

accounts differed considerably, however, in attributing either 800 or 1,400 soldiers
to Prince Rupert's force at Market Drayton on 5 March 1644.[115] The Royalist field
army defeated near Stokesay on 8 June 1645 numbered 1,500-2,000 men, comprising
detachments from the garrisons of Shropshire, Worcestershire, Hereford and
Monmouth.[116] Finally, newsbook reports suggest that by March 1646 there were 700-
800 regulars in the three Royalist garrisons remaining in Shropshire, at High Ercall,
Bridgnorth and Ludlow, reduced by May to just the 100 horse and 250 foot blockaded
in Ludlow.[117]

Parliamentarian forces in Shropshire
The First Civil War, 1642-6
During summer 1642 militia bands were formed in support of the execution of
Parliament's militia ordinance in at least 35 towns across England, including
Shrewsbury. There, by mid-July, volunteers were meeting outside the town to practise
arms drill under Thomas Hunt's leadership.[118] On 2 August the Parliamentarian

115 *Mercurius Aulicus*, w/e 9 Mar. 1644, p. 870; Lewis, *Fire and Sword*, p. 70.
116 *The Perfect Occurrences of Parliament And Chief Collections of Letters*, 13-20 June 1645, unpaginated;
    Intelligence From Shropshire of Three Great Victories obtained by the Forces of Shrewsburie (1645), p. 2; Walker,
    Discourses, p. 129.
117 *A Copy of the Summons from Sir William Brereton, Col. Morgan, and Col. Birch sent in for the surrender of the
    City of Worcester* […] *Also the taking of High-Arkall, the Lord Newports House by the Shropshire Forces* (1646),
    p. 2; *The Kingdomes Weekly Intelligencer*, 28 Apr.-5 May 1646, p. 84; *Perfect Occurrences of Both Houses of
    Parliament and Martiall Affairs*, w/e 8 May 1646, unpaginated.
118 Fletcher, *Outbreak*, pp. 353-6; *JHL*, V, pp. 221-2, 19 July 1642.

MPs Corbet, More and Pierrepont viewed at Shrewsbury a muster of around 300 of Hunt's 'orderly men', whilst the same day the commissioners of array inspected two companies of the Trained Bands at nearby Atcham and Montford bridge. Hunt – whom local Royalists derided for having assumed 'the name of captain to the militia of Shrewsbury' – fled upon the arrival of King Charles in Shropshire, and his followers were disarmed and threatened with imprisonment.[119] Thus the first organised armed body raised in Shropshire in support of Parliament was suppressed. It would take eight or so months for new units to be established, recruited mostly in and around London.

With his Cheshire forces under threat of Royalist attack, in February 1643 Sir William Brereton sought military support by lobbying Parliament to hasten Sir John Corbet and Sir Thomas Myddelton to raise regiments and advance into Shropshire and Denbighshire respectively, where Brereton expected enthusiastic recruits would be found. By June, Corbet had recruited a cadre of officers who, together with any soldiers under them, were transferred to Colonel Thomas Mytton and other committeemen when they assumed command on 4 July of what became the Shropshire forces.[120] Meanwhile, in May 1643 the Earl of Essex had commissioned Mytton to raise a regiment each of horse, dragoons and foot, in which at least three of the Shropshire committeemen served as officers – Humphrey Mackworth, Andrew Lloyd and Thomas Hunt as captains of troops of horse, and Hunt also as a captain of a company of foot.[121] Mytton's Regiment of Foot left London in late August accompanied by several troops of horse, of Mytton's own regiment and others recruited by the Earl of Denbigh.[122] In the meantime Sir Thomas Myddelton, with a colonel's commission to raise a regiment each of horse, dragoons and foot as Parliament's major-general of North Wales, had also recruited in London and the Southeast, although the reported 'great forces' he brought to Nantwich around 19 August 1643 comprised just a regiment of foot and some horse.[123]

Myddelton's, Mytton's, and Brereton's forces together occupied and fortified Wem in September, and from 14 to 18 October undertook the campaign for the town's defence and relief against Lord Capel's army.[124] Royalist assaults on the 17th and 18th were repelled by the garrison numbering around 300, mostly half of Colonel Mytton's Regiment of Foot, some 170 men, and a scratch militia company of townsmen.[125] Meanwhile, Myddelton's and the rest of Mytton's Foot remained with Brereton's main body in pursuit of Capel's army around Nantwich and Wem. The Wem campaign was conducted by a coalition of Parliamentarian forces, setting a precedent for the vital supportive role that auxiliary units – in this instance mostly Brereton's Cheshire forces, but also including Myddelton's units and some Staffordshire Horse – would play throughout the war in sustaining the Shropshire forces (Table 7). The Cheshire

119 *JHL*, V, pp. 269-70, 6 Aug. 1642; SA, 6000/13291.
120 HMC, *Thirteenth Report, Appendix Part I*, pp. 94-6; *JHC*, III, p. 155.
121 BDL, Tanner Mss 60, f. 463; Baxter, *Reliquiae Baxterianae*, p. 45; WRO, CR2017/C9, f. 18; BRL, Additional Mss 18981, f. 69.
122 *A Perfect Diurnall of some passages in Parliament*, 28 Aug.-4 Sept. 1643, p. 54.
123 Malbon, *Memorials*, p. 72.
124 HMC, *Thirteenth Report, Appendix Part I*, pp. 141-3, 157; Malbon, *Memorials*, pp. 75-84; WRO, CR2017/C10, f. 60.
125 HMC, *Thirteenth Report, Appendix Part I*, p. 142; WRO, CR2017/C10, f. 60.

Trained Bands in particular played a key role at Wem as a garrison and also in building fortifications.[126] It was reported that 'whilst the Cheshire soldiers continued in Wem (which were about 500 musketeers besides horse) the enemy did forbear to make any attempt against the town'.[127] Several companies of Cheshire Foot remained at Wem into November, where on the 23rd their impending withdrawal was reported with trepidation by the Shropshire committeemen.[128]

Units of Horse and Dragoons	Units of Foot
Cheshire Horse and Dragoons (1643, 1645)	Cheshire Foot (1643-5)
Staffordshire Horse (1643, 1644, 1645)	The Earl of Denbigh's Regiment of Foot (1644-5)
The Earl of Denbigh's Regiment of Horse (1644)	Sir Thomas Myddelton's Regiment of Foot
Sir Thomas Myddelton's Regiment of Horse	(1643-4)
(1643, 1644)	Sir William Myddelton's Regiment of Foot
Sir Thomas Myddelton's Dragoons (1644)	(1644)
Yorkshire Horse (1644, 1645)	Staffordshire Foot (1644-5)
Colonel John Birch's Horse (1646)	Colonel John Birch's Foot (1646)
Montgomeryshire Horse (1646)	Montgomeryshire Foot (1646)
	Radnorshire Foot (1646)

Table 7: Parliamentarian units serving as auxiliary forces in Shropshire (with service date).

The Cheshire units were withdrawn to bolster Brereton's weakened grip on Cheshire as a result of the precipitate withdrawal of his forces from the hitherto successful advance into north-east Wales made in partnership with Myddelton. The campaign had begun on 8 November when the Parliamentarians stormed the bridge over the River Dee at Holt, an operation including 200 of Myddelton's Foot and one troop of his Horse.[129] In their later retreat from Flintshire the Parliamentarians left Hawarden Castle as an isolated outpost. When the castle's 120-strong garrison capitulated in early December 1643, a Royalist officer described them as 'being all that was left of Sir Thomas Myddelton's Regiment'.[130] However, the remainder of Myddelton's force was active into February 1644, mounting a raid jointly with a detachment from Wem upon Bangor-on-Dee (Flintshire) on the 15th, and occupying several small garrisons astride the Flintshire/Shropshire border.[131] These outposts can be identified as the manor houses of Fens Hall, Hanmer Hall, Emral Hall and Bettisfield Hall, which all quickly surrendered to Lord Byron during the brief campaign he conducted in the area in late March.[132]

Mytton's force at Bangor-on-Dee in mid-February 1644 reportedly numbered 250 foot and 160 horse, while the detachment led by him against Royalists at Ellesmere

126 Malbon, *Memorials*, p. 78; Baxter, *Reliquiae Baxterianae*, p. 43.
127 *Shropshires misery and mercie, Manifested in the defeat given to the Lord Capels ravenous and devouring Armie, by the forces of Cheshire and Shropshire* (1643), p. 4.
128 HMC, *Thirteenth Report, Appendix Part I*, pp. 158-9.
129 Ibid., p. 151.
130 Carte, *Original Letters*, p. 31.
131 *The Kingdome's Weekly Intelligencer*, 20-29 Feb. 1644, p. 363.
132 WSL, SMS 478/13/36; John, Lord Hanmer, *A Memorial of the Parish and Family of Hanmer in Flintshire* (London, 1877), p. 71.

on 12/13 January was probably underestimated by a Royalist officer as 240 strong.[133] These numbers suggest the limited operational capability of Parliamentary forces in Shropshire at this time (mostly the Shropshire forces, comprising Mytton's three regiments) and are commensurate with Royalist intelligence reports in late February 1644. These numbered 150 horse and 400 foot at Wem, 80 or so dragoons garrisoning Ightfield, and probably somewhat underestimated the combined Parliamentarian strength in Shropshire as 700 men, when there were also auxiliary companies of Cheshire and Staffordshire foot garrisoning Longford House and Tong respectively.[134] Furthermore, at this time the Parliamentary cavalry in Shropshire were reinforced by five troops of Yorkshire Horse led by Sir William Fairfax, detached from Sir Thomas Fairfax's forces of the Northern Association still operating in Cheshire after Fairfax's victory at Nantwich in January. They did not remain in Shropshire for long, however, for together with Mytton's cavalry the Yorkshiremen were beaten and scattered by Prince Rupert at Market Drayton on 5 March.[135] That day in London, the Committee of Both Kingdoms reported the strength of the garrison at Wem as 400 foot and 200 horse. This concurs with Royalist estimates of the strength of the composite Parliamentarian force beaten at the engagement near Longford on 25 March, as around 400 foot and nine troops of horse, comprising Cheshire and Staffordshire auxiliaries and units from Wem.[136] This deployment was for several months a high watermark in the size of force the Parliamentarians could field in Shropshire. The Royalists' victory furthered a string of successes under Prince Rupert's leadership that by the end of April 1644 left the Parliamentarians isolated and blockaded in Wem.

Sir Thomas Myddelton had meanwhile returned to London to raise and equip 1,500 infantry and 300 cavalry. This new brigade would include a regiment of foot and a troop of horse raised by Myddelton's cousin Sir William Myddelton, and on 22 March 1644 Sir Thomas agreed to bankroll and equip both units.[137] Recorded in Myddelton's accounts are payments to officers recruiting companies or troops at this time, including £20 each on 1 April to Captains John Weaver and Thomas Judd, for their soldiers 'shortly to march from London'.[138] On 28 March *The Perfect Diurnall* reported 'there is 500 foot and 300 horse already raised in and about the city for Sir Thomas […] who will presently set forth for Shropshire', and during the next month or so Myddelton's brigade gathered at Coventry; Captain Thomas Pope's Company of Sir William Myddelton's Foot, for example, departed London around 1 May.[139] Sir Thomas left London for the Midlands on 24 May 1644, and meanwhile three troops of his Horse and three companies of Sir William Myddelton's Foot were already marching into south Staffordshire with the Earl of Denbigh's army of the

133 *The Kingdome's Weekly Intelligencer*, 20-29 Feb. 1644, p. 363; Carte, *Original Letters*, p. 40.
134 BRL, Additional Mss 18981, ff. 22, 69; *CSPD 1645-1647*, p. 298; Pennington and Roots, *Committee at Stafford*, p. 63.
135 Malbon, *Memorials*, pp. 123-4; *Mercurius Aulicus*, w/e 9 Mar. 1644, pp. 870-1; Firth, *Rupert's Marches*, p. 735.
136 *CSPD, 1644*, p. 34; BDL, Firth Mss C6, f. 353; *Mercurius Aulicus*, w/e 30 Mar. 1644, p. 908.
137 *JHL*, VI, pp. 424-5, 21 Feb. 1644; *CSPD, 1644*, p. 65.
138 TNA, SP28/346 Part 1, ff. 40, 46.
139 *A Perfect Diurnall of some passages in Parliament*, 25 Mar.-1 Apr. 1644, p. 277; *The Perfect Occurrences of Parliament*, 26 Apr.-3 May 1644, unpaginated; TNA, SP28/346 Part 1, f. 50.

West Midland Association.[140] Reinforced by another troop and numbering more than 200 men, Myddelton's Horse were with Denbigh when Rushall Hall was taken on 28 May, but neither Sir Thomas's nor Sir William's regiments of foot contributed much to the brief siege, and the Earl bemoaned their laggardly and mutinous conduct. By 2 June both regiments, each of about 400 men, were with Denbigh at Wednesbury (Staffordshire), although the Earl noted that they had been reduced by desertion like the rest of his army, which also included his own regiments of horse and foot, each around 400 men plus officers.[141]

On 11 June Myddelton led his brigade as part of Denbigh's army at the engagement at Tipton Green, where Colonel Mytton also held a subordinate command. Myddelton's Horse also participated in the capture of Oswestry on 22-23 June, Denbigh's first action in Shropshire and a joint operation involving also his lifeguard and regiment of horse, and 200 foot and some horse from Wem led by Mytton – probably 900 men in all. Much reduced by casualties, sickness and desertion, the foot regiments of Denbigh and the Myddeltons were then put to garrison duty at Oswestry and Wem.[142] However, on 29 June Royalists from Shrewsbury laid siege to Oswestry, causing Sir Thomas Myddelton to return to relieve the town on 2 July leading 1,500-1,700 men. Except for Sir Thomas's Horse these were all infantry, comprising three Cheshire regiments and detachments from Wem including Denbigh's Foot. These units together with reinforcements hurriedly brought up by Denbigh formed the army mustered under his command at Knockin Heath, south-east of Oswestry, early on the morning of 4 July 1644. In skirmishing lasting until nightfall, the Parliamentarians forced the Severn crossing at Montford and reached the westerly defences of Shrewsbury. Denbigh's heterogeneous army comprised Myddelton's brigade, the Cheshire Foot and units of the West Midland Association – detachments of the Shropshire forces, Denbigh's own two regiments and lifeguard, and some Staffordshire Horse and Foot. At 3,500-4,000 men this was, albeit briefly, the largest force the Parliamentarians would deploy in Shropshire during the Civil Wars.[143]

The next day Denbigh's army withdrew or dispersed. Myddelton's and Mytton's forces went into garrison at Oswestry and Wem, while both commanders sought reinforcements. In mid-July, Mytton asked Denbigh's confirmation of the brevet colonelcy of Robert Powell, a local gentleman. Powell then went to London to recruit cavalry, and by October had returned to Oswestry as a colonel of horse. The Committee of Both Kingdoms in turn pressed Denbigh to confirm the commissions of several captains the London-based Shropshire committeemen had recruited and sent to their colleagues at Wem. On 18 June the Earl had granted a captain's commission to Thomas Hunt, enabling him to raise a troop of horse independently of

---

140 *A Perfect Diurnall of some passages in Parliament*, 20-27 May 1644, p. 342; *Newes from Prince Rupert whose forces being discovered by the Earl of Denbigh, The Earle with his forces marched against them* (1644), pp. 4-6.

141 *CSPD, 1644*, pp. 177-8, 194; *JHL*, VI, p. 653.

142 *CSPD, 1644*, pp. 235-6, 284, 286-7; *A happy Defeat Given to the King's Forces, neere Tipton Green in Staffordshire* (1644), unpaginated; *Two Great Victories*, unpaginated

143 *CSPD, 1644*, p. 331, 337-8; *The Perfect Occurrences of Parliament And Chief Collections of Letters*, 5-12 July 1644, unpaginated; Malbon, *Memorials*, pp. 133-5; *A Copy of A Letter sent From Sir Tho. Middleton, to the Honourable, William Lenthall Esq; Speaker of the House of the House of Commons Concerning the Siege at Oswestree* (1644); *JHL*, VI, p. 653.

Mytton.[144] These appointments began the estrangement between Thomas Mytton and the other militarily active committeemen, and the resultant division of the Shropshire forces between Mytton's Oswestry-based units and those of the committee at Wem. Mytton later recollected how during summer 1644 his erstwhile colleagues began to make 'themselves colonels and other officers, and so […] engrossed the whole militia [i.e. the Shropshire forces] into their own regiments'.[145] Mytton seems to have lobbied for support in London against this usurpation of his overall command. On 18 August, Captain Samuel More, one of his adherents in the officer corps at Wem, wrote cautioning Mytton, 'that I think the Parliament will not take away from the committee the power granted them'. Nonetheless, More agreed to help in blocking the appointment to a senior captaincy at Wem of Wilhelm Reinking, one of the committee's new officers and later Mytton's rival. More concluded that when they next met, he would discuss with Mytton 'of such a way that we may make up our own garrisons with such men under your command that may not be subject to other commanders'.[146]

While his regiment of horse left Shropshire for good with him in July 1644, the Earl of Denbigh's Regiment of Foot remained at Wem, where later that month its eight companies numbered just 200 or so rank and file.[147] Although in mid-August the Committee of Both Kingdoms had instructed the committee at Wem to manage the regiment, Denbigh's Foot suffered by the rift between the committeemen and the Earl. Consequently, on 24 September a captain wrote to Denbigh from Wem of the regiment, 'struggling with the want of all things to serve in a place where we are hated for your honour's sake'.[148] The proposed amalgamation of the regiment to just two companies was averted in November, but in January 1645 the Committee of Both Kingdoms proposed its reduction to three. The Committee intervened again two months later, pointing out to the committee at Shrewsbury that Denbigh's Foot should be reinforced and paid in accordance with their other units.[149]

In mid-July 1644 the Committee of Both Kingdoms had granted Sir Thomas Myddelton licence to prosecute a campaign into Wales, provided he continued to support the Shropshire forces. Writing on the 16th, Thomas Mytton informed his wife in coded terms that he planned to transfer troops from Wem to Oswestry, because 'Brother Myddelton and myself intend, God willing, to take a voyage into Wales'.[150] Accordingly, on 4 August the brothers-in-law jointly led around 550 horse, foot and dragoons from Oswestry, together with two Cheshire companies from Nantwich, in a successful cross-border raid the next morning upon Prince Rupert's Regiment of Horse billeted at Welshpool in Montgomeryshire.[151] A month later, Myddelton again led his men into Montgomeryshire in the offensive that culminated on 18 September

144 WRO, CR2017/C10, ff. 6, 16, 38; *CSPD, 1644*, pp. 354-5; SA, 366, f. 181.
145 BDL, Tanner Mss 60, f. 463.
146 NLW, Sweeney Hall Mss A1, f. 21.
147 WRO, CR2017/C10, f. 3.
148 *CSPD, 1644*, p. 429; WRO, CR2017/C10, f. 34.
149 WRO, CR2017/C10, f. 43; *CSPD, 1644-1645*, pp. 259, 370.
150 *CSPD, 1644*, p. 355; NLW, Sweeney Hall Mss A1, f. 20.
151 *CSPD, 1644*, p. 405; *Wareham taken by the Parliament Forces Also Collonel Mittons valiant Exploits certified by two several Letters dated at his Quarters* (1644), pp. 1-3.

in the battle of Montgomery, but by mid-October of the brigade of 650-800 there remained just 300 foot and 50 horse. Notwithstanding Sir Thomas's understandable special pleading to London for reinforcements – in October he asked for 500 Scots infantry from the Earl of Leven's army – his brigade appears somewhat to have regained strength into winter 1644-5. In November the regiment of foot newly raised in Montgomeryshire under Colonel Sir John Price was issued with 340 muskets, and by January 1645 Myddelton could muster at least 235 horse and dragoons.[152]

Sir Thomas in the meantime had continued to cooperate with his colleagues in Shropshire, especially Mytton at Oswestry. Together they mounted an ambitious and successful raid upon the Royalist garrison at Ruthin in Denbighshire in late October 1644, while Myddelton's garrisons at Montgomery and the Red Castle (today Powis Castle, near Welshpool) opened a new front in western Shropshire; a foray from the Red Castle in mid-October seems to have caused the Royalists briefly to abandon their new outpost at Lea, near Bishop's Castle.[153]

But the withdrawal of Myddelton's brigade significantly weakened the garrisons of Oswestry and also Wem, from where on 23 August 1644 Royalist spies reported there were 500 foot and four troops of horse.[154] Responding to appeals from the committee at Wem and the Committee of Both Kingdoms to send reinforcements to Shropshire, during September Sir William Brereton posted four companies of Cheshire Foot to Wem, whose advance parties helped on 8 September to capture the important Royalist stronghold of Moreton Corbet Castle.[155] Not only was Brereton's army a reliable source of timely reinforcements, by the secondment or transfer of a number of officers it also provided the Shropshire forces with experienced leadership. Captain Lord Colvill (or 'Calvin'), for one, jointly led the attack on Moreton Corbet. In 1645 he held a subordinate command at the capture of Shrewsbury, and from June governed the garrison at Broncroft Castle.[156] Similarly, during 1645 Francis Spicer was first a company captain of Cheshire Foot posted to Shropshire, and later became the governor of Lilleshall garrison.[157]

Horse and foot from Cheshire and Staffordshire as auxiliaries under Brereton's direction formed more than half of the around 1,200-strong task force which captured Shrewsbury on 22 February 1645. In January, the committee at Wem had courted Brereton for substantial reinforcements, in part to minimise their reliance on Mytton's forces at Oswestry. Whether by accident or design, in the event only a few of Mytton's horsemen joined in the Shrewsbury operation.[158] On 26 February Brereton entered the county town with another three companies, increasing the number of Cheshire

---

152 *CSPD, 1644-1645*, p. 34; NLW, Chirk Castle Mss 1/Biii, 93.
153 *CSPD, 1644-1645*, pp. 80-1; *The Perfect Occurrences of Parliament And Chief Collections of Letters*, 18-25 Oct. 1644, unpaginated.
154 BDL, Firth Mss C7, f. 150.
155 *CSPD, 1644*, pp. 462-3, 484-5; *LBWB*, I, p. 44; Malbon, *Memorials*, p. 146.
156 *Relation […] by […] William Reinking*, p. 3; *Three Great Victories*, p. 1; Symonds, *Diary*, p. 172; *LBWB*, II, p. 392;
157 *LBWB*, I, p. 325; II, p. 327.
158 Ibid., pp. 33, 44; *Relation […] by […] William Reinking*, p. 2; *A True and Full Relation Of the manner of the Taking of the Towne and Castle of Shrewsbury* (1645), p. 3.

Foot deployed in Shropshire to nearly 600.[159] With 17 companies of Staffordshire and Cheshire infantry still there, towards the end of March Brereton also sent three auxiliary regiments of cavalry into Shropshire, primarily to assist operations against High Ercall Hall. Among them were the nine troops of Lord Fairfax's Yorkshire Horse deployed in Shropshire during April.[160] With the Staffordshire Foot becoming mutinous, by the end of April 1645 the committee at Shrewsbury had released most of their auxiliaries, except for one or two companies from Staffordshire and four from Cheshire. By then the committee had raised several new companies – including one from Warwickshire – in furtherance of their expansion of the Shropshire forces under their own command, the policy of engrossment of the 'militia' criticised by Mytton (Table 8).[161]

Regiments of Horse and Dragoons	Regiments of Foot
Colonel Thomas Mytton's Horse (1643)	Colonel Thomas Mytton's Foot (1643)
Colonel Thomas Mytton's Dragoons (1643)	Colonel Thomas Hunt's Foot (1645)
Colonel Richard Powell's Horse (1644)	Colonel Andrew Lloyd's Foot (1645)
Colonel Thomas Hunt's Horse (1644)	Colonel Humphrey Mackworth's Foot (1645)
Colonel Andrew Lloyd's Horse (1645)	Colonel Roger Pope's Foot (1645)
Colonel Samuel More's Horse (1645)	

Table 8: Parliamentarian regiments raised by local commanders (with date).

In October 1644 Thomas Hunt had received a colonelcy from the Earl of Essex to raise a regiment of horse in Shropshire, and both Humphrey Mackworth and Andrew Lloyd were colonels when Shrewsbury was taken. If not held beforehand, both colonelcies may have resulted from discussions by the Committee of Both Kingdoms on 18 January 1645 of plans for raising forces in Shropshire, which were referred as proposals to the Earl of Essex, still then lord general.[162] As colonels the Shropshire committeemen raised several regiments and troops. Hunt was colonel also of a regiment of foot, in which one George Williams was commissioned a company captain on 1 July 1645.[163] Lloyd commanded a regiment of horse – reported as 300 strong at Stokesay in June – and a regiment of foot, companies from which garrisoned Bridgnorth during 1646.[164] Mackworth's Foot seems to have been a militia regiment recruited in and around the county town; from 2 April 1645 Captain William King commanded one of its five companies, 'of townsmen in this garrison of Shrewsbury'.[165] Colonel Samuel More raised some horse, and his troopers are recorded serving about Chester in November 1645.[166] The county committee may also have authorised the raising of independent companies. It was the committee at Shrewsbury collectively,

159 *LBWB*, I, pp. 44-5, 52-4.
160 Tibbutt, *Letter Books of Sir Samuel Luke*, p. 477; *LBWB*, I, pp. 132-3, 249, 265, 395.
161 *LBWB*, I, pp. 281-2, 291, 303, 324-5.
162 SA, 366/179; *CSPD, 1644-1645*, p. 259.
163 SA, 366/1.
164 *Three Great Victories*, p. 1; Carr and Atherton, *Civil War in Staffordshire*, p. 175.
165 *Three Great Victories*, p. 1; SP28/242 Part 2, Captain King's accounts.
166 *LBWB*, II, p. 204.

rather than a named colonel, who on 1 March 1645 commissioned Samuel Farrington captain of 'a company of foot soldiers in this county of Salop'.[167] The Shropshire forces also included at least one independent body of horsemen, an amalgamated troop of supernumerary officers known as 'reformadoes'. They fought at Stokesay in June 1645, and garrisoned Dawley Castle that December.[168]

Elements of Mackworth's, Lloyd's and Hunt's regiments were reported in action during 1645 at, for instance, Stokesay in June and during December at the siege of Chester.[169] However, regimental distinction probably meant little in practice, because the Shropshire forces usually operated as individual companies and troops, dispersed to garrison duty and brought together only for particular tasks. For example, the task force sent from Shrewsbury in mid-June against the Royalist outpost at Morville Hall was reported as 13 companies of foot and five troops of horse, the infantry led by Colonel Reinking, the cavalry brigaded under the command of Colonel Walter Prince (son of the Royalist Sir Richard Prince of Shrewsbury).[170] Neither officer appears to have had his own regiment, both serving instead as field commanders to whom the county committee could delegate leadership.

As a result of their enlargement and reorganisation by the county committee, the Shropshire forces by later spring 1645 could secure their garrisons and also draw into the field a brigade-size body numbering 1,000 or so. Around 25 April, 900 horse and foot were deployed against a suspected Royalist advance towards Shrewsbury, and the Parliamentarian brigade victorious near Stokesay on 8 June reportedly was of similar size. The Royalists numbered the Parliamentarians beaten at High Ercall on 5 July as 500 horse and 600 foot.[171]

One of Colonel Mytton's officers reported of the defeat at High Ercall that only the Oswestry Horse had put up a fight, indicating the partisanship that began to cloud collaborative operations between Mytton's and the committee's soldiers. The London newsbook carrying the officer's letter also reported disputes between the 'Oswestry forces' and the 'Salop men' engaged in the recent siege of Shrawardine Castle: 'these divisions amongst our selves are not good', the editor concluded, 'I would all the soldiery in England would [look] to Sir Thomas Fairfax['s] [New Model] army for a pattern who being united in affection, we see how they conquer'.[172] The Shropshire forces stayed divided, however, for in June 1645 Mytton succeeded Sir Thomas Myddelton as commander-in-chief for North Wales, and the ambiguous status of the Oswestry garrison, as part of the Shropshire forces but also under Mytton's independent command, became apparent. As with the Earl of Denbigh's Foot, this situation encouraged the county committee's proclivity to neglect those units not under its direct control. Consequently, on 22 July the Committee of Both Kingdoms sent terse instructions to Shrewsbury, for the Oswestry garrison to be strengthened

167 TNA, SP28/174 Part 1, Farrington's account book, unfoliated.
168 *Three Great Victories*, p. 2; *LBWB*, II, pp. 338-9.
169 *Three Great Victories*, p.1; *The Kingdomes Weekly Intelligencer*, 9-16 Dec. 1645, p. 1044.
170 *The Perfect Occurrences of Parliament And Chief Collections of Letters from the Armie*, 20-27 June 1645, unpaginated.
171 *LBWB*, I, p. 291; *Three Great Victories*, p. 1; BRL, Harleian Mss 6852, f. 274.
172 *Perfect Passages of Each Dayes Proceedings in Parliament*, 9-16 July 1645, p. 300.

14. Sir Richard Leveson (1598-1661) depicted reclining in his funerary monument at the church of St. Michael and All Angels, Lilleshall. Leveson during the First Civil War raised units of horse and foot and garrisoned Lilleshall Abbey for King Charles I.

and paid the same as the rest of the Shropshire forces. Nonetheless, in February 1646 Mytton reported to London that the county committee had instead left his men unpaid for almost six months.[173]

In the interim Mytton had exacerbated the fractious relationship with his erstwhile colleagues by poaching men from the committee's units. In early November 1645, two officers offered promotion in the infantry regiment recently raised by Mytton's son-in-law Colonel Roger Pope had defected with their companies from Shrewsbury to Oswestry. Furthermore, a month later the committee complained to Sir William Brereton that many of their men were 'drawn away' by Mytton's officers. As well as Pope's Foot, the regiments under Mytton's direct command at this time were his own horse and foot – in February 1646 the foot numbered 250 at Oswestry – and Colonel Powell's Horse.[174] In addition, Mytton could call upon the remainder of Myddelton's old command in Montgomeryshire. At the leaguer, or besieging encampments, before Chester in early November, clear distinction was made between Mytton's 350 horse and 300 foot, and the 500 horse and 350 foot of the committee of Shropshire serving as auxiliaries in Brereton's army. This deployment marked the impressive overall expansion of the Shropshire forces during 1645.[175]

By Christmas 1645 the number of the county committee's soldiers before Chester had fallen to 350 foot and 150 horse.[176] By early spring 1646 the Shropshire forces were concentrated to reduce the county's remaining Royalist garrisons, although in March some horse and foot were detached to Sir William Brereton's forces besieging

173 *CSPD, 1645-1647*, p. 25; BDL, Tanner Mss 60, f. 461.
174 BRL, Additional Mss 11332, f. 111; *JHC*, IV, p. 337, 10 Nov. 1645; BRL, Additional Mss 11333, f. 36; BDL, Tanner Mss 60, f. 444.
175 *LBWB*, II, pp. 179-80.
176 Ibid., pp. 402-3.

Lichfield.[177] During April, the besiegers of Bridgnorth Castle reportedly numbered 700, while later that month 200 Shropshire Foot joined with the Parliamentarian forces from Hereford, Radnorshire and Montgomeryshire comprising Colonel John Birch's task force investing Ludlow.[178] By June, as the war in England petered out, elements of the Shropshire forces had joined Major-General Whalley's army besieging Worcester.[179]

Disbandment and the Second Civil War, 1646-8

As the siege of Ludlow, the last military operation of the First Civil War in Shropshire, drew to a negotiated conclusion, in the third week of May 1646 the committee at Shrewsbury was preparing to demobilise around half of their forces. Because of the difficulties of maintaining pay and providing for arrears, they planned to disband 500 foot and several troops of horse.[180] Accordingly, on 11 July Parliament authorised the disbandment of the Shropshire forces except for 400 foot and a 60-strong troop of horse (plus officers), a decision ratified by an ordinance passed on 13 August.[181] On 19 February 1647 the standing county forces comprised the horse troop and the remaining garrison companies at Shrewsbury and Ludlow. Six days later, Parliament further approved the disbandment of the remaining foot, leaving a 100-strong company based at Shrewsbury Castle as the county's sole garrison.[182] This reduction of the infantry to a cadre appears to have been achieved, because early the following June the county committee for safety's hurried precautionary military response to the potentially destabilising news that King Charles had been taken into army custody involved just the county troop, the garrison of Shrewsbury Castle and a detachment at Ludlow. In addition, a rather apathetic town militia of four companies under local captains was raised at Shrewsbury that summer.[183]

How was demobilisation achieved? There were widespread mutinies in Parliament's provincial forces across England and Wales during 1646 and 1647 engendered by soldiers' grievances about disbandment, especially over pay and also indemnity against civil prosecution for wartime acts.[184] Concerted rank and file mutinies did occur in the Shropshire region. On 27 March 1647, Samuel Wood, steward of Sir John Trevor's estate at Trevalyn in east Denbighshire, reported how three companies of Colonel Pope's Foot had recently occupied nearby Wrexham. Demanding their pay and a share of the spoils from recent victories in North Wales, the soldiers had seized several officers including Major Sadler (who as a captain had left the committee's employ at Shrewsbury in November 1645) and had fired upon others, including Mytton himself.[185] Similarly in Montgomeryshire, in early May 300 soldiers gathered at

---

177 *CSPD, 1645-1646*, pp. 339, 369; BDL, Tanner Mss 59, f. 10.
178 *CSPD, 1645-1646*, p. 408; *The Kingdom's Weekly Intelligencer*, 28 Apr.-5 May 1646, p. 84; *Perfect Occurrences of Both Houses of Parliament and Martiall Affairs*, w/e 8 May 1646, unpaginated.
179 *The Moderate Intelligencer*, 4-11 June 1646, pp. 482-3.
180 Carr and Atherton, *Civil War in Staffordshire*, p. 267.
181 *JHC*, IV, p. 614; *JHL*, VIII, p. 463.
182 *CPCM*, I, p. 62; *JHC*, V, p. 98.
183 NLW, Aston Hall Estate Records: Correspondence, C2; D1 Mss, 2469-70, 2586.
184 J. Morrill, 'Mutiny and Discontent in English Provincial Armies', *Past and Present*, 56 (1972), pp. 49-74.
185 Flintshire Record Office, D/G/3275, f. 66.

Welshpool and forced the issue of their arrears by holding several local committeemen and a tax collector hostage until their demands were met.[186] Although it cannot be certain that disbandment in Shropshire proceeded without discontent, there appears no evidence of comparably mutinous action by the Shropshire forces. The prompt action taken by the county committee to commence disbandment before hostilities had ended may have forestalled the worst of the soldierly discontent experienced elsewhere. Making what appears to have been judicious use of revenue to provide acceptable remuneration, already by September 1646 the committee had disbanded many soldiers and settled their pay.[187] Moreover, other soldiers found alternative employment. On 1 March 1647 Major Anthony Hungerford agreed a contract with the Committee of Both Kingdoms to raise a regiment of foot for service in Ireland.[188] Hungerford had served with distinction in Shropshire, as a captain in the Earl of Denbigh's Foot and successively as governor of two garrisons, and in autumn 1646 was appointed major of the four standing companies.[189] With the county committee's support Hungerford soon recruited 600 men, mostly from the disbanding units and ex-soldiers of Shropshire, and his regiment crossed from Chester to Dublin in late April/early May, with a further company at least sailing in June.[190] While Hungerford's regiment re-employed many foot soldiers, some of the Shropshire Horse may have enlisted in a new, 600-strong regular regiment commanded by Colonel Needham, formerly the governor of Leicester, ordered to be raised in April 1647 from the disbanding cavalry of Shropshire, Cheshire and several Midland counties.[191]

The renewed hostilities in 1648 saw a hurried partial expansion of the Shropshire forces, a necessary volte-face from the policy of disbandment of the previous two years. Although they were little more than a policing force, the county committee's soldiers managed to suppress the ill-coordinated Royalist insurrections attempted that summer. The hard-tasked County Troop saw most service, supported by a second troop of around 120 horsemen raised hurriedly in July. Nonetheless, Colonel Humphrey Mackworth deployed just 80 troopers – 'all the horse of the county that could be got' – to disperse the most threatening Royalist gathering of the summer, attempted at Wattlesborough Heath on the night of 1/2 August. Mackworth had few foot soldiers and later sought Parliament's sanction and funding to expand his garrison at Shrewsbury to three regular companies.[192] In attempting to reestablish the militia after the disintegration of the Royalist Trained Bands, in early June 1648 the county committee had ordered across Shropshire the compilation of rolls listing male householders and their sons and servants eligible for militia service, in order 'that the said county may be put speedily in a posture of defence of horse and foot'. But by mid-July the implementation of this previously long-delayed plan to raise 1,200 foot

186 *Perfect Occurrences of Every Daies Journall in Parliament*, 7-14 May 1647, p. 148.
187 *CSPD, 1645-1647*, pp. 470-1.
188 Ibid., pp. 528-9.
189 WRO, CR2017/C10, f. 116.
190 *The Kingdomes Weekly Intelligencer*, 27 Apr.-4 May 1647, p. 511; *The Moderate Intelligencer*, 15-22 Apr. 1647, p. 1030; *Perfect Occurrences of Every Daies Journall in Parliament*, 4-11 June 1647, p. 150.
191 *The Weekly Account*, 7-14 Apr. 1647, unpaginated; *The Moderate Intelligencer*, 8-15 Apr. 1647, p. 1010; NLW, Sweeney Hall Mss A1, f. 32.
192 HMC, *Thirteenth Report, Appendix Part I*, pp. 484; *JHL*, Vol. X, pp. 424-5.

had faltered, hindered by public apathy and political infighting among the committee for the militia.[193] The scanty evidence in constables' accounts of militia-related activity suggests that a patchy response in some parts of the shire may have accounted for those volunteers (the 'well affected of the county') who gathered at Wem under Colonel Andrew Lloyd's leadership at the height of the emergency in late July and early August 1648.[194] Indeed, on 7 August his fellow committeemen appointed Lloyd to raise and command a regiment of foot in Shropshire, thereby reviving the plan in hand to reconstitute the county militia.[195]

Conclusions

In Shropshire, as elsewhere in England and Wales during the Civil Wars, both sides recruited their forces in similar ways, by the enlistment of volunteers and conscripts, and by the interchange of prisoners of war and deserters. Many units that served in Shropshire from 1642 to 1648 have been named here, but others may yet remain to be identified. Regular soldiers predominated, but both sides also deployed irregular militias. Many of the opposing leaders among the county gentry raised units in Shropshire, although not all were of regimental size. These and units from elsewhere posted to the county recruited in Shropshire, activity that must have entailed the widespread militarisation of the county's male population.

Given the limitations of the known sources, the reconstruction of orders of battle and of overall numbers remains problematic. On the Parliamentarian side, however, it can be suggested that during 1644 the Shropshire forces, not counting auxiliaries, numbered 700-1,000 men, and (excluding Colonel Mytton's units) during 1645 and into 1646 increased to around 1,900. The largest of the small field armies to see action in Shropshire were Lord Capel's 3,000 Royalists engaged around Wem in October 1643, and the Earl of Denbigh's 3,500-4,000 Parliamentarians briefly brought together in early July 1644. Both armies included substantial reinforcements from further afield, and throughout the First Civil War in Shropshire outsider or auxiliary forces – often outnumbering the local units – played key supportive roles. Units of the Royalist regional armies of Lord Capel and later Prince Rupert were based in Shropshire and sustained the local war effort. On the other hand, local Royalist forces were somewhat diminished by the departure of officers and units serving elsewhere. This was not, however, a one-way process: the Prince of Wales's Lifeguard, for example, returned to Shropshire in autumn 1643 and remained there. Among the Parliamentarian auxiliaries, detachments from Sir William Brereton's army played a vital role in their repeated and often long-standing deployments to Shropshire. After what appears to have been the relative success of the county committee's policy of disbandment after the First Civil War, in 1648 the small Parliamentary county force and some volunteers were able to suppress piecemeal the local Royalist insurrections, largely because their opponents failed to coordinate and concentrate their manpower.

193 SA, BB/C/8/1/6; HMC, *Thirteenth Report, Appendix Part I*, pp. 484-5.
194 SA, P314/M/1, ff. 40-3, Worfield constables' accounts; SA, P270/B/1/1, ff. 60-1, Stockton constables' accounts; *JHL*, Vol. X, p. 425.
195 NLW, Aston Hall Estate Records D1 Mss, 2468.

Having explained the organisation of the armed forces in Shropshire in detail, their funding will now be considered as part of a wider analysis of the financial aspects of the war effort.

4

Contributions and Assessments: Financing the war effort

Money is a thing not spoken of.

The English Civil Wars were fought at a time when the cost of waging war had increased exponentially during the previous 100 years, and would continue to do so for the remainder of the seventeenth century. With costs outstripping revenue, financing war effort could result in national indebtedness.[1] In 1638, for example, the estimated cost of raising and maintaining a 40,000-strong English army for a one-year campaign against the Scots was £900,000 – almost double Charles I's annual crown revenues.[2] Ten years later, even if Parliament's monthly £60,000 assessment had been collected in full across England and Wales, it would have barely covered the ongoing costs of the 24,000-strong standing army and regional garrisons.[3] The financial burden of civil war was immense because both sides exploited the same national economy. As an Essex churchman prophesied in a tract published in 1642: 'civil war exhausts the exchequer, or brings the treasures or riches of the land into an hectic fever, being like a vessel tapped at both ends, which quickly runs out'.[4] Financing war effort, in Morrill's phrase, set the kingdom on a 'fiscal treadmill', as both sides sought sustainable alternatives to indiscriminately living off the land.[5] During 1642 the forces of King and Parliament were funded by more or less voluntary contributions. During 1643 more systematic means of securing revenue were put in place, including general taxation, excise and the sequestration of enemy assets. Westminster led the way, by enacting a series of fiscal ordinances that created a legal framework (albeit of questionable constitutional validity) to finance the Parliamentarian war effort in the longer-term.

Money was required to finance vital aspects of war effort, including great expenditure on armaments bought from arms dealers, contractors and individual craftsmen. At Shrewsbury in February 1644, for instance, the local carpenter George Nicholls received £2 for working on gun carriages; meanwhile in London 550 firearms and 500

---

1   Parker, *The Military Revolution*, pp. 61-4; Wheeler, *World Power*, pp. 2, 14-16, 70-6.
2   M.C. Fissel, *The Bishops' Wars, Charles I's Campaigns Against Scotland, 1638-1640* (Cambridge, 1994), p. 111.
3   Wheeler, *World Power*, p. 113.
4   R. Ward, *The Anatomy of Warre, Or Warre with the woefull, fruits, and effects thereof, laid out to the life* (1642), p. 9.
5   Morrill, *Revolt*, p. 121.

swords purchased on the arms market for Sir Thomas Myddelton cost £640.[6] Military wages were the largest and least sustainable charge, with few soldiers on either side being paid regularly or in full; a case in point being Sir Michael Ernle's complaint to Prince Rupert in October 1644, that despite the near mutinous discontent over pay of four Royalist regiments at Shrewsbury, he 'could get nothing settled nor paid for the subsistence of this garrison'.[7] As examples of the wages of common foot soldiers, Royalists at Ludlow in 1643 were paid 6d daily, while in 1645-6 Parliamentarians based around Shrewsbury fared slightly better, receiving 4s per week.[8] Parliamentarian captains of foot like John Brett expected 15s per day, but Brett actually received less than one third of his pay in 1644 and 1645 while serving in Shropshire, and later claimed arrears of £172.[9] Like Brett, at the end of the First Civil War the generality of Parliament's soldiers were due large amounts of back pay, to the extent that by spring 1647 total army arrears may have amounted to £2,800,000.[10] Senior officers were proportionately better off, but they too accrued large deficits. Despite Sir Francis Ottley's governorship of Royalist Shrewsbury commanding a weekly salary of £20, he received just £326, less than a quarter, during the 17 months from October 1642 to March 1644.[11]

The financial machinery of both sides, in terms of administrative bodies and personnel was touched on in chapter two. The present chapter more fully examines the financing of war effort in Shropshire – the various expedient and more systematic methods of gathering revenue. Looting and the taking of 'free quarters' (whereby soldiers were compulsorily billeted with civilians) served to subsidise the combatants, and these practices are given due attention here. Because of the lack of extant financial records, more will be said of the methods used to acquire money than of the overall sums demanded, raised and disbursed.

The Royalists

The Royalist cause in Shropshire during the First Civil War is unlikely to have received direct financial support from the exchequer at Oxford. According to one of his officers, when Lord Capel took command at Shrewsbury in March 1643 he did so without bringing any money from the Royalist capital. Prince Maurice similarly arrived at Worcester in January 1645 without a war chest, and so immediately demanded a monthly £100 subscription for subsistence from Shropshire and the other counties of his new command.[12] On the other hand, Shropshire probably made few significant payments to the Royalist centre after early 1643. Instead, funds gathered by the Royalist administration sustained an agreed number of soldiers based there and paid for the fortification of their garrisons. Greater numbers of troops, however,

6   SA, 3365/588, f. 95; TNA, SP28/300 Part 1, f. 93.
7   BRL, Additional Mss 18981, f. 299.
8   SA, LB7/2015; SP28/174 Part 1, Capt. Farrington's account book, unfoliated.
9   SP28/34 Part 4, ff. 468, 470, Brett's accounts.
10 I. Gentles, 'The Arrears of Pay of the Parliamentary Army at the End of the First Civil War', *Historical Research*, 48 (1975), p. 55.
11 SA, 6000/13316.
12 HMC, *Twelfth Report, Appendix Part IX*, p. 39; 'Ottley Papers' (1896), p. 271.

magnified the financial strain. As Sir Michael Ernle found in early January 1645, the enlarged military establishment that he considered essential was to 'the gentlemen of the county' a force 'they really say they will not maintain'.[13] All that can be said about any funding for the short-lived Royalist insurgency in Shropshire during summer 1648 is that it came from the pockets of activists and from sympathisers proffering clandestine backing.

Concentrating on the First Civil War, then, and adopting a thematic approach, the main sources of Royalist revenues will be examined in turn, beginning with the recourse first made to donations and loans.

Gifts, loans and subscriptions

King Charles's three-week stay in Shropshire during September and October 1642 allowed time and opportunity to finance an army. Denied money by Parliamentary means, the King relied on benefaction and also expediency. This included the contrivance of summoning Catholics and other known Recusants in Shropshire and Staffordshire to pay their fines two or three years in advance, thereby generating almost £5,000 within 12 days. Charles meanwhile received cash in exchange for honours awarded to his wealthy supporters in Shropshire, among them Sir Richard Newport, who paid £6,000 for his elevation to the peerage, and Sir Thomas Lister of Rowton Castle, who reputedly gave a purse of gold coin for his knighthood on 1 October.[14] Local supporters and those further afield were encouraged to gift or loan cash and silver plate. Individual subscriptions were requested of Shropshire's gentry, among them Humphrey Walcot who was summoned to lend £5,000. How much Walcot paid is unknown but on 9 October he gave a warhorse and arms to Prince Rupert, for donations of war matériel were as acceptable as cash.[15] A bequest of plate arrived from the University of Oxford, and other public donations included cash and part of the corporation silver proffered by the aldermen of Ludlow, transported to Shrewsbury at a cost of 13s and dutifully presented to the King by Bailiff Colbatch.[16] Meanwhile, after presenting the royal entourage with a shared gratuity of almost £20 upon their arrival in town, Shrewsbury's corporation set about levying public subscriptions for the King, although on 28 September the aldermen permitted a one-week extension, 'because of the weak estate of the town'.[17] Shrewsbury Grammar School loaned £600 to the King on 11 October.[18]

As a result of warrants circulated on 22 September 1642 by High Sheriff John Weld to Shropshire's high constables, summoning them to encourage donations from among the gentry, clergy and freeholders, what became, in effect, a fund-raising rally was held on the riverside meadows at Shrewsbury on the 28th.[19] There, Charles I

13   BDL, Firth Mss C6, f. 303.
14   Clarendon, *History*, II, pp. 365-7; Owen and Blakeway, *Shrewsbury*, I, p. 423.
15   J.R. Burton (ed.), 'The Sequestration Papers of Humphrey Walcot', *TSANHS*, 3rd Series, V (1905), pp. 314-15.
16   Clarendon, *History*, II, p. 364; SA, LB8/1/162, f. 3; SA, LB/Fiche 4677.
17   SA, 3365/586, f. 1; SA, 6001/290, f. 133.
18   Anon, *A History of Shrewsbury School* (Shrewsbury and London, 1889), p. 105.
19   SRO, P593/P8/1/4, warrant to the high constables of Bradford hundred.

15. Denominations of the silver coinage minted at Shrewsbury from October until December 1642. In later December the mint was relocated to Oxford, King Charles I's wartime capital. (© Shropshire Council/Shropshire Museums)

spoke of undertaking a financial commitment alongside his loyal subjects in order to combat the rebellion. After promising to expend his personal financial reserves, the King urged the gathering to

> Not suffer so good a cause to be lost, for want of supplying me with that which will be taken from you by those who pursue me with this violence. And whilst these ill men sacrifice their money, plate and utmost industry to destroy the commonwealth, be you no less liberal to preserve it.

The means of obtaining the anticipated donations were deferred to the sheriff and commissioners of array, as perhaps their first task as wartime financial officials.[20]

One eyewitness to the events at the Gay Meadow commented 'there was no money or plate parted with that I did see', but on 18 October another correspondent noted the 'abundance' of plate arriving at Shrewsbury.[21] By then a royal mint was operating there under the supervision of Sir Thomas Bushell, a wealthy entrepreneur and superintendent of the mint and of the royal mines in Wales. It was Bushell who had overseen the transfer of plant and tooling, together with several skilled artificers, from the mint at Aberystwyth in west mid-Wales. Until it was relocated to Oxford in January 1643 the Shrewsbury mint converted plate into silver coinage at up to £1,000

---

20 Rushworth, *Historical Collections*, V, p. 23.
21 *Some Late Occurrences in Shropshire and Devonshire* (1642), p. 4; *The true copie of a letter importing divers passages of high and dangerous consequence. Written by one Master Tempest a grand recusant, to his brother master John Tempest, likewise a papist and an officer in the Kings army* (1642), p. 5.

per week, the first supply arriving with the army on 21 October when the common soldiers each received a half crown (30d).[22] Given the sums raised by these initiatives and seized from neutralists and Parliament's supporters, according to Clarendon at this time the Royalist field army usually received weekly pay and did not go unpaid beyond a fortnight.[23]

Loans and gifts remained the mainstay of Shropshire's financial contribution to the Royalist war effort into winter 1642-3, when Sir Vincent Corbet's Dragoon Regiment was at first funded by public subscription.[24] Further demands for individual donations were made as the war intensified. In April 1643, Lord Capel ordered the identification of persons deemed able to fund the Royalist cause, and it was probably the sum of this initiative that in late June encouraged King Charles to write of his generously 'well-affected subjects of the gentry of Salop'.[25] Further loans were demanded from Oxford in early 1644 in another attempt to exploit the King's supporters. A device agreed by the Royalist parliament to avert more widespread taxation, from mid-February standard letters demanding individual loans proportionate to wealth were sent under cover of the privy seal to Royalist gentry across England and Wales. Among Shropshire's recipients were one Mr Mitton of Shipton, summoned to pay £30, and Humphrey Walcot, who by May had paid £150 in instalments.[26] The privy seal letter subscription was intended to raise £100,000 in coin and plate to finance the Oxford-based field army during the forthcoming campaigning season, but lobbying on his behalf ensured that instead Prince Rupert was allocated most of the money raised from Shropshire and the six counties of North Wales.[27] Accordingly, in a petition to King Charles in later June 1644 the sheriff and certain Shropshire gentry requested the further retention of privy seal loan money in order to lessen the burden of military taxation.[28] Committed Royalists also contributed what they could in other ways to finance the war effort. Among them was Captain Edward Lloyd, who claimed he spent £800 in raising and equipping a troop each of horse and dragoons.[29]

Sequestration

The next step from taking donations from supporters was to seize the assets of opponents and their sympathisers. Sequestered property could be sold or rented out to generate income, but King Charles was at first reluctant to sanction the appropriation of his adversaries' wealth without robust legal justification. In March 1643, however, Parliament forced the issue by enacting an ordinance regulating the sequestration of their antagonists, and so the following June the King and his Council of War at

---

22 *Letter […] by one Master Tempest*, p. 5; R. Lloyd Kenyon, 'History of the Shrewsbury Mint', *TSANHS*, 2nd Series, X (1898), pp. 251-72.
23 Clarendon, *History*, II, p. 373.
24 'Ottley Papers' (1895), pp. 254-6.
25 Ibid., p. 312; NLW, Llanfair-Brynodol Letters, 54.
26 HMC, *Tenth Report, Appendix Part IV*, p. 407; Burton, 'Sequestration Papers of Humphrey Walcot', pp. 315-16.
27 Hutton, *War Effort*, pp. 92, 135; BRL, Additional Mss 18981, ff. 113-14, 204; Anon., 'Correspondence of Archbishop Williams', *Archaeologica Cambrensis*, 4th Series, I (1870), pp. 64-5.
28 *CSPD, 1644*, pp. 282-3.
29 NLW, Sweeney Hall Mss A4 (Vol. II), f. 93, Captain Lloyd's narrative.

Oxford agreed a similar policy that Royalists in the shires soon formally adopted.[30]

Hutton found that the scarcity of evidence left Royalist sequestration 'shadowy', and questions regarding its effectiveness 'unanswerable'.[31] The evidence from Shropshire, although tending to those conclusions, does suggest, however, that Royalist finances benefitted by the systematic exploitation of enemy assets. It was not long after the King had departed Shropshire that in later 1642 the Royalist leadership at Shrewsbury sought his approval, to 'seize upon the goods and chattels of such persons his majesty hath deemed traitorous'. Consequently, Sir John Corbet was among several Parliamentarian MPs whose restitution was the subject of a Commons debate on 5 April 1643, 'for the losses they have sustained by the King's forces, by having their estates and goods violently taken from them'.[32] By way of a proclamation printed at Shrewsbury, two days before Lord Capel had announced his approval of the sequestration of 'disaffected persons', provided that due process was followed.[33] Accordingly, by July Capel was encouraging his subordinates to use sequestration as the preferred means of funding Royalist forces in the region.[34] In Shropshire meanwhile the estates of enemy exiles were being sequestrated, while suspected Parliamentarian sympathisers were made to pay Royalist taxes.[35]

By later 1643 Royalist sequestration was better organised, a development of their fiscal apparatus seen in the example of Lord Capel's orders concerning Thomas Mytton's assets.[36] That spring the Royalist military had seized Mytton's chattels including his livestock, an act indistinguishable from plundering. By November, however, a commission sitting at Shrewsbury was managing sequestration more systematically, including the collection of rental from Mytton's estates. Samuel More, Mytton's fellow committeeman, later recollected that by early 1644 his family's lands in south Shropshire had been similarly appropriated by the Royalists.[37] The orders given on 23 March 1644 by a Shrewsbury-based commission, instructing the receivers of sequestered wealth from across Shropshire to submit accounts for audit and directly to pay the proceeds to the commission, demonstrate the ongoing importance of Royalist sequestration and the extent of the administrative machinery.[38] Sequestration remained of sufficient value to the Royalists in Shropshire and adjacent counties into early 1645 that it was proposed as a prime source of funding for the Marcher Association under the commissioners' control. At the local level, in May 1645 the Royalist leadership at Bridgnorth directed that further work on the town's fortifications should be funded from sequestration.[39]

30 Hutton, *War Effort*, p. 89; Morrill, *Revolt*, p. 11; Engberg, 'Royalist Finances', pp. 92-3.
31 Hutton, *War Effort*, p. 90.
32 SA, 6000/13293; *JHC*, III, p. 31.
33 *Arthur Lord Capell Lieutenant Generall under the Prince His Highnesse of His Majesties forces, in the counties of Worcester, Salop, and Chester, and the six northern counties of Wales. To all commanders, officers, and souldiers, and to all other His Majesties subjects whatsoever* (1643).
34 NLW, Crosse of Shaw Hill Mss, 1123; WRO, CR2017/C9, f. 22.
35 'Ottley Papers' (1895), pp. 298-9, 309, 353-4.
36 NAM, 8812-63, ff. 1-2.
37 HMC, *Calendar of the Manuscripts of the Marquis of Bath*, I, p. 36.
38 SA, 3365/2711, f. 26.
39 Townsend, *Diary*, II, p. 193; BDL, Dugdale Mss 19 [second part], f. 105; SA, BB/C/1/1/1, unfoliated.

Taxation

In Shropshire Royalist taxation assumed three forms. Firstly, regular payments and irregular impositions were levied in the fashion of the pre-war local rates. Secondly, monthly contribution was levied across the shire. The third instrument, excise duty, can briefly be dealt with first. County commissions to levy duty on certain 'wares and commodities' were appointed at Oxford from mid-April 1644. Accordingly, in early May Edward Baldwin of Diddlebury, James Lacon of West Coppice and Richard Studeley of Shrewsbury were appointed as the superintending commissioners for the excise in Shropshire.[40] The reach of the Royalist excise nationally appears to have been patchy and its yield mediocre, but, as in Shropshire, there is little evidence upon which to base these conclusions. However, the levy in Shropshire was not wholly a dead letter; in early 1645 half of excise revenue was to be diverted to the Marcher Association, and the excise commission for Shropshire was reappointed that March.[41]

Local rates were levied for the wages and upkeep of soldiers in Royalist service. At Bridgnorth, the aldermen set lewns for the townsfolk to pay the local trained bandsmen on duty elsewhere. A lewn for £20 was laid on 26 December 1642, and another agreed on 25 March 1643. Ludlow's inhabitants claimed to have spent almost £367 on the town's militiamen during 1642/3.[42] Because voluntary subscriptions proved insufficient to finance Sir Vincent Corbet's Dragoons – as one Royalist lamented to Sir Francis Ottley in January 1643, would-be contributors tended to 'say much and do nothing' – in addition each allotment was charged a proportionate allocation.[43] Bridgnorth as one allotment had to provide nine dragoons, 'to be maintained at the general charge of the town', towards which the corporation laid a lewn for £20 on 25 January 1643. In a further example of ad-hoc taxation by allotments, in March 1643 a rate of 40s per allotment to pay for ammunition was levied in the southerly hundreds of Overs and Munslow.[44]

Ongoing levies to finance fortifications imposed long-term fiscal demands on the inhabitants of the Royalist garrison towns. As early as August 1642 the corporation of Bridgnorth had set a lewn for £20 to improve the town defences, and the following November Shrewsbury's corporation imposed a rate of £250 for similar measures.[45] By late 1644, nearly £2,800 (at least) in public assessments had been raised to fund the fortification of the county town.[46] Similarly at Ludlow, during June 1644 114 townsfolk contributed to an assessment ordered by Sir Michael Woodhouse to fund further strengthening of the town walls. Other supernumerary charges also had to be met. Sometime in later 1644 Ludlow's inhabitants complained of the costs of distributing military warrants and of providing coal and candles for the garrison.[47] In a petition to the governor Sir Michael Ernle dated 12 October 1644, Shrewsbury's

40 BDL, Dugdale Mss 19 [second part], ff. 49, 59.
41 Ibid., ff. 105, 110.
42 SA, BB/C/1/1/1, unfoliated; SA, LB7/2105.
43 'Ottley Papers' (1894), p. 64.
44 SA, BB/C/1/1/1, unfoliated; SA, LB7/2235.
45 SA, BB/C/1/1/1, unfoliated; SA, 6001/290, f. 135.
46 SA, 3365/587, f. 1; SA, 3365/588, f. 4; SA, 3365/591, f. 1.
47 SA, LB7/2250; SA, LB8/1/164, f. 8; SA, LB7/2319, unfoliated.

aldermen alike complained that after paying for fortifications, for the purchase of eight cannon and towards military taxes and privy seal loans, 'the whole revenue of the town would not pay the coals and candles of the sentries'. Previous levies at Shrewsbury had included rates that raised £550 for Lord Capel in 1643, and £100 as a gift welcoming Prince Rupert in February 1644.[48]

In addition to ad hoc imposts, from early 1643 systematic military taxation was enforced in Royalist-controlled areas as a sustainable means of financing war effort. Levied first on Oxfordshire from late December 1642 as a weekly loan arrangement to pay for regiments of the field army, henceforth a weekly or monthly rate of contribution, in the form of a sweeping tax agreed between the military and civilian authorities, was to be collected in each shire to fund a commensurate number of soldiers based there.[49] Accordingly, in early 1643 a monthly rate had been set in the neighbouring Royalist counties of Worcestershire and Herefordshire, in January and February respectively, before contribution was demanded from Shropshire in late March.[50] The inception of the tax on Lord Capel's arrival seems coincidental, for already by early March the commissioners of array were planning a county levy. Accordingly, on the 25th the corporation of Bridgnorth set a lewn for £46, 'charged to the town toward £4,500 for the defence of the country [county]'.[51] Other evidence – of the petty constable of Halesowen (then an enclave of Shropshire lying within Worcestershire) who by June had failed three previous payments 'concerning the £4,500', and the £112 to be paid by the town of Ludlow in November as 'part of the £4,500 contribution' – confirms that Shropshire's monthly target for contribution during 1643 was £4,500, apportioned between the 100 allotments very much in the fashion of the ship money levies of the 1630s.[52]

Writing on 23 June 1643 to the Royalist commissioners in Caernarvonshire, King Charles endorsed 'the good example of our good subjects of our county of Salop' in raising 'competent monthly contribution'. And it may well have been the efficacy of Royalist taxation at this time that had provoked ten days previously a counterblast in a London newsbook, describing Shropshire's inhabitants as 'much embittered against the Lord Capel, for his excessive and unreasonable taxes and impositions'.[53] Later evidence suggests, however, that popular discontent and administrative neglect caused the payment of contribution, and indeed Royalist finances in general, markedly to decline in Shropshire during the two-month hiatus in high command between Capel's return to Oxford in December 1643 and Prince Rupert's arrival in February 1644. In the meantime Capel's 300-strong cavalry regiment remaining in Shropshire was funded only with great difficulty, by emergency subscriptions from loyal gentry and latterly out of his own pocket by the high sheriff. From Shrewsbury on 2 February

48   SA, 6001/290, f. 144; SA, 3365/587, f. 2; SA, 3365/588, f. 2.
49   Engberg, 'Royalist Finances', pp. 89-90; Morrill, *Revolt*, pp. 112-13
50   For Worcestershire, *Mercurius Aulicus*, w/e 21 Jan. 1643, p. 7; for Herefordshire, *A Perfect Diurnall of the passages in Parliament*, 30 Jan.-6 Feb. 1643, unpaginated.
51   'Ottley Papers' (1895), p. 269; SA, BB/C/1/1/1, unfoliated.
52   'Ottley Papers' (1895), p. 329; SA, LB7/1932.
53   NLW, Llanfair-Brynodol Letters, 54; *Certaine Informations from Several Parts of the Kingdom*, 12-19 June 1643, p. 170.

1644 Sir John Mennes wrote to Prince Rupert that many Royalist soldiers were unpaid and mutinous. 'Money', Mennes declared, 'is a thing not spoken of', grumbling that during his eleven-month posting to Shropshire he had been paid just £20.[54]

On arriving in the county Prince Rupert immediately set about reforming the contribution. A warrant to Ludlow's bailiffs dated 24 February 1644 signalled a more equitable approach: 'The great inequalities heretofore used in the assessing and collecting the payments of this county coming to our notion and knowledge occassioneth us to endeavour the prevention of having any payments or money raised […] in that unequal way'.[55] The Prince's intent, however, was more to broaden the reach of the tax. Henceforth contribution would be levied as a monthly penny rate in the pound, 'out of all men's estates, in which there can be no partiality or excuse', as Rupert reiterated in early April to the Royalist commissioners of neighbouring Montgomeryshire.[56] During 1644, a 6d in the pound rate was levied in Shropshire from March to May, 4d from June to September, 6d in October and November, and 7d in December and into January 1645.[57] Further evidence for 1645 comes from Colonel Devillier's garrison at Caus Castle, which received contribution at the rate of 4d in February and March, and 6d in May and June.[58] However, the monthly target of the county levy remains obscure. In 1644, the amount for March was £6,000, while monthly sums of £4,400 and £4,700 are also documented.[59] But it remains uncertain whether these were totals for contribution, or were monthly targets embracing all revenue, including privy seal loans and sequestration.

Rupert's reforms shifted the focus of assessment from the allotments to individual townships. This required a countywide programme of reassessment by an increased number of parochial assessors.[60] By the end of March 1644 there were 142 in the town and liberties of Shrewsbury alone, while during 1644 the parish of Stockton had five assessors.[61] Assessors were entrusted under oath to 'take the true values of all the lands, messauges and tenements, tithes and ecclesiastical livings […] as the same were really and indifferently worth and valued by the year three years since'.[62] In the example of Battlefield, three miles north of Shrewsbury, this retrospective valuation amounted to £101 10s based on the assessed worth of 15 inhabitants. Accordingly, at the 4d rate the township paid £1 13s 10d monthly in summer 1644. All but 10s was charged to Pelham Corbet, a local gentleman. Assessed at £70, he was taxed £1 3s 4d. Meanwhile the evaluation of the small village of Acton Scott was £299. There, the hall and seat of the local squire was rated at £60 (so paying £1 per month at the 4d levy), and the parsonage £40, with the remainder of the assessment charged to 15 villagers, six of

54 BDL, Firth Mss C6, f. 80; BRL, Additional Mss 18981, f. 25.
55 SA, LB/8/3/75.
56 Order cited in G. Sandford (ed.), 'Incidents in Montgomeryshire during, and also before and after, the Civil War in the time of Charles I, and during the Commonwealth', *Collections Historical and Archaeological relating to Montgomeryshire and its Borders*, XIV (1881), p. 299.
57 SA, LB/8/3/75; Townsend, *Diary*, II, p. 82; SA, 3365/224, unfoliated; SA, 3365/589, f. 3.
58 HRO, CF61/20, ff. 569, 571, 573.
59 SA, LB/8/3/75; *CSPD, 1644*, pp. 282-3.
60 SA, LB/8/3/75; SA, 3365/2711, f. 25.
61 SA, 3365/2711, f. 23; SA, P270/B/1/1, ff. 55-6.
62 Townsend, *Diary*, II, p. 164.

whom were classed as freeholders. In March 1644 the combined valuation of almost 400 inhabitants of eight parishes in northerly parts of Purslow hundred was £5,205, which would have yielded £130 monthly at the 6d rate.[63]

Instead of land, in urban areas personal income was taxed. Accordingly, the inhabitants of High Street and Old Fish Street at the heart of Shrewsbury were assessed on the basis of 'poundage and personal estate'.[64] Appeals to the authorities during 1644 by some of their fellow townsfolk, most of whom were tradesmen, complained mostly of unfair assessment of personal estate expressed in money – as cash or investments, in goods and stock, or even tied to 'good debts'.[65] The shoemaker John Betton, for one, remonstrated to the commissioners not against his assessment, calculated on 'ability both for his house and shop and for his personal estate', but against vindictive neighbours who alleged that he had failed to declare an investment – a 'by estate of some moneys at interest'.[66]

Because a regular supply of food for soldiers and horses was just as important to the Royalists as cash flow, since Prince Rupert's overhaul of the tax (if not before) up to half of contribution could be paid in kind, in provisions or provender, at a set cash-equivalent rate. Thus in June, July and August 1644 together the township of Harlescott paid £2 18s 11d in cash and gave £3 1d worth of provisions towards contribution for those months of £7 11s 6d.[67] The proviso allowing payment in cash or kind ensured that the contribution reached far down the socio-economic scale, so those who were cash-poor gave produce instead. Two individuals with very modest land holdings in Purslow hundred who nonetheless paid contribution were Thomas Watkis of Moreswood, assessed at £1, and Nathaniel Matthews of Acton, assessed at £1 10s, who paid 6d and 9d respectively at the 6d monthly rate.[68] Both were probably small freeholders, but tenants were also taxed, either in their own right or towards their landlord's assessment. When, in the autumn of 1646, Charles Bright, bailiff of the manor of Lydham, audited his tenants' rent arrears for the first time since 1642 he generously allowed eight between them a rebate of £22 for contribution payments they had made.[69]

Prince Rupert succeeded in reforming the reach and partiality of the contribution in Shropshire, but it remained an inefficient tax because it was administratively burdensome and its yield depended on the accumulation of a profusion of small payments. Money dribbled in, in an unpredictable way. The fullest extant set of accounts, for contribution paid in cash in parts of Shrewsbury and in 52 outlying townships from late September 1644 until shortly before the fall of the county town in February 1645, record 370 separate payments.[70] The collectors of the township of Astley, for

63 SA, 3365/224, unfoliated; WSL, 350/40/5, unfoliated, transcript of 'An account of the pound rate of the township of Acton Scott'; SA, 1079/Box 13, Item 14, 'The upper end of Purslow hundred valuation of lands by a warrant of Prince Rupert, ann. 1643'.
64 SA, 3365/224, unfoliated.
65 SA, 3365/2711, ff. 1-16, 21.
66 Ibid., f. 16.
67 SA, 3365/224, unfoliated.
68 SA, 1079/Box 13, Item 14, unfoliated.
69 Ibid., Item 12, Bright's account book, unfoliated.
70 SA, 3365/589, ff. 1-3.

example made 21 payments, seven of which in October amounted to just £1 11s 9d, while nearby Hadnall paid on 27 occasions. Payments were inconsistent and variable. In rounded figures, monies received at Shrewsbury (towards a now unknown monthly target) amounted to £164 in October and just £104 in November. Contribution for December 1644 and January 1645 received by February came to £193, which with arrears from October and November amounted to £209. In October 45 places paid, 34 in November, but just 22 in February. While some places, such as Acton Reynald and Grinshill, paid regularly on a monthly basis, many others did so sporadically – Great Hanwood, for example, only in October and January. The townships of Edgebold and Blackbirches each made their sole recorded payments in January 1645.

Achieving a consistent yield of contribution became all the more difficult in the face of local non-cooperation or forceful dissent. In December 1644, for instance, it was reported that inhabitants of Newport and Much Wenlock had refused warrants to levy contribution and had arrested four civilian collectors.[71] This partisan account of concerted tax refusal at this time is substantiated by Sir Lewis Kirke's report to Prince Rupert from Bridgnorth dated 22 February 1645, that the garrison there had received 'no contribution from the county these three months, nor like to receive any'.[72] Those constables of Chirbury hundred who, from autumn 1644 until mid-1645, provided contribution to Colonel Devillier's garrisons at Leigh Hall and later Caus Castle seem to have followed a calculated policy of hindrance. They accumulated substantial arrears but made sufficient timely payments in cash and provisions to avert Devillier's threats of punitive action against their constablewicks. The perceived indolence of the petty constables of Stockton, a hamlet five miles south-west of Leigh Hall, provoked the high constable to write to them in exasperation on 23 January 1645, that if they did not settle their accounts and bring in arrears, he would 'burn all the books and make you pay all anew'.[73] Nonetheless, Devillier's account with Stockton ran substantial cash arrears into March.

The constables of Stockton personally delivered contribution to Devillier's garrisons, and it generally seems to have been the case in Shropshire that the Royalist military was not routinely involved in tax collection. This contrasts with the situation in the East Midlands for example, where Royalist officers routinely served as tax collectors – albeit in a region generally more administratively unstable for the Royalists than Shropshire.[74] The record of contribution from the Shrewsbury area in 1644 and into 1645 shows that civilian collectors paid into the mayor's office, from where money was allotted to the military's receiving officer on a hand to mouth basis.[75] Similarly, during 1644 the petty constables of townships owing contribution to Bridgnorth delivered their payments to the garrison, among them the constables of Stockton parish who also made at least two journeys to Shrewsbury to pay contribution there. Meanwhile during 1644, the collector for the village of Buildwas sent contribution to garrisons at Madeley and Wellington, and paid October's money to a servant of Sir Francis

71 *The Weekly Account*, 25 Dec. 1644 -1 Jan. 1645, unpaginated.
72 BRL, Additional Mss 18982, f. 36.
73 HRO, CF61/20, f. 567.
74 Bennett, 'Contribution and Assessment', p. 4.
75 SA, 3365/589, f. 2.

16. The tree-grown and fragmentary remains of one of the D-shaped towers
once forming the gatehouse of Caus Castle. Caus was held as a Royalist
garrison in 1644-5. From here Colonel Devillier levied contribution
in cash and provisions from settlements in west Shropshire.

Ottley.[76]

If the Royalists sought to avoid the direct involvement of soldiers in tax collection, how did the military respond to non-compliance, given the balance to be struck between ensuring the soldiery were paid and fed without engendering non-cooperation or hostility amongst the populace? Colonel Devillier impatiently issued intimidating warrants threatening action for non-payment and arrears, such as that dated 26 November 1644 directed to the petty constables of Stockton and Walcot, that 'if any mischief befall you by my soldiers going forth you must blame yourselves for it'.[77] Devillier also threatened to impose higher payments, but there is no evidence of his men actually taking forceful retributive action. In what seems to have been a measured response to non-payment, it was not until Shifnal had failed to pay contribution for several months that in August 1644 Sir Lewis Kirke finally sent soldiers to collect the village's arrears. In the event, the small detachment from the nearby garrison at Tong was set upon by the locals, disarmed and imprisoned for several hours.[78]

On the other hand, evidence of a more forceful military response to non-payment comes from Shrewsbury sometime during 1643, when dragoons were sent to arrest

76   SA, BB/D/1/2/1/53-4; SA, P270/B/1/1, ff. 55-6; 'Ottley Papers' (1896), pp. 256-7.
77   HRO, CF61/20, f. 563.
78   BRL, Additional Mss 18981, f. 225.

persons 'who refused cessments'.[79] These individuals may well have then faced a period of incarceration, like others imprisoned for failing to pay personal arrears, such as the rector of Harley who in January 1646 was held at Ludlow, or else because as prominent local individuals they were scapegoats held accountable for the indebtedness of the community – the fate at some point in 1644 of the husband of one Eleanor Cound, who petitioned Lady Ottley to secure his release.[80] Another means of enforcement was the distraint of an individual's chattels. Distraint was employed in the Ludlow area in November 1643, for example, but the sluggish local economy made it difficult for the bailiffs to resell goods and livestock seized from defaulters in lieu of their contribution payments.[81] Among those subject to distraint during 1644 were Samuel France of Ludlow, whose shovel and horse tack were confiscated for failing to pay 4s contribution, and one Mrs Allenson of Sutton, who during October had possessions seized on four occasions to the value of £4.[82] Civil officials were, however, often ill prepared to enforce distraint or were reluctant to do so, being fearful of retribution. Richard Baxter's father during 1644 collected Royalist taxes, 'but he would not forcibly distrain of them that refused to pay, as not knowing but they might hereafter recover it all from him'.[83] While no firm conclusion can be drawn as to the extent or severity of the Royalist military's coercive role, these examples show, however, that threatened or actual punishment went hand-in-hand with taxation.

The Marcher Association movement encouraged administrative changes to the contribution in Shropshire in January 1645, when certain gentry proposed the replacement of the 'levy by poundage' with a reformed version of the 'old division of allotments', but nonetheless the pound rate remained in force.[84] By later 1645, with just three Royalist bases in Shropshire the concomitant loss of territory led to an irrecoverable decline in revenue. By December this resulted in a situation where at Bridgnorth Sir Lewis Kirke reportedly found that he had to negotiate and 'entreat hard' with the locality in order to continue to receive reduced contribution, while at the same time the garrison at High Ercall had resorted to coercion and robbery, including waylaying the collectors of Parliamentary taxes.[85]

The Parliamentarians
Overview
The first of Parliament's many legislative measures to finance military operations against Charles I was the ordinance of 9 June 1642, 'for bringing in plate, money and horses', the so-called Propositions. Thereby Parliament called upon its adherents voluntarily to contribute plate and cash, while promising reimbursement and interest. Accordingly, by 20 September 1642 Richard More, MP, had delivered £120-worth of silver plate

79   SA, 3365/587, f. 14.
80   'Ottley Papers' (1896), pp. 210, 297.
81   SA, LB7/1932.
82   SA, LB7/2148; SA, 3365/589, f. 1.
83   Baxter, *Reliquiae Baxterianae*, p. 40.
84   'Ottley Papers' (1896), p. 267.
85   *The Weekly Account*, 10-17 Dec. 1645, unpaginated; BDL, Tanner Mss 60, f. 444.

to London's Guildhall.[86] The Royalist response suggests that, like More, many of Parliament's supporters in Shropshire donated generously towards the Propositions. Having been detained on suspicion of using their mercantile connections to send plate to London, that October several leading Shrewsbury drapers were summonsed by the Royalist leadership to reveal the extent of local donations to Parliament.[87] Further, King Charles's proclamation at Bridgnorth on 14 October 1642 acknowledged that 'many of our subjects, inhabitants of this county', had contributed money and plate to aid the rebellion, 'contrary to their duty and allegiance'.[88] A correspondent had reported from Bridgnorth on 1 October how the high sheriff had seized there 'certain thousands of pounds', collected by Shropshire Parliamentarians and intended to be smuggled down the River Severn to Bristol.[89]

The Propositions were an important source of Parliamentarian revenue, and further individual contributions were exacted under a national ordinance of 7 May 1643. Thereby, individuals with an annual income exceeding ten pounds or a personal estate valued greater than £100 who had not given to the Propositions were compelled to make a donation of up to one-fifth of their income and one-twentieth the value of their estate.[90] But fines and donations were insufficient to sustain war effort in the long term. Parliament responded during 1643 by enacting further national fiscal ordinances enabling its generals and the various London-based and county committees to exact revenue more widely, by taxation and from enemy property. But the exiled leadership of Parliament's cause in Shropshire was ill placed to implement levies most effectively administered in areas sympathetic to Parliament or held under Parliamentarian military control. Precariously established in their foothold at Wem, in autumn 1643 the Parliamentarians faced the difficulty of raising income from largely enemy territory – a task that Sir Thomas Myddelton, in a dispatch written from Wem on 6 October, gloomily reported was all but impossible.[91] Parliament acknowledged in the preamble to the ordinance of 13 June 1644 – 'For raising monies for maintenance of the forces in Shropshire' – that 'all other ordinances made this present Parliament for the advance of monies in the several counties of the kingdom […] never could be put in execution in the county of Salop, in regard it hath been and is under the command of the King's forces'.[92] Subsequently, because both sides increasingly taxed Shropshire's inhabitants, the Parliamentarians had to contend with diminishing returns. In April 1645 and again the following August, the committee at Shrewsbury reported (albeit, perhaps, with a degree of special pleading) the chronic difficulty of imposing levies on an impoverished populace repeatedly taxed and otherwise exploited by the combatants.[93]

Regional Parliamentarians pressed Westminster to grant additional fiscal powers and allocate scarce funds, requests that were subject to protracted lobbying and

86   *JHL*, V, pp. 121-2; *JHC*, II, p. 774.
87   SA, 6000/13291.
88   Clark Maxwell, 'King Charles I's Proclamation', pp. xxv-vi.
89   *A True and exact Relation of the Proceedings of His Majesties Army*, p. 4.
90   *A&O*, I, pp. 145-55.
91   HMC, *Thirteenth Report, Appendix Part I*, pp. 134-5.
92   *JHL*, VI, p. 586.
93   *LBWB*, I, pp. 265-6; HMC, *13th Report, Appendix Part I*, p. 236.

1. The tower house (or keep) of Hopton Castle that in March 1644 became the final refuge of Captain Samuel More's garrison. The garderobe outlet that Royalist pioneers entered in order to place a gunpowder mine is at the base of the nearest (south-west) wall.

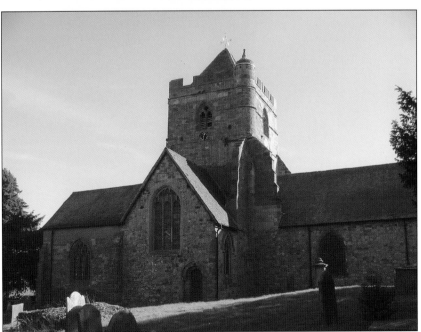

2. During the Civil Wars churches were often garrisoned and used as strong points, of which the church of St. Peter at Wrockwardine is one example from Shropshire. In late 1645 St. Peter's was occupied by a Parliamentarian detachment that on 19 December beat off attacks by a Royalist force led by Sir William Vaughan. The main structure of the church has not been significantly altered since the seventeenth century.

3. The Parliamentarian defence of Wem, October 1643.
(Painting by Peter Dennis, © Helion & Company Limited)

Facing page: a reconstruction painting depicting the Parliamentarian defenders
of Wem beating off attacks against the fortified town by units of Lord
Capel's Royalist army on the afternoon of Tuesday 17 October 1643.

The Parliamentarians conducted a successful defence by concentrating their firepower against
the Royalist assault parties. Shown here firing from the defensive earthworks, reinforced
by earth-filled wicker baskets called gabions, that enclosed Wem, in the foreground a
townsman of the militia hesitatingly aims his musket, while behind him a musketeer of
Colonel Thomas Mytton's Regiment of Foot fires against the retreating Royalists. Both
are armed with matchlock muskets, the standard infantry firearm of the period, for which
a measured charge of gunpowder for an individual shot is held in each of the cylindrical
containers suspended from their shoulder-slung bandoleers. The soldier of Mytton's regiment
steadies and aims his musket using a forked rest, a piece of equipment that declined in use
during the war as lighter, handier, muskets became widespread. The townsman wears his
workaday clothes, and while a 'regular' regiment like Mytton's is likely to have had some
uniformity in dress, the red coat - a colour adopted by units on both sides – is conjectural.

Behind the musketeers a light cannon, of an improved type known as a Drake in
use at the beginning of the Civil Wars, discharges a round of hail shot; a form of
anti-personnel ammunition (later known as case shot or canister) that scattered
lead bullets of musket calibre, or sometimes small, angular pieces of metal
known as dice, against the enemy at short range with devastating effect.

Sheltering behind the defensive rampart a townswoman assists in the defence by loading
muskets. According to an eighteenth-century local antiquarian, during the short siege
'the women particularly distinguished themselves, which gave occasion to this rhyme:
"the women of Wem and a few musketeers beat the Lord Capel and all his Cavaliers".

4. Royalist cavalry relieve High Ercall Hall, July 1645.
(Painting by Peter Dennis, © Helion & Company Limited)

Facing page: a reconstruction painting depicting Sir William Vaughan leading the all-mounted Royalist force that early on the morning of 5 July 1645 routed the Parliamentarians besieging the garrison of High Ercall Hall. The success of Vaughan's fast-moving 'flying column' in relieving High Ercall was a notable regional victory for the Royalists after the disastrous defeat of King Charles's main field army at Naseby (Northamptonshire) on 14 June. The well-defended garrison was not only an important Royalist outpost in Shropshire, but was also a key staging post in maintaining a line of communication between Royalist bases in the Midlands and those at Chester and in North Wales.

Much of Vaughan's life remains obscure, but he probably came from a minor gentry family of the mid-Welsh borderlands, and is assumed to have pursued a career as a professional soldier in the Continental wars. Returning to England before the outbreak of Civil War, Vaughan went to Ireland in spring 1642 as captain of a troop of horse, where he campaigned until being posted back to the British mainland to join the Royalist forces, probably with the rank of colonel, in command of his own cavalry regiment in February 1644. Although aged around sixty, Vaughan was an active, able and sometimes ruthless cavalry and field commander. With his regiment, he was based and frequently campaigned in and around Shropshire into 1646.

Vaughan is depicted dressed as a typical well-equipped cavalryman of the period, wearing a lobster pott helmet and further protected by a leather buff coat, with decorative metallic lace on the sleeves befitting his rank, worn under a steel breast and backplate. Vaughan's was regarded as one of the best regiments of horse in the Royalist army, and so his charging troopers in the background are shown similarly well accoutred.

Nothing is yet known of the uniform worn by the Parliamentary Shropshire forces, and so although 'grey' clothing - representing the various hues of undyed wool - was widely worn on both sides, the grey coats of the foot soldiers depicted here fleeing before the Royalists are conjectural.

5. Francis (later Sir Francis) Ottley (1600/01-1649), depicted in a pre-war family portrait. Shropshire's leading Royalist, Ottley throughout the First Civil War was an active supporter of King Charles I as an administrator and soldier. However, his capture together with other local Royalists by Parliamentary forces at Dawley Castle in July 1648 soon ended Ottley's involvement in the Second Civil War. (© Shropshire Council/Shropshire Museums)

6. As Parliament's major-general for North Wales from June 1643, Sir Thomas Myddelton (1586-1666) with his brigade was significantly involved in the fighting in and around Shropshire during the First Civil War. (© National Trust Images)

7. The impact scar of a cannon ball above a now blocked north door at St Mary and St. Bartholomew's, Tong, is evidence of the Royalist assault on the Parliamentarian garrison occupying the church in April 1644.

8. The probably originally fourteenth-century gatehouse at Moreton Corbet Castle, with the Elizabethan range partly visible in the background. During the First Civil War Moreton Corbet served both sides as an important garrison. Strategically situated between Parliamentarian Wem and Royalist Shrewsbury, the castle exchanged hands on four occasions.

9. View from the castle mound at Shrawardine across the site of the inner bailey towards the likely remains of the Civil War outer defensive earthworks (crowned by trees in the middle of the photograph). Shrawardine Castle was a Royalist garrison that fell to the Parliamentarians after a short siege in June 1645. It was slighted, or dismantled, soon after.

10. The probable site of the battle of Montgomery. Fought on 18 September 1644 just over the Shropshire border with Wales, Montgomery was the largest engagement in both the Principality and the Shropshire region during the First Civil War. A resounding Parliamentarian victory, the battle had damaging repercussions for the Royalist war effort in Shropshire and elsewhere in the Welsh borderlands.

17. Photographed during archaeological excavation, a Civil-War period coin hoard discovered in south Shropshire. Money may have been hoarded and hidden to evade wartime taxation or as a safeguard against plundering soldiers. (Courtesy of Peter Reavill/© the Portable Antiquities Scheme)

committee-room debate. A joint appeal from Wem on 21 October 1643 by Sir Thomas Myddelton and Sir William Brereton soliciting the Commons for a grant of £3,000 resulted some five weeks later in the formation of a Parliamentary committee, including the Shropshire MPs, tasked with procuring £2,000 for Myddelton.[94] Lobbying by this committee eventually secured additional financial powers for the major-general, by way of an ordinance enacted on 21 February 1644.[95] There was no guarantee, however, that funds granted at Westminster would be paid quickly or in full. Payment was referred to Parliament's executive committees, which raised money largely on credit and advanced it in installments, a protracted process necessitating lobbying on the recipients' behalf. As a case in point, after the report of the capture of Shrewsbury was read in the Commons on 27 February 1645 a grateful House pledged £4,000 from excise receipts to the committee of Shropshire, but the onus of securing payment from the excise commissioners was firmly placed on three committeemen in London, Thomas Nicolls and the MPs Pierrepont and Corbet. But almost a year later half of the grant remained unpaid, so on 8 January 1646 an ordinance was passed

94 HMC, *Thirteenth Report, Appendix Part I*, pp. 134-5; *JHC*, III, p. 321, 27 Nov. 1643.
95 *JHL*, VI, pp. 424-5.

directing the commissioners to release the remaining funds.[96]

The difficulties the Parliamentarians faced in funding war effort in Shropshire were therefore threefold: firstly, the county committee initially operated in exile and so was restricted in implementing Parliament's pecuniary levies; secondly, once established in Shropshire the Parliamentarians had to contest revenues with the Royalists; and thirdly, reliance could not be placed on subsidies from London.

The finances of Sir Thomas Myddelton, the Earl of Denbigh's West Midland Association and the committee of Shropshire will now be considered in turn. Parliament's cause in Shropshire was also partly funded by Sir William Brereton, who subsidised the Cheshire forces serving in the county and in later 1645 also funded the Shropshire forces operating around Chester.[97] However, Brereton's finances are not considered here on the grounds of space, and also because his war effort was firmly focused on Cheshire.

Sir Thomas Myddelton's finances

Funding Sir Thomas Myddelton's objective of recovering the six counties of North Wales for Parliament would also assist the recovery of Shropshire. Therefore, two days after Parliament's authorisation of Myddelton's commission as major-general, on 14 June 1643 the Earl of Essex pressed the Committee of Safety to relieve 'the distressed and miserable condition of the county of Salop and parts adjacent' by hastening the despatch from London of forces led jointly by Myddelton and the Shropshire committeemen. Meanwhile, in order to help finance this expeditionary force the Earl ordered the sequestration of the timber yard at Hammersmith owned by the Royalist merchant and ship-owner Sir Nicholas Crisp.[98] On 13 June 1644 Myddelton's appointment to the enlarged sequestration committee for Shropshire gave him an executive say in financing the war there.[99] Emboldened by this mandate and Sir Thomas's leading role on 2 July in breaking the Royalist siege of Oswestry, in mid-July his supporters at Westminster sought a Commons vote to commit for the maintenance of Myddelton's forces for the duration of the war rental sequestered from the estates of Lord Newport and his son Sir Francis, the MP and Royalist officer who had been captured in the fighting for Oswestry. However, by 19 July this fiscal coup attempted on Myddelton's behalf had been blocked, by the Earl of Denbigh's supporters in Parliament and by Sir John Corbet acting to protect the interests of the county committee.[100]

The episode showed that competition for scarce financial resources could provoke conflicts of interest amongst the Parliamentarians in the Shropshire theatre of war. A year earlier, however, Sir Thomas Myddelton had embarked on his major-generalship with a degree of financial self-determination. Although his commission empowered him to tax Royalist-controlled North Wales it was clearly impossible to do so, or for Myddelton to gather revenue from his Denbighshire estates. However, the

96 *JHC*, IV, p. 64; *JHL*, VIII, pp. 91-2.
97 *LBWB*, II, p. 204.
98 WRO, CR2017/C9, f. 5.
99 *JHL*, VI, pp. 586-7.
100 WRO, CR2017/C10, ff. 14-15, 18.

previous generation of the wider Myddelton family, being ambitious entrepreneurs, had established themselves as land-owning merchant adventurers, manufacturers and financiers in London and south-eastern England.[101] This enabled Sir Thomas by drawing on credit via the Myddelton's mercantile and political connections topped up from his and the wider family's wealth soon to advance £5,000 towards his war effort, which the Commons pledged to underwrite from sequestration revenues.[102] Myddelton used this money to recruit the few soldiers and to purchase the military supplies and artillery train with which he arrived at Nantwich in August 1643, and which sustained his participation in the campaign for Wem in September and October and in the abortive offensive in partnership with Sir William Brereton into north-east Wales in November.[103] By early October, however, Myddelton's borrowings were spent. Moreover, he was no longer considered creditworthy because the Committee of Safety had failed to reimburse his lenders; as the Commons acknowledged in early January 1644, just £1,000 of Myddelton's £5,000 capital had been repaid.[104]

The ordinance of 21 February 1644 revived Myddelton's war effort by consolidating his fiscal powers with the objective of financing a fresh brigade for six months. It allowed the major-general to solicit for subscriptions and to appoint officials to implement the four main national imposts introduced by Parliament during 1643, namely the assessment, the sequestration ordinance, the fifth and twentieth part and the excise. But given Myddelton's strategic situation, these powers for the most part were effective only in writing. It was little more than Parliamentary bluster to demand, by way of the assessment re-enacted on 2 August 1643, a weekly levy of £175 from North Wales. (This did, however, set a precedent for levying arrears in the future). However, Myddelton also gained practical dispensations: he eventually received £1,500 from the New River Company, a venture his late uncle Sir Hugh had pioneered thirty years previously to supply London with fresh water; and the right to retain up to £3,000 from any unaccounted revenues from sequestration he could discover in and around the capital within a month of the ordinance.[105]

Sir Thomas Myddelton's accounts record receipts up to his relinquishment of the major-generalship in June 1645.[106] These show that in addition to the first advance of £5,000 his war effort was financed to the total of £22,179. This seems mostly to have been the funding for the second brigade, from its raising in London in early 1644, to its deployment, from May, into Staffordshire and Shropshire, and from September into Montgomeryshire. However, the overall cost of Myddelton's war effort was undoubtedly much higher, because his accounts omit monies volunteered or gathered by officers of his brigade. Captain Hercules Hannay, for one, who served under Myddelton during 1644, later certified the payment out of his own pocket of

101 *ODNB*, 40, pp. 44-7, 50-3; Anon., 'The Myddelton Family of Denbighshire', *The Cheshire Sheaf*, 2nd Series, I (1895), pp. 114-15, 118-19, 144-6.
102 *JHC*, III, p. 278, 17 Oct. 1643; *JHC*, III, p. 361, 8 Jan. 1644.
103 Malbon, *Memorials*, p. 72.
104 HMC, *Thirteenth Report, Appendix Part I*, pp. 134-5; *JHC*, III, p. 361, 8 Jan. 1644.
105 *JHL*, VI, pp. 424-5, 164.
106 TNA, SP28/139 Part 18, f. 203.

almost £325 towards the maintenance of his troop of horse.[107]

According to his accounts, Myddelton's war effort was funded mostly by sequestration and subscriptions. Sequestration provided most, generating almost £11,000. This included £804 taken from the fund for repairs to St. Paul's Cathedral that King Charles had sponsored before the war, a seizure sanctioned by the House of Commons on 30 September 1644, while the largest sum, eventually amounting to £2,000, came from the estates of the recently deceased Lady Jane Shelley, heiress of the Catholic Shelley family of Sussex.[108] Subscriptions generated the second largest amount, £7,425 in all, from monies volunteered under the original terms of the Propositions or otherwise coerced as fifth and twentieth part fines. Myddelton's agents gathered his subscriptions mostly from the Parliamentarian heartlands of London, the Home Counties and East Anglia. Furthermore, in February and again in June 1644, Myddelton benefitted from support at Westminster, when the Commons issued appeals to ministers across London to urge their congregations to volunteer subscriptions to fund Myddelton's recovery of North Wales.[109]

Sir Thomas also gained money from small Parliamentary grants and by individual loans, while ransom payments generated nearly £140. Several county committees between them gave £314, including £50 from Shropshire, but only two of the six Welsh counties of his command contributed directly to Myddelton's exchequer – £157 from the committee of Montgomeryshire and a paltry £6 from Merionethshire. Finally, there was £350-worth of 'fines and compositions', £300 of which came, it seems, from the townsfolk of Whitchurch in Shropshire. This was probably a one-off emergency communal contribution to forestall plundering, similar to that paid in June 1644 by the inhabitants of Oswestry who reportedly gave £500 to appease the Parliamentarian soldiers who had captured the town.[110]

Financing the West Midland Association

An undated memorandum emanating from Parliament around the time of the Earl of Denbigh's commission as general in June 1643 foresaw the need for his Association to be put on a sound financial footing.[111] Detailing the support to be accorded him as was customary for a commander-in-chief, it noted:

> A considerable army [of the Association] may upon any occasion be put into a body and maintained at the charge of those counties where the contributions being to be levied […] it will be necessary to have some foundation to put such ordinances of Parliament in execution, as may conduce to the maintaining of the army.

However, the Earl was unable adequately to fund a unified army and thereby strengthen Parliament's position in Shropshire. Indeed, Denbigh's inability to impose financial control over the West Midland Association was in stark contrast to the

---

107 TNA, SP28/41 Part 4, ff. 472-3, 476, 480, 483.
108 *JHL*, VII, p. 4; G.E. Cokayne (ed.), *Complete Baronetage*, 5 vols. (Exeter, 1900), I, p. 25; *JHC*, III, p. 424.
109 *CSPD, 1644*, p. 661; *JHC*, III, pp. 405, 538-9.
110 *Two Great Victories*, unpaginated.
111 WRO CR2017/C9, f. 8.

Earl of Manchester's Eastern Association during 1644, the exemplar of a fiscally well-organised Parliamentarian army. With the support of allies in both Houses, Manchester was, in Holmes's words, 'given the opportunity to create a centralised fiscal and military administration'. In accordance with an ordinance of 20 January 1644, the counties of the Eastern Association relinquished their financial independence to a standing committee with a central treasury at Cambridge, which in turn was superintended by the Association's Parliamentary committee at Westminster and also by Manchester himself.[112]

Denbigh meanwhile had little fiscal authority over his Association other than the deference he might expect as general. As Holmes concluded: 'Denbigh strove to secure some measure of central control […] but was unable to tap the financial resources of the area ostensibly subject to his command'.[113] Denbigh's commission did not address fiscal matters, apart from vaguely pointing to his powers as lord lieutenant of Warwickshire.[114] With its authority derived from the royal prerogative rather than Parliamentary statute, the lieutenancy was in any case an uncertain platform from which to finance war effort. Lacking licence to levy money on his own initiative or by Parliamentary ordinance, the Earl did seek financial powers. A draft ordinance to enable his execution of Parliament's main imposts within the West Midland Association was read in the Commons on 30 October 1643, and on 2 November referred to a committee including Sir John Corbet and Richard More.[115] By December Denbigh sought to hasten the ordinance, writing to More on the 1st to press the Commons for 'the same honour and power which they have conferred upon others of my quality employed in matters of the same nature'.[116] But over the following weeks debate instead revolved around Denbigh's acrimonious relationship with the county committee of Warwickshire, rather than his hoped-for empowering ordinance. As Hughes has shown, although in spring 1644 Denbigh once more pressed his allies at Westminster to secure powers for him like those of the Earl of Manchester, neither this nor another attempt by Denbigh that August came to fruition.[117]

While Denbigh lacked sustained support across both Houses, his Association was not militarily robust enough for Parliamentary taxation to be effectively implemented there. The Eastern Association, on the other hand, had benefited since its formation in December 1642 by remaining for the most part firmly under Parliamentarian control, allowing Cambridgeshire, Norfolk, Suffolk, Essex and Hertfordshire consistently to provide revenue. Similarly, when a South-Eastern Association was re-enacted in November 1643, although, like Denbigh, its commander Sir William Waller lacked financial powers, tax-raising committees were at least assigned to his support, in Hampshire, Sussex, Surrey and Kent.[118] However, as has been seen, much of the West Midland Association was contested territory, so that by the end of 1643

112 Holmes, *Eastern Association*, pp. 119, 122, 130-1.
113 Ibid., p. 1.
114 *JHL*, VI, p. 92, 12 June 1643; WRO CR2017/C9, f. 7.
115 *JHC*, III, pp. 295, 298-9.
116 BDL, Tanner Mss 62, f. 402.
117 Hughes, *Warwickshire*, p. 232; *JHL*, VI, pp. 652-4.
118 *A&O*, I, pp. 333-9.

Parliamentarian administrations were firmly established in only Staffordshire and Warwickshire

Denbigh understandably hoped to rely on the successful Parliamentarian organisation in Warwickshire. However, in early September 1643 the county committee saw their fiscal arrangements endangered by the arrival in Coventry from London of the nucleus of Denbigh's Association forces – several hundred foot, a few troops of horse and some gunners.[119] Frustrated by the Earl's prolonged stay in London, within weeks the county committee tired of subsidising his men. Disregarding Denbigh's instructions to them to care for his soldiers until his arrival, the committee instead unilaterally ordered their disbandment. In a letter to the Earl dated 16 October they justified their action, describing Denbigh's men as 'burthensome to our small treasury […] the [established] diverse garrisons being as many as the county can well bear'.[120] Localism shaped the Warwickshiremen's stance: 'nor did we believe your lordship meant them a sole charge to this county', they added, 'who we considered came down for the service of the Association'. The incident set the tone for the Earl's vitriolic relationship with the committee of Warwickshire, and he was undoubtedly right in thinking that they saw themselves as the reluctant 'purse bearers of the Association'.[121] The committee continued – albeit because of their own necessity – to deny Denbigh the regular revenues from Warwickshire, which instead maintained the county forces. In May 1644 the Earl complained to the Committee of Both Kingdoms that this situation was the main cause of his financial plight and a justification for additional powers.[122] Denbigh received some support from the county committee at Stafford, who in June 1644 permitted him to levy £20 from each of Staffordshire's administrative divisions.[123] But by mid-July just £500 of the anticipated £2,000 had been collected, although faltering efforts to collect the arrears continued into winter 1644-5.[124]

The Earl's attempts to gather revenue elsewhere in his Association met with little success. Some money was raised from northerly Worcestershire, although in doing so Denbigh quarreled with his subordinate Colonel John Fox, who from his base at Edgbaston Hall near Birmingham was already taxing the same area.[125] Turning to Shropshire, although Denbigh taxed the enclave of Halesowen there seems no evidence that he attempted to tax the county proper.[126] Here, as elsewhere, the state of the relationship between commander-in-chief and county committee determined their financial cooperation. In July 1643, during the honeymoon period after Denbigh's appointment, six leading Shropshire committeemen had joined with him to underwrite £1,000 as surety for £2,000 loaned by a wealthy Parliamentarian supporter. On 20 February 1644 William Crowne, Denbigh's secretary and agent, serviced the loan, paying £40 to the lender as 'the interest of £1,000 for three months borrowed

119 Hughes, *Warwickshire*, pp. 181-2; TNA, SP28/131 Part 12, *passim*; SP28/34 Part 2, f. 291, undated memorandum by William Crowne.
120 WRO CR2017/C9, ff. 31, 33.
121 BDL, Tanner Mss 62, f. 456, Denbigh to the committee of Warwickshire, Coventry, 15 Dec. 1643.
122 *CSPD, 1644*, pp. 161-2.
123 WRO CR2017/C9, f. 122; TNA, SP28/242 Part 3, f. 457, Madeley parish accounts, Aug. 1644.
124 WRO CR2017/C10, f. 14; Pennington and Roots, *Committee at Stafford*, p. 242.
125 *CSPD, 1644*, pp. 161-2; WRO CR2017/C9, ff. 58, 76a.
126 TNA, SP28/174 Part 1, unfoliated, arrears in Halesowen, undated.

by his Lordship and the Shropshire gents'.[127] That summer, however, the relationship between general and committee had soured. Consequently the committeemen made little or no attempt, despite the House having entrusted them with doing so, to fulfill the Commons' pledge of 28 June for £1,000, together with 600 pistols, to be provided for Denbigh's soldiers as reward for their success at Oswestry. Although in the meantime and with some backing in the Lords William Crowne had lobbied on Denbigh's behalf, neither cash nor firearms had been supplied when the matter briefly resurfaced in the upper chamber in mid-November.[128]

On 20 June 1643 the Commons had reported how the Earl of Denbigh had obtained 'credits and securities' to raise £6,000, which Parliament would underwrite and repay from that December. This sum with funds gathered within the West Midland Association was expected to allow the Earl to raise horse and foot as the mainstay of a field army.[129] However, two years later, on 2 July 1645, Denbigh submitted for audit personal accounts showing revenues amounting to just £5,328.[130] Of this, £440 was obtained from small donations, forced loans and minor acts of sequestration. The remaining £4,888 had been raised on credit, of which the London-based Treasurers of Sequestration had reimbursed £2,478.[131] The Earl later feared that as a result his estates and family jewellery would be 'either lost, or eat themselves out with interest'. The extent of Denbigh's reliance on credit raised against his assets, although demonstrating a considerable personal commitment, revealed the underlying fiscal weakness of the West Midland Association as an organisation.[132] Yet in early September 1644 a London newsbook had commended Denbigh's military achievements amid financial adversity: 'He hath never had pay for his soldiers, yet he hath done better service for nothing, than some others that have spent the country 100,000 pounds'.[133]

The finances of the Committee of Shropshire
Fiscal expediency, 1643-4

Without the hold on Shropshire that from 1646 to 1648 enabled it to put Parliament's imposts more fully into effect, the county committee for at least the first two years of the conflict relied mostly on financial expediency and personal contributions. The leading committeemen collectively were not a conspicuously wealthy body, their financial circumstances varying considerably. Nonetheless, and despite their financial interests in Shropshire being threatened by Royalist sequestration, they managed to raise money on credit – as in the example of the joint loan with the Earl of Denbigh. In writing to William Lenthall, the Speaker of the Commons, in July 1644 the committeemen acknowledged their dependence on loans. They may also have continued to receive clandestinely some revenue from their Shropshire lands, as suggested by a Royalist

127 NLW, Aston Hall Estate Records D1 Mss, 2148; TNA, SP28/131 Part 12, irregular foliation.
128 *JHC*, III, p. 545; WRO CR2017/C10, f. 15; *JHL*, VII, pp. 23, 64.
129 *JHC*, III, pp. 137-8; WRO CR2017/C9, f. 8.
130 *JHL*, VII, pp. 589-90.
131 Cited in the Lords by the Committee for taking the Accounts of the Whole Kingdom on 20 Sept. 1645, these figures are verified by an undated note – 'Balance of the Earl of Denbigh's debt' – in the Commonwealth Exchequer Papers: TNA, SP28/34 Part 2, f. 290.
132 *JHL*, VII, p. 590.
133 *The Scottish Dove*, 20 Aug.-6 Sept. 1644, p. 376.

initiative in October 1643 to call to account the factors of Thomas Mytton's estates.[134] Although it is unknowable to what extent the committeemen personally funded their war effort, the ordinance of 13 June 1644 pointed out that they had raised forces 'at their own charges'.[135] Mytton, for example, was in early 1646 still obliged to take out a personal loan of more than £400 to pay his garrison at Oswestry. Like the committeemen, other officers also contributed to the cause and provided for their soldiers. For example, in April 1645 a gentleman preparing to serve in Shropshire as an officer under Myttton pledged £400 to the war effort.[136]

The committee of Shropshire also sought to obtain revenue from a broader body of contributors. Donations made by Salopians under the Propositions during 1642 were absorbed into the wider nascent Parliamentarian war effort. However, eight days after the introduction of fifth and twentieth part fines, on 15 May 1643 a Commons committee including Sir Thomas Myddelton and the MPs More and Pierrepont was tasked with calling to account defaulters of subscriptions for Shropshire.[137] The ordinance that embodied the committee of Shropshire that April had required the preparation of rolls, listing the 'names, and surnames and places of abode of every person charged', enabling the committee to solicit subscriptions from expatriate Salopians – those exiled by the conflict or otherwise residing elsewhere – and perhaps also from likely contributors remaining in the Royalist-controlled shire.[138] In mid-1644 the county committee also received a windfall donation from the estate of Daniel Oxenbridge, a merchant who had willed £1,000 to Parliament. Accordingly, on 28 June the Commons directed Oxenbridge's executors to pay the first tranche of £500 to William Spurstowe, MP, on behalf of the committee.[139]

The committee of Shropshire's other main source of revenue during 1643 and 1644 was sequestration, mostly by seizing cash and portable assets. This varied from small sums, like the £50 taken from a Catholic Royalist officer that the Commons on 14 April 1643 ordered to be paid to Sir John Corbet for the purchase of arms, to the probably much larger amount generated as a result of the Commons on 1 March 1644 permitting the London-based committeemen to sell by public auction appropriated goods belonging to the Herefordshire Royalist James, Viscount Scudamore. Furthermore, in a dispensation similar to that granted to Sir Thomas Myddelton in February 1644, the ordinance of 13 June enabled the committee for four months to sequester hitherto undiscovered enemy assets found in and around London to the value of £3,000.[140]

Other financial expedients embraced by Shropshire's committeemen included a proposal in May 1643 to secure credit against revenue from the Welsh cloth trade, and an initiative that October to revive the powers of the Coquet Office – the customs house of the port of London. Merchants who supported this proposal were prepared

---

134 HMC, *Sixth Report, Part I*, p. 19; NAM, 8812-63, f. 2.
135 *JHL*, VI, p. 586.
136 BDL, Tanner Mss 60, f. 461; NAM, 8812-63, f. 6.
137 *JHC*, III, p. 86.
138 *A&O*, I, p. 127.
139 *JHC*, III, pp. 545; NLW, Sweeney Hall Mss A1, f. 25.
140 *JHC*, III, pp. 44, 412; *JHL*, VI, p. 586.

to pay an administrative levy of 2s per transaction to obtain the Office's seal as verification of legal trading and the payment of appropriate duties.[141]

The Assessment

Levied in each county as a widespread military tax, the weekly or monthly assessment became a long-standing Parliamentary impost, and eventually the largest single source of funding for Parliamentarian and the later Commonwealth armies. Since its introduction in February 1643, Shropshire's weekly share of the assessment had been set at £375.[142] But then and later this was an impossible target and more a commitment of Parliament's intent. Towards that year's end, two committeemen wrote from Wem that 'the country refuse to pay any money', expressing the impracticability of administering Parliamentary taxation at that time in the county war.[143] Although Parliament had designed the assessment to be paid into the central treasury at London's Guildhall, instead the proceeds mostly remained in the shires, where the committees used what they collected as a regular source of funding for local forces. This was the case in Shropshire during 1644 and into 1646, where the weekly assessment was levied upon allotments assigned to a particular Parliamentarian garrison or unit, as the following examples suggest. By autumn 1644 the allotment of Stoke, lying within north Bradford hundred, was allocated to the garrison of the fortified manor house at Stoke upon Tern. Similarly, from April to November 1645 Captain King's was one of five companies of foot paid out of the assessment of the allotments comprising the town and liberties of Shrewsbury. The garrison of Oswestry meanwhile levied the assessment from allotments within the hundreds of Oswestry and Pimhill.[144]

The account books of captains of foot King and Farrington provide insight into the working of the assessment in Shropshire.[145] Some comparisons with the Royalist contribution can also be drawn from the three-monthly interim accounts, for July to September 1644, surviving from a handful of townships in Shrewsbury liberties which were later assigned to King's and Farrington's companies (Table 9). The Parliamentarians also taxed each township at a monthly rate in the pound according to land and property ownership. Thus the evaluation of Astley – a township four miles north-east of Shrewsbury assigned to Farrington from mid-November 1645 to February 1646 – would have been £181 10s, derived from rating 25 wealthier inhabitants who between them paid the monthly sixpenny rate of £4 11s 8d. The wealthiest area assigned to King during summer 1645 was Stoneward, the southerly ward of Shrewsbury. Here, 172 townsfolk contributed to a monthly levy of £29 8s 3d at the sixpenny rate, hence Stoneward's assessment can be calculated as £1,176 10s. Both captains calculated their assessment on a monthly basis, although King's collectors had leeway to collect the 'several sums […] charged and assessed monthly, weekly or otherwise'.

141 *JHC*, III, p. 86, 15 May 1643; *JHC*, III, p. 278, 17 Oct. 1643.
142 *A&O*, I, p. 87.
143 WRO, CR2017/C9, f. 37.
144 TNA, SP28/242 Part 2, f. 300, Capt. Hungerford's accounts; TNA, SP28/242 Part 2, Capt. King's account book; BDL Tanner Mss 60, f. 461.
145 TNA, SP28/174 Part 1, Capt. Farrington's account book; SP28/242 Part 2, Capt. King's account book.

Townships	Royalist valuation, summer 1644	Royalist percentage collected, 4d rate	Parliamentary valuation, June1645–February 1646	Parliamentary valuation, April-June 1646	Parliamentary percentage collected, 6d rate
Acton Reynald	£209	77%	£216	£151	95%
Albright Hussey & Battlefield	£101	Unknowable	£100	£100	95%
Betton, Sutton, Alkmere & Longner	£477	Unknowable	£477	Unknown	22%
Great Berwick	£151	Unknowable	Unknown	£147	65%
Harlescott	£151	78%	Unknown	£136	67%
Haston	£86	100%	£90	£51	75%
Smethcott	£115	79%	£75	£54	88%

Table 9: Analysis of contribution and assessment paid by townships within the liberties of Shrewsbury, 1644-6.[146] Calculations rounded to the nearest £.

Table 9 suggests that the Parliamentarian assessment at first tended to adopt the same valuations that the Royalists had calculated to levy contribution. Reevaluation, however, was the most likely reason for the reduction of the levy in 1646 on three of the five townships for which there is comparative data. In June 1645 the assessment was being revised in the Shrewsbury area at least, and by the end of the year the county committee was overseeing a countywide reevaluation.[147] Table 9 also implies that given a favourable military situation both sides could achieve respectable collection rates. Captain King gathered 63% of the £575 assigned to him for June to November 1645, while Captain Farrington collected 72% of the £520 allotted to his company from mid-November 1645 until June 1646. Furthermore, both captains also received subsidies from the county committee's treasury. From the date of his commission, 2 April 1645, until 2 July following when he began to levy the assessment, King was allocated £6 weekly for his and his officers' pay, of which he received just over half. Farrington fared better, receiving £206 in several cash payments, and the committee paid his company in full for February/March 1646. Overall, Farrington's accounts show that his company received much of their pay. This may reflect an improvement in the county committee's finances from late 1645 and into 1646, resulting from a more pragmatic approach to taxation (widespread reassessment providing a realistic appraisal of what the county could deliver), and greater opportunity for collection and enforcement as the Parliamentarians gained control over much of Shropshire.

146 Sources: TNA, SP28/242 Part 2, Capt. King's accounts; SP28/174 Part 1, Capt. Farrington's accounts; SA, 3365/224, unfoliated.
147 SA, P250/Fiche 326, Churchwardens' accounts of the parish of the Holy Cross, 1645/6; *LBWB*, II, pp. 420-1.

Indeed, the Parliamentarian military – in contrast to the Royalists – appears to have been directly involved in tax administration and collection. Captains King and Farrington were responsible for gathering and accounting their allotted assessment. King's five collectors were authorised to enforce distraint, and at least three of them were officers in his militia company. In November 1645 the committee at Shrewsbury acknowledged their reliance on military enforcement to gather the assessment, when complaining to Sir William Brereton about the prolonged deployment of many of the Shropshire Horse around Chester: 'The want of our men is extremely prejudicial to our own country', the committeemen admitted, 'which hinders us of that contribution that otherwise would have been fore-gotten [i.e. collected previously]'.[148] Once a unit was allocated the assessment from a particular allotment it regarded the territory as its fiefdom, and would be mindful of the revenue accordingly. Hence, in October 1645 the Shropshire Horse complained that because of their prolonged absence on campaign receipts of money from the districts allotted to them were diminishing.[149] The quarrel between Colonel Mytton and the committee at Shrewsbury over soldiers' pay and allocation of assessment revenue flared up in February 1646 as a territorial dispute, when rival troops of horse from Oswestry and Shrewsbury collecting the assessment in the same parts of northerly Shropshire confronted each other in an armed standoff at Ellesmere.[150] The continued active involvement of the Parliamentarian military in the collection of the assessment during 1647 and 1648 is suggested by the example of the experience of Worfield, a parish centred on the village three and a half miles north-east of Bridgnorth. Here, on several occasions, the parishioners had to provide food and lodging for soldiers come to collect the assessment before it was due.[151]

In June 1647 Parliament re-enacted the monthly assessment, intending to reclaim the tax as a national levy to finance the New Model Army and the war in Ireland. However, the ongoing political and fiscal crisis over army pay and soldiers' arrears led to two national ordinances being passed on 24 December 1647 which gave tacit approval for assessment revenue to be allocated to the disbandment of the remaining supernumerary county forces and to the pay of regional garrisons.[152] To retain some control over the tax and prevent its dissipation at local level, Parliament the previous day had appointed audit commissioners for each shire, those for Shropshire being the recruiter MPs Colonel Robert Clive, Sir Humphrey Briggs and Esau Thomas. The Westminster-based Committee of the Army, acting on behalf of the Treasurers at War, also appointed regional superintendents including one Robert Baddeley, the committee's agent for bringing in the assessment in Shropshire and Montgomeryshire during 1648.[153]

During 1647 and 1648 Shropshire's monthly assessment was £554, proportionately 37 per cent of the sum demanded by the weekly assessment in 1643. The levy was

148 BRL, Additional Mss 11332, f. 94.
149 *LBWB*, II, pp. 184-5.
150 BDL, Tanner Mss 60, ff. 444, 461; *CSPD, 1645-1646*, p. 359; *The Scottish Dove*, 26 Feb.-4 Mar. 1646, pp. 582-3.
151 SA, P314/M/1, ff. 40-1.
152 Wheeler, *World Power*, pp. 189-91; *A&O*, I, pp. 1048-9, 1053-4.
153 TNA, SP28/50 Part 3, f. 467, Papers of the Committee of the Army.

apportioned to the county's 100 allotments, including the town of Ludlow, assessed to pay £5 13s monthly as one allotment.[154] Papers of the Committee of the Army provide a probably incomplete record of how Shropshire's assessment was disbursed during 1648, payments reflecting the changing priorities Parliament confronted that year, from back pay and disbandment, to sustaining forces during the Second Civil War. During the political turmoil of 1647 much of the assessment nationally went unpaid, although a forceful final demand for Ludlow to pay arrears by 10 August suggests that Shropshire's commissioners collected the tax with some vigour.[155] By February 1648 the commissioners were able to authorise payment of £2,000 from Shropshire's assessment towards the disbandment of two regiments in Herefordshire.[156] Furthermore, from March 1648 to February 1649 Shropshire contributed at least £2,100 to the pay of Colonel Robert Duckenfield's Cheshire-based Regiment of Foot. Upwards of £400 was also paid to the standing garrisons in Wales, at the Red Castle, Denbigh, Conway and Caernarvon.[157] In addition, in July 1648 the county committee imposed an ad-hoc levy across Shropshire to fund the additional troop of horse raised to counter the Royalist insurgency. At £10 10s, each allotment was charged double the monthly army assessment. Alternatively, an allotment could make payment in kind by providing a horse, with tack and arms, and one month's pay for a trooper. The levy was extended into August and re-enacted in November to raise additional disbandment money.[158] It is unclear whether at this time the monthly army assessment was suspended or was appropriated for the county's use.

Finally in this examination of Parliamentarian assessments, Shropshire seems to have remained exempted from the ordinances enacted from 1644 to provide for Lord Leven's Scots army while it served in England allied to Parliament. However, Shropshire did contribute to national assessment ordinances in 1644 and 1648 to fund Parliamentary forces campaigning in Ireland. The ordinance of 18 October 1644 demanded £62 10s per week from the county for 12 months for the 'British Army in Ireland'. When it was re-enacted on 17 February 1648, Shropshire had to pay almost £185 monthly for six months towards a national monthly total of £20,000.[159] Wheeler concluded that during 1644 and 1645 this tax was collected very irregularly, and this appears to have been so in Shropshire, for in February 1646 the Committee of Both Kingdoms instructed the county committee to make greater effort in collecting arrears.[160] The 1648 assessment for the Irish war was being enforced in Shropshire by April when rates were being calculated in the Shrewsbury area, while on the 10th the county committee demanded that Ludlow pay the current levy and also imposed arrears from 1645 and 1646, when the town was Royalist controlled.[161]

154 *A&O*, I, pp. 959, 1109; SA, LB7/1946.
155 Wheeler, *World Power*, pp. 113, 189; SA, LB7/1946.
156 TNA, SP28/50 Part 1, f. 81, Part 3, ff. 309-10, Papers of the Committee of the Army.
157 C. Firth, *The Regimental History of Cromwell's Army*, (Cranbury, 2006), p. xxiv; Papers of the Committee of the Army: SP28/52 Part 1, f. 21; SP28/55 Part 1, ff. 15, 17, 21, 23, 39, Part 2, ff. 339, 406; SP28/58 Part 4, f. 550.
158 SA, LB7/1936-7, 1943-4.
159 *A&O*, I, pp. 553, 1074.
160 Wheeler, *World Power*, p. 181; *CSPD, 1645-1647*, p. 360.
161 SA, P250/Fiche 328; SA, LB7/1933.

Sequestration and Compounding

Sequestration varied in both form and degree. In 1643 and 1644 the committee of Shropshire benefited from windfalls and chance seizures of enemy property and cash. Systematic Parliamentarian sequestration embraced the financial management of businesses and landed estates, entailing the collection of rental income and the leasing and sub-letting of assets to third parties.[162] Sequestration was part of a wider regime of financial punishment imposed on Parliament's enemies that embraced appropriation, loans forced under the Propositions or the fifth and twentieth part or composition fines. By August 1644 the Parliamentarians were applying these penalties to levy income from the north Shropshire estates around Wem of the Royalist exile Robert Howard, Earl of Arundel. His tenants' rents were sequestrated under the pretext of the Earl's obligations under the fifth and twentieth part, and his woodland was felled and the timber sold for profit.[163] This appears to be the earliest evidence of methodical Parliamentarian sequestration in Shropshire, supporting Humphrey Mackworth's contention in 1649 to the London-based Committee of Compounding, that it was not until mid-1644 that the county committee had been able to impose sequestration to any significant effect. Even so, the Parliamentarians' reach had been limited to northerly Shropshire and to suspected Royalists like Sir Arthur Mainwaring, who in November 1644 was assessed to pay £400, his manor at Ightfield lying discomfortingly close to the Parliamentarian garrisons at Wem and Stoke upon Tern.[164]

Victories during 1645 and 1646 resulted in the consolidation of Parliament's authority over previously contested territory, enabling a concomitant increase in the imposition of fines and sequestrations. Shropshire reflected the prevailing national situation. Valuations for sequestrations in the Shrewsbury area were being prepared during August 1645, with the result that in 1646 Captain Farrington's monthly assessment included rents and tithes sequestered by the county committee from the estates of Royalist gentry.[165] By June 1645 the properties of Sir Basil Brooke, a Royalist activist and notable Catholic, were within reach of sequestration by the Parliamentarian garrison at Benthall Hall near the absent Brooke's estates at Madeley, where lay his coalmines and iron works. On 9 June – the day after the Parliamentarian victory near Stokesay in south Shropshire – the Benthall garrison seized the works and more than £600-worth of stock. Acting under the direction of the committee at Shrewsbury, two captains of the Benthall garrison managed the iron works until the end of the year, when it was handed over to the Staffordshire ironmaster Richard Foley. Brooke's coalmines were also sequestrated, and for the next four years let on one-year leases and exploited for short-term profit.[166] Accordingly, in 1650 one local master collier despondently related how the pits, denied investment, had fallen into disrepair: 'Much wrong was done to the said works since they came into Parliament's possession […] to gain from what they can out of the said works for their satisfaction,

162 Morrill, *Revolt*, p. 111.
163 HMC, *Sixth Report, Part I*, p. 25.
164 *CPCC*, I, p. 157; *CPCM*, I, p. 486.
165 SA, P250/Fiche 326; SP28/174 Part 1, Capt. Farrington's accounts.
166 SP23/105, ff. 199, 201, 209, 225.

though to the destruction of the same'.[167]

Other Shropshire Royalists suffered similar punitive measures, among them Sir William Whitmore. Between December 1646 and October 1647 sequestration agents made at least five inspections of Whitmore's estate at Apley in order to compile the detailed inventories that in early 1648 allowed the sale of £583-worth of goods, from which £116 was deducted as Whitmore's payment of the fifth part. The sequestrators also sub-let his land and received the rental. At this time the county committee for safety seems to have employed a permanent staff of three agent-collectors in each hundred. It seems likely, therefore, that John Llewellyn, Richard Hawkshead and Thomas Achelley, who administered Whitmore's sequestration, were the agents for Brimstree hundred.[168] The Newport family alone contributed a substantial proportion of the revenue the county committee received from local Royalists. On 18 October 1645 Parliament allotted Sir Francis Newport's fines to the committee, and on 24 July 1646 instructed the Committee of Compounding to advance £3,500 towards the disbandment of the Shropshire forces against the surety of revenue from Sir Francis's fines. By spring 1649 the county committee appears to have received more than £8,000 from penalties imposed on Sir Francis and his father in exile Sir Richard.[169]

The Newports paid much of their fines by composition, and were among the 130 or more Shropshire Royalists who eventually compounded for their involvement in both Civil Wars.[170] A Royalist could seek financial settlement with Parliament by applying to compound for a one-off fine rated according to the degree of his militancy: whether he was considered a less significant 'delinquent', or else a more committed, hard-line 'malignant'. Paying the resultant fine would lift or prevent sequestration. On 12 August 1645 the Commons agreed that a composition fine should be calculated retrospectively, according to the pre-war worth over two years of the applicant's estate. Sir Thomas Eyton, for example, who compounded in February 1647 was the following 18 March fined £818 as one-tenth of his estate, reduced to £500 two months later.[171] Towards the end of the First Civil War the county committee had agreed temporary compositions with a growing number of local Royalists, among them Richard Oakeley, who paid £250 by December 1645, and Sir Thomas Whitmore, who had paid the committee £500 by September 1646 when he formally applied to compound.[172] Other Royalists negotiated a local financial settlement with the county committee by paying subscriptions, either under the pretext of the Propositions – towards which John Pierce of Westbury paid £55 in January 1646 – or the fifth and twentieth part, for which Humphrey Walcot paid £300 two months later.[173]

Such fines for the most part went into the coffer of the committee at Shrewsbury.

167 SP23/105, f. 227.
168 Fletcher, 'Sequestration […] of Sir Thomas Whitmore', pp. 308-14; Wanklyn, 'Landed Society & Allegiance', p. 266; *CPCC*, pp. 266-7.
169 *JHC*, IV, pp. 314, 627-8; Phillips, 'Sequestration […] of Sir Richard […] Newport', pp. 37-8.
170 Figure calculated from the cases in the calendared volumes of the *Proceedings* of the Committees for Compounding and Advance of Money, cross-referenced against the Shropshire entries in T. Dring (ed.), *A Catalogue of the Lords, Knights and Gentlemen that have compounded for their Estates* (1655).
171 *JHC*, IV, p. 237; *CPCC*, II, p. 1674.
172 *CPCM*, I, p. 657; *CPCC*, II, p. 1483.
173 *CPCC*, II, p. 1159; *CPCM*, I, p. 658.

However, the Committee for Compounding sitting at London's Goldsmith's Hall was the central agency entrusted with administering compositions and receiving the resultant fines. The revenue a county committee received from composition would thus diminish without gaining dispensations, like that allowing the committee of Shropshire to receive the Newports' fines. This awkward arrangement between local and central authority led to dispute in 1647 over Sir Richard Leveson's composition. Having paid £50 of his £400 fine in Shropshire, Leveson went to London to pay the rest. On 19 June, however, the committee at Shrewsbury demanded the fine in full, and when it went unpaid, retaliated in September by sequestrating Leveson's Shropshire estates, despite vociferous objections from the authorities in London.[174] Similarly, the coalmines jointly-owned by Lawrence Benthall and James Lacon that the county committee had seized in 1646 remained sequestered and leased to third parties while both undertook the protracted process of compounding during 1647 and 1648.[175] In order to enforce fines sequestration was often an inextricable part of the process of compounding, as in the case of Sir Richard Prince of Shrewsbury. Having in May 1645 paid £200 to the county committee for his fifth and twentieth part, Prince in December 1646 applied to compound and on 11 May 1647 was fined £800, but five months later his sequestration was ordered for non-payment.[176]

Plunder and free quarter

Looting and compulsory billeting were universal practices of the Civil Wars that subsidised war effort. According to Gentles, a 'massive resort to free quarter and plunder' typified the conflict.[177] Unauthorised plundering was condemned, but booty could be resold, or else provided the soldiery with basic essentials, such as clothing and bedding, which otherwise had to be purchased and were often in short supply. By lodging soldiers amongst civilians the burden of providing food and shelter for them was placed upon the householder. Plunder and free quarter compensated for inadequate logistical support and for shortfalls in pay. Indeed, in April 1645 one would-be Parliamentarian officer promised Colonel Mytton that he with 30 recruits would at first 'do duty [at Oswestry] for free quarter (requiring no pay)'.[178] Morrill's assertion that these 'incidental costs of war [nationally] exceeded the formal fiscal burdens' is supported by the local example of Astley, near Shrewsbury. Here, if we take their claims at face value, the near £27 that 10 inhabitants between them accrued in debts for billeting Royalist soldiers during 1643 can be compared to the village's total recorded cash contribution payments from October 1644 to February 1645 of only £4 18s.[179]

174 CPCM, I, p. 428.
175 CPCC, II, p. 1041.
176 CPCM, II, p. 735; CSPD, 1645–1647, p. 483.
177 Gentles, English Revolution, p. 445.
178 NAM, 8812-63, f. 6.
179 Morrill, Revolt, p. 120; SA, 3365/2566, unfoliated; SA, 3365/589, ff. 1, 3.

Plunder

Military appropriation carried varying degrees of legality, but the effect was much the same on those who experienced requisitioning by warrant, commandeering or outright looting. Such was the lot of those Ludlow townsfolk who in 1644 relinquished bedding to furnish the quarters of Royalist soldiers garrisoning the castle. Although they may well have been served official warrants beforehand, these people doubtless felt violated, among them a householder who reported the loss of a bed and linen, 'taken out of my house by musketeers by violent means'.[180]

Plundering was feared in England as a destructive vice imported from contemporary Continental warfare. There, because the ostensibly more legitimate means of military finance and supply often proved inadequate and unsustainable, as one appraisal of seventeenth-century logistics has put it, often 'more or less well-organised plunder was the rule rather than the exception'.[181]

The understandable tendency of victims to overstate losses and the often propagandist intent of reporting makes it impossible to determine the extent of plundering in Shropshire. What seems clear, however, is that from the beginning of the conflict looting was a chronic underlying problem for the civilian population. Richard Baxter described how his father and Godly neighbours in Shropshire 'that were noted for praying and hearing sermons, were plundered by the King's soldiers so that some of them had almost nothing but lumber left in their houses'.[182] Baxter may not have over exaggerated the worst effects of looting. A household near Shrewsbury apparently ransacked by Royalists around Easter 1643 sustained damages amounting to almost £50, including stolen silver, brass and pewter ware, bed linen, clothing, books, and provisions, and broken furniture and fixtures.[183] Countermeasures adopted by the corporation of Bishop's Castle at the beginning and towards the end of the First Civil War show that plundering by both sides was a persistent threat. On 6 December 1642 the townsmen were ordered to attend an armed night watch, to guard against the 'eminent dangers […] by reason of divers soldiers now remaining within this county'. In April 1646 the watch was reappointed on the 14th, because of fear of 'a continued concourse of soldiers at all times'.[184] In March 1645 Sir Thomas Myddelton found that the central Marches generally had been despoiled by both sides to such an extent, that 'the licentiousness of the soldiers in plundering and wasting the country make most people that have no relation to arms to hate the very name of a soldier'.[185]

Partisan reports of the fighting often contained accusations of looting. According to the Royalist organ *Mercurius Aulicus*, a Parliamentarian force operating out of Wem in mid-March 1644 had intended to 'plunder the country', but the booty they later abandoned in their retreat was by the King's men 'safely returned to the honest owners'. In early February 1646 a London newsbook similarly reported how Sir William

---

180 SA, LB7/2156.
181 M. van Crefeld, *Supplying War: Logistics from Wallenstein to Patton* (Cambridge, 1977), p. 8.
182 Baxter, *Reliquiae Baxterianae*, p. 44.
183 SA, 336/2566, unfoliated.
184 BCHRC, First Minute Book, ff. 202v, 207v.
185 BDL, Tanner Mss 60, f. 41.

Vaughan's horsemen had recently 'plundered very much' around Bishop's Castle.[186] Both reports were probably substantially true, because the combatants sporadically harried ostensibly enemy territory. During April 1643, for instance, Royalist patrols operating from Lord Capel's field headquarters at Whitchurch seized livestock and goods from several Cheshire villages. But on 30 May Sir William Brereton struck back by storming Whitchurch itself. The Parliamentarians seized Royalist military supplies and looted the town, and a week later Brereton's men returned to take back to Nantwich what remained; although according to Thomas Malbon, a committeeman at Nantwich, they plundered 'no man's goods but only the Cavaliers'.[187] Cattle were among the commodities most frequently seized upon, either to provide meat on the hoof or for resale. Because of the notoriety of his troops in this respect, by June 1643 the capital's press had dubbed Lord Capel 'that great cow stealer'. A year later, however, a London newsbook was pleased to report how Parliamentarian soldiers had rustled livestock in the hill country near Oswestry and sold the animals on for 'good pennyworths'.[188] The resale and redistribution of looted or sequestered goods in this way was part of a wartime economy from which some benefitted. As Samuel Garbet remarked in the case of the Parliamentarian headquarters at Wem, 'Great was the plunder brought into Wem, which never flourished more than in these times of confusion'.[189]

Notwithstanding their acceptance of officially sanctioned acts of plunder, both sides recognised the damaging effect that unauthorised pillage and extortion by their own soldiers had on popular support. On the Royalist side for example, the notorious depredations of Colonel Johan Van Geyrish's troopers in south-west Shropshire during autumn 1644 caused many country people to withhold contribution. Consequently, as the de facto area commander, an exasperated Sir Michael Woodhouse wrote from Ludlow on 5 October complaining to Prince Rupert, that Van Geyrish was 'quartered to destroy and not advance the service'. Although billeting bills suggest that part or all of the regiment was withdrawn into Ludlow, the hostility that Van Geyrish's men engendered against the Royalist military triggered the clubman activity in south Shropshire during winter 1644-5.[190] With similar detriment to the Parliamentarian cause for the short time that they campaigned in Shropshire, the Earl of Denbigh's Horse, in summer 1644, and detachments of the Yorkshire Horse, during April 1645, were notorious freebooters whose behaviour alienated many from Parliament's cause. The latter unit's especially violent conduct caused the Shropshire committeemen to demand that Sir William Brereton withdraw and replace them, with 'such as will not plunder otherwise the country will rise against them'.[191]

It was generally assumed that the cooperation they gave one side or the other allowed civilians a certain degree of protection from extortion by the enemy, as Sir Michael

186 *Mercurius Aulicus*, w/e 23 Mar. 1644, p. 890; *The Weekly Account*, 4-11 Feb. 1646, unpaginated.
187 Malbon, *Memorials*, pp. 46-60; HMC, *Twelfth Report, Appendix Part IX*, pp. 39-40.
188 *The Kingdome's Weekly Intelligencer*, 30 May-6 June 1643, p. 174; *Two Great Victories*, unpaginated.
189 Garbet, *History of Wem*, p. 223.
190 BRL, Additional Mss 18981, f. 284. Bills for quartering Van Geyrish's regiment at Ludlow at this time include SA, LB7/2066, for £62.
191 HMC, *Sixth Report, Part I*, p. 20; BRL, Additional Mss 11331, f. 4.

Ernle acknowledged in later October 1644. Having dispersed the Royalist cavalry to garrisons across Shropshire, Ernle was unable entirely to safeguard the hinterland of Shrewsbury, and so some locals, 'for want of protection', began 'to forsake their dwellings and seek shelter amongst the enemies'. The Parliamentarian committeemen voiced similar concerns to Sir William Brereton in November 1645: 'We suffer much in the opinions of the best for leaving our country so naked' they declared, being unable to prevent plundering forays by the Royalist garrison at High Ercall because most of the Shropshire Horse were in Cheshire.[192]

Marauding was condemned as a capital offence in the published articles of war regulating the armies of both sides, and also in particular standing orders. On 21 September 1642 High Sheriff John Weld circulated to Shropshire's civil authorities Charles I's reassuring declaration of his 'especial care' of the county, against 'the adverse army or by such straggling and disorderly soldiers of our own'. The King pledged to impose martial discipline, and restitution for 'damage or plunder'.[193] In a later initiative endorsed by Charles and his parliament at Oxford, the pamphlet of *Orders* published in spring 1644 to regulate the conduct of Royalist forces in dealing with civilians sanctioned the prosecution under the common law of soldiers accused of theft or robbery, an important dispensation seized upon by the townsfolk of Ludlow in their petition that year, for protection against 'the rapine and plunder of soldiers and other mutinies'.[194]

The orders given on 21 February 1645 to the Parliamentarian task force preparing to assault Shrewsbury were intended to forestall plundering. The soldiers were promised a share of a bounty worth up to £4,000, but any man caught looting would 'not only lose his present reward but be proceeded against for trial of his life according to the martial law'.[195] Incentive and threat notwithstanding, on the following day, in the largest single act of plunder in Shropshire during the Civil War, the soldiery instead set to ransack the town before it was fully secured. The acting commander-in-chief Colonel Reinking recollected how 'both horse and foot for most part contemning both order and command, fell to plunder all before them', some disciplined soldiers having to be deployed to protect leading Royalists and their property. On the 23rd the committeemen could do little other than exercise forbearance whilst the looting and disorder continued, admitting the following day that Shrewsbury had been 'exceedingly plundered' – the soldiers (unsurprisingly) having rejected their offer of a reduced bounty. Order was not fully restored until the 25th, with the arrival of Sir William Brereton accompanied by some disciplined Cheshire Foot.[196] By then, Brereton reckoned, Shrewsbury had been 'damnified to the value of £4,000'. Repairs to the damaged mayor's chambers were still being made seven months later.[197] Learning by this unfortunate lesson, in April 1646 the committee of Shropshire delivered on a

192 BRL, Additional Mss 18981, f. 299; BRL, Additional Mss 11332, f. 94.
193 SA, LB7/2318.
194 *Orders Presented to His Majesty By advice of the Lords & Commons of Parliament Assembled at Oxford* (1644), p. 8; SA, LB7/2139.
195 NLW, Sweeney Hall Mss A1, f. 24.
196 *Relation […] by […] William Reinking*, p. 6; *LBWB*, I, pp. 38-9, 45-6, 49-50.
197 Tibbutt, *Letter Books of Sir Samuel Luke*, p. 465; SA, 3365/591, f. 18.

modest pledge to pay just £1 (a bonus of around a month's pay for an infantryman) to each soldier undertaking the assault on Bridgnorth. As a result the soldiery mostly exercised restraint, and, as the committeemen thankfully reported, 'the town was generally saved from plunder'.[198]

Billeting and free quarter

While the garrisoned castles, manor houses and other strong points provided some accommodation, soldiers otherwise were dispersed to lodge amongst civilians, in churches, inns, or private houses and outbuildings. With the King's army in town, in early October 1642 a Shrewsbury resident reported 'the multitude of soldiers daily billeted upon us', adding disconsolately, 'I have had of these guests all this week and expect little better next week'.[199] Although published as anti-Royalist propaganda, this statement captures the resentment forced billeting engendered as an intrusion into private life. It was always a most unpopular practice – probably even among civilians who otherwise favoured the soldiers' cause – and especially so when soldiers were disorderly. In January 1646 householders at Bridgnorth complained to the Royalist commissioners about the ill-disciplined soldiers living amongst them. The minutes of the meeting of the town corporation on the 15th noted that, 'the towns men implored to those gentlemen their grievances of great spoil and detriment they say is sustained by the soldiers unruliness and distress in their houses'.[200]

Such behaviour exacerbated civilian fears of the arrival of numbers of soldiers requiring food and accommodation. In November 1648, one of the county committee's officials for the assessment played on these apprehensions, urging the bailiffs of Ludlow to hasten the collection of arrears to avert the billeting of the county troopers in their town: 'I pray you if you want to save the horse from quartering on you, that you would cause the petty constables to be very careful to gather that assessed'.[201] On the other hand, communities sometimes banded together in a hostile stance against unwarranted billeting. In August 1644, the townsfolk of Much Wenlock and then Bridgnorth opposed the arrival of Colonel Van Geyrish's Regiment by turning on the troopers and forcing them to seek accommodation elsewhere.[202] Van Geyrish's Horse had been posted to Shropshire on Prince Rupert's orders, and it was the unexpected arrival of outsiders and the unanticipated burden they placed on local resources that provoked most hostility. In December 1645 the county committeemen cautioned Sir William Brereton against sending auxiliaries from Lancashire into Shropshire: 'for should any strange force be quartered upon our county it would be imputed to our disregard of the welfare thereof'. The committeemen feared the effect on popular support of 'bringing others upon them to devour and eat them up'.[203]

Billeting had, quite literally, a consuming effect because householders often bore the full financial burden of providing for military lodgers. The soldiery was supposed

198 BDL, Tanner Mss 59, f. 10.
199 *Occurrences in Shropshire and Devonshire*, p. 4.
200 SA, BB/C/1/1/1, unfoliated.
201 SA, LB7/1944.
202 BRL, Additional Mss 18981, f. 216.
203 BRL, Additional Mss 11332, f. 24.

to pay its way, but the military's perennial problems with cash flow encouraged the widespread practice of free quarter. Thereby soldiers received board and accommodation on credit at the expense of their host, who was promised reimbursement at some later date. Because bills often remained unpaid and it was imposed in addition to taxes and other levies, free quarter has been singled out by historians as 'the most widespread grievance of all' during the Civil Wars, and as a system 'universally detested among the civilian population'.[204]

The record of Royalist billeting in Shropshire survives in the form of bills and petitions for arrears, so that little is known of what the military *did* pay. Documents from Ludlow and Shrewsbury show that as regional commanders during 1642 and 1643 the Marquis of Hertford and Lord Capel set tariffs for billeting against which civilians were to be reimbursed.[205] Similarly, the regulations issued by the Oxford parliament in spring 1644 published a tariff for weekly board and lodging that allowed 3s 6d for a common foot soldier, for example. Richard Brasier of Ludlow claimed this rate for providing for one garrison soldier for a fortnight, another for six weeks and a third for 20 weeks.[206] There were, however, periods when soldiers paid their way or were provided for by other means. In March 1644 Prince Rupert rescinded free quarter in Shropshire, and Royalist soldiers instead were given modest but sustainable pay and weekly rations. At Bridgnorth the garrison disliked the new regime and complained of poor victuals and remuneration, but the governor Sir Lewis Kirke acknowledged that the town was then too impoverished to sustain free quarter.[207] From the opposing side, there is evidence that in spring 1645 Parliamentarian garrison soldiers at Shrewsbury paid billeting charges out of their wages, probably by deduction.[208] The bills of several Royalist units billeted at Ludlow in 1642 and 1643 were paid in part, among them the local dragoons commanded by Captain Edward Baldwyn, who 'paid for all the billets until that 26 of May [1643]'. Nevertheless, local officials calculated that the town's arrears for billeting to the end of June 1643 still amounted to £370.[209] Communities and individuals elsewhere also accrued large debts in providing free quarter for Royalist soldiers, much of which probably went unpaid. Nine companies of the King's army, for example, between them left debts of £117 when they marched from Shrewsbury in October 1642, while Roger Ambler, a local baker, reckoned he was owed £1 14s for having provided for officers' servants as well as soldiers. On 6 December 1642 Bailiff Farr of Bridgnorth journeyed to Shrewsbury seeking remittance for his town's cumulative arrears for billeting amounting to almost £407.[210]

In order to ease the problems of billeting, the *Orders* of the Oxford parliament in spring 1644 prohibited Royalist soldiers from taking free quarter where contribution was also paid. Consequently, in their petition that year Ludlow's townsfolk concluded it would be lawful 'to deduct out of their monthly contribution all such sums of money

204 Pennington, 'War and the People', p. 117; Hutton, *War Effort*, p. 30.
205 SA, LB7/2015; SA, 3365/2566, unfoliated.
206 *Orders […] of Parliament Assembled at Oxford*, pp. 5-6; SA, LB7/2067.
207 BRL, Additional Mss 18981, ff. 117, 153.
208 *LBWB*, I, p. 281.
209 SA, LB7/2015.
210 SA, 3365/2566, unfoliated; SA, BB/C/8/1/14-3.

18. The actual text (or a copy, or draft) of a petition by the inhabitants of Ludlow expressing grievances against the Royalist military, dating to later 1644 or very early 1645. Clause six, in the left hand column, stated that 'it may be lawful for all the inhabitants of this town to deduct out of their monthly contribution all such sums of money which shall be due for quartering either foot or horse'. (Courtesy of Shropshire Archives, ref. LB7/2139)

which shall be due for quartering either foot or horse'.[211] This intent notwithstanding, surviving records from Ludlow, dating from later 1644 and into January 1645, present a litany of grievances relating to free quarter. These suggest that even in a long-standing garrison town irregular payment and long-standing arrears often prevailed (although we lack a corresponding record of settled accounts). Typically, William Bagley received just 3s 6d for providing food and lodgings for a garrison soldier for nine weeks, leaving him £1 18s in arrears. His fellow townsman Richard Soloman declared that he had provided for one soldier for a month, another for six weeks and a third for three months, all without recompense. At Shrewsbury in the meantime, by later 1644 free quarter had been reintroduced but without the exemption for paying contribution.[212]

The burden of free quarter eased, but did not end with the First Civil War. In addition to Parliament's standing county force and the soldiers awaiting disbandment, detachments of the New Model Army were posted to Shropshire, as in May 1647

211 Orders […] of Parliament Assembled at Oxford, p. 6; SA, LB7/2139.
212 SA, LB7/2158, 2164; 'Ottley Papers' (1896), p. 243.

when five companies of Colonel John Okey's Regiment of Dragoons were based there.[213] A case study of the burden and local response to billeting and free quarter at this time is provided by the two-year accounts from September 1647 of the constables of Worfield parish.[214] There the parishioners often provided individual soldiers and small detachments with accommodation of one or two nights' duration. On one occasion it cost the parish 8s to provide a party of horse with free quarter for a night. Furthermore, Constable William Billinglsey reimbursed himself from parochial funds the 3s 4d it cost him to provide overnight accommodation for five soldiers, and other householders received compensation from the parish for similar losses in providing free quarter.

More troubling for Worfield was the arrival on 21 November 1647 of troopers led by one Captain Young, a detachment of Colonel John Birch's old regiment that had served in and around Herefordshire since December 1645. These cavalrymen and Birch's foot soldiers had mutinously opposed disbandment, and communities across Herefordshire and neighbouring Radnorshire had been disrupted and intimidated by their lingering presence during 1647. That autumn, some of Birch's horsemen were also billeted at Bridgnorth.[215] In late September one of the town chamberlains journeyed the 13 miles to Diddlebury to seek out their commanding officer, Major Hopton, to facilitate the removal of his men from Bridgnorth. The townsmen also solicited the help of the local high constable, but in November they succumbed to paying Captain Young a bribe of £21 to take his troopers elsewhere.[216] This probably resulted in their arrival at Worfield, where the parishioners sought to remove them by making representations to the authorities at Bridgnorth and Shrewsbury in December, and in January 1648 by sending another delegation to Shrewsbury to lobby Major Hopton. The parish later sought restitution by submitting to the local justices of peace accounts of their losses sustained during the troopers' unwarranted stay.

Conclusions

In financing war effort in Shropshire, unsurprisingly the combatants adopted similar methods, some of which, such as taxation at parish and county level, followed pre-war precedent. Other measures, such as sequestration, took root in expediency but became important and sustained sources of revenue. Both sides at first took recourse to the wealth of their confirmed or supposed supporters, given as donations or proffered hopefully as loans; as the Royalist leadership at Shrewsbury optimistically noted in their planning sometime in late 1642, 'this is but advance monies and when things are settled his majesty will repay'.[217] Many activists, army officers especially, continued to make donations in a voluntary way, but payments were also coerced from wealthier individuals using devices such as the privy seal loans and the fifth and twentieth part. Sequestration and composition fines were the punitive culmination of attempts to

---

213 C.H. Firth (ed.), *The Clarke Papers, Volumes I & II* (London, 1992), p. 58.
214 SA, P314/M/1, ff. 40-1.
215 Parker, *Radnorshire*, pp. 131-2. In January 1648 the regiment had at least four troops, see TNA, SP28/50, Part 1, f. 81.
216 SA, BB/D/1/2/1/57.
217 SA, 6000/13290.

acquire the wealth of the better off.

Both sides increasingly turned to general taxation. Royalist and Parliamentarian taxation of property and income, in the form of the contribution and assessment respectively, used similar methods to engage large numbers of taxpayers. At certain stages of the conflict both sides achieved reasonably successful rates of collection, but administrative difficulties and the increasing reluctance or inability of an over-exploited and war-weary populace to continue to pay meant that taxation never produced the anticipated returns. Consequently, soldiers were usually in arrears of their pay or went unpaid, and this encouraged the prevalence of free quarter and looting, practices that were probably as widespread in Shropshire as elsewhere in England during the First Civil War.

The Royalists were placed to exploit Shropshire's financial resources and they succeeded in establishing mechanisms for doing so, while being able to effect necessary financial reform. Although sequestration remains a shadowy facet of Royalist finance, this study has suggested its effectiveness. However, as the Royalists lost both territory and support, including those gentry who sought financial settlement with the Parliamentarians, opportunities to gather revenue withered alongside the administrative structure for doing so. This increased the incidence of plunder and other coercive acts by Royalist soldiers as the First Civil War drew to an end.

Denied the territory that sustained the Royalist war effort, the Parliamentarians first drew resourcefully on expedient fiscal measures enacted away from Shropshire, largely in and around London. Although they lacked collective financial organisation – and the Earl of Denbigh's inability to impose financial control over the West Midland Association was more typical of Parliamentarian attempts at regional financial organisation than was the success of the Eastern Association – by tacit cooperation the committee of Shropshire and Sir Thomas Myddelton, backed at times by Denbigh and Sir William Brereton, financed war effort from scratch without much of a territorial base to draw on. Despite the limitations of their financial resources – the £27,000 or so that directly funded Sir Thomas Myddelton's brigade for the best part of two years seems insignificant against the near £34,000 per month required in 1644 to finance the (greatly larger) army of the Eastern Association[218] – the Parliamentarians maintained forces in the field until being more able to implement taxation and to extract revenue from their disheartened or defeated opponents. The county committee in particular achieved considerable success as a money-raising body, although it lacked very wealthy members and for much of the conflict could only obtain limited revenues from Shropshire.

Apart from soldiers' wages, money was otherwise mostly spent in purchasing military supplies and funding logistical activity. These actions of war effort are the subject of the following chapter.

---

218 Holmes, *Eastern Association*, p. 117.

5

Logistics: Supplying the war effort

That we may have no muskets forged but what shall be for the King.

Logistics – the coordinated provision of military supplies – was the vital connective activity underpinning the overall war effort, enabling the armed forces to be equipped and to be sustained in the field. Logistical activity involved the acquisition, transportation and distribution of supplies and war matériel purchased or otherwise obtained from a variety of widespread suppliers and locations. The ways in which both sides provided for their forces in Civil War Shropshire are examined in this chapter. Addressed, in turn, are the methods used to procure arms and munitions, equipment, provisions, horses and provender, and the movement and distribution of military supplies around the theatre of war.

Arms and munitions procurement

Obtaining armaments was of course a pre-eminent activity of war effort. The regular soldiers of all armies of the English Civil Wars were similarly armed and accoutred, with the majority of them being equipped with firearms. It was the norm for two thirds and sometimes more of the foot to be musketeers. Dragoons, as mounted infantry, also carried muskets. The horse were armed with pistols, some also with carbines. The remaining foot soldiers and their officers carried staff weapons, mainly pikes, and most soldiers, mounted or on foot, wore a sword. The ordnance, cast mostly in iron but sometimes in bronze, in a range of calibres comprised cannons and a smaller number of mortars, which all required an array of ancillary equipment. Match, a slow-burning cord, as a fuse was the means of ignition for the predominant type of infantry firearm, the matchlock musket, and also for artillery. Gunpowder was the propellant for ammunition, in the form of lead bullets for firearms, and cast-iron solid round shot and hollow grenades for cannon and mortars respectively.[1]

---

1   Among the plethora of publications dealing with general and particular aspects of the arming (and also the equipping and clothing) of English Civil War armies the most informative, especially for their illustrations, include: K. Roberts, *Soldiers of the English Civil War (1): Infantry* (London, 1989), and the companion volume, J. Tincey, *Soldiers of the English Civil War (2): Cavalry* (London, 1990); P. Haythornthwaite, *The English Civil War, 1642-1651, An Illustrated Military History* (Poole, 1983); and D. Blackmore, *Arms & Armour of the English Civil Wars* (London, 1990). For the artillery, see S. Bull, '*The Furie of the Ordnance*',

19. The general area where the seventeenth-century and later foundry at Leighton was situated that manufactured shot and grenades during the Civil War. Remains of the charcoal-fired blast furnace were revealed by archaeological investigation to the rear and under the car park of the hotel at top right of the photograph.

Apart from the equipment kept by individuals or in town or parish armouries for the trained militia, in Shropshire on the eve of civil war arms were also held in private ownership. In July 1635, three of his deputy lieutenants in Shropshire had reported to the Earl of Bridgewater their efforts to determine the weaponry available to equip the county's able men in the event of a wider call to arms:

> We […] have spoken to those of the better sort to provide themselves of arms for their particular uses and divers gents have some arms besides those for the use of the trained bands, but what the number of them is we know not, nor of any other arms in readiness for arming of untrained men.[2]

Whilst practicably unquantifiable in terms of numbers, then, arms in private ownership were fairly widespread. However, probate inventories compiled before the Civil War show the somewhat limited military usefulness of many of these weapons. Husbandmen and yeomen, gentlemen and lesser gentry owned bladed and staff weapons such as swords, daggers, bills and halberds. Those with firearms tended to own fowling pieces rather than muskets, while some individuals still had longbows and arrows.[3] The spare equipment stored in parish armouries was probably often obsolescent. At Shrewsbury in 1637, for example, the arms of the parish of the Holy Cross included a sword and two old helmets as well as the well-maintained modern equipment for two trained bandsmen. Small supplies of munitions for exercising the Trained Bands were kept by town and parish officers, like the petty constables of Stockton who spent £2 on match and gunpowder to be used in training during 1640.[4]

On 13 January 1642 Parliament instructed the shires to take precautionary measures for security and defence.[5] Accordingly, four days later a quorum of Shropshire's justices of peace, the high sheriff and the mayor of Shrewsbury met there in response. Their resultant directives suggest the state of the county's military preparedness.[6] The county magazine at Shrewsbury then held 30 barrels of gunpowder (a barrel normally holding 100 pounds of powder) and proportionate supplies of bullets and match (for which the standard measure was usually the hundredweight). Orders were given that all arms kept on the county's behalf were to be returned to Shrewsbury, apart from the personal weapons of the trained bandsmen. The individual subscribers, parishes and town authorities who maintained the Trained Bands were commanded to provide the musketeers with ammunition, while wealthier gentry were instructed to 'provide a convenient quantity of arms, powder and munition in their house for the defence of themselves and the county according to their several abilities'.

The Royalists
Local sources and manufactures

The demands of civil war on Shropshire's arms-holdings began in earnest with the arrival of the King's army in the third week of September 1642. In other counties weapons had been taken from the militia to equip the army's recruits, but Shropshire's Royalist gentry lobbied to ensure that the shire's Trained Bands kept their equipment. Therefore arms had to be found elsewhere, so on 21 September High Sheriff John Weld issued warrants calling for public donations of weaponry to the magazine at Shrewsbury.[7] This and similar appeals for the contents of private armouries resulted, according to Clarendon, in the accumulation of arms that were often 'very mean', the sort of obsolescent weaponry and elderly equipment like the four sets of pikeman's armour, four swords, a halberd and a pair of daggers taken from the town hall at Bridgnorth by officers of Colonel Pennyman's Regiment on 29 September.[8] Although the King's army commandeered a quantity of local weaponry, after its departure in mid-October much probably still remained. Shropshire's Royalist leadership therefore made intermittent appeals for arms in private hands. In March 1643, men from south Shropshire summoned for militia service were to bring whatever weaponry they

3   SA, 'Wem Probate Inventories, 1535-1650', 2 vols. (undated); SA, 'Whitchurch Probate Inventories, 1535-1650', 2 vols. (undated).
4   SA, P250/Fiche 321-2; SA, P270/B/1/1, ff. 46-7.
5   JHC, II, pp. 377-8.
6   SA, LB7/2315.
7   Clarendon, History, II, p. 373; SA, LB7/2317.
8   Clarendon, History, II, p. 373; SA, BB/C/8/1/7.

owned, from which assemblage the most useful arms would be allocated to the chosen recruits. Responding to Lord Capel's demand for horses and arms the following June, one William Young explained that he could donate only a fowling piece, having already armed a trooper and a dragoon.[9]

Arms given up by individuals were a diminishing resource, so the Royalist leadership in Shropshire soon sought alternative supplies. In October 1642 they ordered all gunsmiths in the county to work at Shrewsbury, 'so that we may have no muskets forged but what shall be for the King'. By January 1643 firearms were being manufactured (and probably also reconditioned) there, although not in sufficient quantity to provide a surplus to supply demand from Oxford. Output was superintended by Sir Francis Ottley, who in early April 1643 was entrusted by Lord Capel with overseeing all supplies of arms in Shropshire.[10] The production of small arms continued at Shrewsbury into 1644, in which a local joiner was engaged making musket stocks from stockpiled seasoned timber.[11]

Ottley's remit extended to the manufacture of bullets, and volume production was underway by April 1643 when Capel ordered the casting of a further half-ton of musket ball.[12] Soldiers often cast their own shot, but plumbers had the necessary lead-working skills and the equipment to manufacture larger batches of ball to order. Thus bullets were made at Bridgnorth in 1642 by the plumber Richard Broadfield, and during a production run at Ludlow in 1643 two hundredweight of ball was cast by a local plumber working in the vestry of St. Leonard's church.[13]

Metal and wood workers at Shrewsbury also adapted their skills to warlike production, including the manufacture and refurbishment of swords. In early 1643 a consignment of 43 new swords was made for 6s apiece, while the charge to fit a new hilt and guard to a reconditioned blade was 1s. From 1642 into 1644 the wooden and iron components for gun carriages and trails were made and assembled, along with gunnery tools including rammers, linstocks, sponges, budge barrels and gunpowder horns. Gunpowder cartridges for the cannon were made from hempen cloth produced locally.[14]

The Royalists also developed local production of match and gunpowder. The cultivation, processing and spinning of hemp and flax to make cord, rope and coarse cloth was a widespread productive cottage industry in Shropshire.[15] Recognising the county's potential as a source of raw material for the production of match for the wider Royalist war effort, in April 1643 King Charles instructed Sir Francis Ottley to send regular supplies to Worcester. That match was also manufactured in Shropshire is suggested by a request in May 1644 by Sir John Watts, governor of Chirk Castle, to Sir Abraham Shipman, then governor of Oswestry, for his help in obtaining a supply of

9   SA, LB7/2235; 'Ottley Papers' (1895), p. 338.
10   SA, 6000/13292; 'Ottley Papers': (1894), pp. 57, 59, 71-2; (1895), p. 304.
11   SA, P250/325.
12   'Ottley Papers' (1895), p. 304.
13   SA, BB/D/1/2/1/52; SA, LB8/1/163, f. 4.
14   SA, 6000/13281; SA, 3365/587, ff. 19, 34, 58; SA, 3365/588, ff. 45, 95.
15   P. Edwards, 'Shropshire Agriculture 1540-1750' in *A History of Shropshire Volume IV, Agriculture*, (ed.) G.C. Baugh (Oxford, 1989), p. 147.

match from the magazine at Shrewsbury. By way of exchange Watts promised a fresh supply of raw material – 'as much, or much more good flax'.[16]

The large-scale production of gunpowder was an industrialised operation requiring water-driven mills. Local processing was dependant on the availability of gunpowder's three ingredients – charcoal, sulphur and saltpetre (potassium nitrate). Charcoal was readily made in Shropshire, but sulphur (brimstone) could be obtained only as an import from the Mediterranean region. Saltpetre as the main constituent of gunpowder was also imported, but could be made locally in a lengthy process involving the extraction, distillation and crystalisation of the nitrogen-enriched soil dug from latrines, stables, barns, dovecotes and middens. Evidence for the wartime extraction of raw material for saltpetre production at Shrewsbury appears in the accounts of the churchwardens of St. Mary's parish, who in 1646 paid 6s for transporting 'earth to repair after the saltpetre men'.[17] While production of gunpowder or its ingredients was underway at Shrewsbury by December 1642, by April 1643 the mills built at Shrewsbury and Chester that Lord Capel expected would supply the region were nearing completion. The Shrewsbury 'powder work' incurred operational costs of £177 between October 1643 and April 1644, when on the 13th there were eight barrels in stock.[18] Output was locally and regionally important but limited by the availability of raw materials, especially sulphur, delivered to Shropshire via lengthy and vulnerable supply lines. By autumn 1644 gunpowder production at Shrewsbury was becoming unsustainable, as Sir Michael Ernle despondently reported, 'for the want of brimstone and other materials'.[19]

These local initiatives to manufacture war matériel had varying success, but the most significant contribution Shropshire industry made to the wider Royalist war effort was the production of ordnance and shot, and also bar iron and steel. In 1611 John Speed wrote that Shropshire had iron and abundant woodland, 'which two […] continue not long in league together', an allusion to the by then well-established county iron industry in which local and imported ore was smelted, cast and worked in charcoal-fired blast furnaces and forges.[20] During the sixteenth and early seventeenth centuries a scattering of upwards of 40 foundries, forges and slitting mills operated along Shropshire's river valleys under the auspices of some of the county's entrepreneurial landed families. Shropshire's iron industry was of growing national importance at the outbreak of civil war, although output was modest compared to England's main iron-production region, the Weald of Sussex and Kent.[21]

Whether or not there was warlike production in Shropshire before 1642 remains unknown. However, the local iron masters quickly adapted to the demands of the Royalist war effort, including mastering the technically exacting process of gun

16   'Ottley Papers' (1895), p. 316; WRO, CR2017/C9, f. 106.
17   SA, P257/B/3/2, unfoliated.
18   'Ottley Papers' (1894), p. 49; NLW, Crosse of Shaw Hill Mss, 1097; SA, 3365/588, f. 18.
19   BL, Additional Mss 18981, f. 253.
20   Speed, *Great Britaine*, p. 71.
21   R. Hayman, 'The Shropshire Wrought-Iron Industry, c. 1600-1900' (PhD thesis, University of Birmingham, 2003), pp. 28-31; W.H.B. Court, *The Rise of the Midland Industries, 1600-1838* (London, 1965), p. 82; B. Trinder, *The Industrial Revolution in Shropshire* (Chichester, 2000), p. 20.

founding. In this transition the enigmatic Mathias Gervase played an important, if now unknown, supervisory role. Gervase may have been a foreign expert who brought Continental expertise to the Shropshire industry. By March 1643 he was superintending the foundry at Leighton, nine miles south-east of Shrewsbury beside the River Severn, where cannon shot and grenades – both mortar shells and hand grenades – were being cast by the ton for the Royalists at Chester, Oxford and in Staffordshire.[22] During 1643-4 Gervase held authority from King Charles's Council of War at Oxford to regulate the production of foundries in Shropshire and Staffordshire. The furnace at Leighton meanwhile continued to specialise in casting shot and shells, and during April 1644 increased production to meet demand from Oxford for the forthcoming campaigning season.[23] Shot was also cast at the foundry operated by Francis Walker at Bouldon, in the lee of the iron ore-bearing Clee Hills north-east of Ludlow. Walker had pre-war operational experience of the county iron industry and successfully introduced gun founding at Bouldon, and also to the blast furnace he had operated under lease in the 1620s at Bringewood, on the Shropshire/ Herefordshire border.[24] During 1643, at least 43 medium and heavy iron cannon in three calibres were cast at Bouldon for Royalist garrisons as far afield as Shrewsbury, Worcester, Oxford and South Wales, for which Walker charged £965. Four pieces were sent to equip a Royalist warship fitted out at Chester.[25] Meanwhile, ordnance for the defence of Ludlow and Shrewsbury was also cast at Bringewood.[26] During 1644 Walker fulfilled further orders for cannon and munitions for Royalist garrisons in Worcestershire – at Hartlebury, Evesham and Worcester – and Sudeley Castle in Gloucestershire.[27] But production had probably ceased at Bouldon before June 1645 when enemy garrisons were established nearby.

In July 1645 Walker was paid for supplying bar iron to make fittings for the drawbridges defending Ludlow.[28] Probably one of Walker's last orders, it provides evidence of the production of finished raw material by Shropshire's iron industry. This supplied manufactories of armaments for the Royalist war effort at Worcester and Oxford, and in what later became the industrialised Black Country of southern Staffordshire and northern Worcestershire, particularly the forges clustered along the Stour valley on Shropshire's south-eastern border. Three tons of bar iron and nine tons of shot delivered at Oxford from Worcester on 18 May 1644, for example, were most likely cast in Bouldon's foundry.[29] The forge on the River Roden near Moreton Corbet also produced bar iron, and during a raid on the area in May 1644 the Parliamentarians reportedly captured 'six loads of iron'.[30] Little is known of the wartime production of Sir Basil Brooke's ironworks at Madeley, but the haul of finished iron and steel, including nine tons of annealed plate, taken when the Parliamentarians seized the

22   'Ottley Papers' (1895), pp. 287-92.
23   BL, Harleian Mss 6804, f. 226; BL, Additional Mss 18981, f. 130.
24   Hayman, 'Iron Industry', p. 28.
25   *CSPD, 1641-1644*, p. 488; *CSPD, 1644*, p. 22; NLW, Llanfair-Brynodol Letters, 58.
26   *CPCC*, II, p. 1484; SA, 3365/587, f. 14.
27   BL, Harleian Mss 6802, ff. 72, 113, 218; *CSPD, 1644*, p. 22; Townsend, *Diary*, II, p. 257.
28   SA, LB8/1/165, f. 1.
29   Hayman, 'Iron Industry', p. 23; *ROP*, I, pp. 35-6, 134.
30   Hayman, 'Iron Industry', p. 31; Malbon, *Memorials*, p. 131.

works in June 1645 had probably been intended for the Royalist war effort.[31]

Other sources of supply

Because local producers could provide only some of the armaments they required, the Royalists in Shropshire relied on supplies from further afield – especially from Oxford, Worcester and Bristol. Oxford, the Royalist wartime capital, became a centre for the manufacture and distribution of armaments. Arms and munitions supplied from Oxford for Lord Capel's forces in Shropshire included the 150 muskets, 20 barrels of gunpowder, and match and bullets delivered to Shrewsbury in November 1643. Similarly, the 21 firkins of gunpowder and 20 bundles of match received at Shrewsbury on 10 April 1644 were among the deliveries from Oxford for Prince Rupert's command.[32] Worcester was an entrepôt for consignments from Oxford and also for the output of regional arms manufacturers. When Prince Rupert was briefly based at Ludlow in March 1645 he intended to equip his infantry with pikes fitted with the points stockpiled at Worcester forged in Worcestershire and Staffordshire.[33] Bristol, second only to London as the kingdom's most important seaport, after the Royalists captured it in July 1643 became a major arms manufacturing centre and a vital point of entry for imported armaments.

In fact imports played a major part in sustaining the Royalist war effort nationally. Much of the arms and munitions passing through Oxford and Worcester to Shropshire would have been obtained on the Continent by the King's agents and shipped to Bristol and other Royalist-held ports in south-western England. An arms consignment from Leiden in Holland landed at Dartmouth in late February or early March 1644 provides a revealing example of the scale and diversity of these imports. This shipment included 6,280 matchlock and 52 flintlock muskets, 350 musket locks and 900 gun flints, 838 cavalry pistols, 100 carbines, 600 swords and five hundredweight of the fine-grained gunpowder required for priming pistols.[34]

One of his aides at Oxford was hopeful that Prince Rupert would receive a share of this shipment, for the Prince had taken up his regional command early in 1644 with the intention of supplying his forces in and around Shropshire from such imports. At Chester, his deputy Lord Byron anticipated receiving a proportion of the 2,000 muskets Rupert hoped to receive, but in practice optimistic expectations were confounded by shortages caused by irregular shipments and demand from strategic imperatives elsewhere. In January 1644, Bristol's stock of gunpowder was diminished and awaited replenishment from a 500-barrel consignment from the Netherlands recently landed at Exeter. Accordingly, on 13 February one of Rupert's officers wrote to him from Bristol to temper his expectations of receiving munitions from there: 'I am afraid you will find yourself very much mistaken in the quantity which you believe here, and more in the care which should provide them'.[35] Delays in sending from Bristol to Shrewsbury by mid-March just 200 muskets and 100 barrels of gunpowder

31   TNA, SP23/105, f. 201.
32   TNA, WO55/459/Part 3, f. 481; *ROP*, II, p. 305; TNA, WO55/459/Part 1, f. 53.
33   Warburton, *Prince Rupert*, III, p. 68.
34   BL, Additional Mss 18981, f. 204.
35   Ibid., ff. 60, 11, 36.

– considerably less than half the consignment that had seemed deliverable a month before – caused much apologetic back-peddling at Oxford by Lord Percy, the Master-General of Ordnance, and by the influential courtier Henry Jermyn. Priority had instead been given to equipping the Oxford army and Lord Hopton's western army, which between them during March had received most of the new muskets available.[36]

However, Prince Rupert's resounding victory at Newark on 21 March 1644 provided a twofold solution to his shortage of armaments. Firstly, the victory reconfirmed Rupert's military and political standing at Oxford, so that by the 28th he had been allocated 140 barrels of gunpowder at Bristol and supplies of sulphur there and at Oxford.[37] Secondly, the Prince's field army could be equipped from the arms and munitions surrendered by the defeated Parliamentarians. On 28 March, from Leicester the Earl of Denbigh reported the imminent departure from the East Midlands of the Royalists for Shropshire, with the armaments taken at Newark loaded onto requisitioned carts, a haul that a Royalist officer at Shrewsbury estimated as including 40 barrels of gunpowder and 5,000 weapons.[38] As the war continued Royalist stocks of arms and munitions in Shropshire were also supplemented by local captures, like the 22 pairs of new pistols reportedly taken by Sir William Vaughan's Horse in December 1644 in a cavalry skirmish near Welshpool. In another successful action by Vaughan's forces, by their victory at High Ercall on 5 July 1645 the Royalists secured supplies of gunpowder, match and bullets, along with probably several hundred muskets and pikes.[39]

The Parliamentarians

It remains uncertain to what extent local manufacture contributed to the Parliamentarian war effort. The production of grenades, at least, ceased when the Royalists lost control of the foundries, for by December 1645 the Parliamentarians in Shropshire could not obtain mortar shells.[40] Parliament's forces campaigning in and around the county were equipped instead mostly from London. Purchases were made on the arms market, while under the direction of Parliament and its executive committees supplies were issued from central magazines operated by the Committee of Safety and the Ordnance Office. These arsenals were replenished in turn by home manufactures and by Continental imports.

Lobbying was a prerequisite to obtaining Parliament's centrally kept supplies. Responding to an appeal from the committee of Shropshire in February 1644, on the 26th the newly formed Committee of Both Kingdoms recommended to Parliament the provision of 20 barrels of gunpowder and one ton of match for Colonel Mytton. The Commons concurred on 1 March, ordering the release of powder and match from the Committee of Safety's magazine. The Commons the same day also allotted arms and munitions to Sir Thomas Myddelton, including 40 barrels of gunpowder and a

36 Warburton, *Prince Rupert*, I, pp. 503, 508, II, pp. 380, 388; BL, Additional Mss 18981, f. 92; Day, *Pythouse Papers*, pp. 58-9, 60-2.
37 BL, Additional Mss 18981, f. 113.
38 *CSPD, 1644*, pp. 75-6; Lewis, *Fire and Sword*, p. 71.
39 *Mercurius Aulicus*, w/e 5 Jan. 1645, p. 1325; BL, Harleian Mss 6852, f. 274.
40 *LBWB*, II, p. 349.

half-ton of match from the Committee of Safety's magazine, and petards (demolition charges) from the Ordnance Office's stores in the Tower of London.[41] In a further example of this procedure, a warrant from the Committee of Both Kingdoms allowed Sir John Corbet on 2 April 1645 to take delivery for the Shropshire forces of 30 barrels of gunpowder from the Ordnance Office stores and quantities of match and bullets soon after.[42] However, these central supplies were not always forthcoming. On 8 December 1645 the Committee of Both Kingdoms directed the Ordnance Office to provide Corbet with a demi-cannon and a mortar, together with 20 barrels of gunpowder, match and bullets. But due to oversight, carelessness or shortage, the Committee had to re-submit the warrant on 10 March 1646. A further warrant from the Committee of the Army was required for Corbet to receive the mortar piece on 10 April, along with some match. But it was not until 4 May that Corbet finally took delivery of the brass demi-cannon.[43] The siege gun came from the Ordnance Office stores, and, because armaments from the central arsenals were often charged for, it cost the committee of Shropshire £76. During summer 1643, munitions provided for the Earl of Denbigh from the Committee of Safety's magazine had similarly been charged to his account.[44]

However, the central magazines were an unpredictable source of supply because of administrative delays, shortages and competition from other Parliamentary armies. Therefore the Parliamentarian war effort in Shropshire was also sustained by purchases made on the open market, from producers or their intermediaries and from arms merchants and dealers. Armaments were bought from leading manufacturers supplying Parliament's wider war effort. In August 1643, for instance, the Earl of Denbigh purchased bullet moulds and 16 hundredweight of ball from John Montgomery, one of the capital's most productive shot casters.[45] Sir Thomas Myddelton meanwhile bought pole-arms from Anthony Webster, the prominent London pike maker who later supplied the New Model Army. The cutler Stephen Heard, another long-term contractor to Parliamentary forces, delivered 400 swords at 6s apiece to Myddelton's London storehouse in early April 1644.[46] That month Myddelton's agents also purchased grenades from the London agent of John Browne, the pre-eminent gun founder with works in the Weald who before the Civil War held the royal monopoly to supply shot and iron ordnance.[47] The London market also provided artillery and associated equipment. In 1643, as well as ordnance received from the Tower armoury the Earl of Denbigh purchased six small cannon, known as drakes, at £22 per pair. A light cannon supplied to Sir Thomas Myddelton's brigade in April 1644 cost almost £6. Meanwhile John Arundel, Myddelton's master gunner, purchased the tools of his trade, including fuses, artillery tools and nine hundredweight of round shot.[48] The

41   *CSPD, 1644*, p. 26; *JHC*, III, p. 412.
42   WSL, SMS 463, unfoliated; *CSPD, 1644-1645*, p. 404.
43   *CSPD, 1645-1646*, p. 252; WSL, SMS 463, unfoliated.
44   TNA, SP28/34 Part 2, f. 291.
45   Ibid., f. 287; Edwards, *Dealing in Death*, p. 103.
46   TNA, SP28/346 Part 1, f. 57, Part 2, f. 49; Edwards, *Dealing in Death*, pp. 72-3.
47   TNA, SP28/34 Part 2, f. 49; Edwards, *Dealing in Death*, pp. 95-6.
48   TNA, SP28/34 Part 2, ff. 239, 264; TNA, SP28/346 Part 1, unfoliated, Part 2, f. 47.

capital was also the main source of firearms; by the end of August 1643 the Earl of Denbigh had acquired around 1,000 small arms there. Arms shipments from London to Coventry under Denbigh's direction were ongoing, including a consignment of 80 new muskets delivered in January 1644.[49] Firearms purchased for Sir Thomas Myddelton's brigade during 1644 included a batch of 250 new matchlock muskets at 15s 6d apiece, and 121 reconditioned muskets costing £27 11s. From September 1644 to January 1645 Myddelton's brigade received in all 1,150 matchlock and flintlock muskets.[50]

In May 1645 the committee at Shrewsbury awaited the arrival by way of Coventry of 400 muskets from London, and also expected a consignment of firearms imported via the Parliamentarian port of Hull – an example that armaments were obtained elsewhere than the capital.[51] By April 1645 the committee was also buying gunpowder and match from the Manchester-based dealer William Sunderland. An order for 50 barrels of gunpowder at £6 each was then in hand, although Sunderland's price for match was an expensive £50 per ton.[52] Another example of a provincial supplier was Robert Porter, a cutler from West Bromwich near Birmingham, who made swords for the West Midland Association. On 6 May 1644, for example, Porter delivered a consignment of 200 swords with belts, at 7s 1d apiece. That April one of Denbigh's commissary officers at Coventry had received 31 new firearms from another local manufacturer, the gunsmith John Launder.[53]

The bulk purchases of arms by Parliamentarian commanders were supplemented by the private purchases made by junior officers to equip their own troops or companies. Lieutenant Thomas Perkins, for example, on joining the major's troop of the Earl of Denbigh's Horse in March 1644 bought 27 pairs of wheel lock pistols with holsters, for which he paid £53 6s 6d. The Parliamentarians also benefited from the reuse of captured arms. While serving in Shropshire Captain Anthony Hungerford armed his company in part by buying weapons captured by his own men or other soldiers, paying a bounty of 5s for a flintlock musket, 2s for a matchlock and 1s for a pike.[54]

Clothing and equipment

In addition to clothing and footwear, standard items of soldiers' personal equipment included sword belts, knapsacks, body armour, helmets and the bandoliers worn by musketeers. As with armaments, local producers in Shropshire provided the Royalists with much of what they needed. At Ludlow, during 1643 tradespeople supplied soldiers' clothing, stockings, boots, shoes and other items of personal equipment, while in 1644 the tailor Owen Jones clothed Colonel Van Geyrish's horsemen. At Shrewsbury during 1643 leather workers and other craftspeople supplied the garrison with scabbards, and also bandoliers at 2s apiece. Armour and helmets were refurbished, and there was also some small-scale production of armour; in May a local blacksmith

49   TNA, SP28/34 Part 2, f. 191; WRO, CR2017/C9, f. 44.
50   TNA, SP28/300 Part 1, f. 93; SP28/346, Part 1, f. 91; NLW, Chirk Castle Mss. 1/Biii, 93, unfoliated.
51   *LBWB*, I, p. 343.
52   Ibid., pp. 278-9; SP28/225, Part 4, f. 723, Sunderland's tariff for county forces.
53   TNA, SP28/34 Part 2, f. 272; WRO, CR2017/C9, f. 91; TNA, SP28/131 Part 12, f. 23.
54   WRO, CR2017/C10, f. 72; TNA, SP28/42 Part 2, f. 298, Hungerford's accounts.

supplied a cavalry officer with a new breast and backplate.[55]

From Shrewsbury in early February 1644 Sir John Mennes reported that shoes and stockings for 1,700 Royalist foot soldiers could be made locally, while 500 finished suits of clothes (probably comprising caps, coats, breeches and shirts, together with stockings and shoes) were already in store.[56] Before the Civil War Shrewsbury, and Oswestry to a lesser extent, were regional centres for finishing and marketing woolen cloth produced in Mid and North Wales. A directory of mercantile trade published in 1638 had noted that Shrewsbury was 'much enriched by their trade for cottons and friezes, with their neighbours the Welsh'.[57] Notwithstanding the disruptive and depressing effect of the war on trade, the Royalist war effort provided an alternative market for the wares of Welsh cloth producers, made into military clothing at Shrewsbury and elsewhere. In early August 1644, coats and caps in uniform colours made in Montgomeryshire (and perhaps further afield) for two of Prince Rupert's infantry regiments were stored in the Royalist garrison at the Red Castle near Welshpool, along with a batch of red cloth for clothing the Prince's Regiment of Horse. However, the loss of Oswestry and later Shrewsbury and the inroads into Wales made by Myddelton's brigade from autumn 1644 denied the Royalists such sources of cloth and centres of manufacture. Consequently, when Prince Rupert was at Ludlow in March 1645 attending to logistical matters he had to request soldiers' clothing to be sent from Oxford and Bristol.[58]

The Parliamentarians also made some use of Welsh cloth. A large consignment they captured at Oswestry in June 1644 intended for Price Rupert's army instead went some way to clothe the Shropshire forces and the Earl of Denbigh's Regiment of Foot.[59] However, the capital remained the main source of equipment for Parliamentarian forces campaigning in and around Shropshire. Coats for Sir Thomas Myddelton's foot soldiers were made in London in October 1644, and among the other purchases there during 1644 for Myddelton's brigade were 300 bandoliers at 14d each, and the 300 knapsacks bought off James Gough, a leading supplier of leather ware to Parliamentary forces. In April, another London-based supplier, Gyles Smart, was paid £23 for providing 20 drums for Myddelton's companies of foot.[60] Equipment acquired by the Earl of Denbigh in London during summer 1643 included 83 sets of cavalryman's armour – enough, perhaps, to equip fully half of the four troops then being raised – and 300 'Swedish feathers', a defensive stake used by musketeers. Meanwhile, the Greenwich-based master armourer Thomas Stevens made Denbigh's own amour. An example of the use of regional suppliers was the purchase by the Shropshire committeeman Thomas Hunt of 74 pairs of soldiers' shoes at Nantwich on 1 December 1644.[61]

---

55   SA, LB7/2015; SA, LB7/2081; SA, 6000/13281.
56   Warburton, *Prince Rupert*, II, pp. 373-4.
57   L. Roberts, *The Merchants Mappe of Commerce* (1638), p. 230. Cottons and friezes were kinds of woolen cloth.
58   *The True Informer*, 10-17 Aug. 1644, pp. 319-20; Warburton, *Prince Rupert*, III, p. 64.
59   *The Perfect Occurrences of Parliament And Chief Collections of Letters*, 28 June-5 July 1644, unpaginated; *CSPD, 1644*, p. 429.
60   TNA, SP28/300 Part 1, f. 93; SP28/346 Part 1, unfoliated, Part 2, ff. 45, 56.
61   TNA, SP28/34 Part 2, f. 291; WRO, CR2017/C10, f. 68; TNA, SP28/225 Part 4, f. 723.

The supply of provisions

An adequate and reliable supply of food was of course essential to military operations, to maintain the effectiveness, wellbeing and loyalty of the soldiery. Hunger lowered morale and induced desertion, as Sir John Mennes found in early February 1644 when he reported that Royalist cavalry at Shrewsbury were 'ready to disband for want of victuals'.[62] Because Civil War armies obtained most of their foodstuffs locally, Shropshire agriculture had to sustain this vital function of war effort.

The occasional dearth caused by poor harvests notwithstanding, farming in Shropshire in the mid-seventeenth century was productive and well developed. Commentators noted the county's agrarian prosperity. In 1611 John Speed described Shropshire as a near-idyllic land, 'very fruitful for life'; the air was 'wholesome', and the climate 'delectable and good, yielding the spring and the autumn, seed time and harvest, in a temperate condition'. Cornfields and woodland flourished on the fertile soil of a 'fruitful' land. Sixty years later Richard Blome, another geographer, more prosaically echoed Speed's assessment of Shropshire: 'It is a fertile soil, both for tillage and pasturage, abounding in wheat and barley, is well clothed with wood, feedeth store of cattle'.[63]

Cattle were indeed the mainstay of Shropshire's farming economy.[64] Pastoralism predominated on the central and northern lowlands and there were strong ties to the Welsh cattle-rearing trade. Traditionally cattle had been kept for beef, but during the seventeenth century the north Shropshire plain became a notable dairying region. Sheep were of secondary importance, and large flocks were kept on the county's uplands and heath land. Shropshire wool was noted for its fineness, and there was growth in mutton production. Pig keeping was being developed on a commercial scale, often in association with dairying.

Early modern Shropshire has been characterised as 'a good example of a cattle rearing, meat-producing county'. But notwithstanding the primacy of livestock keeping, by the 1640s arable farming was expanding in an increasingly mixed agriculture. At the close of the seventeenth century Richard Gough found his own parish, in a predominantly pastoral district, yielding corn as good as the notably productive fields on the plain above the River Severn near Wroxeter, which together with the valley of the Tern and easterly parts of the county were becoming important arable areas.[65] The enclosure of land and the improvement of marginal areas encouraged more widespread development of arable. In 1649, a proponent of agricultural betterment cited Shropshire as noteworthy for the 'improvements made upon coarse lands', to the extent that he considered it among several agriculturally improved shires that had become 'as gallant corn countries as be in England'.[66] Wheat was grown for flour, but in Shropshire bread was more often made from barley and rye. Barley was also grown

---

62 BL, Additional Mss 18981, f. 25.
63 Speed, *Great Britaine*, p. 71; Blome, *Britannia*, p. 192.
64 This summary of Shropshire's agricultural economy at this time draws on Edwards, 'Shropshire Agriculture', pp. 119-68, and D.G. Hey, *An English Rural Community: Myddle under the Tudors and Stuarts* (Leicester, 1974), pp. 57-70.
65 Hey, *Rural Community*, p. 57; Gough, *Myddle*, p. 265.
66 W. Blith, *The English Improver, Or a New Survey of Husbandry* (1649), pp. 54-5, 72.

for malt, while oats and peas were often cultivated as fodder crops.

Notwithstanding a developing inter-regional trade in livestock and produce, most transactions in animals, corn and provisions were made at the seasonal fairs and weekly markets held at Shropshire's 18 market towns and larger villages.[67] On Thursdays at Wem, for example, there was a large market for cattle and produce, while the Wednesday market at Market Drayton specialised in horses and cattle.[68] Shrewsbury's six annual fairs and the livestock markets held regularly at Ellesmere, Oswestry, Bridgnorth and Ludlow were important for animal husbandry. During the Civil Wars markets and fairs were vulnerable to military action. Trade was threatened by unlicensed plundering, and events were sometimes targeted to deny provisions to the enemy and as calculated acts of retribution. This occurred on 1 August 1644, when Colonel Mytton led a party of Parliamentary horse to disrupt the Lammas, or harvest, fair at the county town, beforehand having 'charged the country not to carry provisions to the enemy into Shrewsbury, which many malignants did'. In a cross-country sweep to the south of the town Mytton's troopers reportedly 'drove away to a great number of horse, cows and sheep and did much hinder the fair'. The unsuccessful raid attempted by Royalists from Ludlow upon the fair at Bishop's Castle on Saturday 30 August 1645 appears to have been a similarly deliberately punitive action against the by then largely pro-Parliamentary townsfolk.[69]

Sometimes food was forcibly taken from civilians as well as livestock. Thomas Crosse of Ludlow, for one, complained of Royalist soldiers 'throwing open my larder and spoiling all that was in it'.[70] However, soldiers were usually fed by more legitimate ways, taking board in their billets from civilian hosts, or issued rations by the commissariat on campaign or in garrison. Accordingly, during 1643 and 1644 Shrewsbury and Ludlow householders claimed a daily allowance of six pence for providing two meals and drink for each Royalist infantryman lodging with them.[71] The Royalist force that besieged Oswestry from 29 June 1644 carried with it a supply of provisions, much of which was abandoned in their retreat on 2 July. Consequently Sir Thomas Myddelton reported the capture of several vehicles 'loaded with provisions, [such] as beer, bread and other necessaries'. From November 1644 to January 1645 Colonel Devillier's Royalist garrison at Leigh Hall regularly received victuals from the surrounding countryside, including quarters of beef and sides of mutton and bacon, cheese, butter and poultry. Bread does not appear to have featured among these supplies, but the garrison received deliveries of rye and so baked its own. Local bakers were sometimes required to provide this staple of the military diet, and accordingly sometime in 1644

---

67   In 1673, Blome, in *Britannia*, pp. 193-4, identified 15 Shropshire market towns, namely: Shrewsbury; Church Stretton; Oswestry; Ellesmere; Whitchurch; Market Drayton; Wem; Newport; Wellington; Much Wenlock; Bridgnorth; Shipton; Cleobury Mortimer; Ludlow and Bishop's Castle. To these can be added the small town of Clun, and also Prees and Tong, which as larger villages had held fairs since the middle ages. This total of 18 market centres in seventeenth-century Shropshire is corroborated in J. Thirsk (ed.), *The Agrarian History of England and Wales, Volume IV, 1500-1640* (Cambridge, 1967), p. 471.

68   Blome, *Britannia*, p. 194.

69   *Wareham taken […] Also Collonel Mittons valiant Exploits*, p. 4; HMC, *Thirteenth Report, Appendix Part I*, pp. 95-6.

70   SA, LB7/2156.

71   SA, 3365/2566, unfoliated; SA, LB7/2067, 2126.

the parish of Stockton supplied the Royalist garrison at Tong Castle with 220 lbs of bread.[72]

| Township (17 in total) | Sorts of Provision By weight or volume/number of consignments | | | | | | |
	Cheese lbs	Butter lbs	Bacon lbs	Wheat strikes	Barley strikes	Rye strikes	Cash Equivalent Sum
Alkmond Parva [Park]	283/3	-	-	-	-	-	£2 7s
Allbright Lee	-	-	-	-	-	15/1	£1 13s
Astley	72/2	-	-	-	-	-	12s
Battlefield	96/2	5/1	-	1/1	-	-	£1 3s
Clive	327/4	12/1	-	-	-	-	£2 7s
Coton	-	-	-	-	5/1	26 ½/3	£10 12s
Great Berwick	183/1	-	-	-	-	-	£1 11s
Great Hanwood	108/1	25/1	-	3/1	-	-	£1 10s
Hadnall	240/5	-	-	1/1	-	-	£2 4s
Harlescott	343/7	4/1	-	-	-	2/1	£3 5s
Hencott	300/7	21/1	26/1	1/1	-	13 ½/2	£5 4s
Little Berwick	264/3	25½/2	-	-	-	-	£2 13s
Newton and Edgebold	478/12	8½/1	6/1	-	-	-	£4 6s
Newton on the Heath	77/4	-	-	-	-	2/1	£1
Nobold	346/2	8/2	-	5/1	-	-	£3 11s
Stone Bridge	50/2	-	-	-	-	2/1	15s
Wollascott	-	7/1	-	-	-	3/1	10s
Totals	3,167/55	116/11	32/2	11/5	5/1	64/10	£45 3s

Table 10: List of sorts, quantities and cash-equivalent values of provisions supplied as contribution from the Shrewsbury area, 1644.[73] Sums rounded to the nearest shilling.

The provisions the local constablewicks provided for Devillier's men were given in part payment of contribution taxes. As already noted, by 1644 up to half of contributions could be made with food or provender. In Shropshire the equivalent cash value per pound weight for cheese was 2d, for butter 4d and bacon 3d. Wheat, at 4s per strike, was the most expensive bread corn, with barley the cheapest at 2s 2d per strike.[74] Table 10 lists produce given in lieu of cash as contribution delivered into the Royalist garrison at Shrewsbury, from one town ward and 16 rural townships within a seven-mile northerly radius. The table is compiled from the loose folios of

72 *A Letter sent From Sir Tho. Middleton*, p. 5; HRO, CF61/20, ff. 561-7; SA, P270/B/1/1, f. 55.
73 Source: SA, 3365/2572, ff. 1-3.
74 Townsend, *Diary*, II, p. 164; SA, 3365/2572, ff. 1-3.

an incomplete and undated ledger. Its association with other documents relating to contributions in the Shrewsbury area indicates that the surviving entries represent a three-month accounting period over high summer 1644. These records are dominated by deliveries of what amounted to more than 28 hundredweight of cheese, which together with bread was a staple in the diet of the Civil War soldier. Evidence elsewhere suggests that Shropshire's productive dairying economy was able to meet the military's demand for this important commodity. In July 1644, for example, one ton of Shropshire cheese was sent to Bridgnorth and on to Worcester in order to supply the Oxford army. Furthermore, the following September farmers in the Buildwas area sent 12-hundredweight of cheese to Shrewsbury as part-payment of contribution at the usual twopenny rate per pound.[75] Table 10 also lists smaller quantities of butter and bacon, characteristic products of local dairying. The predominance of rye among cereal crops in Shropshire is also apparent.

Grain or milled flour and other preserved foodstuffs such as cheese and bacon could be kept in magazines to provide a reserve of provisions. By March 1646 the besieged Royalist garrison of High Ercall Hall depended on such supplies, subsisting on powdered meat and bread made from their stored grain.[76] Prince Rupert in particular recognised the importance of securing food supplies, whether to sustain field operations or to endure a prolonged siege. Although on 2 February 1644 Sir Richard Newport had written forewarning him that Shrewsbury was 'altogether un-provided of a magazine of victuals', after the Prince arrived in Shropshire provisions were amassed at the main Royalist garrisons. During March, warrants were sent into the countryside around Bridgnorth to deliver provisions there, and on the 30th Rupert's Commissary General Sir William Bellenden optimistically reported that at Shrewsbury, 'there comes in great store of provisions, so that we do promise your highness a full magazine of corn at your return'. Foodstuffs contributed from the easterly hundreds of Stottesdon and Brimstree went to Bridgnorth, while Ludlow received supplies from southerly Overs hundred.[77]

Shropshire agriculture fed soldiers there and also supplied military operations further afield. Before the Civil War the county had met its obligation for purveyance by paying cash in lieu of produce. In March 1643, however, food rather than money was demanded, when a Royalist commissary officer arrived at Shrewsbury from Oxford bearing a royal warrant, to 'bring thence divers provisions for our household and army'.[78] In early June 1644 provisions were sent from Bridgnorth downriver to Bewdley in Worcestershire to supply a division of the Oxford army led by King Charles then operating in the region. That month Sir Michael Woodhouse also agreed to regularly send provisions from Ludlow to Royalist Worcester, giving orders on the 17th for a 'good store of victuals, bakers' goods, quantities of butter, cheese, bacon and malts to be provided and sent forthwith'.[79] The Parliamentarians in turn could eventually

75 'Ottley Papers' (1896), pp. 247, 253.
76 *A Copy of the Summons […] Also the taking of High-Arkall*, p. 2.
77 BL, Additional Mss 18981, ff. 24, 117; SA, 3365/2711, f. 22, order of Prince Rupert's commissioners at Shrewsbury, 2 May 1644.
78 BL, Harleian Mss 6851, f. 143.
79 SA, BB/D/1/2/1/54; SA, LB7/2251.

spare supplies to support operations elsewhere, so in November 1645 provisions from Shropshire were sent to Sir William Brereton's army besieging Chester.[80]

It remains to consider the war effort's impact on the Shropshire cattle trade, and here again the evidence is of Royalist activity. The herds appropriated by the military provided a ready supply of fresh meat. In 1644, for example, around 60 head of cattle kept by the garrison at Ludlow were grazed at the expense of the townsfolk's pastureland. The Royalists sought to control the cattle trade but found it difficult to regulate, as an anonymous memorandum to Prince Rupert, undated but probably written in later 1644, makes clear.[81] It disclosed a widespread clandestine trade, in which oxen, steers and dairy cows driven from Wales into south Shropshire were exchanged in deals struck surreptitiously away from the established livestock markets. The cattle were then herded from Shropshire into south Staffordshire in small numbers so as to avert suspicion, and (with the alleged connivance of Royalist garrisons nearby) driven through Warwickshire to Parliamentarian Coventry or onward to London. The report named two chief middlemen from south Staffordshire, who had recently been 'to Bridgnorth […] and went up and down the county and bought many cattle and have many agents for them', and stressed the strategic importance of controlling trade: 'If those cattle were brought to Worcester there happily they might be better fed at the spring and so conveyed to Oxford unto the King's friends'. The memorandum concluded by recommending to Prince Rupert that unauthorised trading should be suppressed and the cattle seized. It is therefore likely that in March 1645 Sir Lewis Kirk acted with the Prince's authority when obstructing the spring droves heading for Staffordshire passing within reach of his garrison at Bridgnorth. In south Shropshire meanwhile Sir Michael Woodhouse also adopted a characteristically ruthless policy of containment. This prompted the Archbishop of York, from his fastness at Conway in north-west Wales, to protest in January 1645 to Prince Rupert against Woodhouse's 'oppression' of the Welsh cattle droves, which he described as 'the Spanish fleet of North Wales which brings hither the little gold and silver we have'.[82]

Obtaining horses and provender

Like most pre-mechanised armies, those of the Civil Wars depended on horses for their mobility in combat and on the march. Cavalry and dragoons took their place in the line of battle, and undertook more routine duties such as reconnaissance, convoy escort and raids upon enemy outposts. Consequently a large proportion of the opposing armies were horse soldiers, in comparison to the usually more numerous and cheaper to equip foot. At the battle of Edgehill in 1642 the ratio of horse to foot was probably around one to two point five, while by 1645 the balance in the field armies on both sides was nearer one to one.[83] Sometimes substantial numbers of horsemen were deployed in Shropshire, as in July 1645, when, on the 4th, in an all-mounted engagement in Corvedale around 400 Royalist horse defeated seven Parliamentarian

80 *LBWB*, II, pp. 206-7, 222.
81 SA, LB7/2125; WSL, SMS 5513.
82 Warburton, *Prince Rupert*, I, p. 503, II, p. 386, quotation from III, p. 56.
83 Foard, *Naseby*, p. 207.

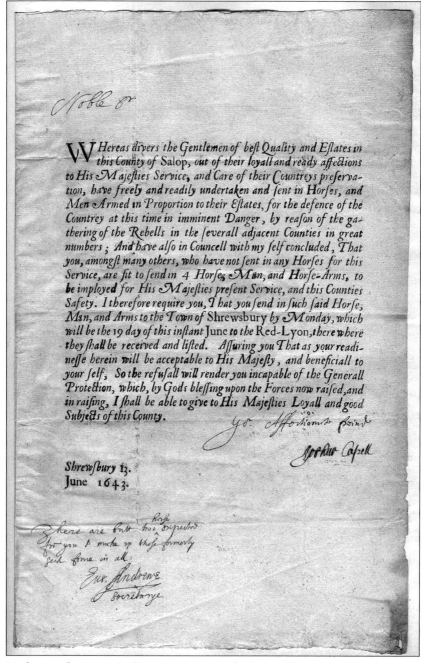

Noble Sr

WHereas divers the Gentlemen of best Quality and Estates in this County of Salop, out of their loyall and ready affections to His Majesties Service, and Care of their Countreys preservation, have freely and readily undertaken and sent in Horses, and Men Armed in Proportion to their Estates, for the defence of the Countrey at this time in imminent Danger, by reason of the gathering of the Rebells in the severall adjacent Counties in great numbers ; And have also in Councell with my self concluded, That you, amongst many others, who have not sent in any Horses for this Service, are fit to send in 4 Horses, Man, and Horse-Arms, to be imployed for His Majesties present Service, and this Counties Safety. I therefore require you, That you send in such said Horse, Man, and Arms to the Town of Shrewsbury by Monday, which will be the 19 day of this instant June to the Red-Lyon, there where they shall be received and listed. Assuring you That as your readinesse herein will be acceptable to His Majesty, and beneficiall to your self, So the refusall will render you incapable of the Generall Protection, which, by Gods blessing upon the Forces now raised, and in raising, I shall be able to give to His Majesties Loyall and good Subjects of this County.

yor Affectionate friend

Arthur Capell

Shrewsbury 13.
June 1643.

There are but two Horse expected for you & make up those formerly send some in all:

Exr Andrews
secretarye

20. A printed warrant, in this example sent to Sir Richard Leveson, directing certain Shropshire gentry to send horses, men and arms to Shrewsbury by 19 June 1643 for service in Royalist forces. (By courtesy of Staffordshire Record Office, ref. D868/2/45)

troops. The battle at High Ercall the next day may have involved around 1,500 horsemen. In addition to mounting the cavalry and dragoons, horses were used as draught animals in the artillery, baggage and supply trains of the armies, and also for other ancillary tasks. In October 1644, for example, Shrewsbury's corporation hired mounts locally for Prince Rupert's tax collectors.[84]

Large numbers of suitable animals were essential to military operations, so horse procurement became a vital activity of war effort. In this respect the outbreak of war in 1642 was propitious, for by then, as Edwards's research in particular has demonstrated, the combatants could draw upon a substantial stock of horses. During the 100 years preceding the Civil Wars there had been significant improvements in both the number and quality of horses across England and Wales, in what was of course an era of popular horse-ownership for riding and for haulage. These national developments were reflected in Shropshire. Here, during the early Stuart period horse breeding on a small-scale was widespread, with most animals being reared by yeomen farmers. However, wealthier individuals also bred and kept larger numbers of horses. Sir Andrew Corbet (the father of Royalist colonel Sir Vincent), for example, on his death in 1637 owned 28 horses, including two stallions and ten colts.[85]

The military preparations for the defence of the kingdom required by the Privy Council of the shires of Caroline England involved horses. While ensuring that the county horse troop was mounted adequately, a lord lieutenant and his deputies were also entrusted to maintain muster rolls of vehicles and teams, and also of 'nags to mount shot on' – a reserve of horses that could be used to mount musketeers as a corps of dragoons.[86] Accordingly, in summer 1635 Shropshire's deputy lieutenants dutifully sent the Earl of Bridgewater rolls of draught and riding horses, while a muster of the County Troop was planned for 10 September. In 1640 Shropshire also had to provide 40 draught horses for the royal army during the Second Bishops' War.[87]

Civil War armies obtained horses in five ways: via donation; via requisitioning; via outright theft; via purchase; and via the enemy. Early in the war the Royalists exploited Shropshire's equine population to mount locally raised units and also to provide remounts for horse soldiers posted to the county like Sir Henry Crowe's Dragoons, who during summer 1643 received horses obtained by Sir Francis Ottley. Later of course the Parliamentarians found it commensurably more difficult to obtain horses in Shropshire, hence in October 1643 Sir Thomas Myddelton could see no possibility of obtaining horseflesh in the vicinity of Wem.[88] Therefore the capital and the Home Counties became important sources of horses for the Parliamentarians campaigning in and around Shropshire. However, local horseflesh was a finite resource only slowly replenished: a colt born in 1642 would not achieve maturity to serve as

84   SA, 3365/588, f. 45.
85   P. Edwards, 'The Supply of Horses to the Parliamentarian and Royalist Armies in the English Civil War', *Historical Research*, 68 (1995), pp. 53-6; Edwards, *Dealing in Death*, pp. 155-7; Edwards, 'Shropshire Agriculture', p. 160; SA, 322/4/5, Corbet's probate inventory.
86   HHL, Ellesmere Mss 7639: Bridgewater's instructions of 9 May 1635 to Shropshire's deputy lieutenants, referring to the Privy Council's standing orders from July 1626.
87   HHL, Ellesmere Mss 7639, 7671, 7673; SA, 1831/1/5/8, order to the Drapers' Company of Shrewsbury, Apr. 1640.
88   'Ottley Papers' (1895), pp. 345-6; HMC, *Thirteenth Report, Appendix Part I*, pp. 134-5.

a cavalry horse until later 1646.[89] As a result of local shortages, by April 1644 Prince Rupert was seeking riding and draught horses for his Shropshire-based forces from as far afield as his fellow-general Sir Henry Hastings's command in the East Midlands.[90]

Both sides at first looked to voluntary donations from the gentry, the horse-owning class with the most suitable animals. Along with the horse, donors were often expected to provide tack, horseman's weapons and sometimes also the rider. An individual's response was also seen as a mark of loyalty. On 5 December 1642, in repeating an earlier warrant the Royalist leadership at Shrewsbury ordered gentlemen in the Ludlow area to send horses with tack and weaponry to be enlisted at Shrewsbury on the 15th. Previous donors were thanked, but the recalcitrant were threatened with their names being 'informed to his majesty as ill affected'. In another forced appeal for donations in June 1643 Lord Capel requested horses, arms and riders for enlistment, while threatening to deny military protection to those failing to cooperate. Among the expected donors was Sir Richard Leveson, who, although he had previously given two horses, was required to send two more, together with tack and arms, to the muster at Shrewsbury on the 19th.[91]

Parliament also expected its supporters to donate horses. The Propositions of June 1642 called for the contribution of horses, arms, and horsemen, besides plate and cash.[92] Given the early predominance of the Royalists in Shropshire Parliament's forces probably received few horses from there, but in 1643 Parliamentarian commanders raising units in London for service in the region benefitted from revised legislation. Parliament's ordinance of 10 May – 'to redress the abuses in taking horses for the supply of the army' – empowered the deputy lieutenants and committee for the Propositions in each county to regulate the collection of horses. An amendment on 29 May sanctioned the levying of horses by county quota.[93] Thereby, in June 1643 the Earl of Denbigh was authorised to obtain horses in London and Middlesex, while Sir Thomas Myddelton gained 100 horses from Surrey and Sussex.[94] This helped several troops of horse to be raised for service in Shropshire and the West Midlands, which departed the capital for Coventry in late August.[95] During 1644, Myddelton's London agents continued to receive horses by way of the Propositions: eight were brought in on 18 August by a gentleman of Maidstone, Kent, for example.[96] The Earl of Denbigh also recruited some horses and horsemen by voluntary parish quotas and contributions in his home county of Warwickshire. In spring 1644 Denbigh benefitted from quotas enforced in Staffordshire, when the county committee ordered four horses from each of the shire's divisions to be sent to the Earl's stable at Stafford.[97]

During winter 1642-3 the Shropshire Royalists in addition to voluntary subscriptions used a quota system to raise dragoons, certain allotments having to provide a number

89   Edwards, *Dealing in Death*, p. 155.
90   WSL, SMS 550/17, SMS 550/20.
91   SA, LB7/2234; SRO, D868/2/45.
92   *JHL* V, pp. 121-2, 9 June 1642.
93   *JHL*, VI, pp. 39-40, 10 May 1643; *JHL*, VI, pp. 68-9, 29 May 1643.
94   WRO, CR2017/C9, f. 9; *CSPD, 1641-1643*, p. 467.
95   *A Perfect Diurnall of some passages in Parliament*, 28 Aug.-4 Sept. 1643, p. 54; TNA SP28/34 Part 2, ff. 291-2.
96   TNA, SP28/139 Part 20, Captain Sontley's accounts, unfoliated.
97   WRO, CR2017/C9, f. 18; Pennington and Roots, *Committee at Stafford*, pp. 60, 77, 93.

of horses and armed riders. The allotments of the southerly hundreds of Clun and Purslow, for example, were each to contribute eight horses and horsemen.[98] Meanwhile eight Bridgnorth townsmen between them provided nine horses under contract to the town corporation, which undertook to pay 12d for the daily hire of the horses on active service and also compensation for loss or injury. Accordingly, in December 1643 the corporation duly paid Thomas Glover, who had supplied two horses with tack, the modest sum of £4, 'towards his losses in horses, bridles and saddles'.[99] During the Second Civil War, in July 1648 a similar quota system by allotments was introduced to mount the additional troop of horse raised by the county committee.[100]

Horses were also requisitioned by warrants subscribed and executed by the civil and military authorities; in this way a mare belonging to Thomas Heath of Ludlow was taken from him by a town constable accompanied by four Royalist soldiers. Because Civil War armies did not retain large numbers of draught horses they requisitioned additional animals as and when required. This exploited the pool of working horses owned by common people, like John Aston of Bridgnorth. Described as 'a poor man and not able to brave the loss', Aston was compensated by the corporation in October 1645 for the horse he lost by Royalist impressment. The requisitioning of their animals was an ongoing grievance of Ludlow's townsfolk, who in their petition of 1644 declared 'that no horse or teams may be gone after presses but that payment may be first made'.[101]

Unpaid requisitioning was, in effect, legitimised theft, but soldiers also arbitrarily stole horses for their own use or resale. Horse thieving was widespread and recurrent. In July 1643, for instance, Sir Thomas Wolrych, as governor of Bridgnorth, was informed that Royalist troopers had taken 'by violence' four horses from a loyal local farmer. In December 1644, on the evening of the 4th Royalist troopers leaving Stanton Lacy near Ludlow broke into a stable and took two mares, and on their march north also stole a horse from Richard Burnell of Acton Scott parish. Burnell enterprisingly tracked the thieves to their destination, the garrison at High Ercall.[102] Both sides officially condemned and sometimes severely punished horse thieving – Edward Preece, a Royalist soldier from Myddle, for example, was hanged for it – and occasionally there was restitution. In January 1644 the county committee at Stafford ordered that a horse stolen by a trooper from Wem and sold to a Parliamentarian captain should be returned to its rightful owner.[103] Horses were branded to counter theft, as in May 1644 when one John Salisbury received 14s for 'marking' horses of Sir Thomas Myddelton's brigade, while at Shrewsbury Royalist mounts were seen branded with a stylised royal crest – described as 'CR and the print of a wheel'.[104]

Many animals were obtained legitimately through the established channels of horse-trading. Cavalry officers made occasional purchases while on campaign, like

98   BCHRC, First Minute Book, f. 203
99   SA, BB/C/1/1/1, unfoliated; SA, BB/D/1/2/1/53.
100 SA, LB7/1936-7.
101 SA/LB7/2130; SA, BB/C/1/1/1, unfoliated; SA, LB7/2319, unfoliated.
102 'Ottley Papers' (1895), pp. 347-8; SA/LB7/2136.
103 Gough, *Myddle*, p. 71; Pennington and Roots, *Committee at Stafford*, p. 42.
104 TNA, SP28/346 Part 1, f. 50; SA, 3365/2566, unfoliated.

Lieutenant Tayler, a Warwickshire horseman who served in Humphrey Mackworth's troop in Shropshire in 1643-4, who spent a small allowance of £13 on horses.[105] But horseflesh was also purchased in larger numbers. Mounts for Sir Thomas Myddelton's brigade were bought at Smithfield, London's main livestock market, from leading dealers such as Harvey Conway. On 4 April 1644 Conway was contracted for £150 to deliver 20 'able and serviceable' troop horses to one of Myddelton's captains. Similarly, early the following May Benjamin Ash, another prominent dealer, was paid almost £132 for the purchase and livery charges of 20 horses. London's saddlers meanwhile supplied tack for Myddelton's horses. Parliament's armies generally relied on the manufacturing capacity of the London industry for the bulk of their saddlery ware, and between January and May 1644 Myddelton's officers and agents purchased more than 480 sets of tack from the leading producers Ellis Parry, Benjamin Potter and William Pease.[106] There is little extant evidence of the Civil War horse trade in Shropshire, although Royalist soldiers bought mounts at the annual livestock fairs held around 22 July at Bridgnorth in 1644 and in 1645. Among them was a dragoon who acquired a 'grey nag' in a part-exchange deal with a gentleman from Herefordshire at the fair in 1645.[107]

The opposing army was a lucrative source of horses. Captured horses were habituated to military service, and might be taken with tack and other equipment. Their loss also weakened the enemy's mobility and offensive capability. Horses were usually part of the victor's spoils after every action, as in June 1645 when those surrendered by the Royalist garrison of Caus Castle were reportedly 'delivered up to the [county] committee for the public service'.[108] A characteristic action of the Civil Wars in which taking horses was an objective was the so-called 'beating up of quarters' – a raid on the enemy's camp. An example of this kind of operation, to which a unit of horse at rest was especially vulnerable, was the raid on 5 August 1644 by Myddelton's and Mytton's forces upon Prince Rupert's Regiment of Horse recuperating at Welshpool. With his men dispersed to billets in the town and surrounding countryside, and most of their horses unsaddled and put to grass during daytime, Major Dallison on 4 August wrote fearing a sudden 'blow' against his scattered command. His fears were realised before dawn the next morning, when the Parliamentarians attacked. Offering little resistance Dallison and most of his men escaped, but the enemy reportedly captured around 200 of their horses.[109] Back in March the Royalists had achieved similar success at Market Drayton, when Prince Rupert's men gained 100 horses after routing the Parliamentarian Shropshire and Yorkshire Horse.[110] Horses were also vulnerable to enemy raids when put to grass outside a garrison's protective perimeter because nearby pasture had been denuded by over grazing or stripped of turf for building earthwork defences. In August 1644 a patrol led by Colonel Mytton reportedly seized upon by

---

105 WRO/CR0285, f. 172.

106 TNA, SP28/346 Part 1, irregular foliation.

107 SA, BB/C/6/1/1-6, unfoliated

108 *The Kingdomes Weekly Intelligencer*, 25 June-2 July 1645, p. 844.

109 Dallison's dispatch to Prince Rupert was found by the Parliamentarians and published in transcript in *The True Informer*, 10-17 Aug. 1644, pp. 319-20; *CSPD, 1644*, p. 405.

110 *Mercurius Aulicus*, w/e 9 Mar. 1644, pp. 870-1.

chance some Royalist cavalry horses grazing on the Monkmoor beyond the easterly defences of Shrewsbury, and in July 1645 Parliamentarian cavalry similarly attempted to rustle horses kept outside town by the Royalists at Bridgnorth.[111]

Feeding and caring for horses to keep them fit and serviceable had a significant logistical and financial impact on the war effort. Horses were routinely shod and when unwell treated by army farriers, like the Royalist John Bromley at Bridgnorth in 1644, while civilian tradesmen also provided services for the upkeep of army horses. In summer 1644, for example, Sir Thomas Myddelton's wagon master paid for the shoeing and for running repairs to the harnesses of draught horses on convoy work between Stafford, Wem and Oswestry.[112] Because working horses need a nourishing diet, including cereals and pulses as well as grass or hay, Civil War armies had regularly to gather and purchase large supplies of provender. Livery bills for horses in garrison or awaiting deployment soon accumulated. John Ward, a London ostler, was owed £145 and fell into debt after stabling horses for the Earl of Denbigh during his recruiting drive in the capital in 1643. Meanwhile, Sir Richard Prince found over two months that providing stabling and grazing on his paddocks outside Shrewsbury for nearly 100 Royalist cavalry horses had cost him £32. Householders providing free quarters for horse-soldiers also had to provide provender, like the Shrewsbury leather worker Thomas Betton who for six days in March 1643 fed four Royalist troopers and bought oats and hay for their horses.[113]

Fodder was stockpiled in the magazines of the garrisons by commissaries like John Duckett, who later recollected his employment by the county committee 'to get in oats and such like provisions'. Similarly responding to warrants issued by the Royalist garrison at Bridgnorth during 1644 and 1645, Stockton's parish constables delivered hay and oats there by the cartload, and sometime in 1645 also sent oats and peas to nearby Worfield where Royalist horsemen from Lichfield were billeted.[114] The Royalists also accumulated provender given as contribution in lieu of cash payments. During 1644 the cash equivalent for hay was 1s 8d per hundredweight and 1s 4d pence per strike for oats and peas. In late summer 1644 townships in the liberties of Shrewsbury fulfilled their contributions in this way. Hencott, for example, supplied seven hundredweight of hay, and Coton six strikes of peas, while Hadnall and Great Berwick between them provided seven strikes of oats. Individual landowners also contributed fodder, such as Francis Burton of Longner Hall near Atcham, who in early February 1645 received a warrant from the Royalists at Shrewsbury to provide up to 50 loads of hay.[115]

The opposing garrisons coveted supplies of provender, especially in mid-winter when stocks were limited. In January 1645, a London newsbook reporting how Parliamentarian Oswestry was endangered by the equidistant Royalist strongholds at Shrawardine and Chirk described how: 'neither is there any hay left there, save what is

111 *The Perfect Occurrences of Parliament And Chief Collections of Letters*, 9-16 Aug. 1644, unpaginated; *The Moderate Intelligencer*, 10-17 July 1645, p. 156.
112 SA, BB/C/6/1/1-6, unfoliated; TNA, SP28/346 Part 1, f. 79.
113 WRO, CR2017/C10, f. 75; SA, 3365/2566, unfoliated.
114 SA, 3365/2263, unfoliated, Duckett's petition, *c.* 1646-7; SA, P270/B/1/1, ff. 55-8.
115 Townsend, *Diary*, II, p. 164; SA, 3365/2572, ff. 1-3; Warburton, *Prince Rupert*, III, p. 58.

as much under the power of the enemy, as under the command of Colonel Mytton'.[116] Foraging expeditions were mounted to secure supplies, as in February 1644 when soon after arriving in Shropshire Prince Rupert sent a strong detachment of horse and foot from Shrewsbury into the countryside around Wem, which returned with 30 cartloads of hay. In harvest-time 1645 a party of Parliamentarian horse reportedly captured 22 cartloads of hay and corn by intercepting a similar sortie by Royalists from High Ercall and Lilleshall.[117]

The relentless and apparently insatiable demand for provender imposed great demands on local supplies. In 1644, Ludlow's townsfolk called for the removal of 'the troops of horse […] in regard of the scarceness of hay and provender for their accommodation', while after that year's harvest officials of Shrewsbury's corn market reported how demand by the Royalist military for local yields of corn, especially oats taken for fodder, had caused toll revenues to collapse.[118] Such problems were exacerbated when the military disrupted farming and caused damage to crops. In July 1643 Lord Capel had reportedly infuriated Oswestry's husbandmen, by putting 'all his horse into their meadows, which hath eaten and spoiled all their grass'. During 1644 Thomas Tipton of Frankwell, Shrewsbury, also complained of the damaging loss of pasture, cut from his tenants' land as forage for Royalist cavalry.[119]

Transportation and distribution

War matériel once procured had to be transported to and around the theatre of operations. The key entrepôts for armaments were Oxford and Bristol for the Royalists, and London for the Parliamentarians. However, because Shropshire was far from these centres long-distance supply lines had to be established. Military supplies brought to Shropshire or obtained locally were distributed to the various magazines, while units took reserve stocks of munitions and provisions with them on campaign. All of this activity – involving riverine and road transport and the procurement of vehicles and draught animals, and requiring the services of large numbers of personnel, including military commissary officers and civilian carters, porters and boatmen – was shaped by the pre-existing routes of trade and communication.

The Severn navigation

The River Severn was the single most important means of transportation for finished goods and raw materials into and out of Shropshire during the seventeenth century. A usually toll-free arterial trade route of great regional importance connecting the county to the major ports of Gloucester and Bristol, the Severn was commercially navigable throughout its course in Shropshire by sailing barges and other, larger, shallow-draught trading vessels called Trows. Hence, both Shrewsbury and Bridgnorth were locally important inland ports.[120] In February 1634 Bridgnorth's

---

116 *The Perfect Occurrences of Parliament And Chief Collections of Letters,* 10-17 Jan. 1645, unpaginated.
117 HMC, *Thirteenth Report, Appendix Part I,* pp. 170-1; *Heads of Some Notes of the Citie Scout,* 28 Aug. 1645, p. 5.
118 SA, LB7/2319; SA, 3365/2263, unfoliated.
119 *Certaine Informations from Severall Parts of the Kingdom,* 10-17 July 1643, p. 202; SA, 3365/2263, unfoliated.
120 Court, *Midland Industries,* pp. 6-9; T.S. Willan, 'The River Navigation and Trade of the Severn Valley, 1600-1750', *The Economic History Review,* 8 (1937), pp. 68-9, 77-8; Trinder, *Industrial Revolution,* pp. 7, 10.

aldermen, in declaring their opposition to a scheme to improve the navigability of the Warwickshire Avon, described the Severn's vital economic importance to Shropshire, to 'common commerce and traffic which we have with other countries [counties]'; by 'carrying away coals and other fuels, and butter and cheese which is the life and chief supportation of the same'.[121]

King Charles's army used the Severn as a military highway from autumn 1642, when towards the end of September six cannon were shipped from Shrewsbury for the defence of Bridgnorth. Foot soldiers and supplies took the same passage in October, when Bridgnorth was the main mustering point for the army in its advance out of Shropshire. Accordingly, boatmen and their vessels were hired or commandeered, including Abram Gyles, a Shrewsbury bargeman, who on or around 12 October shipped a Captain Boles's company to Bridgnorth.[122] In March 1644 Prince Rupert also used the Severn for troop deployment, when 1,100 commanded musketeers were lifted downriver from Shrewsbury to rendezvous with the Prince at Bridgnorth on the 15th, thence embarking on the campaign to relieve Newark.[123]

However, Parliamentarian strongholds restricted the use that the Royalists could make of the River Severn as a supply route into and out of Shropshire. Bristol was under Parliamentarian control by December 1642, when a Royalist there wrote advising Sir Francis Ottley that enemy riverine patrols prevented arms being smuggled from the port.[124] Although Bristol fell to the Royalists seven months later, they were still denied access to the lower Severn because Gloucester remained a vital Parliamentarian garrison throughout the First Civil War. The middle Severn from Shrewsbury to Worcester, however, was useful to the Royalists for transporting the armaments made in Shropshire, because ordnance and shot were more easily carried by water than by road. In April 1644, for instance, river craft were used in preference to a wagon convoy to carry from Bridgnorth to Worcester cannon shot and grenades urgently needed at Oxford. Offloaded at Worcester, the munitions then went overland to the Royalist capital.[125] This ammunition had been made at Leighton, where the foundry's location beside the Severn allowed output to be directly shipped downstream to Bridgnorth and Worcester, or upstream to Shrewsbury, where on 8 June 1643 a boatman delivered 900 round shot. The Royalists also hired a Severn barge for several days in September 1643 to transport turves cut from surrounding fields into Shrewsbury, to be used as revetments in the town's earthwork fortifications.[126]

The important pre-war trade in transporting coal from the east Shropshire coalfield to Shrewsbury and Worcester also continued despite the fighting. However, by December 1645 the combatants were engaging in mutually damaging economic warfare by blockading, as was reported, the riverine 'free trade in coals' from the pits close by the Severn at Benthall, Broseley, Dawley and Madeley. The Parliamentarian

121 SA, BB/C/1/1/1, unfoliated.
122 *The Latest Remarkable Truths From Worcester, Chester, Salop, Warwick, Stafford, Somerset, Devon, Yorke and Lincoln Counties* (1642), p. 8; SA, 6000/13285-6, 13298.
123 *Mercurius Aulicus*, w/e 23 Mar. 1644, p. 894.
124 'Ottley Papers' (1894), p. 54.
125 BL, Additional Mss 18981, ff. 130, 153.
126 SA, 6000/13314; SA, 3365/588, f. 4.

garrison at Benthall disrupted downstream deliveries heading for Bridgnorth and Worcester, while roving Royalist patrols from High Ercall and Bridgnorth attempted to obstruct the passage to Shrewsbury by intimidating or seizing the boatmen.[127]

Local overland routes and carriers

While the River Severn was of some importance as a supply route to the Royalists in Shropshire, for both sides most war matériel was transported overland.

John Ogilby's *Britannia*, an atlas of the kingdom's main roads published in 1675 and an important development in cartography, identified the 'principal roads' traversing seventeenth-century Shropshire.[128] (The wider regional main road network identified by Ogilby is reconstructed in Map 7). The main north-south route through Shropshire was the Chester to Bristol road, through Whitchurch and Shrewsbury and on to Ludlow, with a north-westerly spur heading via Ellesmere into Flintshire. The southerly of the two other 'principal' roads, crossing Shropshire 18 or so miles apart on an approximately parallel south-easterly to westerly course, was the London to Montgomery road, via Worcester and Tenbury, which entered Shropshire south of Ludlow and traversed the southerly hill country. The second cross-county route, to Shrewsbury, led from Bridgnorth, where a spur of the London to Holyhead road crossing northern Warwickshire and southern Staffordshire, and another southerly London route via Oxfordshire converged. From the county town this London to Shrewsbury road continued westerly to the Welsh border. Beyond these and other thoroughfares lay a network of lesser roads and trackways, following often-ancient courses determined by the interconnection of market places and the movement of livestock. Drove roads from Wales crossed Shropshire, and livestock was driven locally to common grazing along driftways and straker routes. Richard Gough in describing some of the lesser ways crossing Myddle parish left an impression of seventeenth-century Shropshire's mazelike network of local routes: 'the Linch Lane, the lane that leads from Haston to Balderton, the Sling Lane, Bald Meadow Lane, Whitrish Lane … '.[129]

The condition of Shropshire's thoroughfares was probably as variable as the differing ways that historians have interpreted the state of the roads of Stuart England. Crofts considered that roads were often 'thought of as a strip of land' not to be farmed or quarried, rather than treated as permanent structures. On the other hand, Chartres pictured an expansive seventeenth-century road network supporting widespread carrying services.[130] Ogilby's laconic itineraries offer a vague impression of the state of Shropshire's principal routes: the London road from Oxfordshire approaching Bridgnorth was good, 'a well accommodated and frequented road', while the London to Montgomery road was 'to Ludlow indifferent, but better to Bishop's Castle', the

---

127 *The Weekly Account*, 10-17 Dec. 1645, unpaginated; *LBWB*, II, pp. 206-7.

128 J. Ogilby, *Britannia, or an Illustration of the Kingdom of England and Dominion of Wales by a Geographical and Historical Description of the Principal Roads thereof* (1675).

129 T. Rowley, *The Shropshire Landscape* (London, 1972), pp. 241-2; Gough, *Myddle*, pp. 68-9.

130 J. Crofts, *Packhorse, Waggon and Post: Land Carriage and Communications Under the Tudors and Stuarts* (London, 1967), p. 14; J.A. Chartres, 'Road Carrying in England in the Seventeenth Century: Myth and Reality', *The Economic History Review*, 30 (1977), p. 87.

latter stretch being 'much up hill and down dale'. Ogilby depicted Shropshire's main roads as unenclosed along much of their course, allowing them to broaden into driftways across open fields or heath: 'so that', as Crofts considered elsewhere, 'the line of the road evaporated into an abstract right of way'.[131] The stretches of roadway near to bridges and market towns were most likely to benefit from the statutory obligation upon each parish to provide highway maintenance. In February 1641, for example, Bridgnorth's corporation authorised repairs for a mile or so from the town to a westerly stretch of the London to Shrewsbury road. But the national road network deteriorated during the First Civil War because only militarily essential repairs were made. For that reason, in late 1645 the Chester road through Coton, Shrewsbury's northerly suburb, was reported by a local petty constable to be 'very much out of order'.[132]

Despite uncertain maintenance and variable construction, frequently worsened by the weather, roads and trackways became military supply lines. Civil War armies for road transport relied mostly on civilian hauliers and carriers, conscripted or hired on a more or less makeshift basis. Accordingly, by 8 October 1642 horses and vehicles commandeered as transport for the King's army for the forthcoming campaign were being gathered at Shrewsbury, including the two carts provided by distant Stockton parish.[133] When the army moved into the Bridgnorth area, on 13 October further warrants were circulated for the surrounding areas to provide additional transport. However, the limitations of relying on coerced civilian drivers reluctant to leave their locality were becoming apparent, so that day King Charles instructed his Lieutenant-General of Ordnance, Sir John Heyden, to order that 'no carts, wains, horses taken up for the use of the artillery shall depart the service upon pain of death'.[134]

However, civilian hauliers also entered into paid contractual arrangements, like Edward Colbatch of Ludlow and John Lewis of Bridgnorth who were both paid for transporting ammunition, during 1642-3 and in February 1645 respectively.[135] Indeed, the regulatory orders published by the Royalist parliament at Oxford stipulated the rates for mileage – at 2d for a horse, and 1½d for an ox, per mile – that the army should pay for civilian transport.[136] The tariff for oxen was particularly relevant to Shropshire, where they were used for haulage and often preferred by farmers instead of horses for plough work. Oxen, then, were also used for military transport work, and so Sir Richard Prince sent two drivers, with a team of four oxen, and one of two horses, to Lord Capel's army for five days in 1643.[137] William Jordan of Acton Scott parish was an occasional carter whose petition, complaining of being unpaid by the Royalist military for most of his work during 1644, provides insight into the workload of civilian hauliers. With his wain and team Jordan ferried ammunition from Ludlow to Church Stretton, transported timber to the garrison at Stokesay Castle, and in

131 Ogilby, *Britannia*, pp. 23, 87-8; Crofts, *Packhorse, Waggon and Post*, p. 15.
132 SA, BB/C/1/1/1, unfoliated; SA, 3365/1267, f. 20.
133 *Continuation of the late proceedings of His Majesty's Army*, p. 4; SA, P270/B/1/1, f. 51.
134 SA, BB/D/1/2/1/52; *ROP*, I, p. 152.
135 SA, LB8/1/163, f. 3; SA, BB/D/1/2/1/55.
136 *Orders […] of Parliament Assembled at Oxford*, p. 8.
137 Crofts, *Packhorse, Waggon and Post*, pp. 133-4; SA, 3365/2566, unfoliated.

March delivered provisions to the forces besieging Hopton Castle.[138]

In Shropshire at this time the vehicles used to carry freight hauled by oxen or horse teams were carts and tumbrils and the heavier load-bearing wains and wagons, all generally two rather than four-wheeled types.[139] While Civil War armies relied on such requisitioned civilian vehicles, they also kept small permanent transport parks, particularly for the artillery trains. Hence several wagons and carriages with draught harnesses were purchased in London in March 1644 for Sir Thomas Myddelton's brigade, while wagons from the artillery park of the Oxford army carried munitions to Shropshire for Prince Rupert's forces.[140]

Vehicles seem to have been the predominant means of military transport, but packhorses had excellent mobility over rough ways and hill country and had been important to Shropshire's pre-war economy, especially the ponies indigenous to Wales and the Marches used as pack animals in the cross-border cloth trade. Evidence of Royalist military packhorse traffic during 1644 is found in the petitions of three Ludlow townsmen: Walter Lea, whose horse, with 'a [pack?] saddle and a collar', was lost during the Montgomery campaign; Samuel France, who had a horse commandeered that died in carrying ammunition to Chester; and William Bagley, who provided fodder for a packhorse convoy – described as 'twelve horses with munition to carry to Shrewsbury'.[141]

Long-distance supply lines

Beyond these local transportation arrangements, the bulk of the war matériel upon which both sides depended arrived in Shropshire via long-distance supply lines. These routes of communication are reconstructed in Map 7.

The Parliamentarians' main supply line led firstly from London to Coventry, Parliament's stronghold in the central Midlands since the city had barred it gates to King Charles in August 1642. Soldiers and supplies took the London to Holyhead road, described by Ogilby as following Watling Street from St. Albans to Towcester, and thence, via Daventry or Northampton, to Coventry – thereby skirting Royalist Oxfordshire and Worcestershire. London-based carriers and waggoners delivered supplies to Coventry for the West Midland Association and for Sir Thomas Myddelton's brigade. In February 1644, for example, three carriers employed by the Earl of Denbigh between them delivered two and a half tons of gunpowder, charging 8s per hundredweight. In April, another carrier transported three and a half tons of ammunition for Myddelton.[142] From Coventry, supplies were transferred to Parliamentarian Stafford via Meriden, Tamworth and Rugeley, the route taken by Denbigh's army in May 1644. In January 1646, armaments stockpiled at Coventry for Thomas Mytton's campaign into North Wales were also convoyed along this route to Stafford.[143] In its final stretch through Staffordshire the route from Stafford to

138 SA, LB7/2144.
139 Edwards, 'Shropshire Agriculture', pp. 149-50.
140 TNA, SP28/346 Part 1, f. 45; SP28/346 Part 2, f. 50; BL, Additional Mss 18981, f. 60; *ROP*, I, p. 342.
141 SA, LB7/2112, 2148, 2158.
142 TNA, SP28/34 Part 2, f. 251; SP28/346 Part 1, f. 51.
143 *Newes from Prince Rupert […] The Earl with his forces marched against them*, pp. 1-5; *CSPD, 1645-1647*, p. 297.

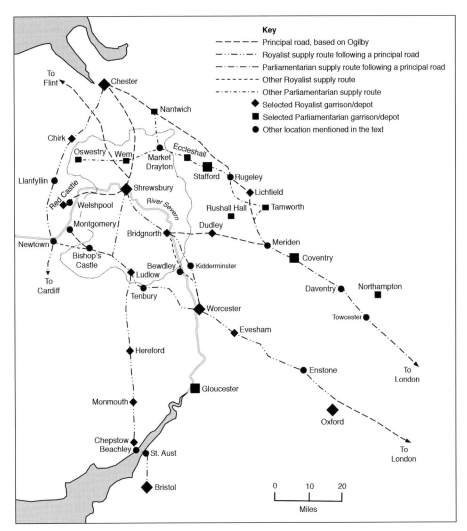

Key

- - - - - Principal road, based on Ogilby
- · - · - · - Royalist supply route following a principal road
- · - · - · - Parliamentarian supply route following a principal road
- - - - - Other Royalist supply route
- · - · - · - Other Parliamentarian supply route
◆ Selected Royalist garrison/depot
■ Selected Parliamentarian garrison/depot
● Other location mentioned in the text

Map 7: Main supply lines into Shropshire as they may
have operated during summer 1644.

Wem passed the Parliamentarian garrison at Eccleshall Castle. Here, in 1644 the nearby village of Yarnfield provided teams and carters to relay Sir Thomas Myddelton's supplies en route to Wem.[144] Crossing into Shropshire, at Market Drayton convoys were routed northward to Sir William Brereton's Cheshire stronghold at Nantwich or on to Wem.

The Royalists could threaten this London to Shropshire route along much of its course. Accordingly, in October 1643 the committee of Warwickshire warned the Earl of Denbigh against sending artillery from London to Coventry because of enemy activity.[145] However, the threat from Royalist garrisons in Staffordshire lessened after Denbigh captured Rushall Hall, near Walsall, in May 1644. A London newsbook reported the Earl's success: 'this will appear a very considerable service, and of great benefit to the country [Staffordshire] in opening the passage to Coventry and London'. But the way to Wem was often endangered by Royalist blockade. In the third week of December 1643 his colleagues there wrote instructing Humphrey Mackworth to suspend the movement of supplies from Coventry, because the 'passages are now so stopped'.[146]

Two long-distance Royalist supply lines led to Shropshire. Along the first supplies were conveyed from Oxford. The organisation and route of one such convoy, bringing munitions to Shropshire in early October 1643 escorted by the returning infantry regiments of Sir Michael Woodhouse and Richard Herbert, can be reconstructed from the papers of the Oxford-based Royalist Office of Ordnance.[147] Leaving the city on 29 September, two conductors (Ordnance Office transport officers) led the convoy, of one wagon and two carts drawn by horses from the Oxford artillery train, via Woodstock to Enstone, 14 miles north-west of Oxford on the Worcester road. With fresh teams provided at Enstone, the convoy resumed the 35-mile journey to Worcester on the London to Montgomery road, crossing the northern Cotswolds and continuing via Evesham. Arriving at Worcester on 2 October, the convoy was met by carts and fresh teams from Shropshire sent in advance by Colonel Robert Ellice; fortuitously so, it seems, because at Worcester Sir Michael Woodhouse found 'much confusion to get a horse'. With the loads transferred, supervised by one of the Oxford conductors the convoy continued to Ludlow, arriving on 12 October. After crossing the Severn at Worcester this convoy would have followed the London to Montgomery road along the valley of the River Teme, via Tenbury, to Ludlow, the route taken in mid-February 1644 by a four-wagon ammunition convoy from Oxford. Upon arriving at Worcester, the conductor in charge sent orders ahead for the authorities at Ludlow to requisition two carts and eight horse teams to allow the convoy's ongoing journey to Shrewsbury. Convoys to Bridgnorth from Worcester could travel either side of the Severn valley, on the east bank along the London road via Kidderminster and Quatt, or by the bridge at Bewdley taking a lesser road on the west bank; in April 1644 several unescorted

144 Pennington and Roots, *Committee at Stafford*, p. 281.
145 WRO, CR2017/C9, f. 33.
146 *CSPD, 1644*, pp. 177-8; *A Perfect Diurnall of some passages in Parliament*, 27 May-3 June 1644, p. 351; WRO, CR2017/C9, f. 37.
147 TNA, WO55/459/Part 3, ff. 477-9, 481.

wagons went by this latter route from Bridgnorth to Worcester.[148]

In 1644 supplies from Bristol for Prince Rupert's command were first routed via Oxford and Worcester. A consignment of munitions reported on 16 March as being delayed in departing Bristol had arrived at Worcester by the 28th, where preparations were made for its journey onward to Shrewsbury.[149] But stores from Bristol also went by an alternative route, through the Welsh Marches along the Royalists' second main supply line. This followed the Bristol to Chester road described by Ogilby. From Bristol, supplies were carried north nine miles to the Severn crossing at St. Aust and ferried across the estuary to Beachley Head near Chepstow. From there, the route traversed Monmouthshire and Herefordshire, to Ludlow and Shrewsbury, and on to Chester. Around 20 June 1644 a Chester-bound convoy from Bristol taking this route narrowly avoided interception by Parliamentarians near Oswestry. The Royalists after losing Oswestry diverted their convoys further westward into Wales, along the northerly stretch of the Cardiff to Chester road. A Chester-bound munitions convoy from Bristol captured at Newtown in Montgomeryshire on 4 September by Myddelton's brigade had been diverted at Ludlow to follow this supposedly safer but more laborious passage, via Llanfyllin to the key Royalist garrison and staging post at Chirk Castle.[150]

By autumn 1644 this overextended line of communication along the Welsh Marches had become increasingly vulnerable to enemy action and other disruption. In September, the Gloucester garrison followed up a raid on the Severn landing at Beachley Head by capturing Royalist Monmouth on the 26th, which remained in Parliamentarian hands for the next two months. By mid-October Royalist communications were further obstructed by Myddelton's garrisons in Montgomeryshire, so that on the 13th one of Prince Rupert's aides wrote despairing for the safety of any supplies sent from Bristol into the Marches. In early March 1645, ammunition sent from Bristol for Prince Rupert at Ludlow was stranded at Chepstow because the locals refused to provide transport; meanwhile an uprising of clubmen against the Royalist military in Herefordshire had endangered supply lines there.[151]

Shortages of supplies, and their loss or capture, could have a significant effect on the military situation. Considerable effort was made, therefore, to protect or intercept convoys, as in the example of two such actions in Shropshire. Notwithstanding the Royalist ammunition convoy sent from Shrewsbury in early January 1644 to Lord Byron's army besieging Nantwich having a strong escort of 400 cavalry, when the convoy halted overnight at Ellesmere on the night of the 12th/13th it was surprised and captured by a smaller Parliamentarian force from Wem. The following August, Royalist horse operating out of nearby Whittington attacked a Parliamentarian munitions convoy from Wem bound for Oswestry, but were beaten off by the escort and mounted reinforcements from Oswestry's garrison.[152]

148 SA, LB7/2249; BL, Additional Mss 18981, f. 153.
149 Day, *Pythouse Papers*, p. 28; WSL, SMS 537.
150 *CSPD, 1644*, p. 258; WRO, CR2017/C9, ff. 131, 133; BL, Additional Mss 18981, f. 245.
151 Phillips, *Civil War in Wales*, I, pp. 257-60, 272-3; Carte, *Ormond*, VI, p. 206; BL, Additional Mss 18981, f. 83.
152 Carte, *Original Letters*, I, p. 40; *The Perfect Occurrences of Parliament And Chief Collections of Letters*, 6-13 Sept.

Magazines

Convoys delivered to the magazines that served as storage and distribution centres for military supplies. Even small strong points kept a magazine, for example Longford House near Newport. When the Parliamentarian garrison surrendered to Prince Rupert on 3 April 1644 it yielded provisions, four barrels of gunpowder, supplies of match and bullets, some hand grenades, 40 pikes and 100 muskets.[153]

The pre-war county magazine had been located at Shrewsbury and the Royalists kept their main regional depot there. The Parliamentarians found the garrison well supplied when they took the town in February 1645, and reported the capture of nearly 2,000 weapons and 14 cannon, along with 100 barrels of gunpowder.[154] The repair and refurbishment of Shrewsbury Castle as an arsenal had been completed soon after Prince Rupert's arrival in February 1644. On 25 January Rupert had written forewarning Sir Francis Ottley, demanding 'the covering of the castle of Shrewsbury, and the dividing and disposing thereof into rooms capable and fitting to receive the stores'. Ottley responded by hastening building work there and arranging temporary storage facilities.[155] After Shrewsbury fell, Bridgnorth and Ludlow remained as Royalist supply depots. Provisions and ammunition were received at Bridgnorth in May 1645 during the northerly advance of the main Royalist field army, for example.[156] Prince Rupert had gathered military supplies at Ludlow in early March 1645, and when the castle was surrendered in 1646 the Parliamentarians found it still well provisioned and holding a number of pieces of ordnance and 37 barrels of gunpowder.[157]

After the First Civil War the county magazine remained at Shrewsbury Castle, with a subsidiary depot at Ludlow. On 5 June 1647, the day after King Charles had been taken into army custody, the county committee took the precaution of ordering the transfer of the Ludlow magazine to Shrewsbury, and the confiscation and delivery into the castle of all arms in private ownership. That August, the arsenal at Shrewsbury Castle was well enough supplied to allow the equipping of the town militia with 400 muskets and pikes and 20 barrels of gunpowder.[158]

During the First Civil War the Parliamentarians had kept regional magazines at Nantwich and Stafford. By May 1644 the magazine of the West Midland Association had been established at Stafford, and a large consignment of armaments delivered there on the 16th included 682 matchlock muskets with 740 bandoliers, and 59 barrels of gunpowder. Stafford in turn supplied the magazine kept at Wem jointly by the committee of Shropshire and Sir Thomas Myddelton. Deliveries into Wem from late June to mid-July 1644 included 200 muskets, three hundredweight of match, 20 barrels of gunpowder, two petards, and three cannon with 200 rounds of ammunition.[159] Immediately after the fighting for Oswestry, on 2 July six barrels

1644, unpaginated.
153 *Mercurius Aulicus*, w/e 6 Apr. 1644, p. 921.
154 Tibbutt, *Letter Books of Sir Samuel Luke*, p. 465.
155 Phillips, *Civil War in Wales*, II, pp. 257-60; BL, Additional Mss 18981, f. 19.
156 SA, BB/D/1/2/1/55.
157 Warburton, *Prince Rupert*, III, pp. 68-9; Carr and Atherton, *Civil War in Staffordshire*, p. 267.
158 NLW, Aston Hall Estate Records: Correspondence, C2; D1 Mss 2470, 2586.
159 TNA, SP28/15 Part 1, ff. 42-3; SP28/242 Part 3, ff. 440, 447-8, 450, 452.

21. The remains of the Civil War gatehouse or barbican at Shrewsbury
Castle completed in early 1644, when under Prince Rupert's direction
the Royalists had adapted the castle for use as a magazine. Note the
embrasures in the walls to allow forward or flanking defensive fire.

of gunpowder, six hundredweight of match and a thousand-weight of bullets were
transferred there from Myddelton's stores at Wem. By mid-October arsenals had also
been established at Myddelton's Montgomeryshire garrisons. On the 10th and 12th,
the magazines at Montgomery Castle and the Red Castle between them received 22
barrels of gunpowder and nine hundredweight of match.[160]

Both sides also made use of more temporary storehouses, including private residences.
In London, in summer 1643 the Earl of Denbigh rented a 'chamber and warehouse
for the ammunition', where he employed a staff of waggoners, porters and watchmen
to deliver, handle, pack and oversee military supplies. From there armaments were
delivered to Denbigh's town house at Coventry. Sometimes during 1644 Humphrey
Mackworth's house at Coventry was also used to provide temporary accommodation
for military supplies delivered from London. At Shrewsbury, in March 1644 a Royalist
commissary officer delivered gunpowder and match to Sir Richard Leveson's town
house, where it was re-packaged and transferred to Leveson's garrison at Lilleshall.[161]

Magazines were supervised by commissary officers and their deputies, who
managed the procurement and also the delivery and distribution of supplies. One

160 NLW, Chirk Castle Mss 1/Biii, 93, unfoliated.
161 TNA, SP28/34 Part 2, ff. 238, 291; SP28/346 Part 1, f. 51; WRO, CR2017/C9, f. 44; SRO, D593/R/1/3/2,
      unfoliated.

David Maurice was chief commissary to Sir Thomas Myddelton's brigade throughout 1644 and into 1645, and in later 1644 John Taylor was Maurice's sub-commissary officer at the Red Castle. The ex-Royalist quartermaster John Visgate later claimed to have been commissary of the ammunition magazine at Shrewsbury under Sir Francis Ottley's governorship.[162]

Conclusions

Because of the widespread support for King Charles in Shropshire and the region, from the onset of civil war the Royalists exploited the military resources available to them. They used existing industries to produce armaments and equipment, of which Shropshire's iron industry was of most importance to the wider Royalist war effort. However, because residual stocks and local and regional manufactures could not supply all their needs, increasingly the Royalists drew supplies from much further afield. The Parliamentarians were denied local resources for most of the First Civil War and so obtained military supplies mostly in London, by purchase and also by grants from central stores. As the war progressed they established a wider supply network, involving importers and regional producers. Both sides made extensive use of captured armaments.

Shropshire agriculture to a great extent became a militarised command economy linked to taxation. Producers had to provide sufficient provisions for the day-to-day consumption of the garrisons and for their reserve magazines. By supplying animals and feed the county also enabled the combatants to maintain their essential stocks of horses. During the First Civil War the Royalists were the more successful in exploiting local reserves of horseflesh, forcing the Parliamentarians to obtain most of their mounts much further afield.

Military supplies were moved around a network of routes that, despite some use being made of the navigable River Severn, depended on the vagaries of the local and national road network. Both sides obtained much of their war matériel far from Shropshire, so that military success or failure often depended on the timely arrival of supplies shifted along long and vulnerable lines of communication. Tactical operations were undertaken to protect or harass supply convoys, to acquire resources and to deny them to the enemy.

Logistical activity therefore fuelled the intermittent skirmishing that characterised garrison warfare. This aspect of the fighting in Shropshire is the subject of part of the final chapter, which also deals more widely with operational aspects of war effort.

---

162 NLW, Chirk Castle Mss 1/Biii, 93, unfoliated; *OT List*, p. 319.

6

Engaging the Enemy: Military operations

They fell upon us with more than reported […] charged the foot to the very muzzle, having before routed the few horse.

While this book so far has looked at the war effort in terms of organisation, manpower and war matériel, this final chapter turns to the operational conduct of the Civil War in Shropshire, when leadership, manpower and military resources were all put to the test in the theatre of war. The larger field engagements fought in the county are reconstructed here in some detail for the first time, before moving on to consider garrison warfare – the activity of the forces occupying the opposing strongholds. Because of the importance of garrisons to both sides in Shropshire, and the great effort made to defend and to take them, the view of these fortified places is broadened to examine the means of fortification and the methods of siege-craft. Given also the importance to Civil War armies of intelligence gathering and medical services, these often overlooked operational aspects of war effort are given due attention here. Because the fighting in Shropshire in 1648 during the Second Civil War was limited and on a small scale, this chapter on the whole is concerned with the widespread military activity from 1642 to 1646 during the First Civil War.

However, before considering how both sides set about engaging the enemy, mention should be made of an overriding factor beyond the combatants' control, one that at all times has affected and even determined military operations: the weather. Inclement weather could hamper marching and manoeuvre, and if prolonged would weaken both the health and the morale of the soldiery, who on campaign often had to bivouac outdoors, usually without tents and with little other shelter. Fine weather of course made life somewhat easier for the armies, but long or forced marches in summer heat could induce debilitating fatigue. This limited the effectiveness of a long-distance raid by Parliamentarian forces from Montgomeryshire into adjacent Radnorshire in late July 1645. Their advance was slowed by the 'tediousness of the march of the foot', and when the Parliamentarians eventually reached and attacked Royalist-occupied Radnor only some of their horse were engaged, 'the rest not being able to march so far'.[1]

The immediate effect of bad weather in hampering military operations was to

1   *Perfect Passages of Each Dayes Proceedings in Parliament*, 30 July–6 Aug. 1645, p. 324.

worsen the usually already poor and rutted state of the mostly unmetalled roads and trackways. This was the reason why a unit of Parliamentarian cavalry gave up tailing some of Sir William Vaughan's Horse near Ludlow in February 1646, reportedly because of 'being wearied before with the long march, and the ill ways made more heavy by the thaw, which more deeply did corrupt them'.[2]

Rainfall during September 1644 affected campaigning in and around Shropshire. On the 3rd and 4th, Sir Thomas Myddelton found that the advance of his brigade from Oswestry into Montgomeryshire was slowed by the muddied roads and by being unable to ford the swollen rivers and watercourses. Later in the month, after the battle of Montgomery, Sir John Meldrum, who had commanded the combined Parliamentarian army in the battle, was wary of taking the offensive into Shropshire because of the continuing poor weather and the rising rivers. Soon after Meldrum was sent orders by the Committee of Both Kingdoms, cautioning against commencing any siege operations against Shrewsbury or Bridgnorth because the onset of autumnal weather was bringing the traditional campaigning season to an end.[3] Although neither side fully adhered to a formal campaigning season, the weather and the concomitant state of the roads meant that in practice Civil War field armies generally dispersed to winter quarters in October, and resumed full-scale operations later in the following spring.

However, the onset of winter did not bring military operations wholly to an end. This can be seen in Shropshire, for example, by Sir William Vaughan's attack in December 1645 on the Parliamentarian garrison at Wrockwardine; by Colonel Mytton's raid in January 1644 on the Royalist convoy halted at Ellesmere; and by the Parliamentarian assault on Shrewsbury in February 1645. Furthermore, the two latter actions were conducted wholly or in part under cover of darkness. Severe winter conditions could, in fact, be put to military advantage. During a prolonged deep frost in December 1645, the Parliamentarians at Shrewsbury feared that the freezing over of the River Severn, which in a loop enclosed most of the town, made it no longer an obstacle, and instead could allow a Royalist assault party an uninterrupted approach to the town walls. However, Sir William Brereton's base at Nantwich in Cheshire was a more tempting target for the Royalists. Accordingly, in mid-December they considered a plan (though not executed) in which a mobile force from Shropshire led by Sir William Vaughan, marching overnight and rapidly across the frozen landscape under moonlight, would storm Nantwich, its defences being weakened by the freezing of the water-filled ditches of the earthworks that enclosed the town, and of the River Weaver, which covered Nantwich to the west.[4]

The nature of warfare in Shropshire
The larger field engagements or battles
The major battles of the Civil Wars did not occur in Shropshire, although the regionally important battle of Montgomery – the largest battle in Wales during the First Civil

2   *The Citties Weekly Post*, 10-17 Feb. 1646, p. 5.
3   HMC, *Sixth Report, Part I, Report and Appendix*, p. 27; *CSPD, 1644*, pp. 524, 538.
4   *LBWB*, II, pp. 356-7, 369.

22. The porch at St. Michael's, Loppington, was erected in 1655 to replace
the one burnt during the Royalist attack on Parliamentarians occupying the
church in September 1643. The notable internal feature of the church remains
the mid seventeenth-century re-roofing, also replacing Civil War damage.

War – was in 1644 fought within yards of the county border. However, seven larger
field engagements in Shropshire can be identified, fought over more or less open
country and involving more than 1,000 combatants, all during the First Civil War.
These took place at Loppington on or around 28 September 1643; at Market Drayton
on 5 March 1644; in the Longford/Lilleshall area on the following 25 March; near
Oswestry on 2 July 1644; to the west of Shrewsbury two days later; near Stokesay on
8 June 1645; and at High Ercall on the following 5 July.

The fighting for Wem on 17-18 October 1643 was not an open field engagement.
However, because the Royalist assault on the fortified Parliamentarian-occupied town
was the climax of a six-day campaign of manoeuvre, and was a key action and a turning
point in the war in Shropshire, it is also described at some length here.

None of the engagements in Shropshire are particularly well documented. Because
the contemporary written accounts are usually brief, lacking in detail and partisan
there is insufficient balanced reporting from both sides. Furthermore, these accounts
rarely provide sufficient topographical detail to closely locate the fighting to a certain
area within the landscape. Because of the limitations of the documentary record and
the lack of archaeological investigation – typically in a Civil War context, where

23. The probable site between Longford and Lilleshall of the engagement fought
on 25 March 1644. A Royalist account described how 'his majesty's forces
retreated somewhat carelessly in disorder through Brockton and into Lynshall
field' - the likely general area in the centre and foreground of the photograph.

systematic metal detecting may reveal evidence of military action in the form of
projectile distribution, of scatters of musket, carbine and pistol balls – none of the
'battles' in Shropshire have, at the time of writing, been securely and tightly located
on the ground. The author therefore accepts in attempting to reconstruct the likely
course of these engagements that other interpretations may be drawn from the written
record, and that archaeological work may, in time, shift or more precisely identity the
location of the battlegrounds described here.

'Battleground' is perhaps an imprecise term to use in the context of the larger Civil
War engagements in Shropshire, for these actions fall into the awkward to define scope
of military combat that includes large skirmishes and small-scale battles. However, a
recent archaeological study of battlefields in England has characterised battles (of
all historic periods) as being fought between military forces numbering more than
1,000 men on each side, on the basis that with more than 2,000 soldiers engaged,
for command and control reasons both 'armies' would have to deploy in battle array
according to the tactics of the time.[5] With the caveat that in fact forces and individual
units of all sizes and across all periods, even the sometimes very small numbers involved
in minor skirmishes, will, unless taken wholly by surprise, adopt some form of tactical

5   G. Foard and R. Morris, *The Archaeology of English Battlefields: Conflict in the Pre-Industrial Landscape* (York,
2012), pp. 5-6.

formation in order to engage the enemy, this is a useful benchmark against which to categorise the Civil War engagements in Shropshire, and indeed elsewhere during the Wars. By this criteria, then, with a total of more than 2,000 men of both sides present, if not wholly engaged, the engagements at Loppington in 1643, at Oswestry and soon after nearer to Shrewsbury in 1644, and in 1645 at Stokesay and (just, in terms of likely numbers) at High Ercall, can be considered as small battles. However, although in all of them tactical formations would of course have been adopted, none of these field engagements closely followed the formula of a set-piece battle of the period – fought over an area of generally open country between opposing armies carefully arrayed in linear battle formation, with the infantry in the centre, interspersed with any available artillery, and with the cavalry and any dragoons deployed on the wings. Instead, the actions in Shropshire were less coordinated encounters.

Loppington, September 1643

Such was the case in autumn 1643, when Lord Capel's Royalist army numbering around 2,000 men and intending to assault nearby and recently Parliamentarian occupied Wem, instead became bogged down in first attempting to clear the enemy from Loppington, the village having been occupied by two or three companies of Parliamentary dragoons. The fighting centred on the church, which the dragoons defended as a strong point. Capel's men appear to have eventually taken the church, but a vigorous counter attack by a relieving force of 500 or more Parliamentarian horse and foot sent hastily from Wem seems to have caught the numerically superior Royalists by surprise. They broke off the action and withdrew under cover of nightfall, leaving Wem secure for the time being.[6]

The significance of the battle at Loppington, the least clearly documented of the larger engagements in Shropshire, was that the edge and morale of Lord Capel's forces was blunted for a while, allowing the Parliamentarians a respite of a further two weeks or so in which to organise and improve the defences of Wem. The anonymous writer of a Parliamentarian dispatch reporting the campaign for Wem also reflected on the significance of the action at Loppington:

> I need not mention again God's former mercy at Loppington when […] the [Royalist] army so possessed with fear, but had the day served & the whole body of forces been ready to pursue, we had wholly routed them as they them selves have acknowledged. After that defeat where some persons of quality were slain, the enemy retreated to Shrewsbury.[7]

The Wem campaign, October 1643

Lord Capel spent two weeks reorganising and reinforcing his army, and on 13-14 October 1643 led from around Shrewsbury upwards of 3,000 men into the mere and heath land country of north-west Shropshire.[8] Expecting Wem to be Capel's objective,

---

6   Williams, 'Notebook of William Maurice', p. 35; *Shropshires misery and mercie, Manifested,* pp. 2-3; Malbon, *Memorials,* pp. 76-7.

7   WRO, CR2017/C10, f. 60.

8   The following reconstruction of the Wem campaign is based on: HMC, *Thirteenth Report, Appendix Part I,* pp. 141-3, 157; HMC, *Twelfth Report, Appendix Part IX,* p. 41; Malbon, *Memorials,* pp. 75-84; WRO,

in order to slow his advance on Saturday 14th the Parliamentarians deployed a body of cavalry near the ford over the River Roden at Blackhurst, five miles north-west of Wem. This did not bring about an engagement, however, because, as the Parliamentarians reported, the Royalists 'came not as we expected';[9] Capel's army instead resumed its march in a north-easterly direction, and after crossing the open expanse of Fens Moss entered Whitchurch on Sunday. By advancing to Whitchurch Capel's strategy had been to interpose his army between Wem and Parliamentarian Nantwich, threatening both garrisons while drawing enemy forces away from Wem. On Sunday evening Capel's plan remained opportunistic: from Whitchurch he wrote to Sir Abraham Shipman, left in command at Chester, that 'I am come to Whitchurch, my design as for tomorrow's march somewhat depending on intelligence'. However, he ordered Shipman with most of the garrison to make a diversionary march from Chester towards Nantwich early on Monday morning.[10]

Meanwhile, leaving a small garrison at Wem, Sir William Brereton and Sir Thomas Myddelton with the rest of the Parliamentarian forces in the area, forming a field army of perhaps 2,000 men (the sources are silent in this respect), had marched north from Wem, and by daybreak on Monday were deploying in battle order on Prees Heath, two miles south of Whitchurch. The Royalists, however, had left Whitchurch well before sunrise, and entering Cheshire, marched the 11 miles to Nantwich before mid-day. It remains uncertain whether Capel intended to make a serious assault on Nantwich – whether the skirmishes with the Parliamentary garrison to the west of the town on Monday afternoon were meant to test the defences, or were just a feint. Come the evening Capel disengaged and about turned to Whitchurch, his army having suffered around 40 casualties. In the meantime, the Parliamentarians who that morning had been left flat-footed outside Whitchurch, instead of pursuing Capel had cautiously withdrawn 12 miles to the south-east to Market Drayton, where they rested Monday night.

Having rested his own men for a few hours at Whitchurch, on the morning of Tuesday 17 October Capel made a forced 11-mile march south to Wem. Advance units of the Royalist army began to arrive near the fortified town after mid-day. With some limited artillery support, from mid-afternoon the Royalist vanguard attempted to take Wem by storm, launching attacks against the northern and eastern defences where the ground was more suitable. However, because the Parliamentarian garrison effectively concentrated its firepower, which included several small cannon, against the two points of their attack, the Royalists were unable to gain the earthworks and the assault petered out at nightfall. Furthermore, the Royalist effort may have become increasingly uncoordinated, as units arriving late from the line of march from Whitchurch were drawn piecemeal into the assault. The Royalists mounted further attacks on the morning of Wednesday 18th, but Capel broke off the action around mid-day without success. His assault parties had sustained heavy lossess – a Parliamentarian estimate that the enemy suffered more than 200 casualties may

CR2017/C10, f. 60.

9   HMC, *Thirteenth Report, Appendix Part I*, p. 141.

10   WRO, CR2017/C9 f. 32.

not have been too inflated – and the killing or wounding of several senior officers depressed morale among the Royalist rank and file.

The Parliamentarian field army, meanwhile, had marched from Market Drayton early on Tuesday to relieve Nantwich. However, upon news that Nantwich was no longer threatened the soldiers, to the point of mutiny, demanded a period of rest, and so the Parliamentarians spent the remainder of Tuesday billeted between Nantwich and Market Drayton. With reinforcements from Nantwich, the Parliamentarian army mustered on Wednesday morning and finally marched to the relief of Wem. In the afternoon Capel received intelligence of their approach, and to avoid a disadvantageous field engagement ordered his blooded and weary army to withdraw. With their immediate line of retreat towards Shrewsbury blocked by the River Roden, in order to preserve their artillery and supply and baggage train the Royalists made a circuitous march of about five miles to the bridge over the Roden at Lee Brockhurst, south-east of Wem. In late afternoon Parliamentary units caught up and skirmished with them, but the Royalist rear guard effectively covered the withdrawal over Lee Bridge, and with nightfall most of Capel's army made good its retreat towards Shrewsbury.

Market Drayton and Longford/Lilleshall, March 1644

Turning to the engagements in 1644, in March the Royalists under Prince Rupert's overall command achieved two victories in the field in north-east Shropshire. An attack on Parliamentarian quarters by a fast-moving Royalist force led by Rupert himself took place at Market Drayton on 5 March, against the Shropshire and Yorkshire horse. Although some of the Parliamentarian cavalry were hastily deployed on heath land to the south of the market town to oppose the Prince's rapid approach march, the Royalist horse and foot soon drove them back through Market Drayton and onto another body of Parliamentarian horse formed to the east of the town. Taking advantage of the enemy's disarray the Royalists renewed the attack, causing the Parliamentarian horsemen wholly to break and scatter to the north-east.[11] Another encounter engagement was fought near Longford on 25 March. This developed when around 650 Royalists, commanded jointly by Colonels Robert Ellice and Sir William Vaughan, advanced against a larger Parliamentarian force, numbering perhaps 850 men and apparently commanded by Colonel Thomas Mytton, mustered at their garrison at Longford in preparing to attack the Royalist garrison at nearby Lilleshall. Being unable to draw the Parliamentarians from their defensive position, the Royalists withdrew in some disorder followed at a distance by the Parliamentarians. The Royalists rallied on a large open field near Lilleshall and then attacked and broke the Parliamentarians, who in turn had become disordered in advancing across enclosed ground.[12]

The outcome of both engagements reflected the improving Royalist military situation in Shropshire and elsewhere in the region as a result of Prince Rupert's leadership. Thus defeated twice in the field, the Parliamentarians during March also lost or abandoned garrisons in Shropshire at Moreton Corbet, Acton Reynald, Ightfield, Apley and Hopton, and in April surrendered the garrisons at Longford

---

11   Lewis, *Fire and Sword*, p. 70; *Mercurius Aulicus*, w/e 9 Mar. 1644, pp. 870-1.
12   *Mercurius Aulicus*, w/e 30 Mar. 1644, pp. 908-9; BDL, Firth Mss C6, f. 353.

and Tong. With the capitulation of Tong Castle, the end of April 1644 found the Parliamentarians in Shropshire restricted to a small enclave in the north of the county centred on Wem, their sole stronghold.

Oswestry and Montford/Shrewsbury, July 1644

With the departure from Shropshire in mid-May 1644 of Prince Rupert with units of his field army, embarking on a campaign into Lancashire with the eventual strategic objective of intervening in Yorkshire and securing the city of York, the immediate threat against Wem was lifted. Resupplied, the Parliamentarians were able to range more widely in north Shropshire. With the long-delayed, though, given Prince Rupert's absence, the timely arrival of the Earl of Denbigh in Shropshire, on 22/23 June the Parliamentarians captured the border town of Oswestry. Taking care to leave an adequate garrison at Oswestry, Denbigh soon left for Cheshire and then briefly into Lancashire, to join the Parliamentarian provincial forces being brought together to guard against the movements of Prince Rupert's army.

The Shropshire Royalists meanwhile had resolved to recapture Oswestry, and on 29 June 2,000 or more horse and foot, with at least two heavy cannon, gathered outside the town and began to lay siege to it. With the approach from the north-east of a Parliamentarian relief force led by Sir Thomas Myddelton, the battle for Oswestry on 2 July 1644 began precipitately in the afternoon up to two miles beyond the town. A reconnaissance by cavalry from the Royalist siege lines developed into unsupported attacks against Myddelton's task force by the entire Royalist horse, led by the usually Cheshire-based Colonel John Marrow. With substantial close infantry support the fewer Parliamentarian cavalry checked and eventually routed the Royalist horse, but Royalist infantry defending enclosures and narrow lanes nearer Oswestry obstructed Myddelton's advance. This delaying action enabled the Royalist main body, led by Colonel Fulke Hunckes, with the siege artillery to withdraw towards Shrewsbury protected by a screen of rallied horse organised by Marrow, although with considerable loss in casualties, prisoners and abandoned supplies. Hunckes, in overall command of the operation against Oswestry, later blamed Marrow for the near disaster, for having engaged the enemy in force against his orders, and consequently for the horse having being routed 'before I knew anything of it'. The Parliamentarian commanders had acted successfully in unison, and in his post-battle dispatch Myddelton praised the three colonels of Sir William Brereton's army who had led the Cheshire Foot comprising most of his force, and commended the conduct of 'the rest of the officers and soldiers, full of resolution and courage'.

Soon after the fighting around Oswestry ended, the Earl of Denbigh returned there from Manchester bringing reinforcements. On 3 July Denbigh and Myddelton paused to rest and to organise what had become an army 3,500-4,000 strong. Next day the Parliamentarians set out to capitalise on their victory at Oswestry by advancing against Shrewsbury. Their advance on 4 July 1644 provoked a series of skirmishes throughout the day that developed into a 'running' battle. During the morning units of Denbigh's army stormed and captured the bridge over the River Severn at Montford, and in the afternoon renewed their advance across heath land until they engaged Royalist horse, dragoons and foot defending more enclosed ground nearer Shrewsbury. Here Colonel Marrow played an effective role in delaying the Parliamentary advance, by deploying his mounted units more carefully and with greater control than at Oswestry. Nonetheless, by evening the Parliamentarians had come so far as to engage the defences of Shrewsbury's westerly suburb at Frankwell, exchanging volleys of musket fire with Royalists defending the outlying earthworks. The Parliamentarians broke off the attack and withdrew at nightfall, although one Royalist report suggests that they succeeded in forcing a breach and for a while fought their way into the fortifications.[13] If there had been a breakthrough Denbigh had not reinforced it, and instead baulked against mounting a more concerted attack upon Shrewsbury. After having reconnoitred 'the strength of their works', Denbigh concluded that 'our forces no way proportionable in number to the greatness of the design, I held it unsafe to engage in a siege'. The following day the Parliamentarian army withdrew towards Wem.[14] It was the Earl's last military operation in Shropshire.

Stokesay, June 1645
The battle for Parliamentarian-occupied Stokesay Castle fought on Sunday 8 June 1645 similarly extended over a wide area, involving (including the garrison of the castle) around 3,000 combatants.[15] Taking advantage of the weakening of Royalist forces in Shropshire by the withdrawal of units led by Sir William Vaughan to join the King's main field army, advancing from Shrewsbury in later May Parliamentarian forces for the first time moved into mid-south Shropshire and to the Stokesay area. Commanded jointly by the committeemen Colonels Humphrey Mackworth and Andrew Lloyd, and by Colonel Wilhelm Reinking, and numbering about 1,000 men, the Parliamentarian brigade took Royalist-held Stokesay Castle without a fight, and a detachment also occupied the castle a few miles to the north-east at Broncroft in Corvedale.

Responding to this incursion into hitherto Royalist territory, which threatened his garrison at Ludlow, Sir Michael Woodhouse urgently requested and soon received reinforcements from Worcestershire, Herefordshire and further south from Monmouthshire, led by Colonels Samuel Sandys, Barnabus Scudamore and Sir Thomas Lunsford, respectively the Royalist governors of Worcester, Hereford and Monmouth. They joined forces at Ludlow with Woodhouse and his garrison and probably also a detachment from Bridgnorth, and around 4/5 June the combined Royalist army, numbering upwards of 2,000 men, marched from Ludlow almost due north into Corvedale. The sources are unclear as to whether the Royalists stormed Broncroft Castle, or whether the small Parliamentarian garrison simply abandoned the place in the face of overwhelming numbers and fled to the main body of the brigade remaining in the Stokesay area. Leaving a garrison in Stokesay Castle, in turn the

---

13   Rushworth, *Historical Collections*, V, p. 745; *A Letter sent From Sir Tho. Middleton*, pp. 4-5; *CSPD, 1644*, pp. 332, 337-8; *Great Victories Obtained by the Earle of Denbigh at Shrewsbury, Chulmely, and other parts in Cheshire* (1644), unpaginated; BRL, Harleian Mss 6802, f. 248.
14   *CSPD, 1644*, p. 338.
15   The main sources for the engagement are: *Three Great Victories*; Walker, *Discourses*, p. 129; and *Perfect Passages of Each Dayes Proceedings in Parliament*, 25 June-2 July 1645.

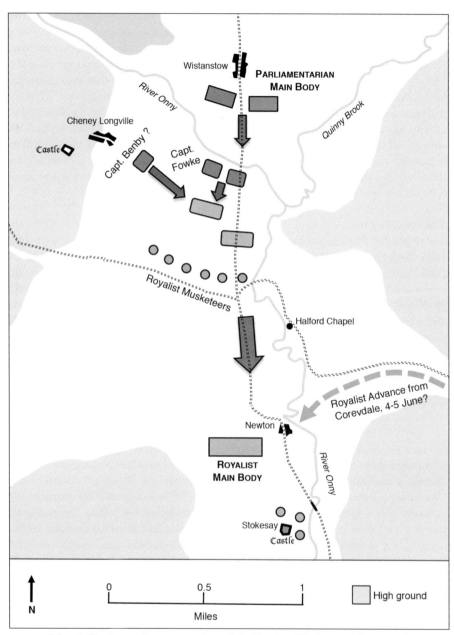

Map 8: Conjectural reconstruction of the Battle of Stokesay, 8 June 1645.

remainder of the Parliamentarian brigade, to avoid being outflanked by the Royalists advancing from the east over Wenlock Edge, withdrew a couple of miles northwards to Wistanstow, the village providing a defensive position given some protection to the south by the confluence of the River Onny with the Quinny Brook.

Contrary to their enemies expectation, rather than force an immediate engagement the Royalists instead prepared to lay siege to Stokesay Castle, thereby allowing the Parliamentarians time to receive some reinforcements from Oswestry. On 8 June the Parliamentarians advanced from Wistanstow and having crossed the River Onny, on open uncultivated ground immediately engaged two bodies of horse deployed as the Royalist vanguard (Map 8). By a frontal charge combined with a probable surprise flank attack by horse led by one Captain Benby, perhaps launched from the direction of nearby Cheney Longville where Benby's troop may have been billeted (one report described how 'Captain Benby received the alarm in his quarters accidentally, fell upon the flanks and body which were in the field'), the Royalist horse were forced to retreat onto a supporting unit of musketeers posted along a hedgerow or among enclosures. From these more concealed defensive positions, or 'ambuscades', the Parliamentarians drove the Royalists back onto their main body covering the castle, and a more general, perhaps hour-long, engagement developed in the Stokesay/ Newton area (today occupied by the town of Craven Arms) until the Royalists broke. Sir Michael Woodhouse, his horse being killed, narrowly evaded capture, and Colonel Sir William Croft, one of the leading Herefordshire Royalists, was killed. Relaying to a fellow Parliamentarian officer the following day the news of this 'great battle', Colonel John Fox reported, probably accurately, that 'after a short fight [the Royalists] were routed and lost all their carriages and foot, but their horse ran quite away'.[16] Disputed leadership and poor coordination between the four governors in command of the Royalist army contributed to what came to be recognised was a regionally significant Parliamentarian victory. As Sir Edward Walker, King Charles's Secretary of War, and at the time with the King's field army campaigning in Northamptonshire six days before the battle of Naseby, later wrote of the battle of Stokesay, that:

> This defeat was subscribed to the ill conduct and strife of these colonels about superiority and command. And although when we had the first intelligence of it we could not see the sad effects of this loss, yet after the battle of Naseby, when we retreated into those parts and had occasion to use them, we too soon felt it.[17]

High Ercall, July 1645

Notwithstanding these 'sad effects' on the Royalist cause in the region, the defeat at Stokesay was to some extent, in Shropshire at least, offset by Sir William Vaughan's success in relieving the garrison of High Ercall Hall on the morning of the following 5 July by routing the besieging Parliamentarians in a short decisive battle. This would be the last of the larger field engagement fought in Shropshire.

After the battle of Naseby, fought on 14 June 1645, Vaughan with his regiment of

---

16 Tibbutt, *Letter Books of Sir Samuel Luke*, pp. 562-3.
17 Walker, *Discourses,* p. 129.

horse seems to have withdrawn with Prince Maurice's forces to Worcester. Marching from Worcester, and on route probably having paused at Bridgnorth, on 4 July Vaughan led upwards of 400 horse back into Shropshire, in a raid, or 'beating up of quarters', into Corvedale. There the Royalists took by surprise and so scattered seven troops of Shropshire Horse billeted near Broncroft Castle and elsewhere in the dale. Reporting the action four days later, a Parliamentarian captain of horse explained now 'the enemy fell upon them before they had knowledge of them and spoilt the greater part of Gatherill's troop, many of Colonel Mackworth's and [Captain] Fowkes […] in all (as it is reported) about 80'.[18] More conservatively, the Royalists accurately numbered the enemy losses as two officers and 47 troopers taken prisoner and five troopers killed.

Continuing what seems to have been a larger pre-planned operation, at a rendezvous that evening or at some point overnight Vaughan and his horsemen joined with reinforcements detached from Bridgnorth, Ludlow, Worcester and, operating much further afield, also from Lichfield. Probably having crossed the River Severn at Buildwas, forcing aside any small Parliamentarian detachment that may have been guarding the bridge, the next morning, probably around dawn, Vaughan's combined task force of 900 horsemen, including 40 dragoons, fell upon the 1,100 Parliamentarians only recently returned to resume siege operations against High Ercall Hall. Although beforehand the Parliamentarians had received some intelligence of the enemy's advance, they failed to act upon it. As a result the Royalists kept the advantage of surprise and their attack was wholly successful. The Parliamentarians in their encampment were overwhelmed, with a substantial loss of military supplies and with more than 500 casualties and prisoners of war – including a number of fugitives killed or drowned in the pursuit in attempting to cross the River Roden, a mile to the south of High Ercall. Colonel Wilhelm Reinking, the Parliamentarian commander, was among the captured.[19] The same Parliamentarian officer who reported the skirmish in Corvedale fought at High Ercall. Having managed to escape the defeat by pretending to be a Royalist and so riding to safety, he later related how:

> The next morning we had intelligence of the enemy, but not believed till they fell upon us with more than reported, fell on us desperately, charged the foot to the very muzzle, having before routed the few horse […] there is great fault laid upon Reinking, but he is taken prisoner […] and almost all our foot in general are taken. I lost only one man and four horses, other troops lost more. I took on me to be one of them, and so escaped.

On the day Vaughan's was a complete victory. The important Royalist garrison at High Ercall was relieved and the Parliamentarian Shropshire forces suffered a heavy defeat. Some units from Colonel Mytton's Oswestry garrison and from the county committee's base at Shrewsbury were routed and entirely broken. Soon after, however, Vaughan with his regiment left Shropshire to rejoin the King, and by the late summer the Parliamentarians had reorganised and were gaining territory. Towards the end of August they took the Royalist garrisons in central east Shropshire at Lilleshall and

18   *Perfect Passages of Each Dayes Proceedings in Parliament*, 9-16 July 1645, p. 300.
19   BL, Harleian Mss 6852, f. 274; *Mercurius Aulicus*, 13-20 July 1645, pp. 1661-2.

Dawley. By that time the Shropshire Foot may have been brought up to strength by the return of the more than 300 officers and rank and file captured at High Ercall. They had been taken prisoner to Bridgnorth, and soon after the Royalists had proposed that could be exchanged for men of the King's Lifeguard of Foot taken as prisoners of war at Naseby.[20]

Garrison warfare

Notwithstanding the importance of these larger actions, the common currency of the fighting in Shropshire was more the skirmishing between garrisons and the attack and defence of fortified paces. Indeed, apart from the action at Market Drayton, the main field engagements resulted from the defence, attempted capture or relief of a stronghold. The proliferation of places occupied and defended more or less permanently by bodies of troops was a distinctive feature of the wider Civil Wars that to a great extent determined the course of the fighting. In particular, the First Civil War in England soon became a territorial conflict, as both sides vied to control and hold towns and countryside, in order to secure and to gain resources and to sustain support and allegiance. As Hutton and Reeves have pointed out: 'The characteristic military action of the British and Irish Civil Wars was an attack upon a fortified strongpoint'.[21] The war in Shropshire was no different from this trend, and indeed several historians since the Webbs, who listed 30 strongholds here during the First Civil War, have commented on the large number of garrisons in Shropshire.[22] Parts of the shire were heavily garrisoned, and in researching this book 37 places were identified as having been under military occupation for sufficient length of time to be recorded as garrisons, although clearly not all were occupied simultaneously (Map 9). Accordingly, warfare in Shropshire during the First Civil War was characterised by small engagements between garrison forces; the intermittent skirmishing and raiding conducted to suppress enemy activity, to control territory and the local resources of war effort. Garrison warfare provoked many clashes of this kind across Shropshire, such as the skirmish involving about 100 men altogether fought near Oswestry on 20 June 1644, which Colonel Thomas Mytton reported in a dispatch to the Earl of Denbigh.[23] On the lookout for enemy activity in the area, upon receiving reliable intelligence that a party of around 30 Royalist musketeers led by a lieutenant was a mile or so away, Mytton

> took some 25 troopers and about as many dragoons [and] after I went as fast as I could. When we came in sight of them our dragoons alighted to charge them in the rear, they being not aware of us, but one of our troopers discharged a pistol by what means I know not and gave them an alarm. We had no way then but to charge them presently with our

20 BL, Harleian Mss 6852, f. 277.
21 R. Hutton and W. Reeves, 'Sieges and Fortifications' in *The Civil Wars A Military History*, (eds.) Kenyon and Ohlmeyer, p. 195.
22 J. Webb and J.T. Webb, *Civil War […] as it affected Herefordshire*, II, p. 131; Pennington, 'War and the People', p. 123; C. Carlton, *Going to the Wars – The Experience of the British Civil Wars* (London, 1992), p. 151; Atkin, *Worcestershire Under Arms*, p. 61.
23 WRO, C2017/C9, f. 131.

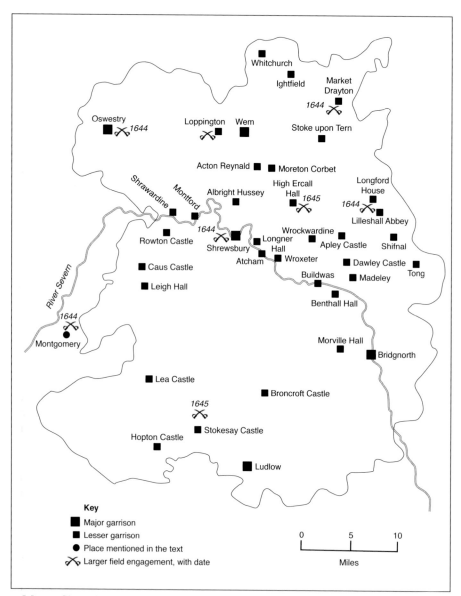

Map 9: Shropshire garrisons during the First Civil War, also showing the battles and larger field engagements. References to these garrisons are found within this chapter and elsewhere in the book, with two exceptions. Firstly, Wroxeter (probably St. Andrew's church) was listed as one of 20 Royalist garrisons 'taken (by the Shropshire Committee and their forces) from the King since they took the field', in Perfect Occurrences of Parliament And Chief Collections of Letters, 22-29 Aug. 1645, unpaginated; secondly, 'Shifnal House' (most likely Shifnal Manor, a house of the Earl of Shrewsbury) was noted as a Royalist garrison in *Mercurius Aulicus*, w/e 23 Mar. 1644, p. 891.

25 horse who went on very resolutely, though in a very disadvantageous place for the horse in respect of the enclosures they were in, being in wood grounds and very many hedges, and instead of 20 we found 54, whereof after a few shots they made at us, we took between 20 and 30 besides two or three slain.

Notwithstanding the local importance of such small-scale actions, the spread of garrisons became 'an unavoidable liability', creating problems for the opposing war efforts.[24] For example, garrison duty unprofitably withheld many soldiers from offensive operations, who by consuming local resources often over-exploited civilians, triggering disputes among fellow commanders. As Sir Michael Ernle tetchily reported in autumn 1644, the outlying Royalist garrisons 'upon the skirts' of Shropshire were absorbing the contribution to the detriment of his main garrison at Shrewsbury. The attack and defence of garrisons also tended to prolong local conflicts as an undercurrent to the wider war. This was recognised by a newsbook reporting the fighting around Wellington in later March 1644, which saw the Royalists occupy, lose, and then regain Apley Castle and the local church: 'Thus our present wars are likely to be prolonged, by this vicissitude and gaining and losing', concluded the editorial.[25]

Garrisons were, however, established for sound operational and local strategic reasons: to hold ground; to control routes of communication and as staging posts; to harass the enemy and to hinder his movements. The latter were the reasons for locating those Royalist garrisons mentioned above by Sir Michael Ernle as recently established or reinforced in west Shropshire. The outposts at Caus Castle, Leigh Hall and Lea Castle would obstruct an advance from Montgomeryshire by Sir Thomas Myddelton's brigade. Garrisons were also sited to secure local taxes and sources of supplies, whilst concurrently denying them to the enemy. Accordingly, part of the role of the Parliamentarian garrison planted at Benthall Hall in spring 1645 was to conduct economic warfare, by denying resources to the Royalists at Bridgnorth less than seven miles away. In this it seems to have succeeded: 'This garrison doth much annoy the enemy', said one partisan report, preventing 'the enemy from gathering contributions in their country' and stopping 'coals [from the nearby pits] from coming thither'.[26]

Outlying satellite garrisons guarded the major strongholds as a screen against enemy incursion while controlling a wider territory. The loss of these outposts, however, had the reverse effect, a corollary acknowledged by Colonel Mytton in early March 1644. The Parliamentarians' recent abandonment of their outer garrisons at Acton Reynald and Moreton Corbet, the result of a planned retrenchment, had, as Mytton put it, 'besieged us already [at Wem] having given the enemy the command of the country close to our walls'.[27]

24   Hutton and Reeves, 'Sieges and Fortifications', p. 199.
25   BRL, Additional Mss 18981, f. 299; *The Military Scribe*, 26 Mar.-2 Apr. 1644, irregular pagination.
26   *The Weekly Account*, 10-17 Dec. 1645, unpaginated.
27   WSL, SMS 558.

Garrisons and fortification

The prevalence of garrison warfare resulted in many places in Shropshire being occupied and fortified, of which towns will be considered first. As economic and political centres of their localities and hubs for trade and communications, towns were highly prized militarily throughout the wider Civil Wars. Defensible towns especially assumed strategic importance. Oswestry, for example, in Sir Thomas Myddelton's opinion was 'a very strong town, and if once fortified, of great concernment, and the key that lets us into Wales'. Arguably the local turning point in the First Civil War in Shropshire was the capture of Shrewsbury by the Parliamentarians in February 1645, which, as Clarendon concluded, 'was a great blow to the King, and straightened his quarters exceedingly, and broke the secure line of communication with Chester, and exposed all North Wales, Hereford and Worcester to the daily inroads of the enemy'.[28]

The course of the First Civil War in Shropshire was determined largely by the occupation and contestation of four other towns – Ludlow, Bridgnorth, Oswestry and Wem. Apart from Whitchurch and Market Drayton, which were garrisoned and fortified by the Royalists in early 1643 but later abandoned, no other Shropshire towns were held as long-term garrisons. Towns were, nonetheless, often and repeatedly used as billets, and sometimes held under short-term occupation. By the third week in August 1645, for example, a party of Parliamentarian horse was posted 'to lye constantly to secure Bishop's Castle (a well affected town but no garrison, which with parts adjacent have appeared well for the Parliament)'.[29]

During September 1642 King Charles's cause became firmly rooted in Shropshire by the Royalism of Shrewsbury, Bridgnorth and Ludlow. These towns once garrisoned were usefully situated to allow jurisdiction over much of the shire. Shrewsbury and Bridgnorth also controlled strategically important bridged crossings of the River Severn. All three as medieval walled towns had developed alongside castles sited on naturally defensible positions, on high ground bounded in part and thus defended by rivers. In the seventeenth century these remained tactically advantageous sites, especially because each town was still circuited by medieval walls and its castle could serve as a citadel. Although in 1642 these ageing defences were not in an immediately defensible state of repair, once strengthened and improved they made effective fortifications. The extensive renovations to Shrewsbury Castle, for example, included new accommodation and ancillary buildings for the garrison, and a loop-holed, stone-built barbican with a drawbridge built to fortify the main gate.[30] At Ludlow, in 1643 the town gates were loop-holed to allow musketry fire, and there were phases of extensive repair or enhancement to the walls and gates from July to August 1644, and in May to July 1645.[31] As an additional defensive measure, by October 1644 all but three of Ludlow's seven gateways had been blocked.[32] Turnpikes (a portable spiked barrier, or *Cheval de frise*, of pointed wooden or iron shafts projecting from a timber baulk) and thick iron chains were used as temporary barricades. Spanning and so obstructing

28   *A Letter sent From Sir Tho. Middleton*, p. 5; Clarendon, *History*, III, p. 512.
29   *Heads of Some Notes of The Citie Scout*, 2 Sept. 1645, pp. 3-4.
30   Evidence of this building work is found in SA, 3365/587, ff. 38, 87, 90, and SA, 3365/588, ff. 90, 99, 107.
31   SA, LB8/1/163, f. 4; SA, LB8/1/164, f. 9; SA, LB8/1/165, f. 6.
32   SA, LB8/1/164, f. 5.

24. The objective of Sir William Vaughan's attack on 5 July 1645 upon the Parliamentarians besieging High Ercall Hall was to relieve this important Royalist garrison. Remains of the earthworks that enclosed the Hall can be seen among the trees to the left of the photograph. High Ercall Hall is now a private residence.

entranceways and thoroughfares against an attacking force, these obstacles served the garrison as defensive stop-lines. Turnpikes were deployed at Shrewsbury by mid-1643, while chains were installed at key positions around the town by local smiths such as Clermont Owen, who in December 1644 fitted ten 'great hooks to hang the chains upon at the end of the streets and gates'.[33]

New permanent earthen fortifications were also built according to contemporary military practice. Used to emplace artillery, to strengthen weak points, and to connect positions in a more defensible perimeter, these earthworks were formed of straight or angled lengths of ditch fronting ramparts revetted with turf and timber and sometimes with stone. The ramparts were studded with rows of sharpened timber stakes, set vertically as palisades, or imbedded horizontally and projecting from the earthworks as anti-storm poles. Because these obstacles lay so thickly about the earthworks constructed by the Royalists to defend Shrewsbury Castle, in February 1645 the Parliamentarian assault force included three carpenters with axes, who alongside soldiers wielding sledgehammers broke a way through.[34] The new fortifications built around Shrewsbury also included a detached earthen artillery fort, known as a sconce, built on high ground above the suburb of Frankwell to defend the westerly approaches to the town. When the Parliamentarians captured Shrewsbury this sconce was surrendered last and on separate terms, thereby suggesting its importance.[35] At

33   SA, 3365/587, ff. 20, 24, 26, 114; SA, 3365/591, f. 42.
34   *Relation […] by […] William Reinking*, p. 4; R. Bell (ed.), *Memorials of the Civil War Comprising the Correspondence of the Fairfax Family*, 2 vols. (London, 1849), I, p. 171.
35   Gough, *Myddle*, p. 267; *Relation […] by […] William Reinking*, p. 6.

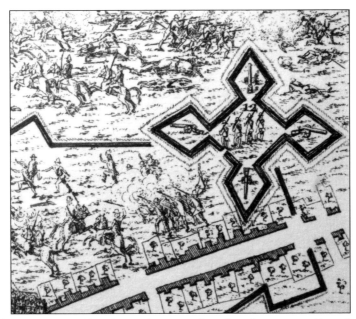

25. The sconce, or artillery fort, and associated earthworks constructed overlooking Frankwell at Shrewsbury may have been similar to star-shaped Fort Royal, Worcester, depicted here in a later engraving. Like the Frankwell sconce, Fort Royal was built on commanding high ground to defend a suburb unprotected by urban medieval walls.

Bridgnorth, improvements to the town defences, including the medieval walls, were set in train in December 1643, and on 1 May 1645 the Royalist leadership ordered further enhancement to the 'works [fortifications] about the town'. The extent of these defences remains uncertain, but the town ditch was re-cut, and the raising of earthworks around the North Gate and the adjacent churchyard of St. Leonard's entailed the destruction of gardens and the demolition of a school house. Accordingly, when the Parliamentarians stormed the town in March 1646 they found that 'the North Gate fort stood some dispute'.[36] Oswestry also still had enclosing medieval walls, but in May 1644 the Royalist leadership at Shrewsbury considered the town remained vulnerable to attack and gave orders for a programme of refortification. That September, however, Oswestry's defences remained incomplete under Parliamentarian control.[37]

Wem made an unprepossessing location for the main Parliamentarian garrison. The town lacked medieval defences and a naturally strong position. Sited above the River Roden, Wem could, however, command a field of fire across the surrounding lowlands (and the Parliamentarians cleared outlying buildings to facilitate this), and was protected to the south by the river and adjacent water meadows. Furthermore, the Parliamentarians appear to have engineered the Roden to flood the pastureland and

36 SA, BB/C/1/1/1, unfoliated; SA, BB/D/1/2/1/53; *The Weekly Account*, 1-8 Apr. 1646, unpaginated.
37 *CSPD, 1625-1649*, pp. 600-1; *CSPD, 1644*, p. 514.

to fill the defensive ditches. Wem was fortified by an enclosing complex of earthworks, incorporating ditches from four to nine yards wide, ramparts and palisades, although when first built in autumn 1643 the defences were somewhat rudimentary, one contemporary report noting 'there had been no time to make sconces [small forts or redoubts]'.[38] In early April 1644 Lord Byron found Wem 'well fortified and advantageously seated', although vulnerable to fire, 'the houses being all thatch and standing very near the works'.[39] Until summer 1644 Wem was sometimes kept under more or less tight Royalist blockade. In mid-April that year, for instance, it was reported that 'The enemy hath not laid close siege against it […] but quarter near about it'.[40] However, the strength of the defences seems to have deterred the Royalists from mounting any concerted attack against Wem after Lord Capel's failed assault in October 1643, apart from an aborted raid attempted on the night of 20/21 May 1645 upon the then 150-strong garrison by a detachment led by Sir Marmaduke Langdale from the main Royalist field army then halted 14 miles away at Market Drayton.[41]

Earlier in May the committee at Shrewsbury had confidently reported that 'Wem is re-fortified and made far more strong than before', improvements they attributed to Colonel Reinking's expertise in military engineering. An engineer skilled in fortification was a valuable asset, and the Royalists in Shropshire benefited from the services of Captain Francis Sandford, a local man and Lord Capel's appointee in March 1643 as his chief engineer. Sandford was empowered to inspect 'castles, forts & works', and 'them to amend & repair, & such other new works to contrive & direct'. His long-term project was overseeing the fortification of Shrewsbury, for which service in 1644 the town corporation paid him a gratuity of £10 – 'for designing the making of fortifications'.[42]

In building fortifications engineers like Sandford directed a mixed local workforce of skilled artisans and conscript labourers. At Ludlow in mid-1645, for example, the local mason John Coffin and his workmen were paid for 14 days' work on the town walls, although one William Brill, a townsman-cum-labourer, had earlier complained of being unpaid after 'constantly working in the castle ditch'. Meanwhile, sometime in 1645 a working party of men from the parish of Stockton supervised by a local petty constable spent 12 days labouring on the fortifications at Bridgnorth.[43] There, the townsmen had been expected to work at the defences in person or send substitutes in their stead, while Bridgnorth's wealthier inhabitants were assessed to find a quota of labourers or else pay the wages of others in lieu, at a day rate of 6d, or 11d in the winter. A similar weekly subscription to pay workmen was enforced on the better-off at Shrewsbury during 1644 and into 1645, paid to 'the collectors for the labourers at

38 HMC, *Thirteenth Report, Appendix Part I*, pp. 170-1; Garbet, *History of Wem*, pp. 217-18; M. Charles and L. Jones, *Land Off Aston Street, Wem, Shropshire, Archaeological Excavations 2007 & 2008* (Birmingham, undated), pp. 2-3, 14-15; *A True Relation of a Great Victory Obtained by the Parliaments Forces Against the Cavaliers neere Chester* (1643), unpaginated.
39 BRL, Additional Mss 18981, f. 118.
40 *A Continuation of Certain Special and Remarkable Passages Informed to the Parliament*, 18-25 Apr. 1644.
41 Symonds, *Diary*, p. 175.
42 *The Kingdomes Weekly Intelligencer*, 6-13 May 1645, p. 796; SA, 465/697, Sandford's commission; SA, 2265/588, f.2.
43 SA, LB8/1/165, f. 6; SA, LB/2147; SA, P270/B/1/1, ff. 57-8.

the works'.[44]

As often the largest stone-built buildings in a locality, churches often served as Civil War strongholds. Church towers made advantageous observation posts and firing positions, whilst the rest of the building provided secure accommodation for soldiers and even stabling for their horses. An advance force could establish itself in unoccupied or hitherto enemy territory by holding a church, as in April 1645 when a Parliamentarian detachment garrisoned St. Michael's, Madeley.[45] Oswestry's parish church, St. Oswald's, being sited outside the town walls became a strong point during the fighting in summer 1644. On 22 June Parliamentarian infantry stormed the place and pursued the Royalist defenders into the steeple. When the Royalists in turn laid siege to the town a week later they made recapturing St. Oswald's their first objective, the place being, as Sir Thomas Myddelton noted, 'the strongest hold about the town'.[46] A church near a garrisoned manor house would be incorporated into the defences, or else rendered indefensible if it stood too far beyond the perimeter. At High Ercall Hall, St. Michael's was linked to the defences because the tower provided the Royalists with a defensible vantage point. The consequential damage the church sustained in the several sieges was estimated in 1655 to cost £800 to repair. Standing within yards of much-contested Moreton Corbet Castle, St. Bartholomew's was left similarly badly damaged until repairs estimated at £500 began in 1662.[47] Sir Richard Leveson's garrison at Lilleshall Abbey was established in what had been the ecclesiastical buildings. After the Dissolution, the Augustinian house had been purchased and converted to secular use by the Leveson family, and by the Civil War the buildings remained in good repair. After a short investment towards the end of August 1645 Leveson's stronghold fell to the Parliamentarians, who in turn garrisoned Lilleshall Abbey into 1646.[48]

St. Eata's church by the bridge at Atcham, within four miles of Shrewsbury, accommodated the Royalist garrison guarding this important crossing of the River Severn, a detachment numbering 32 officers and men in May 1644. The Parliamentarians also recognised the local strategic significance of Atcham and garrisoned it in March 1645, probably once the Royalists had abandoned the place after Shrewsbury fell.[49] The Royalists had also garrisoned the other bridged crossings of the Severn. At Shrewsbury, towers and drawbridges defended both bridges as part of the town's originally medieval defensive circuit. Meanwhile, five miles upriver at Montford the bridge was broken, fitted with a draw section and guarded by a small garrison that numbered 43 foot in May 1644. Although reinforced by some horse, the following 4 July this detachment could not prevent the Earl of Denbigh's army from storming the bridge, and later in retreating from Shrewsbury the Parliamentarians destroyed the drawbridge.[50] Downriver towards Bridgnorth, the bridge at Buildwas was barricaded with turnpikes and defended by a sentry house. At Bridgnorth the

44 SA, BB/C/1/1/1, unfoliated; SRO, D593/R/1/3/2, unfoliated.
45 SA, P180/Fiche 1.
46 *Two Great Victories*, unpaginated; *A Copy of A Letter sent From Sir Tho. Middleton*, p. 5.
47 Lloyd Kenyon, *Sessions*, I, pp. 19, 78.
48 Malbon, *Memorials*, p. 180; Symonds, *Diary*, p. 249; *LBWB*, II, pp. 327, 388-9.
49 *CSPD, 1625-1649*, p. 283; *The London Post*, 11 Mar. 1645, p. 3.
50 *CSPD, 1625-1649*, p. 283; *CSPD, 1644*, p. 338; *JHL*, VI, p. 653.

Royalist garrison controlled the Severn crossing at the Low Town, and chains had been fitted across the bridge since 1642. In May 1643 orders were given also to fortify the fords in the district.[51]

The places most often fortified and converted to garrisons were the country houses of the gentry, which for the military purpose of controlling territory were conveniently scattered across Shropshire. These buildings provided a garrison with accommodation for men, horses and supplies, and protection against attack. Despite residential modernisation some medieval castles retained much of their former character as formidable strongholds. These included the originally thirteenth-century masonry castles at Caus and Shrawardine, owned by the Royalists Sir Henry Thyne and Henry Bromley respectively. Both castles had probably been garrisoned before autumn 1644 when they were occupied by Sir William Vaughan's Regiment. Fourteenth-century Broncroft Castle was more a fortified manor house, home during the Civil War of the Catholic Luttley family. Although in May 1645 a Parliamentarian detachment found that Broncroft Castle had been left 'much demolished' by Royalists, nonetheless they repaired and fortified the place to command Corvedale, 'a rich and fertile part of the county'.[52]

Protected by enclosing water-filled ditches, late medieval moated manor houses also remained defensible. Those known to have been garrisoned were Apley Castle, Dawley Castle, High Ercall Hall, Leigh Hall, the castle at Stoke upon Tern, the house at Albright Hussey, and also Ightfield Hall, a Parliamentarian garrison by early 1644 described as a 'brick house and moated'.[53] Dawley Castle had been fortified around 1316 under a licence to crenellate, and the Compton family owned the 1640s manor house. Abandoned by the Royalists towards the end of August 1645 (reportedly after having burnt it), Dawley Castle became a Parliamentarian garrison under the governorship of Captain Fowke.[54] Several Elizabethan mansions lacking moats also proved defensible, including Sir Basil Brooke's court at Madeley, a Royalist garrison by September 1644 which they abandoned soon after Shrewsbury fell; the Smythe family's house at Morville, under Royalist occupation by April 1645; and, apparently, Longner Hall near Atcham, home of the Burton family and another Royalist garrison.[55] The Earl of Shrewsbury's house at Longford, a Parliamentarian outpost by early 1644, was described in May 1645 by Symonds as 'a large brick house […] spoiled and abused', although it still housed a Royalist garrison.[56]

Like the towns, garrisoned houses were often strengthened by new earthen fortifications. At Moreton Corbet the thirteenth-century masonry castle stood in awkward juxtaposition to the Corbets' Elizabethan mansion, so the defences were consolidated by re-cutting and expanding the outer ditch and by building ramparts

51 SA, 3365/587, f. 20; 'Ottley Papers' (1896), p. 257; SA, BB/C/1/1/1, unfoliated.
52 Symonds, *Diary*, pp. 256, 258; *CPCC*, IV, p. 2931; *Three Great Victories*, pp. 1-2.
53 BL, Additional Mss 18981, f. 69.
54 *CPCC*, IV, p. 3043; *The True Informer*, w/e 30 Aug. 1645, p. 150; Malbon, *Memorials*, p. 181; Symonds, *Diary*, p. 249.
55 *Mercurius Civicus*, 19-26 Sept. 1644, p. 660; *LBWB*, I, pp 49-50, 243-4; Probably the 'Longnar House' listed as one of 20 Royalist garrisons taken by the Shropshire Forces, in *The Perfect Occurrences of Parliament And Chief Collections of Letters*, 22-29 Aug. 1645, unpaginated.
56 Symonds, *Diary*, pp. 171-2.

26. The largely Georgian character of Corve Street, Ludlow, is a result of property destruction during the First Civil War, and of the replacement of insubstantial buildings erected in the period of post-Civil War rebuilding.

incorporating projections known as 'flankers'.[57] The stone-built late sixteenth-century Hall at Benthall was not otherwise readily defensible. Accordingly, when the Parliamentarians planted a garrison there in mid-April 1645 they quickly fortified the place with enclosing earthworks, which within a month were reported as 'perfected [...] against any sudden assault'.[58] Archaeological survey has indicated that ramparts incorporating angled bastions were built at Shrawardine Castle, while excavations at High Ercall Hall have revealed evidence of the deepening and widening of the enclosing moat during the Civil War, and of an accompanying formidable earthen bulwark built over the former boundary wall.[59]

Throughout the Civil Wars it was common practice of garrisons to dismantle or demolish buildings within the vicinity of their defences. This was done in order to allow the construction of outer fortifications, to clear a field of fire, and to deny cover and shelter to an attacking force. Natural obstacles in the landscape were also removed: at Ludlow, for example, an apple orchard was felled during the clearance and re-cutting of the town ditch.[60] The most telling examples from Shropshire are of precautionary defensive destruction wrought by Royalist garrisons under threat of

57 Vicars, *Burning-Bush*, pp. 24-5; Gough, *Myddle*, p. 159; *The Weekly Account*, 18-24 Sept. 1644, p. 447.
58 *LBWB*, I, pp. 241-2, 393.
59 N.W. Jones, *Shrawardine Castle, Shropshire, Archaeological Survey* (Welshpool, 2012), p. 9 and appendices; Shropshire Historic Environment Record No. 00140, 'High Ercall Moat', available at www.heritagegateway. org.uk.
60 SA, LB7/2147.

attack during 1645 and 1646. In 1645 the garrison at Shrawardine levelled the castle's outbuildings, had the nearby parish church pulled down in two stages (after the fall of Shrewsbury, on 24 February, and in early June), and shortly before they were besieged, around mid-summer's day torched the village.[61] At Ludlow, the Royalist garrison hurriedly and partially burnt the suburbs before withdrawing into the town around 24 April 1646, although much property had already been destroyed by 10 April when the corporation ordered the compilation of a rent roll recording the demolished houses. Suburban properties outside the town gates were cleared, and by early November 1645 destruction had been so thorough along the street leading from the northerly Corve Gate that the town surveyors positioned marker stones to delineate where the buildings and plots had stood. The granting of a lease in December 1647 for one Francis Phillips to build on a plot where had stood a 'house burnt down to the ground by the wicked command of Sir Michael Woodhouse' is evidence of the clearance of property in Ludlow's westerly suburb beyond the Galdeford Gate.[62]

In 1644 there had been widespread clearance of property at Bridgnorth. The income lost by property owners, 'from the several rents for houses, shops, dwellings which are now demolished and pulled down in this time of war', was acknowledged by the town corporation, which detailed its own losses in rental from buildings and plots of land, in and around the castle and the town wall and ditch, cleared or given over to fortifications. Further precautionary defensive demolition took place at Bridgnorth during 1645. In March, on the order of the governor Sir Lewis Kirke the tower of St. Leonard's church was reduced in height. In May, the old town hall was taken apart and the new town hall in July, and the timbers from both were stockpiled in St. Leonard's along with those from other dismantled buildings. In September the town cross was pulled down. This was done so that in the event of the capture of the town the enemy would be denied cover and observational or firing positions that might threaten the castle itself. Furthermore, in November all remaining buildings beyond the North Gate defences were ordered demolished to clear a field of fire.[63]

Siege-craft

The capture of a stronghold could be attempted in various ways, with the outcome determined as much by the belligerents' resolve as their resources. To force a conclusion attackers could use negotiation (conducted as a sporadic or ongoing dialogue, in accordance with the customary rules of war); direct assault, or storm (often preceded by the breaching of the defences by bombardment or undermining); blockade and enforced privation; or a combination of these methods during a protracted siege. From 26 February to 13 March 1644 Royalists employed the full *modus operandi* of siege-craft against the small Parliamentarian garrison holding Hopton Castle in south Shropshire.[64] They launched three assaults, set afire most of the buildings, made breaches using hand tools, deployed a battery of heavy cannon, and eventually forced

---

61 SA, P248/A/1/1, unfoliated.
62 Carr and Atherton, *Civil War in Staffordshire*, p. 175; *Perfect Occurrences of Both Houses of Parliament and Martiall Affairs*, w/e 8 May 1646, unpaginated; SA, LB/Fiche 4679-80.
63 SA, BB/D/1/2/1/54; SA, BB/D/1/2/1/55; *The Weekly Account*, 10-17 Dec. 1645, unpaginated.
64 HMC, *Manuscripts of the Marquis of Bath*, I, pp. 29, 36-40.

the surrender of Captain Samuel More and the 29 surviving members of his garrison by preparing to detonate a gunpowder mine under their refuge in the castle keep. The Royalists had also blockaded the garrison for much of the intermittent siege, by setting outposts near to the castle and billeting their main body in settlements nearby. Captain More in the meantime rejected four opportunities to negotiate terms for surrender, each time lessening his chance of gaining a favourable outcome. When More finally relented, because of his obstinate resistance (the Parliamentarians had had no realistic hope of relief) the Royalist commander Sir Michael Woodhouse would only grant 'mercy', leaving the garrison's fate to his discretion. In the event, apart from More all were summarily put to death, in the circumstances an act permissible under the laws of war.

Elsewhere, recourse to military protocol before a garrison was *in extremis* could avert loss of life. Towards the end of April 1644 the important Parliamentarian garrison at Tong surrendered with precipitate haste. They held the church of St Mary and St. Bartholomew, its adjacent collegiate building and the nearby castle – by the seventeenth century the medieval stronghold had been mostly demolished and replaced by a brick-built mansion. Arriving at Tong on 25 April, once the Royalist commander Colonel Henry Tiller had realised that the church complex and mansion were 'so far asunder that they cannot relieve one another', he promptly ordered the church to be stormed and its defenders retreated into the college. Thus isolated from their comrades in the castle, they next day agreed to Tillier's summons to surrender and marched away with their arms. The Parliamentarians remaining in the castle rejected Tillier's first demand to surrender, but after a further parley on the morning of the 27th they too capitulated on favourable terms.[65] This news was soon received at Oxford, and on 4 May *Mercurius Aulicus* reported with satisfaction that: 'those […] which lay before Tong Castle [have] finished their work in taking that castle on Friday last; which was a great eyesore to his majesty's good subjects […] being in itself scarce to be taken had valiant men been in it'. By a peculiar custom of war the bells from the churches of a captured place were granted to the besieging artillery commander, traditionally so that they could be recast to make ordnance. Accordingly, Tong's churchwardens found that by paying 6s 'to the cannoneer for the redeeming of the little bell' they could reclaim from the Royalists this symbol of victory.[66] In later May 1645 the Royalist garrison of Stokesay Castle offered no more than token resistance to the Parliamentarian brigade that advanced into the district. The governor, Captain Danet, rejected the Parliamentarians' first summons to surrender, but when they prepared to storm the place he quickly capitulated on favourable terms.[67]

The course of the investment of Ludlow in 1646 was also determined more by negotiation than by force. On 24 April Colonel John Birch arrived from Hereford with reinforcements to assume overall command of the Parliamentarian forces that for the previous fortnight or so had occupied positions near to Ludlow. Birch had around 1,000 men, mostly his own contingent from Hereford together with detachments

---

65   BRL, Additional Mss 18981, f. 165.
66   *Mercurius Aulicus*, 4 May 1644, p. 967; SA, P281/Fiche 30.
67   *Three Great Victories*, pp. 1-2.

from the county forces of Montgomeryshire, Radnorshire and Shropshire. After some skirmishing in the outskirts Sir Michael Woodhouse's garrison withdrew behind Ludlow's town walls, leaving Birch, by taking 'up quarters […] at places most convenient for straightening of them', to deploy his forces to blockade both town and castle. An attack upon the Parliamentarian leaguer on 29 April by a Royalist force of detachments from Raglan, Goodrich and Worcestershire was repulsed, and Woodhouse's horsemen were equally unsuccessful in their attempts to break out.[68] Birch summonsed Woodhouse to surrender, pointedly reminding him that as governor of the sole Royalist garrison in Shropshire and one of the few remaining in England, there was 'neither any visible force in the field, nor any garrison unbesieged which can yield you the least hopes of relief'. Appealing to Woodhouse to emulate honourable capitulations elsewhere, Birch added: 'I need not tell you of […] sundry other places of strength, maintained by men of honour, who have conceived it prudent […] to make their places happy by terms of honour'. On 2 May Woodhouse replied rejecting the summons: 'I cannot assent unto it, neither with my allegiance, or honour of a soldier, in the condition I am in now to resist you'. He did, however, request – and receive – Birch's permission to send two gentlemen to seek direction from the King.[69]

While the emissaries were away Birch returned to Hereford, leaving the siege to be conducted by the committee of Shropshire who could redeploy to Ludlow their troops previously engaged at Bridgnorth after the castle was surrendered on 27 April. Meanwhile, an order from mid-April by the Committee of Both Kingdoms for siege guns at Gloucester to be sent to Birch at Ludlow was rescinded, either in expectation of a negotiated surrender or because the Shropshire forces could deploy their own ordnance. Woodhouse's emissaries returned from Oxford on 12 May, and the news that King Charles had given himself up to the Scots army outside Newark hastened negotiations at Ludlow. Birch had returned to the leaguer and by the 15th brokered a deal between Woodhouse and the Shropshire committeemen for the surrender of the town. The committee's soldiers entered Ludlow around 20 May, by which time Birch and Woodhouse had agreed articles for the surrender of the castle on the 31st. Birch again returned to his headquarters at Hereford, leaving the local committeemen, annoyed with the leniency of his terms, to complain about the 'diversity of commands'.[70] His surety of Woodhouse's personal safety appears to have clinched the capitulation – the governor reportedly 'refused to perform the same to any other' – but with Birch's departure the agreement broke down; the Royalists sallied out of the castle into the town, killing several Parliamentarians.[71] Birch was hurriedly recalled to patch up the agreement and Ludlow Castle was surrendered on 1 June, albeit on less honourable terms. Whereas the articles at first had allowed for Woodhouse's men to march away

---

68   Carr and Atherton, *Civil War in Staffordshire*, p. 93; *Perfect Occurrences of Both Houses of Parliament and Martiall Affairs*, w/e 8 May 1646, unpaginated; *The Weekly Account*, 22-28 Apr. 1646, unpaginated. Quotation from the latter.

69   *The manner of the discovering [of] the King at Southwell […] And The Copie of the Summons sent to Ludlow and the Governor's Answer* (1646), pp. 1-4.

70   *The Moderate Intelligencer*, 30 Apr.-7 May 1646, unpaginated; *CSPD, 1645-1646*, pp. 412-13, 432; *Perfect Occurrences of Both Houses of Parliament and Martial Affairs*, w/e 22 May 1646, unpaginated; Carr and Atherton, *Civil War in Staffordshire*, p. 236, quotation from p. 267.

71   *The Moderate Intelligencer*, 28 May-4 June 1646, unpaginated.

with their horses, colours and arms to 'garrisons unbesieged' (effectively, therefore, to disband and disperse with due punctilio), in the event just the senior officers kept their horses and side arms while all other ranks were unceremoniously disarmed.[72]

Negotiation, pragmatism and mutual observance of the customary rules of war brought about the Royalist capitulation at Ludlow. On other occasions, the fluctuating military balance caused the hasty abandonment of strongholds. For example, the loss of Shrewsbury in February 1645 caused the Royalists in panic to abandon several garrisons. Rowton Castle, nine miles west of Shrewsbury, had been deserted and burnt within a day or so of the town's fall, as was Leigh Hall 13 miles to the south-west. Further afield, meanwhile, the Royalists torched and abandoned Tong Castle and deserted Madeley Court.[73] However, the Royalists soon repaired and reoccupied Leigh Hall, provoking the Parliamentarians to send a detachment from Shrewsbury to take the place. On 26 March 1645 the committeemen wrote from the county town to Parliament reporting this expedition, explaining how:

> Since our taking this town, fear did so possess the enemy that they deserted some of their petty garrisons, but upon Prince Rupert's approach they endeavoured to re-garrison Leigh Hall, a place which formerly being possessed by some of Sir William Vaughan's commanders did much impoverish the country. For prevention thereof, we sent a party of horse and foot, and with the loss of one captain surprised the enemy in the house, their number being 18, some whereof were Irish and [were] executed according to the ordinance.[74]

When defenders were less obliged to give up the assailants might use a ruse, although the veracity of reports of such stratagems must remain questionable, given that their intention was to stress the resourcefulness of their own side at the expense of the gullible enemy. For instance, on the night of 18 February 1644 Captain More's detachment reportedly gained Hopton Castle after tricking a Royalist sentry into believing that the Parliamentarians were a party of the King's men. A similarly partisan account described how, also under cover of darkness, on the following 8 September the Parliamentarians attacking Moreton Corbet Castle by scattered musketry fire, drum calls and orders shouted to imaginary units attempted to demoralise the Royalist garrison and trick them into believing they faced a far larger attacking force.[75]

The same report continued to describe how the Parliamentarians were soon engaged in close-quarter fighting, using hand grenades to dislodge Royalists firing from windows and loopholes. A direct attack, or storm, of this kind was launched against a stronghold when attackers held the advantage of surprise or numerical superiority, or when there was neither time nor resources to mount a formal siege. Thus the Parliamentarians reportedly stormed Morville Hall on 14 June 1645 after 'a short dispute', whereas on the following 19 December the small Parliamentarian

72 *Perfect Occurrences of Both Houses of Parliament and Martial Affairs*, w/e 22 May 1646, unpaginated; *A Perfect Diurnall of some passages in Parliament*, 18-25 May 1646, p. 1180.
73 *LBWB*, I, pp. 47, 49-50; Malbon, *Memorials*, p. 165.
74 BDL, Tanner Mss 60, f. 11.
75 HMC, *Manuscripts of the Marquis of Bath*, I, p. 28; Vicars, *Burning-Bush*, pp. 24-5.

garrison occupying St. Peter's church at Wrockwardine successfully beat off hasty Royalist assaults.[76] In March 1646 the Parliamentarians similarly intended to take Bridgnorth by surprise attack on the night of the 27th, but the assault force was delayed and left fatigued by the overlong approach march and so the operation was postponed. The Royalist governor Colonel Sir Robert Howard rejected a summons to surrender, and so on 30 March the Parliamentarians stormed and captured the town by simultaneously attacking the defences at three places, forcing the defenders to take refuge in the castle.[77]

A besieging force could employ several tactics to increase their chances of achieving a successful assault. Ladders to scale walls were used by Royalists at Hopton Castle in 1644 and by Parliamentarians against Shrewsbury in 1645, while at Moreton Corbet the previous September the Parliamentarians had negotiated the castle's outer ditch also using ladders.[78] Against Wem in October 1643 Royalist soldiers made faggots, bundles of brushwood and straw, to use as fascines to infill the town ditch, carrying them in their advance as protection against the defenders' fusillade.[79] Setting buildings or defensive fixtures afire was another tactical option. After capturing Oswestry town on 22 June 1644, the Earl of Denbigh's council of war agreed that an attempt should be made the following morning to breach the still Royalist-held castle by setting the gates alight using pitch. But in the event there was no need for this rather desperate expedient, because the garrison were soon persuaded by their womenfolk to surrender without further fighting.[80] At Loppington, in September 1643 Royalists attacking the Parliamentarian outpost of Wem at St. Michael's church burned the door and the shingle roof, an act of arson in which Lord Capel was reportedly 'the busiest of his soldiers in carrying faggots to the porch'.[81]

An assault would be spearheaded by a vanguard of picked soldiers known as the 'forlorn hope', such as the 80 dismounted Royalist cavalrymen whom led the first attack on Wem on 17 October 1643. Armed with swords and short-range firearms (pistols and carbines) the troopers were considered well equipped for close-quarter fighting.[82] The Parliamentarian forlorn hope against Shrewsbury on 22 February 1645 comprised 30-40 dismounted troopers and a similar number of musketeers armed with firelocks. Their flintlock-operated firearms did not use smouldering match cord, the glow from which in the darkness might have revealed their position. Indeed, Colonel Mytton later criticised Colonel Reinking as commander of this night-time operation for failing to maintain discipline amongst the main body of matchlock-equipped musketeers: 'I came in unto them: and whereas he [Reinking] sayeth that he had only two lit matches, I caused them to put out thirty and above, asking them if

76 *The Perfect Occurrences of Parliament And Chief Collections of Letters*, 20-27 June 1645, unpaginated; *The Weekly Account*, 30 Dec. 1645-6 Jan. 1646, p. 1064; *LBWB*, II, p. 394.
77 BDL, Tanner Mss 59, ff. 10, 28; *The Weekly Account*, 1-8 Apr. 1646, unpaginated.
78 *Relation […] by […] William Reinking*, p. 5; *Collonel Mytton's Reply*, p. 2; HMC, *Manuscripts of the Marquis of Bath*, I, p. 36; Vicars, *Burning-Bush*, p. 24.
79 *A Great Victory […] Against the Cavaliers neere Chester*, unpaginated.
80 *Two Great Victories*, unpaginated.
81 Williams, 'Notebook of William Maurice', p. 35; HMC, *Twelfth Report, Appendix Part IX*, p. 41.
82 HMC, *Twelfth Report, Appendix Part IX*, p. 41.

they would surprise the town with lit matches'.[83]

Notwithstanding this sort of difficulty in maintaining operational control at night, attackers valued the advantage of surprise that the hours of darkness gave them. Indeed, a week before the Parliamentarians had attempted a nocturnal assault against Shrewsbury. However, the expedition was abandoned short of the town before sunrise because, as Colonel Mytton reported, their approach march had been slowed by 'the night being exceeding dark and the ways extremely wet'.[84]

Although surprise attacks were often successful, the deployment of artillery was usually the decisive factor in the subjugation of a stronghold. After the failure of the second Royalist assault against Hopton Castle (launched before dawn on 2 March 1644), Sir Michael Woodhouse acknowledged that the place could only be taken with the use of cannon. Artillery support often gave an attacking force an overwhelming advantage. A single heavy cannon could render a lesser stronghold indefensible and so demoralise its defenders. When the Royalists attacked Parliamentarian Apley Castle in March 1644 the matter was decided by a culverin brought from Shrewsbury; its short bombardment reportedly 'played the rebels so close with shot' that the place fell by storm within two hours.[85] Meanwhile Lord Byron, as he reported, had led an expeditionary force 'with a great piece of battery, into that part of Flintshire which lieth between Bangor [-on-Dee] and Wem […] in regard of the many petty garrisons possessed there by the rebels'. 'Upon the sight of our great gun two of them yielded upon quarter and the other two were quitted before I could come to them', Byron wrote from Ellesmere on 30 March to Prince Rupert, reporting with satisfaction the capitulation of the Parliamentarian outposts.[86]

At Oswestry, on 22 June following the Parliamentarians deployed a pair of field pieces to break one of the town gates. The bombardment had a demoralising effect on the Royalist garrison, who retreated into the castle after a cannon ball disembowelled a townswoman and injured a couple of defenders. Later, however, the Parliamentarian gunners found that shot from the heavier of their two cannon caused inconsiderable damage to the castle.[87] The incident demonstrated that medieval walls remained a formidable defence against all but the heaviest guns or most sustained of bombardments. At Hopton Castle, Captain Samuel More recorded (albeit with unlikely precision) that the Royalists' three heavy cannon took some seven hours and 96 shots to breach the outer wall.[88] Against Wem in October 1643 the Royalist assault was hampered when unluckily they lost the use of half of their artillery – three cannon and a mortar – when the mortar broke after discharging its second bomb, and a cannon was dismounted and its carriage damaged by a chance shot from one of the defenders' guns.[89]

83 *Relation […] by […] William Reinking*, pp. 3–4; Bell, *Memorials of the Civil War*, I, p. 171; *Collonel Mytton's Reply*, p. 3.
84 Bell, *Memorials of the Civil War*, I, p. 170.
85 Warburton, *Prince Rupert*, I, p. 511; *Mercurius Aulicus*, w/e 30 Mar. 1644, p. 905.
86 BRL, Additional Mss 18981, f. 118.
87 *Two Great Victories*, unpaginated.
88 HMC, *Manuscripts of the Marquis of Bath*, I, p. 37.
89 Malbon, *Memorials*, p. 78; *Shropshires misery and mercie, Manifested*, p. 5; WRO, CR2017/C10, f. 60.

27. The surviving masonry and earthwork remains of Hopton Castle. There was a hard-fought and particularly notorious siege here during February and March 1644.

At Bridgnorth, during April 1646 the Parliamentarians deployed artillery in laying siege to the castle. The destruction of nearby buildings in a two-day long conflagration on 31 March and 1 April that devastated much of the High Town, caused by incendiary fire from the Royalist garrison's artillery, appears inadvertently to have enabled the besiegers to site some approaches, or entrenchments, close to the castle. By 10 April the Parliamentarian ordnance – a battery that included at least one mortar – was reported as emplaced and 'ready to play'. Because the twelfth-century earthen ringwork and bailey on nearby Panpudding Hill occupies an advantageous hilltop position separated from Bridgnorth Castle by an intervening valley, it is most likely that during the siege the Parliamentarians adapted it as an artillery emplacement.[90]

Whether they deployed artillery or not, advantage did not always lie with the attackers, however, for defenders could employ various countermeasures. Given time and opportunity they could improve their fortifications. At Hopton Castle, after beating off the first Royalist assault More's garrison 'were as industrious as men could be' in constructing earthworks and adapting the buildings for defence. They later piled earth and timber to block the breach made by the Royalist cannon. At Shrawardine in June 1645, the Royalist garrison at first appears to have conducted an effective forward defence from the cover of the ruins of the church and village before withdrawing into

---

90 BDL, Tanner Mss 59, f. 28; Carr and Atherton, *Civil War in Staffordshire*, pp. 93, 107; G. Bellett, *The Antiquities of Bridgnorth* (Bridgnorth, 1856), p. 171.

the castle.[91] Defending marksmen firing from overlooking vantage points could harass besiegers, by picking off at long-range key personnel such as officers and gunners. The snipers' weapon of choice was the fowling piece, used for game shooting and often rifled for greater range and accuracy. The NCO commanding the eight-man Royalist detachment occupying Albright Hussey House, for example, deterred an attack by wounding the Parliamentarian leader and shooting his horse from under him using a fowling piece. In defending High Ercall Hall, the Royalists were reported to have used 'divers long fowling pieces that kill a great way; which have done them great service'.[92] Artillery also enabled a garrison to conduct a long-range defence. The firepower of their emplaced cannon seems to have been the key factor in the Parliamentarians' successful defence of Wem in October 1643, one report acknowledging 'the mighty execution which our cannons did upon the enemies'. The reported killing there of 50 Royalist soldiers in a salvo by two small cannon, or drakes, was probably an exaggerated relation of the devastating anti-personnel effect of canister shot.[93] In mid-April 1644 the artillery emplaced defending Wem was reported as 'two sakers [medium cannon] and some other pieces of ordnance'.[94]

Lord Newport's residence at High Ercall Hall proved to be the most strongly and resolutely defended of Shropshire's Civil War strongholds. Enclosed by a broad wet moat and substantial defensive earthworks, the Royalist stronghold was, as events proved, aptly described as 'a place of great strength and well fortified […] not thought feasible to be taken by storm'.[95] The intermittent attempts by the Parliamentarians to blockade and besiege High Ercall Hall over the course of a year therefore make an informative case study in contemporary siege-craft.

Recognising the threat from the Royalist garrison just seven miles away, in March 1645 the Parliamentarians recently established in Shrewsbury moved quickly, besieging the Hall by the end of the month once mobile Royalist forces led by Princes Rupert and Maurice had left Shropshire or dispersed to their garrisons. The Parliamentarians hastily erected siege-works, and by 3 April their artillery had already damaged the drawbridge and gatehouse. Sappers meanwhile worked to drain the moat and to dig approaches near to the Hall in preparation for an assault, and a night attack was probably attempted on 10/11 April.[96] However, on the evening of 15 April the Parliamentarians abruptly abandoned the siege and retreated to Shrewsbury, blaming their withdrawal on what turned out to be false intelligence of a Royalist relief force approaching the area. For their part, the Royalists' *Mercurius Aulicus* related how the garrison had withstood a 17-day siege by artillery, mining and assault. It seems likely that an aggressive sally by the garrison in which the Parliamentarians suffered a number of casualties hastened their withdrawal.[97]

91 HMC, *Manuscripts of the Marquis of Bath*, I, pp. 36-7; *Perfect Passages of Each Dayes Proceedings in Parliament*, 9-16 July 1645, p. 300.
92 Gough, *Myddle*, p. 134; *A Copy of the Summons […] Also the taking of High-Arkall*, p. 2.
93 *Shropshires misery and mercie, Manifested*, p. 5; *A Great Victory […] Against the Cavaliers neere Chester*, unpaginated.
94 *A Continuation of Certain Special and Remarkable Passages Informed to the Parliament*, 18-25 Apr. 1644, p. 5.
95 Vicars, *Burning-Bush*, p. 403.
96 *LBWB*, I, pp. 133-4, 141-2, 189-90, 209; BDL, Tanner Mss 60, f. 52; *The London Post*, 1-8 Apr. 1645, p. 5.
97 *LBWB*, I, pp. 241-2, 249; *The Weekly Account*, 16-23 Apr. 1645, unpaginated; *Mercurius Aulicus*, w/e 20 Apr.

28. View from the medieval castle earthworks on Panpudding Hill (foreground), across the intervening valley towards the leaning shattered keep of Bridgnorth Castle (centre left). Parliamentarian artillery positioned here during the siege of April 1646 would have been within effective range of the Royalist stronghold.

An apparently favourable military situation encouraged the Parliamentarians to return in force to High Ercall on 1 July, only for them to be beaten and driven away four days later by Sir William Vaughan's relief force. The Parliamentarians appear also to have abandoned a third siege in mid-August, but a month later the Hall was again besieged or under blockade.[98] During December the Parliamentarians scaled down a blockading operation involving mounted patrols and three of four small encircling garrisons planted in nearby churches, and so were unable to prevent the Royalists being reinforced by some horse and resupplied by Sir William Vaughan around the 20th, while bad weather into the New Year prevented their building an earthwork fort near to the Hall.[99] In early March 1646, however, the Parliamentarians succeeded in entrenching themselves nearby, by completing a strong sconce. This fortification together with a string of four smaller redoubts enabled a 600-strong besieging force effectively to blockade the Hall by the middle of the month. At least six pieces of ordnance brought from Shrewsbury were emplaced, and a sustained bombardment by heavy cannon and mortar fire on 25 March forced the garrison to seek terms. The

1645, p. 1571; Williams, 'Note book of William Maurice', p. 39.
98   *Heads of Some Notes of The Citie Scout*, 19 Aug. 1645, p. 5; *CSPD, 1645–1646*, p. 158.
99   Symonds, *Diary*, p. 276; *LBWB*, II, pp. 915, 325-6, 408-9, 445-6.

Royalists surrendered High Ercall Hall on the 27th, somewhat to the besiegers' relief; they had found it 'a most difficult thing to take the place by storm, and their provision within so great that there was little hope in many months to prevail by famine'.[100]

As the fighting in England drew to a close, Parliamentarian attention turned to their remaining garrisons and to those abandoned strongholds that might provide defensible rallying points for further resistance.

In early April 1646 the committee of Shropshire received general and particular instructions from London with regard to rendering indefensible – or slighting – the county's fortifications. In line with national policy, on the 4th the House of Commons entrusted the committee with deciding which places should be kept as garrisons, or else be demolished. Two days later, the Committee of Both Kingdoms ordered that while the fortifications about High Ercall should be levelled and the moat drained, the Hall itself should be left intact; otherwise, they declared, 'there would then be too many sad marks left of the calamity of this war'. On 11 July following the Commons further directed that with the exception of Shrewsbury and Ludlow Castle, all fortifications in Shropshire should be slighted.[101]

How thoroughly this policy was executed is difficult to ascertain, given that some places had already been rendered indefensible by fighting or precautionary slighting. For example, in May 1645 the Parliamentarians found that damage by Royalists had rendered Holdgate Castle in Corvedale unfit for use as a garrison. The following July the Parliamentarians burnt Shrawardine Castle and then quarried its walls for stone used in the defences of Shrewsbury.[102] The near complete destruction of Bridgnorth Castle by demolition began under Parliamentarian direction in February 1647, but elsewhere potential strongholds were left more or less intact. As a result, in July 1648 Parliament issued emergency orders for the castles at Dawley and Broncroft to be rendered 'untenable' to prevent their use by the enemy during the renewed hostilities.[103]

Military intelligence and communications

In the 1644 edition of his treatise on the cavalry, the military writer John Cruso characterised the exemplary 'good commander', a paragon who, among other martial virtues, formulated strategy not only on the basis of the capability of his own forces, but also with 'the assurance of the condition of the estate of the enemy, his commodities, and necessaries, his councils and designs'.[104] Thereby Cruso pointed to the value of intelligence – meaning all sorts of information, especially news of the enemy's condition, which can inform military planning. Although its importance has previously tended to be overlooked by historians of the Civil Wars, recent scholarship has shown that military intelligence played a vital role in the conflict. Accordingly, intelligence-gathering operations of varying sophistication became an integral part of war effort.[105]

---

100 *The Weekly Account*, 25-31 Mar. 1646, unpaginated; BDL, Tanner Mss 59, f. 5. Quotation from the latter.
101 *JHC*, IV, pp. 500, 614; *CSPD, 1645-1646*, pp. 402-3.
102 *Three Great Victories*, p. 1; SA, P248/A/1/1, unfoliated.
103 SA, BB/D/1/2/1/57; *JHC*, V, p. 631.
104 J. Cruso, *Military Instructions for the Cavallrie* (1644), p. 26.
105 See Donagan, *War In England*, pp. 99-114, and especially J. Ellis, '*To Walk in the Dark' Military Intelligence*

In Shropshire's theatre of operations there is good evidence of the widespread collection of intelligence and of commanders acting upon it. Indeed, in a civil war fought between a largely monolingual people by soldiers who lived amongst civilians of sometimes uncertain loyalty, and when the opposing forces often operated in close proximity, the main difficulty that commanders faced was not obtaining intelligence, but determining its reliability and preventing the leakage of disinformation which might be detrimental to morale. In late July 1643, in letters from Shrewsbury Lord Capel rebuked his deputy at Chester for allowing fallacious and uncorroborated intelligence reports to damage Royalist morale. Capel's warnings to Sir Abraham Shipman could have served as a caution to commanders on both sides: 'Let there be an especial notice taken of those that bring intelligence and news', he ordered, 'and if […] they bring false intelligence severe course be taken with them'; furthermore, 'be assured of the condition of the person, and the probabilities of the relation, before you give too much credit'.[106]

In 1642 the King's party in Shropshire were engaged in gathering intelligence. In late August Bridgnorth's aldermen, fearful that Parliament's army 'would come against this town', sent a townsman, one Richard Adams, on a scouting mission towards Coventry to ascertain the whereabouts of the forces of Lord Brooke and the Earl of Essex. By mid-September the mayor of Shrewsbury was acquiring intelligence from letters intercepted at the town gates, and in November it was reported that 'the high sheriff […] and the mayor of Shrewsbury have commission from the King to open all letters before they be either carried out or brought into that county'. By the year's end bargemen plied the River Severn bound under oath to disclose to the mayor's office any correspondence they carried.[107]

These early intelligence operations by civic authorities were intended more to safeguard life and property in their locality than to further Charles I's cause militarily. However, as the war intensified networks of scouts, spies and informants were integrated into the war effort on both sides. Three examples of Parliamentarian operations illustrate well the importance of intelligence in military planning. In the vicinity of Oswestry, around 20 June 1644 Colonel Mytton employed 'diverse ways to have intelligence' (messengers, spies and prisoners of war), enabling him to monitor the progress of an enemy munitions convoy and later to ambush another detachment. Furthermore, the weakened state of the town's Royalist garrison was identified, so that Oswestry was stormed and captured two days later. In February 1645, the surprise assault on Shrewsbury was made against a weak point in the riverside fortifications identified to the Parliamentarians by two defectors from the garrison.[108] In late July 1648 a clandestine plot, co-coordinated by Lord Byron's agents, for local Royalists to seize the county town was disclosed by an informer to Shrewsbury's governor, Humphrey Mackworth. This led to the arrest of several would-be insurgents, and the confessions that two of them made under interrogation enabled the committee's troopers on the

during the English Civil War 1642-1646 (Stroud, 2011).
106 WRO, CR2017/C9, ff. 25-6.
107 SA, BB/D/1/2/1/52; HMC, Fifth Report, Part I, p. 49; The Effect of all Letters Read in the House of Parliament from the 14 to the 23 of November from all places of the Kingdome (1642), unpaginated; SA, 6000/13290.
108 WRO, CR2017/C9, ff. 131, 133; Relation […] by […] William Reinking, p. 2.

night of 1/2 August to surprise the Royalist gathering at Wattlesborough Heath. Mackworth soon after reported to Parliament how:

> The Intelligence proved true. We were all up in arms in the garrison that night; and our horse were ordered to be at the place somewhat before the time, to crush the several parties as they came, before they should unite; which succeeded accordingly: for, about twelve of the clock, the first troop that came, being about fifty horse, fell before they were aware into our horse, who charged and dispersed them; but Captain Allen, who commanded the [Parliamentary] party, was run through the side, which, with the darkness of the night, hindered the pursuit. Another troop coming on, hearing the report of the pistols, gave back, and in the morning dispersed. […] Thus God, by his providence, made the discovery, and succeeded our endeavours.[109]

An army's reconnaissance and intelligence-gathering effort was directed by its scoutmaster, a role George Davis later claimed to have performed for Lord Capel in Shropshire and Cheshire, while one Theodore Jennings was the Earl of Denbigh's scoutmaster-general.[110] Both sides retained small numbers of mounted scouts as specialists in surveillance to supplement the regular cavalry's intelligence gathering. In May 1643 Lord Capel ordered Sir Francis Ottley to deploy scouts from Shrewsbury widely across the county and its border, 'lest some might fail'. Colonel Thomas Hunt's regiment of Parliamentarian horse similarly included a number of scouts.[111] Parties of horse undertook reconnaissance work during their routine patrols, such as the opposing eight-man detachments from the garrisons at Royalist Shrawardine and Parliamentarian Moreton Corbet who skirmished in the village of Myddle sometime in late 1644.[112] Myddle was seven miles equidistant to both castles, and the range of a garrison's reconnaissance effort was effectively a half-day's ride by its horsemen.

News and hearsay filtered into garrisons from the surrounding countryside and both sides coveted local intelligence. In May 1645 High Sheriff Sir Francis Ottley ordered parish constables in west Shropshire to report to Royalist garrisons any movement of Parliamentarian forces. Similarly, in February 1646 Parliamentary officers at Stokesay Castle pledged their garrison's protection to the townsfolk of Bishop's Castle if they cooperated, in giving 'us at all times what intelligence you can of the motion and approaches of the enemy'.[113] But the flow of intelligence was subject to fluctuating popular support, as the Royalists found to their cost after the battle of Montgomery, a blow to Royalist arms in the region that disheartened the King's supporters and encouraged his opponents. Consequently, in October 1644, a month after the battle, Sir Michael Ernle reported of Shropshire that 'the country being now surrounded by the enemy's forces […] is […] apt to run in unto and serveth the rebels with all manner of things especially intelligence'.[114]

---

109 *JHL*, X, pp. 424-5, 8 Aug. 1648.
110 *OT List*, p. 316; *Mercurius Aulicus*, w/e 24 Aug. 1644, p. 1133.
111 'Ottley Papers' (1895), p. 319; SA, 366, f. 179.
112 Gough, *Myddle*, p. 73.
113 HRO, CF61/20, ff. 573-4; BCHRC, First Minute Book, f. 209.
114 BRL, Additional Mss 18981, f. 299.

29. Gathering intelligence was an important function of garrisons. From mid-1645 until the end of the First Civil War the Parliamentarians monitored Royalist activity in south Shropshire from their outpost at Stokesay Castle, above. The castle is a fortified manor house dating to the thirteenth century.

Garrisons were hubs for intelligence gathering. By the close of 1645, news of activity in the three Royalist strongholds remaining in Shropshire was being relayed from nearby Parliamentarian garrisons to Sir William Brereton and to the committeemen at Shrewsbury.[115] Moreover, the wide-reaching regional intelligence network fostered by Brereton informed Parliamentarian operations generally in Shropshire during 1645. This meant that the Royalist task force Sir William Vaughan led from south Shropshire towards Chester in later October 1645 as it advanced through the northern Marches was closely monitored from Parliamentarian garrisons. Timely and accurate intelligence reports enabled Brereton and his fellow regional commanders to concentrate their forces and intercept and defeat Vaughan outside Denbigh on 1 November.[116]

Garrison commanders could gain useful intelligence from deserters and prisoners of war, whose testimony, although given under duress or to appease their captors, nonetheless might provide valuable insight into the enemy's condition and morale. In late February 1644 the Royalists found that statements by Parliamentarian deserters from Wem, reporting the garrison as weakened and demoralised, were corroborated

115 *LBWB*, II, for example pp. 135, 318, 338-9, 394.
116 Ibid., pp. 98-162, *passim.*

by a spy in the town employed by Sir Vincent Corbet, then governor of Moreton Corbet Castle.[117] Prisoner-taking raids were conducted to acquire intelligence of this kind. For example, on 24 October 1645 five of Sir William Vaughan's soldiers were questioned after being seized from their bivouac near Bishop's Castle by a detachment from Stokesay garrison. But common soldiers were usually ill informed about strategy, and on this occasion all Major Hungerford could glean by interrogating his captives was that 'they are designed to raise a siege but where they know not'.[118]

Both sides also made widespread use of 'intelligencers' – the contemporary term for civilian spies and informers. Because intelligencers could operate more freely in enemy-controlled territory, especially in garrisoned towns, their news was an invaluable supplement to the reports of the military's own horse and scouts. To this end, by December 1645 Captain Lord Colvill, governor of Parliament's garrison at Broncroft Castle, had 'an honest friend for intelligence' within Bridgnorth, and also employed an informant in the Royalist-held city of Worcester.[119] In order to undertake their hazardous clandestine work, intelligencers had to be highly motivated, either out of loyalty to their adopted cause or by attractive remuneration. The contemporary military theoretician John Vernon was in no doubt that trustworthy and quick-witted spies should be well rewarded: 'which will cause them to expose themselves unto all hazards and dangers to give intelligence'.[120] Sir Thomas Myddelton accordingly paid his intelligencers well for their missions into Royalist-controlled Wales, including Piers David, given almost £21 for spying in Montgomeryshire. Espionage was not, however, a male preserve and Myddelton also paid one Jane Evan £5 for intelligence.[121] In early December 1645 one of Sir William Brereton's female informers – who was probably a professional spy and perhaps also a *femme fatale* – on her return from Royalist Worcester visited Sir William Vaughan in his quarters at Bridgnorth. Later the next day she related her meeting with the Royalist general and other news to the Parliamentarian committeemen at Shrewsbury.[122] Judging by the tone of his report, Royalism rather than remuneration inspired an intelligencer dwelling in a township near Wem to send Sir Francis Ottley in early 1644 an estimation of Parliament's forces in the county, based on his own observations and local hearsay. The anonymous informer nervously entrusted Ottley to 'keep this letter very close or else burn it as soon as you have read it'. Potentially the most useful intelligencer was an informer of seniority within the enemy's camp, like the 'one that is a commissioner of array and frequently in Ludlow, yet in affection our friend' who by December 1645 was notifying the committee at Shrewsbury about Royalist activity in south Shropshire.[123]

Given this sort of infiltration by informants and the uncertainties of local allegiance, attempts to maintain military secrecy were often ineffectual and the enemy soon knew about deployments. Moreover, news could be communicated quickly along active

117 HMC, *Thirteenth Report, Appendix Part I*, pp. 170-1; BL, Additional Mss 18981, f. 69.
118 BRL, Additional Mss 11332, f. 14.
119 BRL, Additional Mss 11333, f. 24.
120 J. Vernon, *The Young Horseman or The honest plain-dealing Cavalier* (1644), p. 41.
121 TNA, SP28/346 Part 1, unfoliated.
122 BRL, Additional Mss 11333, ff. 8, 43.
123 BRL, Additional Mss 18981, f. 19; BRL, Additional Mss 11332, f. 113.

intelligence networks. For example, from Wem on the morning of 19 February 1644 Colonel Mytton was able to write with the benefit of corroboration by several local sources to inform Sir Thomas Fairfax of Prince Rupert's arrival at Shrewsbury the previous evening. With similar rapidity, news of the Royalist defeat near Stokesay on 8 June 1645 was being communicated the next day by the Parliamentarian Colonel John Fox from his base at Edgbaston Hall near Birmingham, almost 40 miles from the battlefield in south Shropshire.[124]

Messengers were employed when distance and fear of disclosure made it hazardous to impart intelligence in person. One such was Richard Clarke, a youth who cleverly adopted the guise of a simpleton beggar and secreted messages in a hollow staff when travelling between the Parliamentarians at Wem and their informants in Royalist garrisons. Richard Waker was a less cunning messenger arrested by the Royalist authorities at Ludlow in May 1643 on suspicion of carrying letters to and from Brampton Bryan Castle, the Parliamentarian stronghold in northern Herefordshire.[125]

Mounted couriers maintained long-distance communications between commanders, including the exchange of intelligence reports. Accordingly, during 1644 and 1645 the constables of Stockton parish had to requisition horses for the Royalist courier service operating out of Bridgnorth.[126] Trusted and well-paid civilians were frequently employed as dispatch riders instead of soldiers, as in February 1645 when the anxious Sir Richard Cave intended 'instantly to hire messengers at any price' to carry from Ludlow the news of the fall of Shrewsbury to Prince Maurice at Chester. Bailiffs' accounts show that in 1645-6 civilian couriers often delivered Royalist dispatches overnight from Ludlow and were well remunerated for doing so; one rider received 5s for delivering a letter to Sir William Vaughan, for example.[127] Messages of this sort if intercepted were a most valuable source of intelligence to the enemy. Therefore, in order to mitigate the dangers of capture and disclosure critical information could be omitted from the written report and instead given verbally by the messenger, or else disguised by encipherment. But this was a precaution field commanders often found impracticable. 'For want of a cipher or skill how to use', concluded Lord Capel in a dispatch to King Charles's secretary, Lord Falkland, from Bridgnorth on 26 March 1643, 'I dare not advertise more upon the chance of messengers'. In his hasty situation report to Prince Rupert mentioned above, Sir Richard Cave concluded, 'I have not time to write in cipher, if I had I should say more'.[128]

Given that messengers had to contend with ill-made roads, variable terrain, and unpredictable weather, whilst avoiding interception by the enemy, communications and the exchange of intelligence was often maintained effectively. On 22 March 1643, for instance, three Royalist couriers relayed a packet of letters the 20-odd miles from Chester into north Shropshire in just five hours. Perhaps more typical was the 40-mile passage of an intelligence report from Sir Henry Hastings – addressed 'for his Highness Prince Rupert at Shrewsbury, post-haste, post-haste' – sent from Tutbury Castle in

124 WSL, SMS 557; Tibbutt, *Letter Books of Sir Samuel Luke*, pp. 562-3.
125 Gough, *Myddle*, p. 171; SA, LB7/2320.
126 SA, P270/B/1/1, ff. 55-8.
127 BRL, Additional Mss 18981, f. 40; SA, LB8/1/166, f. 7.
128 WSL, SMS 487; BRL, Additional Mss 18981, f. 40.

north-east Staffordshire at four pm on 12 April 1644 that arrived at Bridgnorth at nine pm on the 13th.[129] Such communications were slowed, hampered and endangered by the proximity of enemy garrisons. After the Parliamentarians captured Oswestry, for example, the Royalists were forced to divert across the Shropshire border into the Welsh hill country their line of communication with Chester. Consequently, at the end of June 1644 one of Prince Rupert's agents ruefully contemplated his southerly journey by this alternative route: 'The Parliament men from Wem surprised Oswestry, which sends me to make a passage to Worcester through more unhallowed countries than the Alps'.[130]

Medical services

In comparison to the plentiful evidence for intelligence gathering, there are fewer references to the care of the sick and wounded in the Shropshire theatre of war. Analysis of the medical services of the opposing forces is therefore problematical; what treatment and nursing care was received by soldiers like John Mould, for example, a Parliamentarian trooper from the parish of Myddle who, according to Richard Gough, after being shot in the thigh remained 'very crooked as long as he lived'? Thomas Ash, a Royalist soldier from the same district, similarly returned home with 'a crazy body and many scars, the symptoms of the dangerous service which he had performed'. Both were fortunate to have survived their wounding and return home from the Wars, for Gough calculated that of the soldiers' 18 fellow parishioners who enlisted for King or Parliament, 13 were killed in battle, or else died of wounds or disease, or otherwise remained missing; a statistic reflecting the sometimes high rate of mortality consequential to Civil War soldiering.[131]

The combatants were under obligation to provide charitable care for their own and enemy sick and wounded, in accordance with military custom and the religious and moral standards of mid-seventeenth-century society. Contemporary military theoreticians also acknowledged that medical practice was a necessary ancillary arm of the military. Cruso recommended that army headquarters should include a six-man medical team, in addition to the surgeons and their assistants of the individual regiments, while Henry Hexham thought that each infantry company should have a 'good barber surgeon', to tend the wounded in the regimental surgeon's absence.[132] However, in reality care for the sick and wounded was often limited by shortages of skilled practitioners and the scarcity of medical supplies. The fullest study of military welfare during the Civil Wars has concluded that while the medical corps of the armies of both sides were at first unprepared and inadequately equipped and staffed, by 1645 Parliament had overseen the development of a reasonably well-resourced and administered medical service. The Royalist army, on the other hand, to the end failed to give the same priority to caring for its casualties.[133] These conclusions were, however,

129 'Ottley Papers' (1895), p. 295; WSL, SMS 550/17.
130 Carte, *Original Letters*, I, p. 53.
131 Gough, *Myddle*, pp. 71-2, 227.
132 Cruso, *Military Instructions*, unfoliated; H. Hexham, *The First Part of The Principles of the Art Military* (1642), unfoliated.
133 E. G. von Armi, *Justice for the Maimed Soldier: Nursing, Medical Care and Welfare for Sick and Wounded Soldiers*

based mainly on the practices of the King's Oxford-based army and of Parliament in south-east and eastern England, while less is known of the medical services of the regional armies and local forces elsewhere.

After the departure of the King's army, in mid-October 1642 Shropshire's Royalist leadership agreed to appoint an experienced surgeon to oversee medical care. Nonetheless, local Royalist soldiers lacked medical support when engaged in cross-border skirmishes with Sir William Brereton's Cheshire Parliamentarians in early 1643. Sir Vincent Corbet's Dragoons were part of the Royalist force routed by Brereton at Nantwich on 28 January. The following day Corbet wrote in desperation to Sir Francis Ottley at Shrewsbury, demanding 'all the surgeons you can possibly provide for we are in great want of them'. But any help Corbet's men received was inadequate or transitory, because in mid-April he again appealed for a surgeon ('with all his implements and necessaries') to be sent to treat the wounded at his field headquarters at Malpas.[134] Notwithstanding such shortages of competent practitioners, it seems that eventually Royalist forces more often included medical staff. A surgeon and a physician were among the prisoners of the Royalist army defeated near Stokesay in June 1645, for example, and in April 1646 there were surgeons among the garrison at Bridgnorth Castle.[135]

On 13 April 1643 Sir Vincent Corbet had specifically requested the services of John Shelvock, a barber-surgeon from Shrewsbury. In exchange for his expertise Shelvock was promised 'remuneration to his content', and it is likely that sporadic care provided by civilian practitioners – hired or otherwise called upon by the military – was the norm. Among the military's medical staff officers was William Thorpe, chief surgeon to the Earl of Denbigh. With his wagonload of medical supplies, Thorpe accompanied the army of the West Midland Association on campaign in Staffordshire and Shropshire from May to July 1644, thereby demonstrating a commitment to medical care even in Denbigh's cash-strapped organisation.[136]

Other aspects of the management of care for the wounded in and around Shropshire can be reconstructed. The casualties of a larger engagement might receive primary surgical treatment at a field hospital, like that set up by the Parliamentarians after the battle of Montgomery. There, however, the surgeons and their mates were noteworthy for their avarice rather than medical skill, the Parliamentarian general Sir John Meldrum reportedly threatening several that he would 'deal with them as with enemies' unless they handed over jewellery removed from the fatally wounded Sir William Fairfax.[137] More often casualties were evacuated further afield to receive treatment (or indeed, to be taken for burial). The Parliamentarians reported after Sir William Vaughan's abortive attack on their garrison at Wrockwardine in December 1645 that the Royalists carried away their dead and wounded in ten commandeered

and their Families During the English Civil Wars and Interregnum, 1642-1660 (Aldershot, 2001), pp. 38, 42, 61-72.
134 SA, 6000/13288; 'Ottley Papers': (1894), p. 68, (1895), pp. 311-2.
135 Three Great Victories, p. 3; 'Ottley Papers' (1896), p. 304.
136 'Ottley Papers' (1895), pp. 311-12; References to Thorpe are found in: TNA, SP28/34 Part 2, f. 288; SP28/48 Part 3, f. 239; SP28/131 Part 12, f. 29.
137 The Kingdome's Weekly Intelligencer, 24 Sept.-1 Oct. 1644, pp. 592-3.

30. For a time in 1644 the Royalists used St. Mary's church, Shrewsbury, as
a temporary hospital or infirmary for wounded and sick soldiers.

farm carts.[138] In their retreat (or rout, according to the solely Parliamentarian reports of the action) the Royalist force defeated outside Bishop's Castle on 30 August 1645 abandoned sixty wounded, but in a humanitarian act of quid pro quo an agreement was made for their exchange with a like number of Parliamentarian captives. It was reported: 'the officers have procured their carrying to Ludlow, to be looked after by their own surgeons, and engaged that so many prisoners of war should (at their coming hither) be exchanged for them'.[139]

Numbers of wounded were sent to Shrewsbury, which, as the county town and principal Royalist and later Parliamentarian garrison, could provide carers and accommodation. In mid-September 1644 Royalist casualties from the siege of Montgomery Castle were carted the 20 or so miles to Shrewsbury to receive medical attention. Similarly, after their defeat at nearby High Ercall on 5 July 1645 around 100 wounded Parliamentarian soldiers may have straggled into the county town. St. Mary's Church at Shrewsbury appears to have served as an infirmary or temporary hospital during October 1644 at least, when Lady Leveson made a charitable donation for the care of wounded soldiers accommodated there.[140]

Local men made casualties might be fortunate enough to be tended by their families,

138 *The Weekly Account*, 30 Dec. 1645-6 Jan. 1646, p. 1064.
139 *Heads of some Notes of the Citie Scout*, 9 Sept. 1645, p. 4.
140 *CSPD, 1644*, p. 533; BRL, Harleian Mss 6852, f. 274; SRO, D593/R/1/3/2, unfoliated.

but in the general absence of hospital facilities it was common practice for wounded and sick soldiers to be dispersed to inns or households to be nursed by ordinary civilians. This was done through the general imposition of billeting and free quarter, or else individuals entered into more amenable arrangements with the authorities to provide paid care. The latter may have been the reason why during 1644 William Shepherd, a householder from Onibury, claimed payment for taking in Royalist soldiers wounded at the siege of Hopton Castle, and again after the battle of Montgomery. In July 1644 an officer at Wem complained that wounded Parliamentarian soldiers went unpaid, but this may well have been because their wages had been stopped to pay instead their civilian attendants.[141] Another example of a householder providing medical care was the unknown Shrewsbury resident who from mid-September 1643 provided quarters for the Royalist Captain Holmes and his servant. The Captain was sometime wounded or fell sick, and so received care at his lodgings until his death on 15 November, during which time – as the householder emphasised when submitting his bill – he received 'all things convenient for him'.

But as a result of their actions many soldiers were not accorded careful treatment. The Royalist cavalry officer Cornet Collins had led repeated forays to plunder the parish of Myddle. As a result of his notoriety, when wounded there in a skirmish Collins was left by the villagers to bleed to death on a mattress he had sought to take from a household the day before.[142] However, because the cornet had been shot in the stomach, there was in any case little that seventeenth-century medicine could have done to treat him.

Conclusions

The several small battles and other larger field engagements fought in Shropshire do not rank highly among the actions of the First English Civil War. However, they were characteristic of the sort of regional clashes that were far more typical of the conflict than were the large, and comparatively rare, set-piece battles such as Edgehill, Marston Moor and Naseby. The larger engagements in Shropshire reflected the changing fortunes of both sides, but although for a while they all had important local outcomes, none proved to be decisive in determining the outcome of the county war.

The capture or successful defence of strongholds in the longer term proved to be more significant, and Shropshire is noteworthy for the numerous garrisons established there by both sides during the First Civil War. Accordingly, the resources of war effort were employed mostly in the defence and subjugation of strongholds. Shrewsbury, Oswestry, Wem, Bridgnorth and Ludlow as fortified garrison towns were of pivotal importance, while many other defensible places, including churches, castles and manor houses, became strongholds. These were often strengthened by earthen fortifications, the physical and documentary traces of which are now mostly fragmentary or lost. The prevailing techniques and tactics of mid-seventeenth-century siege-craft deployed in Shropshire ranged from subterfuge to concerted siege operations. The deployment of small numbers of artillery pieces by both sides often proved decisive. Notwithstanding

141 SA, LB7/2098; WRO, CR2017/C10, f. 19.
142 SA, 3365/2566, unfoliated; Gough, *Myddle,* p. 41.

the measures and counter-measures of attack and defence, the subjugation of a stronghold was often settled by negotiations conducted in accordance with military custom.

Intelligence work and medical care were important ancillary aspects of war effort that at the regional and local level of the Civil Wars have received little scholarly attention. This chapter has shown how gathering and communicating military intelligence in and around Shropshire was an essential activity for both sides. Commanders received a scatter of information, gleaned from patrolling troopers and scouts, prisoners, deserters, spies and gossiping townsmen and country-folk. The evidence – particularly that of Sir William Brereton's regional intelligence network – is slanted to the conclusion that the Parliamentarians more effectively gathered and acted on intelligence. Among Royalist commanders, however, Lord Capel for one sought to imbue his subordinates with an appreciation of the importance of accurate intelligence work.

Both sides provided medical care for the sick and wounded on a more or less ad-hoc basis, with most reliance placed on civilian practitioners and lay nurses. From the limited evidence no conclusions can be drawn regarding the efficacy of the opposing medical services in the Shropshire theatre of war, but clearly neither side wholly neglected this benevolent task of the war effort.

Conclusion

A noted historian of Shropshire, author of a general history of the county, has concluded that the shire 'proved itself so unmilitaristic in the Civil War'.[1] Being more concerned with economic and social developments, rather than military history, it is understandable that he did not look more deeply into a county war that superficially may indeed appear to have been an unremarkable tussle for the possession of a comparatively quiet backwater of the English Civil Wars.

Instead, Shropshire's experience of the First Civil War in particular was in fact remarkable. It was here in 1642 that King Charles I was able to organise an effective army to uphold his cause by force of arms, and in 1646 where some of his most ardent supporters made their last stand. The war in Shropshire for most of the intervening years was more prolonged and intense than in many other English and Welsh counties. Shropshire also experienced armed conflict in 1648 during the Second Civil War, albeit on a much smaller and less significant scale.

By having taken a bipartisan view of the war effort, this book has shown that far from being 'unmilitaristic', Shropshire and its populace was in fact deeply involved in the conflict. By examining in detail the nature of contemporary military enterprise, a much clearer picture of an often hard-fought and, on the whole, capably organised and resourced county war has been revealed. Indeed, Farrow's assertion, written in the 1920s, that within Shropshire, 'better perhaps than anywhere else' could be seen the First, or Great Civil War 'in miniature', seems justifiable. Shropshire has provided an instructive case study of the ways in which Royalists and Parliamentarians directed, organised and prosecuted military operations at the county and regional level. The ebb and flow of these often long-sustained provincial struggles, marked by much skirmishing and a few larger engagements, and by fighting for the many fortified places, was more typical of warfare in Civil War England and Wales than were the pitched battles between the amalgamated field armies. It remains the case, however, that historians still tend to overlook the nature and significance of the regional and local county campaigns, instead often being preoccupied with reanalysing and reinterpreting the major battles, or the careers of the most well-known leaders.

Taken as a whole, the conclusions from Shropshire's theatre of war tend to reinforce what is known about contemporary military affairs.

At county level, war effort for both sides was directed by relatively small numbers of

---

1   B. Trinder, *A History of Shropshire* (Chichester, 1998), p. 67.

leading local activists headed by a few outstanding and highly committed individuals, of whom some also served as military leaders. However, a far greater body was involved in administering the war effort, acting with varying authority as civilian or paramilitary officials (with the fine line distinguishing the two roles often being blurred), or else serving in the military. Given also the involvement of farmers providing provisions and fodder, of artisans engaged in warlike production, of lay men and women proffering intelligence or providing medical care, and of a populace paying military taxes levied on income, property, chattels and produce, Shropshire demonstrates well the widespread militarisation experienced by county communities deeply enmeshed in the war effort.

In addition, the officials and structures of traditional county administration assumed wartime roles and responsibilities, alongside the new militarised leaderships of the commission of array and its sub-commissions and the county committee and its offshoots. Moreover, although historians have often and rightly stressed the extent of Civil War neutralism and the variability of active participation, Shropshire's experience has on the other hand demonstrated the very well organised belligerency of the combatants. At the regional level of military organisation, although Shropshire for much of the war formed part of a reasonably cohesive bloc of Royalist territory, allowing the regional commanders Lord Capel and Prince Rupert to enjoy considerable success in organising the war effort there, the county displayed the difficulties of forming successful regional commands where and when widespread and recurrent fighting hampered administration and prevented local forces from being deployed further afield.

Looking closer at military leadership, Shropshire's war showed the range of contemporary military talent available to both sides: from career soldiers, such as the senior Anglo-Irish army officers who came to prominence there on the Royalist side from 1644, to those commanders who appear to have had little or no pre-war military practice but who nonetheless during the course of the war, and learning by experience, became as much professional soldiers – the outstanding capable figure among them in Shropshire being the Parliamentarian Colonel, later Major-General, Thomas Mytton. Similarly, Shropshire had its share of those foreign career soldiers who, in probably relatively small but not inconsiderable numbers, crossed from the Continent to supplement the indigenous officer corps in English Civil War armies. As examples here we have the Colonels Wilhelm Reinking and Giovanni Devillier, mercenaries in the employ of the Parliamentarians and Royalists respectively.

Turning to material aspects of war effort, the means by which both King and Parliament acted nationally to finance war, by donations, subscriptions, fines, seizure and taxation, were imposed in Shropshire to varying effect. War effort in Shropshire also reflected the national situation, in that while most provisions were obtained locally, indigenous warlike production had to be heavily supplemented with military supplies imported from the Continent. However, the findings from Shropshire have pointed to the extent and organisation of regional production, and to the versatility of local suppliers in fulfilling wartime requirements. The overriding importance to the national Parliamentarian cause of London, as a great city and commercial centre, a source of reserves of manpower and of huge economic and fiscal resources, is demonstrated well by the example of Shropshire, a distant theatre of operations that nonetheless was substantially resourced from the capital.

The composition and role of the armed forces in Shropshire tend to support wider conclusions about military organisation during the First Civil War as expressed by Donagan, in that local forces were 'frequently small, heterogeneous and inadequate', and also that the armies, being mobile and widely distributed, were only rarely 'heavily concentrated for major battles'.[2] Indeed, the great mobility of Civil War armies, not only the mounted units but also those on foot, may be seen in the campaigning in Shropshire. The war there was to a certain extent insular, fought mostly by the opposing county forces heavily supported by auxiliaries detached or posted to Shropshire, rather than being directed by the intervention of the major field armies. Neither the Royalist Oxford army, apart from skirting easterly Shropshire in marching northwards in May 1645 at the outset of what became the Naseby campaign, nor Parliament's main armies, under the Earl of Essex, the Earl of Manchester, Sir William Waller, or, indeed, the New Model Army, ever campaigned in Shropshire. This tends to emphasise the achievement of local Parliamentarian arms, for the Shropshire forces – albeit with considerable auxiliary support – eventually regained the county without the benefit of intervention by an allied army to clear their way (other than the Earl of Denbigh's brief intervention in summer 1644). However, apart from the absence of the large field armies and consequently of pitched battles, warfare in Shropshire from 1642 to 1646 very much typified that elsewhere in England and Wales, in particular the attack and defence of strongholds, with garrisons being particularly widespread in Shropshire. The usual methods of fortification were also employed in Shropshire, entailing the refurbishment of medieval works and the construction of military earthworks of modern pattern. A good example from Shropshire of the frequently makeshift nature of Civil War fortification is Morton Corbet Castle, where the buildings of the medieval castle and the Tudor mansion, together with the nearby parish church, were made defensible alongside new earthen defences.

It is regarding Royalist activity during the First Civil War that Shropshire provides the most distinct findings to inform national interpretations of the conflict. The findings here tend to refute the determinist conclusions drawn by a number of leading modern historians on the outcome of the war; that the overriding inadequacies of the Royalist war effort made the military defeat of King Charles inevitable. Inherent administrative and logistical failings have been attributed to the Royalists by Hughes and Gentles, by Morrill, who saw 'financial thrombosis' destroying Royalist capability, and pointed to most volubly in a chapter by Holmes. He considered that King Charles's response to organising leadership and mobilising resources was confused; that the Royalists' approach was conservative, and too slow to adopt punitive wartime measures, such as conscription and sequestration; that local Royalist administration was divided and argumentative; and, overall, that the Royalists 'never developed as efficient a system for mobilising resources' as their opponents.[3]

2   Donagan, *War in England*, p. 218.
3   Reference to Hughes's determinist view has been made in the introduction; Gentles, in *English Revolution*, p. 127, concluded that 'Financially and logistically the Royalists were less well organised than Parliament';

Plentiful extant records have usually made it much easier for historians to demonstrate the superiority of Parliamentarian organisation than to prove the administrative and fiscal competence of their opponents. However, the rather fuller picture of Royalist activity in Shropshire is one of a considerable level of organisation and, as a result, of effective mobilisation of war effort, involving taxation, recruitment, munitions production and logistical provision. Furthermore, it has been argued here that instead of being unduly hesitant to impose harsh wartime measures, regardless of King Charles's early sensitivity, the Royalists adopted exactions such as widespread taxation, sequestration and impressment before or around the same time as the Parliamentarians. Taking general military taxation as a barometer of administrative effectiveness, in terms of systematic organisation and the involvement as assessors and collectors of large numbers of parochial and higher officials, the Royalist contribution, especially during 1644, seems to have been as more or less viable a money-raising instrument as the Parliamentarian assessments from 1645 to 1648. The failings in contribution can be attributed more to military instability, war weariness and the inherent practical and bureaucratic difficulties of implementing widespread taxation of any sort in the seventeenth century, than to systemic failings in Royalist organisation. Overall, Royalist forces in Shropshire do not seem to have been any less well resourced or equipped than their Parliamentarian adversaries, although clearly both sides experienced shortages and the difficulties of relying on long-distance lines of communication with their main depots. To help overcome these difficulties the Royalists attempted to develop local resources, and the adaptation of the Shropshire iron industry to warlike manufacture is a noteworthy example of successful regional production under Royalist direction.

Were the Royalists more prone to infighting? It is the case that in their correspondence the senior Royalist officers posted to Shropshire often expressed distrust and disrespect for the local men become commissioners and commanders. However, historians pre-occupied with the carping of outsiders to their patron Prince Rupert have perhaps overlooked positive evidence of interdependence and collaborative action, resulting from divisions overcome or patched over, of taxes gathered, resources secured, forces kept in the field and engagements won. By their ad hoc nature, Civil War command structures – of commissions and committees of civilians and soldiers; of regional commanders with few permanent headquarters staff; of locals and outsiders; of career soldiers and those of experience gained during the war – with their often blurred lines of demarcation of duties tended to foster cross purposes and generate rivalry and conflicts of interest.

This study has also presented examples of Parliamentarian disharmony, like the officer on the Earl of Denbigh's staff who believed that the purpose of the county committees was only to provide the soldiers with resources, and not to be involved in fighting the war.[4] Denbigh's own unamiable relationship with the county committees of Warwickshire and Shropshire stemmed from political and religious differences within

---

Morrill, *Revolt*, p. 155; C. Holmes, *Why Was Charles I Executed?* (London, 2006), chapter four, 'Why Did Parliament Win the Civil War?', pp 71-92, quotation from p. 90.

4   *CSPD, 1649-1650*, pp. 444-5.

the Parliamentarian camp, between moderate and radicals. Once King Charles was defeated militarily, in 1646 and 1647 these differences came to the fore in factionalism within Parliament and amongst the army: between the so-called Presbyterians, who advocated a clement reconciliation with the King alongside an established form of national religious practice, and the Independents, who upheld a settlement with the King more restrictive of prerogative powers, and who in religious matters sought disestablishment and greater freedom in worship. It is likely, then, that Denbigh, as a moderate Parliamentarian tending to the Presbyterian camp, was at loggerheads with the more radical and Independent-leaning members of the committee of Shropshire, who also happened to be his social inferiors.

Returning to the King's party, unique failings in the Royalist war effort, then, cannot be proven in Shropshire's theatre of war during the First Civil War, although of course nationally King Charles I's war machine eventually proved unable to settle his crown and restore his kingship. In the Second Civil War of 1648, if a Royalist war effort of sorts can be discerned in Shropshire it was ill-coordinated and disorganised, and so easily broken by the county Parliamentarians, notwithstanding their limited and stretched military resources; a situation which somewhat mirrored the national course of events. While the outcome of both Civil Wars in Shropshire was not determined there but by military events elsewhere – in 1645-6, by the terminal retraction of Royalist arms stemming from Parliament's major victories at the battles of Naseby and Langport in summer 1645, and in 1648, by Parliament's suppression of uprisings in South Wales and south-eastern England and by the destruction of the Royalist-Scots Army of the Engagement as a result of the battle at Preston in later August – nonetheless a protracted war within a war was fought for Shropshire from 1643 to 1646. So, what, then, were some of the strengths and weaknesses of the combatants?

The Shropshire Royalists benefitted from being part of a more cohesive regional command than the Parliamentarians were able to achieve by way of the West Midland Association. However, it can be argued that the Shropshire Parliamentarians benefitted proportionally as much by their unofficial cooperative 'association' with Sir William Brereton's Cheshire war effort and with Sir Thomas Myddelton's campaigns into Wales. Brereton, for example, by assuming, de facto, the role of regional commander during winter 1644-5, brought reinforcements from Cheshire and also from Staffordshire and Yorkshire to Shropshire in early 1645. The Royalist regional commanders, Lord Capel, Prince Rupert, Prince Maurice and Lord Astley, and the deputy commanders, Lord Byron and Sir William Vaughan, collectively were among the most committed, and militarily and administratively able of King Charles's followers, with Rupert being the outstanding resourceful figure. However, their benefit to the local Royalists in Shropshire in the longer-term was patchy. Rupert, for example, attracted considerable forces to Shropshire and achieved military success there, but he, like the other commanders-in-chief, often campaigned further afield or was otherwise preoccupied with organisational matters elsewhere. The objectives of their Parliamentarian opponents, however, were more closely regionally focussed, so that they with their forces and military resources tended to remain in theatre; neither Brereton's well-organised Cheshire army, nor the smaller forces of Myddelton and the

Shropshire Parliamentarians were obliged to fight far elsewhere until spring 1646 – when the outcome of the war was decided, and for the Parliamentarians had become a process of eliminating the few remaining and increasingly isolated Royalist garrisons.

The Shropshire Parliamentarians of the county committee, although their forces were small and often outnumbered, achieved success because they were wholly committed to recovering their home county, while Royalist attention and resources were often distracted elsewhere. Until the winter of 1644/5, on the whole the Royalists had held military advantage in Shropshire, in terms of territorial control and in size of forces, and by successes in the field and in taking strong points. However, in the long term the Parliamentarians gained the three most important victories of the county war: by occupying and successfully defending Wem in autumn 1643; by capturing and holding Oswestry in summer 1644; and by taking Shrewsbury in early 1645.

In 1644 Prince Rupert may well have contemptuously disregarded Parliamentarian-held Wem as a 'crow's nest that would not afford each of his men a piece of bread'; an apocryphal quotation, attributed to the Prince by a local eighteenth-century antiquarian.[5] But it was the case, that their inability to capture the Parliamentarian headquarters was the signal military failure of the Royalists in Shropshire. Had they done so, at pivotal points in the county war, in September 1643, or in April 1644, for instance, the result would have been not only to crush local enemy resistance, but also to weaken the regional Parliamentarian war effort, with possibly wider consequences for the war as a whole.

---

5   Garbet, *History of Wem*, p. 221.

Appendix

A Civil War Coin Hoard from south Shropshire

Coin hoarding historically is associated with periods of social and political instability, conflict and warfare – times when individuals sought ways to safeguard their valuables by concealment. Hoards often comprise collections of coins or treasured valuable objects placed together, sometimes in a container, and deliberately hidden – usually buried – by their owner for safekeeping and later retrieval. Clearly, those hoards that have much later been discovered are those that the owners, as a result of misfortune or death, could not recover.

Coin hoards are not unique to the English Civil Wars, but are a recognised archaeological occurrence associated with the period. One such hoard was discovered in February 2011 in south Shropshire. Known since as the 'Bitterley Hoard', the find was declared treasure in June 2012, and acquired by Ludlow Museum in late 2013. To date, this is one of the most valuable hoards – having the highest contemporary face value – from Shropshire associated with the English Civil War, and the only example that has been studied in detail from an archaeological, numismatic and historical perspective.

Howard Murphy, a hobby metal detectorist, discovered the hoard in a field close to the settlement of Bitterley, a village situated on the lower slopes of the uplands forming Clee Hill, south Shropshire. The find-spot was within a small paddock close to a deep hollow-way of some antiquity leading to common grazing above the village. A distinct house platform (which produced finds of seventeenth and eighteenth-century material) was nearby and the paddock was probably a garden or allotment associated with a building that once stood there. Importantly, when Mr. Murphy discovered the hoard he left it undisturbed *in situ* and immediately called in archaeologists from the British Museum's Portable Antiquities Scheme based with Ludlow Museum Resource Centre. They were able to fully investigate the site and to carefully recover the hoard.

The archaeologists found that the hoard had been placed within a pottery vessel shallowly buried in the field. There was no evidence of any direct built archaeology in association with the hoard, such as being placed within a house or a ditch. Instead, it seems that the hoard was deposited relatively swiftly as there was no variation within the surrounding soil, with the actual cut (edge of the hole) being indistinguishable from its back-fill. This is common to deposits that were quickly covered over and is

31. The Bitterley Hoard conserved and presented ready for display.

32. Gold Britain crown of James I from the Bitterley Hoard, obverse (left) and reverse.

33. Charles I half-crown from the Bitterley Hoard, struck
at Bristol in later 1643, obverse (left) and reverse.
Photographs of the Bitterley Hoard and the coins from it are copyright and by courtesy
of the photographer, Keith Pointon, and Shropshire Council/Shropshire Museums.

indicative of single action events. As there was no surrounding archaeology, the hoard
was left encased in soil and 'block-lifted' for transfer to the conservation department
of the British Museum in London for further study.

Post-recovery excavation revealed that the block of soil in which the hoard was
lifted contained a small black-ware tyg – a multi-handled drinking vessel common
in the late sixteenth and seventeenth centuries. It is thought that tygs were shared
between several people when drinking hot alcoholic beverages – hence the multiple
handles. The Bitterley example was relatively small and squat. Contained within the
tyg were the well-preserved remains of a fine leather purse. It had been preserved by
the anaerobic conditions formed by the vessel, in that as the cup was positioned within
the ground – mouth up – it created a waterlogged pocket preventing bacterial decay
of the leather.

The purse contained 137 silver coins and a single gold one, representing good
quality, unclipped coinage in circulation at the time of deposition. The coins dated to
the reigns of the Tudor monarchs Edward VI and Elizabeth I, and the Stuart Kings
James I and Charles I. Particularly noteworthy within the assemblage was a single
shilling of Edward VI struck between 1549 and 1551, a single gold Britain Crown
of James I, and a single half-crown of Charles I struck at the Bristol mint between
July 1643 and March 1644 when the city was Royalist held. This half-crown dates the
deposition of the hoard, giving it its *terminus post quem*; meaning that it could not have
been buried before July 1643. The coins had been highly selected from the currency
in circulation, with only the larger high denomination coins hoarded. There were no
sixpences in the group – a coin usually found in large numbers among seventeenth-

century coin hoards.

While in contemporary monetary terms the Bitterley Hoard was not highly valuable, worth £9 11s and 6d it represented about eleven months' wages for a day labourer, or about six months pay for a more skilled individual. Therefore the hoard may have been the ready money or savings of a fairly successful husbandman (small farmer). Why the hoard was deposited can never be known for certain. No military engagements are known to have occurred in the Bitterley area during the Civil Wars that might have prompted civilians or soldiers hurriedly to conceal their cash. The presence of the half-crown minted at Bristol is intriguing, as Royalist soldiers who had been based at Bristol were posted to Shropshire in early 1644. Perhaps a soldier who was billeted at Bitterley may have decided to conceal his savings for a while rather than keep it on his person? More likely reasons for the hoard's deposition may be that it was hidden by a civilian as a way of avoiding paying military taxes, or to prevent theft by plundering soldiers. Sadly, the owner was never able to recover it. Like other coin hoards of the period, the Bitterley Hoard is a very personal, albeit anonymous, reminder of the upheaval of the Civil Wars.

There are very few other Civil-War period coin hoards known from Shropshire, and none have been recovered using controlled archaeological techniques. The other known examples are from: Oswestry, discovered in 1909 consisting of 4 gold and 522 silver coins deposited c. 1643-4; Hawkestone Park, near Mark Drayton, discovered in c.1930 and donated to Shrewsbury Museum in 2001, containing 142 silver coins with the contemporary value of £5 18s 0d and deposited c.1643-44; Donnington, discovered in 1938 and comprising 522 low denomination silver coins deposited c.1643; and Priorslee, Telford, of 26 silver half-crowns deposited in c.1646

Shropshire Museums Service acquired the Bitterley Hoard with the intention of it being put on permanent display in the new museum at Ludlow, Shropshire. At the time of writing it is expected that the museum will open in later 2015. The acquisition of the hoard was funded by public donations and by grants, from the Friends of Ludlow Museum, Bitterley Church of England Primary School, The Tuesday Group, The Art Fund, The V&A Purchase Fund and The Headley Trust. The conservation of the hoard was funded by grants from the Ludlow Museum Development Trust, The Worshipful Company of Leathersellers and The Art Fund Treasure Plus Initiative.

Bibliography:
Besly, E., *English Civil War Coin Hoards*, British Museum Occasional Paper 51 (London, 1987).
Besly, E., 'A Civil War Hoard from Shropshire', *British Numismatic Journal*, 72 (2002), pp. 180-2.
Flynn, H., Cook, C. and B. Nenk, *Bitterley, Shropshire Hoard of Post-Medieval Coins and their Container* (Report for HM Coroner by The British Museum, T89, 2011).
Harrington, P., *English Civil War Archaeology* (London, 2004).
Reavill, P., and T. Brindle, *Excavation of the Bitterley Hoard* PAS Excavation Report (2012).
Co-written in May 2015 together with Peter Reavill, Finds Liaison Officer, Portable Antiquities Scheme, based at Ludlow Museum.

Note on Sources

While this book is based primarily on fresh archival research, it is right and fitting to acknowledge the efforts of previous researchers and writers. Their work has provided the essential background to inform and shape this author's approach. Clearly, any new piece of historical writing is necessarily founded on, draws upon, and distils and questions the historiography of its subject.

Of two other books to date that have attempted to encapsulate the history of the English Civil Wars in Shropshire as a whole, the first was Farrow's *Great Civil War in Shropshire* – the product of his university MA thesis. Hitherto the county had lacked a narrative history of the period, and Farrow's work was important in for the first time placing events there within a chronological context. Setting out, as he put it in the preface, to correct 'some current misinterpretations', and to reveal a 'very considerable quantity of new material', Farrow succeeded in a book of moderate (149-page) length to fix the course of the county war, while identifying and generally accurately dating most of the engagements. Farrow's was more than a military narrative, however, commenting also on partisanship and neutralism in devoting a chapter to 'social aspects of the struggle'. Farrow's *Great Civil War* remains a generally reliable account of the period, and it was not until 2000 that a new study appeared, with Bracher and Emmett's attractively produced and illustrated *Shropshire in the Civil War*, which continued the story to the Restoration. Including several maps charting the course of the county war and a useful gazetteer, this is a good introduction to the subject for general readership. A recent third book has considered the long period of the Civil Wars in Shropshire through the lens of the experience of one town. As a military historian Barratt has taken the example of Ludlow – as has been seen, a key Royalist garrison town throughout the First Civil War – as the setting for a wider narrative of military events in south Shropshire and elsewhere in the central borderlands of Wales.[1]

These books form part of a sizeable corpus exploring narrower aspects of Shropshire's Civil War, for the conflict has received considerable scholarly attention since the nineteenth century. The clergymen Owen and Blakeway, and Bellett, as antiquarian authors of local histories of Shrewsbury (1825) and Bridgnorth (1856) respectively, acknowledged the importance of these towns as Civil War strongholds. Owen and Blakeway exercised commendable academic rigour in their *History of Shrewsbury*, although Bellett tended to place undue reliance on folklore. The first attempt to

---

1   J. Barratt, *Cavalier Stronghold: Ludlow in the English Civil Wars, 1642-1660* (Almeley, 2013).

consider the war across the county was published in 1867.[2] While the author freely acknowledged her limitations as a military historian – 'it may lead someone better qualified for the task to collect materials for a history of the Civil War as it affected Shropshire generally' – nevertheless Frances Stackhouse Acton's study of the *Garrisons of Shropshire* drew on primary sources to stress the number and local importance of strongholds. However, the hindsight of later scholarship has revealed factual errors in her work, especially in the dating of events.

The founding in 1877 of the Shropshire Archaeological and Natural History Society enabled learned articles by local historians to be published in the Society's annual journal, the *Transactions*. Eminent among them was William Phillips, whose research, often featuring Civil War material, was published during the last decade of the nineteenth century in the *Transactions* and also in *Shropshire Notes and Queries*, a monthly compilation of miscellanea relating to Shropshire's natural and human history. Like other published Victorian local historians Phillips's achievement was in bringing historical documents to the fore. His published transcriptions of seventeenth-century texts were accompanied by a commentary and detailed explanatory footnotes. Phillips's most important work – still of great use to historians – was the transcription of the papers of Sir Francis Ottley, published in the *Transactions* from 1894 to 1896.[3]

Alfred and John Audens' approach to the study of the Civil Wars in Shropshire was more descriptive, and their work featured in the *Transactions* during the early twentieth century. In 1908, Alfred Auden's view of the war in south Shropshire was the first published local study to combine several sources in a narrative account.[4] John Auden's paper on Royalist activity between 1646 and 1660 was a similarly factual work.[5] On the other hand, his articles in 1912, one based around Prince Rupert's correspondence, the other a biographical listing of Royalist officers, both reflected Phillips's earlier formulaic approach.[6] The Parliamentarian leadership and a Royalist regimental history were the subjects of John Auden's three subsequent papers.[7] In the early 1940s Beaumont followed in similar style, with articles on Lord Capel, and on the outbreak of hostilities in Shropshire in 1642.[8]

Since the Second World War the number of local studies concerned with the Civil Wars have been fewer and far between. Hopkins's article in the *Transactions* for 1957-60 considered the economic impact of the war on landed estates in north Shropshire,

2   F.S. Acton, *The Garrisons of Shropshire During the Civil War, 1642-1648* (Shrewsbury, 1867).
3   W. Phillips (ed.), 'The Ottley Papers Relating to the Civil War', *TSANHS*, 2nd Series: VI (1894), pp. 27-78; VII (1895), pp. 241-360; VIII (1896), pp. 199-312.
4   A.M. Auden, 'Clun and its Neighbourhood in the First Civil War', *TSANHS*, 3rd Series, VIII (1908), pp. 287-336.
5   J.E. Auden, 'Shropshire and the Royalist Conspiracies between the end of the First Civil War and the Restoration, 1648-1660', *TSANHS*, 3rd Series, X (1910), pp. 87-168.
6   J.E. Auden, 'Four Letters from Shropshire to Prince Rupert', and 'The War Services of some Shropshire Officers in the King's Army', both in *TSANHS*, 4th Series, II, (1912), respectively pp. 1-21, 215-92.
7   J.E. Auden: 'Lieutenant Colonel William Reinking in Shropshire', *TSAS*, XLVII (1933-4), pp. 33-47; 'My case with the Committee of Salop', *TSAS*, XLVIII (1934-5), pp. 49-60; 'The Anglo-Irish Troops in Shropshire', *TSAS*, L (1939-40), pp. 49-64.
8   H. Beaumont: 'Arthur, Lord Capel, The King's Lieutenant General for Shropshire, 1643', *TSAS*, L (1939-40), pp. 65-94; 'Events in Shropshire at the Commencement of the Civil War', *TSAS*, LI (1941-3), pp. 11-42.

while Gilbert's 1993 study of clubman activity in 1644-5 more fully examined the events pictured by Alfred Auden in 1908.[9] Elsewhere, Wanklyn did important work by identifying many of the activists on both sides in Shropshire, and his thesis on the allegiance of the gentry also addressed military affairs to some extent.[10] Most recently, an article by this author has considered the defence of Shrewsbury as a case study of urban fortification during the Civil Wars.[11]

This book has drawn almost wholly on written sources, because there is very little artefactual evidence or, to date, archaeological evidence of the Civil War in Shropshire. However, during his research the author has also made many field visits to the buildings or their remains where garrisons were once located, and in search of the Civil War battlegrounds of Shropshire.

The written traces of Civil War military activity in Shropshire are fragmentary and scattered, although not unduly scarce. While there are collections of correspondence and administrative records upon which considerable reliance can be placed, there are very few family papers from the period in the public domain.

Selected manuscript material located in 14 regional and national archives has been consulted. As should be expected from a county-centred study of this kind, much reliance has been placed on documents held at Shropshire Archives, the county record office located in Shrewsbury. Notable for their completeness, the local administrative records surviving from the 1640s for the three main Royalist garrison towns of Shrewsbury, Bridgnorth and Ludlow have proven particularly valuable. Indeed, without the incidental detail provided by these civic records much of the Royalist war effort would remain obscure. Evidence of Parliamentarian activity nationally is in general fuller and more plentiful, but the evidence of Royalist action in Shropshire has gone some way to redress the balance, and to allow a more equitable examination of war effort. This book has also made as much use as possible of parish records, in which, as Bennett's important earlier work on military taxation in the English East Midlands demonstrated, by working (as Bennett put it) 'from the bottom up' detailed information on local aspects of war effort may be found.[12] But while Bennett could draw on up to 21 sets of parish constables' accounts across five shires, despite thorough investigation Shropshire has so far yielded only one – fortunately most informative – equivalent source from the First Civil War, the accounts of the constables of Stockton parish.

On the other hand, the correspondence of regional commanders is reasonably plentiful and has provided important information, on the Parliamentarian side notably the Earl of Denbigh's letter books. Prince Rupert's correspondence has supplemented the local sources in order to more fully explain the Royalists' war. The voluminous

9   E. Hopkins, 'The Bridgewater Estates in North Shropshire during the Civil War', *TSAS*, LVII (1961-4), pp. 307-12; C.D. Gilbert, 'Clubmen in Southwest Shropshire, 1644-45', *Transactions of the Shropshire Archaeological and Historical Society*, LXVIII (1993), pp. 93-8.

10   Wanklyn, 'Landed Society & Allegiance'.

11   J. Worton, "The Strongest Works in England"? The Defences of Shrewsbury During the Civil Wars, 1642-1651', *Transactions of the Shropshire Archaeological and Historical Society*, LXXXVII (2012, issued in 2014), pp. 95-112.

12   Bennett, 'Contribution and Assessment', p. 3.

Commonwealth Exchequer Papers held at The National Archives, London, under the general classification SP28 are a vital, if often unpredictable, source of information on Parliamentarian and later Commonwealth armies. However, the records catalogued in SP28 from Shropshire are extremely sparse, and fuller evidence of the activity of the committee of Shropshire remains elusive. However, SP28 has provided details of the actions of Sir Thomas Myddelton and of the Earl of Denbigh.

Considerable use has been made of the calendared *Reports* of the Historical Manuscripts Commission, and of the *State Papers, Domestic Series, of the reign of King Charles I*. Much information about the Parliamentarian war effort was gleaned from the *Journals* of the Houses of Commons and Lords. William Phillips's aforementioned 'Ottley Papers' collectively remain an invaluable source for Royalist activity in Shropshire throughout the First Civil War.

This book has drawn on the copious printed ephemera from the Civil War period, including the numerous political and military declarations and the weekly news journals printed in pamphlet form. Produced mostly in Parliamentarian London, these journals (which have been referenced here as newsbooks) frequently included reports (or extracts) from the front line. However, these were often unattributed and paraphrased, and editorial was skewed for propaganda effect. As a result, newsbooks are questionable sources that two academic historians, in cautionary notes, have categorised as 'exceptionally dangerous', and as 'dodgy traces of the past'.[13] Sometimes newsbooks did print as fact fallacious or false reports. In early October 1642 it was expected that Shropshire would be the frontline where the decisive battle would occur between King Charles's army based around Shrewsbury and the main Parliamentarian field army, then occupying Worcester, commanded by the Earl of Essex. Accordingly, two London newsbooks published eagerly anticipated but wholly fictitious accounts of imagined Parliamentarian victories in major engagements fought in Shropshire, at Bridgnorth and Ludlow, three weeks before the Battle of Edgehill.[14] However, while Civil War-period journalism must be given due circumspection and compared with other sources, newsbooks cannot be disregarded out of hand. Remarkably few fictitious accounts were encountered in researching this book. Moreover, those reports that obviously had been embellished usually had a quite plausible context. Indeed, traces of a number of the military engagements that occurred in Shropshire can only be found in the sometimes capricious reporting of contemporary newsbooks.

13   Respectively, by Hutton, *War Effort*, p. 252, and by Wanklyn, *Decisive Battles*, p. 10.
14   *Exceeding Joyfull Newes From his Excellence the Earle of Essex Declaring the true manner of his Excellencies proceedings in his march towards Shrewsbury* (1642); *True Intelligence and Joyfull Newes From Ludlow: Declaring a Battell fought by his Excellency the Earle of Essex, against Prince Robert, Prince Maurice, and the rest of the Cavaliers, neere Ludlow, October 1 1642* (1642).

Bibliography

The place of publication for all published works is London unless otherwise stated.

Manuscript Sources

Aberystwyth, The National Library of Wales
(i)   Aston Hall Estate Records:
Correspondence, number C2.
D1 Manuscripts, numbers 2469-70, 2586.
(ii)   Chirk Castle Manuscripts, 1/Biii, 93 [Receipts and muster rolls of Sir Thomas Myddelton's brigade, 1644-5].
(iii) Crosse of Shaw Hill Correspondence, numbers 1097-9, 1102, 1123.
(iv) Herbert Manuscripts and Papers, Series II, Volume IX.
(v)   Llanfair-Brynodol Letters, numbers 54-5, 58.
(vi) Powys Castle Records 3(A).
(vii) Sweeney Hall Manuscripts: A1; A4 (Volume II).

Bishop's Castle, Bishop's Castle Heritage Resource Centre
Bishop's Castle Town Chest, First Corporation Minute Book.

Hawarden, Flintshire Record Office
D/G/3275, Trevor Family Papers.

Hereford, Herefordshire Record Office
CF61/20, Rev. J.T. Webb's Manuscripts, Miscellaneous Extracts [Transcripts of Colonel Devillier's papers, 1644-5].

London, The British Library
(i)   Additional Manuscripts:
11332, Sir William Brereton's Letter Book, October-December 1645.
11333, Sir William Brereton's Letter Book, April-June 1645, December 1645-January 1646.
18980-2, Prince Rupert's Papers.
(ii)   Harleian Manuscripts [Papers retained by Sir Edward Walker when secretary to King Charles I]:

6802, State Papers Caroline I.
6804, State Papers Caroline I & II.
6851-2, Papers Relating to the English Civil War.

London, The National Archives
(i)   SP16/381, State Papers of King Charles I.
(ii)   SP23/105, Papers of the Committee for Compounding with Delinquents.
(iii) Commonwealth Exchequer Papers:
SP28/15 Part 1.
SP28/34 Parts 2 and 4.
SP28/37 Part 1.
SP28/41 Part 4.
SP28/42 Part 2.
SP28/48 Part 3.
SP28/50 Parts 1 and 3.
SP28/52 Part 1.
SP28/55 Parts 1 and 2.
SP28/58 Part 4.
SP28/131 Part 12 [William Crowne's Account Book].
SP28/139 Parts 18 and 20.
SP28/174 Part 1.
SP28/225 Part 4.
SP28/242 Parts 1, 2 and 3.
SP28/300 Part 1.
SP28/346 Parts 1 and 2.
(iv)   War Office Papers, WO55/459/Parts 1 and 3, Papers of the Royalist Office of Ordnance at Oxford.

London, The National Army Museum
8812-63, Thomas Mytton's Papers.

Northampton, Northamptonshire Record Office
Finch-Hatton Manuscripts, 133 [Royalist appointments made at Oxford].

Oxford, The Bodleian Library
(i)   Tanner Manuscripts 59-60, 62, The Clerk of Parliament's Papers.
(ii)   Firth Manuscripts C6-7, Transcripts of Prince Rupert's Papers.
(iii) Dugdale Manuscripts 19, Docket Book of the Clerks of Chancery at Oxford, 1643-6.

San Marino, California, Henry Huntington Library
Ellesmere Manuscripts, numbers 7114, 7443, 7625, 7639, 7671, 7673, The Earl of Bridgewater's Correspondence.

Shrewsbury, Shropshire Archives

(i) Bridgnorth Corporation Collection.

Administrative and Militia Records:

BB/C/1/1/1, Corporation Common Hall Order Book, 1634-85.

BB/C/6/1/1-6, Toll records of horse and cattle fairs, circa 1630-45.

BB/C/8/1/6, Warrant to compile muster rolls.

BB/C/8/1/7, Inventory of arms removed from the Newhouse.

BB/C/8/1/14-3, Statement of unpaid bills of the Royalist army.

Chamberlains' Account Rolls:

BB/D/1/2/1/49, year 1639.

BB/D/1/2/1/50, year 1640.

BB/D/1/2/1/52, year 1642.

BB/D/1/2/1/53, year 1643.

BB/D/1/2/1/54, year 1644.

BB/D/1/2/1/55, year 1645.

BB/D/1/2/1/57, year 1647.

(ii) Family Papers, and Miscellaneous Collections and Papers:

322, Corbet Family of Acton Reynald.

366, Hunt Family [Transcripts].

465, Sandford of The Isle.

1079/Box 13, Oakeley Family.

1831, Records of the Drapers' Company of Shrewsbury.

5460, Cressett of Cound.

SRRU Deeds:

6000/13281, 13285-6, 13288, 13290-3, 13298, 13314, 13316, Civil War papers from Pitchford
   Hall [including Royalist administrative records, 1642].

811/87, Nineteenth-century transcript of the Sequestration Papers of Isaac Martin, Rector of
   Great Bolas.

(iii) Ludlow Borough Collection.

Militia Records:

LB7/1931-3, 1936-7, 1943-4, 1946, 2233-6, 2249-51, 2315, 2317-20.

Billeting Bills and Petitions, 1643-5:

LB7/2015, 2064, 2066-7, 2069, 2081, 2098, 2108, 2112, 2125-6, 2130, 2136, 2144, 2147-8,
   2156, 2158, 2164, 2166.

Bailiffs' Accounts:

LB8/1/162, Year 1641/2.

LB8/1/163, Year 1642/3.

LB8/1/164, Year 1643/4.

LB8/1/165, Year 1644/5.

LB8/1/166, Year 1645/6.

LB8/3/75, Prince Rupert to Bailiffs ordering selection of assistants to collect tax.

LB/Fiche 1816-19, loose Churchwardens' Accounts of St. Leonard's, Ludlow, 1642-4.

LB/Fiche 4677-80, Corporation Minute Book, 1643-7.

(iv) Parish Records:

P81/Fiche 115-28, Condover Parish Records Churchwardens' Accounts, 1631-45.

P94/B/1/1, Donnington Parish Records, Churchwardens' and Overseers' Accounts, 1629-1811.

P161/M/1, Lilleshall Parish Records, Constables' Accounts, 1611-1821.

P177/B/2/1, Lydbury North Parish Records, Churchwardens' and Overseers' Accounts, 1616-1813.

P180/Fiche 1, Madeley Parish Records, General Registers, 1645-71.

P200/Fiche 24, Munslow Parish Records, General Registers, 1637-52.

P248/A/1/1, Shrawardine Parish Records, General Registers, 1637-1751.

P250/Fiche 321-8, Shrewsbury Holy Cross Parish Records, Churchwardens' Accounts, 1637-48.

P257/B/3/2, Shrewsbury St. Mary's Parish Records, Churchwardens' Accounts, 1627-1703.

P270/B/1/1, Stockton Parish Records, Churchwardens' Accounts [including constables' accounts], 1604-76.

P281/Fiche 30, Tong Parish Records, Churchwardens' Accounts, 1639-46.

P303/B/1/1/2, Whitchurch Parish Records, General Accounts, 1630-41.

P314/M/1, Worfield Parish Records, Constables' Accounts, circa 1600-1700.

SRO 2310/1, Transcript of Kenley Parish Churchwardens' Accounts, 1600-80.

(v). Shrewsbury Borough Collection:

3365/224, Assessment for Three Months, 1644.

3365/225, Contributions to King and Commonwealth [miscellaneous administrative papers, circa 1640s].

3365/586, Mayor's Accounts, Year 1641/2.

3365/587, Mayor's Accounts, Year 1642/3.

3365/588, Mayor's Accounts, Year 1643/4.

3365/589, Valuations for Assessments [Receipts for Contribution, 1644-5].

3365/591, Mayor's Accounts, Vouchers, Year 1644/5.

3365/592, Mayor's Accounts, Year 1645/6.

3365/1267, Fines and [Constables'] Presentments, Year 1645/6.

3365/2263, Petitions, circa 1580-1670.

3365/2559, Muster Master's Account, Levies and Assessments, 1618-27.

3365/2566, Papers Relating to Soldiers [Billeting Petitions, 1642-3].

3365/2571, Division of the Town by 'Squadrants' [circa 1643-4].

3365/2572, Receipts for Provisions and Supplies, 1644.

3365/2711, Declaration of Income, 1644 [Royalist administrative records].

6001/290, Corporation Assembly Book, Extracts [Eighteenth-century transcripts from the seventeenth-century assembly book, now lost].

Stafford, Staffordshire Record Office

Sutherland Papers:

D593/P8/1/4; D868/2/35, 37-8, 41, 43, 45, Sir Richard Leveson's Correspondence.

D593/R/1/3/2, Lilleshall and Shrewsbury Houses: Disbursements of the Leveson Family Household [circa 1630-50].

Stafford, William Salt Library
SMS 350/40/5, Hardwick Manuscript Collections for the History of Shropshire, Volume V.
SMS 463, Ordnance Office Warrant Book [1645-6].
Prince Rupert's Papers:
SMS: 478/13/36, 487, 493, 502, 537, 550/17, 550/20, 551/2, 556, 5513.
Fairfax Papers:
SMS: 557-8.

Warwick, Warwickshire Record Office
CR2017/C9-10, The Earl of Denbigh's Letter Books.
CR0285, Wollacombe-Adams Family Papers.

Published Primary Sources

(i)   Contemporary Tracts and Pamphlets

The Petition of Knights, Justices of Peace, Ministers, Gentlemen, Free-holders and others, Inhabitants of the County of Salop, to the number of 10,000 (March 1642).

Two Petitions. The One, Presented to the Honourable House of Commons, from the Countie of Hereford, May the fourth, 1642. The Other, To his Mayestie, and the Parliament, From the Towne of Ludlow in the Countie of Salop (May 1642).

A List of the Old and New Regiments of Horse and Foot under the Command of the Honourable Robert Sidney, Earl of Leicester (June 1642).

The Latest Remarkable Truths From Worcester, Chester, Salop, Warwick, Stafford, Somerset, Devon, Yorke and Lincoln Counties (September 1642).

A Continuation of the late proceedings of His Majesty's Army at Shrewsbury, Bridge North and Manchester (October 1642).

A True and exact Relation of the Proceedings of His Majesties Army in Cheshire, Shropshire and Worcestershire (October 1642).

Exceeding Joyfull Newes From his Excellence the Earle of Essex Declaring the true manner of his Excellencies proceedings in his march towards Shrewsbury (October 1642).

Some Late Occurrences in Shropshire and Devonshire (October 1642).

The true copie of a letter importing divers passages of high and dangerous consequence. Written by one Master Tempest a grand recusant, to his brother master John Tempest, likewise a papist and an officer in the Kings Army (October 1642).

True Intelligence and Joyfull Newes From Ludlow: Declaring a Battell fought by his Excellency the Earle of Essex, against Prince Robert, Prince Maurice, and the rest of the Cavaliers, neere Ludlow, October 1 1642 (October 1642).

The Effect of all Letters Read in the House of Parliament from the 14 to the 23 of November from all places of the Kingdome (November 1642).

Arthur Lord Capell Lieutenant Generall under the Prince His Highnesse of His Majesties forces, in the counties of Worcester, Salop, and Chester, and the six northern counties of Wales. To all commanders, officers, and souldiers, and to all other His Majesties subjects whatsoever (Shrewsbury, April 1643).

A True Relation of a Great Victory Obtained by the Parliaments Forces Against the Cavaliers neere Chester (November 1643).

Shropshires misery and mercie, Manifested in the defeat given to the Lord Capels ravenous and devouring Armie, by the forces of Cheshire and Shropshire (November 1643).

Orders Presented to His Majesty By advice of the Lords & Commons of Parliament Assembled at Oxford (Oxford, 1644).

Newes from Prince Rupert, Whose Forces being discovered by the Earl of Denbigh, The Earl with his forces marched against them (May 1644).

A happy Defeat Given to the King's Forces, neere Tipton Green in Staffordshire (June 1644).

Two Great Victories: On[e] Obtained by the Earle of Denbigh at Oswestry […] The Other Victory by Colonel Mitton (June 1644).

A Copy of A Letter sent From Sir Tho. Middleton, to the Honourable, William Lenthall Esq; Speaker of the House of the House of Commons. Concerning the Siege at Oswestree (July 1644).

Great Victories Obtained by the Earle of Denbigh at Shrewsbury, Chulmely, and other parts in Cheshire (July 1644).

Wareham taken by the Parliament Forces Also Collonel Mittons valiant Exploits certified by two several Letters dated at his Quarters (August 1644).

A True and Full Relation Of the manner of the Taking of the Towne and Castle of Shrewsbury (March 1645).

A More Exact And Particular Relation of the taking of Shrewsbury, than hath hitherto been published, With the manner and performance thereof by Lieutenant Collonel William Reinking (May 1645).

Colonell Mitton's Reply to Lieutenant Colonell Reinking's Relation of The taking of Shrewsbury (May 1645).

Intelligence From Shropshire of Three Great Victories obtained by the Forces of Shrewsburie (June 1645).

A Copy of the Summons From Sir William Brereton, Col. Morgan, and Col. Birch, sent in for the surrender of the City of Worcester To the Parliament […] Also the taking of High-Arkall, the Lord Newports House by the Shropshire Forces (March 1646).

A True Relation By Colonell Morgan In a letter of the totall Routing of the Lord Astley, by him and Sir William Brereton at Stow (March 1646).

The manner of the discovering [of] the King at Southwell […] And The Copie of the Summons sent to Ludlow and the Governor's Answer (May 1646).

The Several Divisions And Persons For Classical Presbyteries In The County of Salop (April 1647).

A Narrative, Together with Letters Presented by Captaine Taylor To the Honourable House of Commons, Concerning the late success obtained by the Parliament forces in Carnarvonshire (June 1648).

A New Rising by divers Knights, Colonels, Gentlemen, and others for the King. To Associate the foure Counties of Stafford, Worcester, Hereford, and Shropshire (July 1648).

Dring, T., *A Catalogue of the Lords, Knights and Gentlemen that have compounded for their Estates* (1655).

Walker, Sir Edward, *Iter Carolinum* (1660).

(ii)   Contemporary Newsbooks

A Continuation of Certain Special and Remarkable Passages Informed to the Parliament, 18-25 April 1644.

A Perfect Diurnall of some passages in Parliament:

28 August-4 September 1643; 25 March-1 April 1644; 20-27 May 1644; 27 May-3 June 1644; 18-25 May 1646.

A Perfect Diurnall of the passages in Parliament, 30 January 1642-6 February 1643.

A True and Perfect Journall of the Civill Warres in England, 30 April 1644.

Certaine Informations from Severall Parts of the Kingdome:

10-17 April 1643; 22-29 May 1643; 12-19 June 1643; 10-17 July 1643.

Heads of Some Notes of The Citie Scout:

19 August 1645; 28 August 1645; 2 September 1645; 9 September 1645.

Mercurius Aulicus (published at Oxford):

14 January 1643; 21 January 1643; 19 November 1643; 9 March 1644; 23 March 1644; 30 March 1644; 6 April 1644; 4 May 1644; 24 August 1644; 5 January 1645; 20 April 1645.

Mercurius Britannicus, 6-13 January 1645.

Mercurius Civicus:

4-11 May 1643; 8-15 August 1644; 19-26 September 1644.

Mercurius Veridicus, 7-14 June 1645.

Perfect Occurrences of Both Houses of Parliament and Martiall Affairs:

10 April 1646; 8 May 1646; 22 May 1646.

Perfect Passages of Each Dayes Proceedings in Parliament:

11-18 June 1645; 25 June-2 July 1645; 9-16 July 1645; 30 July-6 Aug. 1645.

Perfect Occurrences of Every Daies Journall in Parliament:

7-14 May 1647; 4-11 June 1647; 18-25 August 1648.

The Cities Weekly Post, 10-17 February 1646.

The Kingdomes Weekly Intelligencer:

30 May-6 June 1643; 20-29 February 1644; 25 June-2 July 1644; 24 September-1 October 1644; 6-13 May 1645; 2-9 September 1645; 9-16 December 1645; 10-17 March 1646; 28 April-5 May 1646; 27 April-4 May 1647.

The London Post:

11 March 1645; 1-8 April 1645.

The Military Scribe, 26 March-2 April 1644.

The Moderate, 1-8 August 1648.

The Moderate Intelligencer:

3-10 July 1645; 10-17 July 1645; 5-12 March 1646; 30 April-7 May 1646; 4-11 June 1646; 8-15 April 1647; 15-22 April 1647.

The Perfect Occurrences of Parliament, 26 April-3 May 1644.

The Perfect Occurrences of Parliament And Chief Collections of Letters:

28 June-5 July 1644; 5-12 July 1644; 9-16 August 1644; 6-13 September 1644; 18-25 October 1644; 20-27 December 1644; 10-17 January 1645; 13-20 June 1645; 20-27 June 1645; 22-29 August 1645.

The Scottish Dove:

20 August-6 September 1644; 26 February-4 March 1646.

The True Informer:
10-17 August 1644; 30 August 1645.

The Weekly Account:
18-24 September 1644; 25 December 1644-1 January 1645; 26 March-2 April 1645; 16-23 April 1645; 4-11 June 1645; 10-17 December 1645; 30 December 1645-6 January 1646; 4-11 February 1646; 25-31 March 1646; 1-8 April 1646; 22-28 April 1646; 7-14 April 1647.

(iii) Books and Edited Collections of Papers

Anon., *A List of Officers Claiming the Sixty Thousand Pounds, &c. Granted by his Majesty for the Relief of His Loyal and Indigent Party Truly* (1663).

Anon., 'A list of the names of the Indigent Officers certified out of the county of Salop by His Majesty's Commissioners appointed by the Act of Parliament for the purpose', in 'Ottleiana: or letters & c. relating to Shropshire chiefly to Sir Francis Ottley', *Collectanea Topographica & Geneaologica* (1841).

Anon., *Being an Extra Volume containing the Herbert MSS at Powis Castle, Part I, 1586-1735. Collections Historical and Archaeological relating to Montgomeryshire and its Borders*, XX (1886).

Anon., 'Correspondence of Archbishop Williams', *Archaeologica Cambrensis*, 4th Series, I (1870), pp. 62-6.

Anon., *Wem Probate Inventories, 1535-1650*, 2 volumes (Shropshire Archives, undated).

Anon., *Whitchurch Probate Inventories, 1535-1650*, 2 volumes (Shropshire Archives, undated).

Baxter, R., *Reliquiae Baxterianae: Or Mr. Richard Baxter's Narrative of The Most Memorable Passages of His Life and Times* (1696).

Beedham, B.H. (ed.), 'The Unpublished Correspondence Between Archbishop Williams and The Marquis of Ormond', *Archaeologica Cambrensis*, 3rd Series, XV (1869), pp. 305-43.

Bell, R. (ed.), *Memorials of the Civil War Comprising the Correspondence of the Fairfax Family*, 2 volumes (1849).

Blith, W., *The English Improver, Or a New Survey of Husbandry* (1649).

Blome, R., *Britannia: Or, A Geographical Description of the Kingdom of England, Scotland and Ireland* (1673).

Burton, J.R. (ed.), 'The Sequestration Papers of Humphrey Walcot', *TSANHS*, 3rd Series, V (1905), pp. 303-348.

Carr, I. and I. Atherton (eds.), *The Civil War in Staffordshire in the Spring of 1646: Sir William Brereton's Letter Book, April–May 1646* (Bristol, 2007).

Carte, T. (ed.), *A Collection of Original Letters and Papers, Concerning the Affairs of England, from the Year 1641 to 1660. Found among the Duke of Ormonde's Papers* (1739).

Clark Maxwell, W.G. (ed.), 'King Charles I's Proclamation of October 14th 1642', *TSANHS*, 4th Series, X (1925-6), pp. xxv-vi.

Cruso, J., *Military Instructions for the Cavallrie* (Cambridge, 1644).

Day, W.A. (ed.), *The Pythouse Papers: Correspondence Concerning The Civil War, the Popish Plot and a Contested Election in 1680* (1879).

Dore, R.N. (ed.), *The Letter Books of Sir William Brereton, Volume I, January 31st–May 29th 1645*, The Record Society of Lancashire and Cheshire (Gloucester, 1984).

Dore, R. N. (ed.), *The Letter Books of Sir William Brereton, Volume II, June 18th 1645–February 1st 1646,* The Record Society of Lancashire and Cheshire (Gloucester, 1990).

Everett Green, M.A. (ed.), *Calendar of the Proceedings of the Committee for Advance of Money*, 3 volumes (1888).

Everett Green, M.A. (ed.), *Calendar of the Proceedings of the Committee for Compounding*, 5 volumes (1889).

Firth, C.H. (ed.), 'The Journal of Prince Rupert's Marches, 5 September 1642 to 4 July 1646', *The English Historical Review,* 13 (1898), pp. 729-41.

Firth, C.H. and R.S. Rait (eds.), *Acts and Ordinances of the Interregnum, 1642-1660*, 3 volumes (1911).

Firth, C.H. (ed.), *The Clarke Papers, Volumes I & II* (1992).

Fletcher, W.G.D. (ed.), 'The Sequestration Papers of Sir Thomas Whitmore, Knight and Baronet of Apley', *TSANHS*, 4th Series, IV (1914), pp. 265-316.

Fletcher, W.G.D. (ed.), 'The Sequestration Papers of Thomas Pigott of Chetwynd', *TSANHS*, 4th Series, IV (1914), pp. 67-92.

Gough, R., *Antiquityes and Memoyres of the Parish of Myddle,* (ed.) D. Hey as *The History of Myddle* (Harmondsworth, 1981).

Grazebrook, G. and J.P. Rylands (eds.), *The Visitation of Shropshire Taken in the Year 1623,* 2 volumes (1889).

Hamilton W.D. [*et al.*] (eds.), *Calendar of State Papers, Domestic Series, of the Reign of Charles I, 1625-1649*, 23 volumes (1858-97).

Hawkins, E.W. (ed.), *Travels in Holland, The United Provinces, England, Scotland and Ireland, M.DC.XXXIV- M.DC.XXXV By Sir William Brereton, Bart.* (1864).

Hexham, H., *The First Part of The Principles of the Art Military* (Delft, 1642).

Hyde, E., Earl of Clarendon, *The History of the Rebellion and Civil Wars in England*, 7 volumes (Oxford, 1859).

Journals of the House of Lords, Volumes V-X, 1643-8 (undated).

Journals of the House of Commons, Volumes III-V, 1643-8 (1802).

Lewis, J. (ed.), *Fire and Sword along the Marches: The Notebook of Sir William Maurice and the Memoranda of Captain Francis Sandford* (Newtown, 1996).

Lloyd Kenyon, R. (ed.), *Orders of the Shropshire Quarter Sessions,* 2 volumes (Shrewsbury, undated).

Malbon, T., 'Memorials of the Civil War in Cheshire and the Adjacent Counties by Thomas Malbon of Nantwich, Gent.', (ed.) J. Hall, *The Record Society for the Publication of Original Documents relating to Lancashire and Cheshire*, XIX (1889), pp. 21-236.

Ogilby, J., *Britannia, or an Illustration of the Kingdom of England and Dominion of Wales by a Geographical and Historical Description of the Principal Roads thereof* (1675).

Pennington, D.H. and I.A. Roots (eds.), *The Committee at Stafford, 1643-1645* (Manchester, 1957).

Phillips, W. (ed.), 'The Ottley Papers Relating to the Civil War', *TSANHS*, 2nd Series: VI (1894), pp. 27-78; VII (1895), pp. 241-360; VIII (1896), pp. 199-312.

Phillips, W. (ed.), 'Sequestration Papers of Sir Richard, First Baron Newport and Francis, his son', *TSANHS*, 2nd Series, XII (1900), pp. 1-38.

Reed, M., 'Early Seventeenth-Century Wage Assessments for the Borough of Shrewsbury', *TSAS*, LV (1954-6), pp. 136-42.

Robertes, L., *The Merchants Mappe of Commerce* (1638).

Roy, I. (ed.), *The Royalist Ordnance Papers 1642-1646*, Parts I and II (Banbury, 1963, 1975).

Rushworth, J., *Historical Collections of Private Passages of State*, 8 volumes (1721).

Speed, J., *The Theatre of the Empire of Great Britaine* (1611).

Studley, P., *The Looking-Glasse of Schisme* (1635).

Symonds, R., *Diary of The Marches of the Royal Army During the Great Civil War kept by Richard Symonds*, (ed.) C.E. Long (1859).

Thursby-Pelham, A. (ed.), 'The Berrington Love Feast', *TSANHS*, 2nd Series, VII (1895), pp. 203-6.

Tibbutt, H.G. (ed.), *The Letter Books of Sir Samuel Luke, 1644-45* (1963).

Townsend, H., *The Diary of Henry Townsend of Elmley Lovett, 1640-1663*, (ed.) J.W. Willis Bund, 3 volumes (1920).

Vernon, J., *The Young Horseman or The honest plain-dealing Cavalier* (1644).

Vicars, J., *The Burning-Bush Not Consumed Or The Fourth and Last Part of the Parliamentarie-Chronicle* (1646).

Walker, Sir Edward, *Historical Discourses upon Several Occasions* (1705).

Ward, R., *The Anatomy of Warre, Or Warre with the wofull, fruits, and effects thereof, laid out to the life* (1642).

Williams, R. (ed.), 'An Account of the Civil War in North Wales, Transcribed from the MS Notebook of William Maurice, esq., Preserved in the Wynnstay Library', *Archaeologica Cambrensis*, I (1846), pp. 33-41.

Yonge, W., *Walter Yonge's Diary of Proceedings in the House of Commons, 1642-1645*, (ed.) C. Thompson, one volume (Wivenhoe, 1986).

(iv) Reports of the Historical Manuscripts Commission

Fifth Report, Part I, Report and Appendix (1876).

Sixth Report, Part I, Report and Appendix (1877).

Tenth Report, Appendix Part IV (1885).

Twelfth Report, Appendix Part IX, Manuscripts of the Duke of Beaufort (1891).

Thirteenth Report, Appendix Part I, The Manuscripts of his Grace the Duke of Portland, Volume I (1891).

Fourteenth Report, Appendix Part II, The Manuscripts of his Grace the Duke of Portland, Volume III (1894).

Fourteenth Report, Appendix Part VII, Manuscripts of the Marquis of Ormonde (1895).

Calendar of the Manuscripts of the Marquis of Bath, Volume I (1904).

Seventy-Eighth Report, Hastings Manuscripts Part II (1930).

Secondary Sources

Books and Reports

Anon, *A History of Shrewsbury School* (Shrewsbury and London, 1889).

Acton, F.S., *The Garrisons of Shropshire During the Civil Wars, 1642-1648* (Shrewsbury, 1867).

Atkin, M., *The Civil War in Worcestershire* (Stroud, 1995).

Atkin, M., *Worcestershire Under Arms: An English County During The Civil Wars* (Barnsley, 2004).

Barratt, J., *Cavaliers, The Royalist Army at War, 1642-1646* (Stroud, 2000).

Barratt, J., *Cavalier Stronghold: Ludlow in the English Civil Wars, 1642-1660* (Almeley, 2013).

Bayley, A.R., *The Great Civil War in Dorset* (Taunton, 1910).

Bellett, G., *The Antiquities of Bridgnorth* (Bridgnorth and London, 1856).

Bennett, M., *The Civil Wars Experienced: Britain and Ireland, 1638-1661* (New York, 2000).

Blackmore, D., *Arms & Armour of the English Civil Wars* (1990).

Blakeway, J.B. and H. Owen, *A History of Shrewsbury*, 2 volumes (1825).

Bowen, L., *The Politics of the Principality – Wales, c. 1603-1642* (Cardiff, 2007).

Bracher, T. and R. Emmett, *Shropshire in the Civil War* (Shrewsbury, 2000).

Braddick, M., *God's Fury, England's Fire A New History of the Civil Wars* (2008).

Broxap, E., *The Great Civil War in Lancashire* (Manchester, 1910).

Brunton, D. and D.H. Pennington, *Members of the Long Parliament* (1954).

Bull, S., *'The Furie of the Ordnance': Artillery in the English Civil Wars* (Woodbridge, 2008).

Bull, S., *'A General Plague of Madness': The Civil War in Lancashire, 1640-1660* (Lancaster, 2009).

Burne, A.H. and P. Young, *The Great Civil War: A Military History of the First Civil War 1642-1646* (Moreton-in-Marsh, 1998. First published London, 1959).

Carlton, C., *Going to the Wars – The Experience of the British Civil Wars* (1992).

Carte, T., *The Life of James Duke of Ormond*, 6 volumes (new edition, Oxford, 1851).

Charles, M. and L. Jones, *Land Off Aston Street, Wem, Shropshire, Archaeological Excavations 2007 & 2008* (Birmingham, undated).

Coate, M., *Cornwall in the Great Civil War and Interregnum, 1642-1660, A Social and Political Study* (Oxford, 1933).

Cokayne, G.E. (ed.), *Complete Baronetage*, 5 volumes (Exeter, 1900).

Coulton, B., *Regime and Religion, Shrewsbury 1400-1700* (Almeley, 2010).

Court, W.H.B., *The Rise of the Midland Industries, 1600-1838* (Oxford, 1965).

Crofts, J., *Packhorse, Waggon and Post: Land Carriage and Communications Under the Tudors and Stuarts* (1967).

Davies, R.D., *The Sheriffs of Shropshire* (Shropshire, 2013).

Donagan, B., *War In England 1642-1649* (Oxford, 2008).

Eales, J., *Puritans and Roundheads: The Harleys of Brampton Bryan and the Outbreak of The English Civil War* (Cambridge, 1990).

Edwards, P., *Dealing in Death: The Arms Trade and the British Civil Wars, 1638–52* (Stroud, 2001).

Ellis, J., *'To Walk in the Dark' Military Intelligence during the English Civil War 1642-1646* (Stroud, 2011).

Everitt, A., *The Community of Kent And The Great Rebellion* (Leicester, 1966).

Farrow, W.J., *The Great Civil War in Shropshire, 1642-49* (Shrewsbury, 1926).

Firth, C.H., *Cromwell's Army: A History of the English Soldier during the Civil Wars, The Commonwealth and The Protectorate* (1902).

Firth, C., *The Regimental History of Cromwell's Army* (Cranbury, 2006. First published London, 1940).

Fissel, M.C., *The Bishops' Wars, Charles I's Campaigns Against Scotland, 1638-1640* (Cambridge, 1994).

Fletcher, A., *A County Community in Peace and War, Sussex 1600-1660* (1975).

Fletcher, A., *Reform in the Provinces, The Government of Stuart England* (New Haven and London, 1986).

Fletcher, A., *The Outbreak of the English Civil War* (1989).

Foard, G., *Naseby The Decisive Campaign* (2nd edition, Barnsley, 2004).

Foard, G., and R. Morris, *The Archaeology of English Battlefields: Conflict in the Pre-Industrial Landscape* (York, 2012), pp. 5-6.

Garbet, S., *The History of Wem* (Wem, 1818).

Gardiner, S.R., *History of The Great Civil War, 1642-1649*, 3 volumes (1886-91).

Gaunt, P., *The Cromwellian Gazetteer* (Gloucester, 1987).

Gaunt, P., *A Nation Under Siege; The Civil War in Wales 1642-48* (1991).

Gaunt, P., *The English Civil War: A Military History* (I.B. Taurus, 2014).

Gentles. I, *The New Model Army in England, Ireland and Scotland, 1645-1653* (Oxford, 1994).

Gentles, I., *The English Revolution and the Wars in the Three Kingdoms 1638-1652* (Harlow, 2007).

Gratton, J.M., *The Parliamentarian and Royalist War Effort in Lancashire 1642-1651* (Manchester, 2010).

Hamper, W., *The Life, Diary and Correspondence of Sir William Dugdale, Knight* (1827).

Hanmer, Lord John, *A Memorial of the Parish and Family of Hanmer in Flintshire* (1877).

Haythornthwaite, P., *The English Civil War, 1642-1651, An Illustrated Military History* (Poole, 1983).

Hey, D.G., *An English Rural Community: Myddle under the Tudors and Stuarts* (Leicester, 1974).

Hibbert, C., *Cavaliers & Roundheads: The English at War, 1642-1649* (1993).

Holmes, C., *The Eastern Association in the English Civil War* (Cambridge, 1974).

Holmes, C., *Why Was Charles I Executed?* (2006).

Hopper, A., *Turncoats & Renegadoes, Changing Sides during the English Civil Wars* (Oxford, 2012).

Hughes, A., *Politics, Society and Civil War in Warwickshire, 1620-1660* (Cambridge, 1987).

Hutton, R., *The Royalist War Effort 1642-1646* (2nd edition, 2003).

John, T., *The Civil War in Pembrokeshire* (Almeley, 2008).

Jones, N.W., *Shrawardine Castle, Shropshire, Archaeological Survey* (Welshpool, 2012).

Ketton-Cremer, R.W., *Norfolk in The Civil War: A Portrait of a Society in Conflict* (1969).

Kingston, A., *Hertfordshire During The Great Civil War* (Hertford, 1884).

Kingston, A., *East Anglia and The Great Civil War* (1897).

Knight, K., *Civil War and Restoration in Monmouthshire* (Almeley, 2005).

Lockyer, R., *The Early Stuarts – A Political History of England, 1603-1642* (Harlow, 1999).

Matthews, H.C.G. and B. Harrison (eds.), *Oxford Dictionary of National Biography*, 40 volumes (Oxford, 2004).

Morrill, J., *Cheshire, 1630-1660: County Government and Society during the 'English Revolution'* (Oxford, 1974).

Morrill, J., *Revolt in the Provinces: The People of England and the Tragedy of Civil War, 1630-1648* (Harlow, 1999).

Newman, J. and N. Pevsner, *The Buildings of England, Shropshire* (New Haven and London, 2006).

Newman, P.R., *The Old Service, Royalist Regimental Colonels and The Civil War, 1642-46* (Manchester, 1993).

Parker, G., *The Military Revolution, Military Innovation and the Rise of the West, 1500-1800* (Cambridge, 1990).

Parker, K., *Radnorshire from Civil War to Restoration* (Almeley, 2000).

Phillips, J.R., *Memoirs of The Civil War in Wales and the Marches, 1642-1649*, 2 volumes (1874).

Porter, S., *Destruction In The Civil Wars* (Stroud, 1994).

Raven M., *A Shropshire Gazetteer* (2nd edition, Shropshire, 1991).

Richardson, R.C., *The Debate on the English Revolution* (3rd edition, Manchester, 1998).

Roberts, K., *Soldiers of the English Civil War (1): Infantry* (1989).

Robinson, G., *Horses, People and Parliament in the English Civil War: Extracting Resources and Constructing Allegiance* (Farnham, 2012).

Rogers, C.J. (ed.), *The Military Revolution Debate: Readings on the Military Transformation of Early Modern Europe* (Boulder, Colorado, 1995).

Ross, D., *Royalist, But … Herefordshire in the English Civil Wars* (Almeley, 2012).

Rowley, T., *The Shropshire Landscape* (1972).

Sherwood, R.E., *Civil Strife in the Midlands 1642-1651* (1974).

Stoyle, M., *Loyalty and Locality: Popular Allegiance in Devon During the English Civil War* (Exeter, 1994).

Tennant, P., *Edgehill and Beyond: the People's War in the South Midlands, 1642-45* (Stroud, 1992).

Thirsk, J., (ed.), *The Agrarian History of England and Wales, Volume IV, 1500-1640* (Cambridge, 1967).

Thomas-Stanford, C., *Sussex in The Great Civil War and Interregnum, 1642-1649* (1910).

Tincey, J., *Soldiers of the English Civil War (2): Cavalry* (1990).

Trinder, B., *A History of Shropshire* (Chichester, 1998).

Trinder, B., *The Industrial Revolution in Shropshire* (Chichester, 2000).

Tucker, N., *North Wales and Chester in the Civil War* (Ashbourne, 2003).

Underdown, D., *Somerset in the Civil War and Interregnum* (Newton Abbot, 1973).

Underdown, D., *Revel, Riot and Rebellion: Popular Politics and Culture in England, 1603-1660* (Oxford, 1985).

Van Crefeld, M., *Supplying War: Logistics from Wallenstein to Patton*, (Cambridge, 1977).

Von Armi, E.G., *Justice for the Maimed Soldier: Nursing, medical care and welfare for sick and wounded soldiers and their families during the English Civil Wars and Interregnum, 1642-1660* (Aldershot, 2001).

Von Clausewitz, C., *On War*, (eds.) M. Howard and P. Paret (Princeton, 1989. First published 1832).

Wanklyn M. and F. Jones, *A Military History of the English Civil War* (Harlow, 2005).

Wanklyn, M., *Decisive Battles of the English Civil War* (Barnsley, 2006).

Wanklyn, M., *The Warrior Generals: Winning the British Civil Wars, 1642-1652* (Yale, 2010).

Warburton, E., *Memoirs of Prince Rupert and the Cavaliers*, 3 volumes (1849).

Warmington, A.R., *Civil War, Interregnum and Restoration in Gloucestershire 1640-1672* (Woodbridge, 1997).

Webb, J. and J.T. Webb, *Memorials of the Civil War between King Charles I and The Parliament of England as it affected Herefordshire and The Adjacent Counties,* 2 volumes (1879).

Wheeler, J.S., *The Making of a World Power: War and The Military Revolution in Seventeenth Century England* (Stroud, 1999).

Willis Bund, J.W., *The Civil War in Worcestershire, 1642-1646; And The Scotch Invasion of 1651* (Birmingham and London, 1905).

Wood, A.C., *Nottinghamshire in the Civil War* (Oxford, 1937).

Worden, B., *The English Civil Wars, 1640-1660* (2009).

Wroughton, J., *An Unhappy Civil War. The Experiences of Ordinary People in Gloucestershire, Somerset and Wiltshire, 1642-1646* (Bath, 1999).

Young, P., and W. Embleton, *The Cavalier Army* (1974).

Young, P., *Marston Moor 1644 – The Campaign and the Battle* (Moreton-in Marsh, 1997).

Articles and Essays

Anon., 'The Myddelton Family of Denbighshire', *The Cheshire Sheaf,* 2nd Series, I (1895).

Auden, A.M., 'Clun and its Neighbourhood in the First Civil War', *TSANHS,* 3rd Series, VIII (1908), pp. 287-336.

Auden, J.E., 'Shropshire and the Royalist Conspiracies between the end of the First Civil War and the Restoration, 1648-1660', *TSANHS,* 3rd Series, X (1910), pp. 87-168.

Auden, J.E., 'Four Letters from Shropshire to Prince Rupert', *TSANHS,* 4th Series, II, (1912), pp. 1-21.

Auden, J.E., 'The War Services of some Shropshire Officers in the King's Army', *TSANHS,* 4th Series, II, (1912), 215-92.

Auden, J.E., 'Lieutenant Colonel William Reinking in Shropshire', *TSAS,* XLVII (1933-4), pp. 33-47.

Auden, J.E., 'My case with the Committee of Salop', *TSAS,* XLVIII (1934-5), pp. 49-60.

Auden, J.E., 'The Anglo-Irish Troops in Shropshire', *TSAS,* L (1939-40), pp. 49-64.

Barratt, J., 'The Letters of the First Baron Byron of Rochdale (1600-1652), *Journal of the Society for Army Historical Research,* 49 (1971), pp. 127-40.

Beaumont, H., 'Arthur, Lord Capel, The King's Lieutenant General for Shropshire, 1643', *TSAS,* L (1939-40), pp. 65-94.

Beaumont, H., 'Events in Shropshire at the Commencement of the Civil War', *TSAS,* LI (1941-3), pp. 11-42.

Bennett, M., 'Contribution and Assessment: Financial Exactions in the English Civil War, 1642-1646', *War & Society,* 1 (1986), pp. 1-11.

Bennett, M., 'Between Scylla and Charybdis, The Creation of Rival Administrations at the beginning of The English Civil War' in *The English Civil War: The Essential Readings,* (ed.) P. Gaunt (Oxford, 2000), pp. 167-183.

Chartres, J.A., 'Road Carrying in England in the Seventeenth Century: Myth and Reality', *The Economic History Review, New Series,* 30 (1977), pp. 73-94.

Cox, D.C., 'County Government, 1603-1714' in *A History of Shropshire Volume III,* (ed.) G.C. Baugh (Oxford, 1979), pp. 90-114.

Donagan, B., 'The Casualties of War; Treatment of the Dead and Wounded in the English Civil War' in *Soldiers, Writers and Statesmen of the English Revolution*, (eds.) I. Gentles, J. Morrill and B. Worden (Cambridge, 1998), pp. 114-32.

Edwards, P., 'Shropshire Agriculture 1540-1750' in *A History of Shropshire Volume IV, Agriculture*, (ed.) G.C. Baugh (Oxford, 1989), pp. 119-168.

Edwards, P., 'The Supply of Horses to the Parliamentarian and Royalist Armies in the English Civil War, *Historical Research*, 68 (1995), pp. 49-66.

Edwards, P., 'Logistics and Supply' in *The Civil Wars A Military History of England, Scotland and Ireland 1638-1660*, (eds.) J. Kenyon and J. Ohlmeyer (Oxford, 1998), pp. 234-71.

Edwards, P., 'Turning Ploughshares into Swords: The Arms and Equipment Industries in Staffordshire in the First Civil War, 1642-1646', *Midland History*, 27 (2002), pp. 52-79.

Engberg, J., 'Royalist Finances During the English Civil War 1642-1646', *The Scandinavian Economic History Review*, XIV (1966), pp. 73-96.

Gaunt, P., 'Bibliography of Journals', *Cromwelliana; The Journal of the Cromwell Association*, Series III: 1 (2012), pp. 111-138; 2 (2013), pp. 114-20; 3 (2014), pp. 97-106.

Gentles, I., 'The Arrears of Pay of the Parliamentary Army at the End of the First Civil War', *Historical Research*, 48 (1975), pp. 52-63.

Gilbert, C.D., 'Clubmen in Southwest Shropshire, 1644-45', *Transactions of the Shropshire Archaeological and Historical Society*, LXVIII (1993), pp. 93-8.

Hill, L.M., 'County Government in Caroline England, 1625-1640' in *The Origins of the English Civil War*, (ed.) C. Russell (1973), pp. 66-90.

Hopkins, E., 'The Bridgewater Estates in North Shropshire during the Civil War', *TSAS*, LVII (1961-4), pp. 307-12.

Hughes, A., 'The King, the Parliament, and the Localities during the English Civil War', *Journal of British Studies*, 24, (1985), pp. 236-63.

Hutton, R. and W. Reeves, 'Sieges and Fortifications' in *The Civil Wars A Military History of England, Scotland and Ireland 1638-1660*, (eds.) J. Kenyon and J. Ohlmeyer (Oxford, 1998), pp. 195-233.

Langelüddecke, H., "Patchy and Spasmodic"? The response of Justices of the Peace to Charles I's Book of Orders', *The English Historical Review*, 113 (1998), pp. 1231-1248.

Langelüddecke, H., "The Pooreste and Sympleste Sorte of People"? The Selection of Parish Officers During the Personal Rule of Charles I', *Historical Research*, 80 (2007), pp. 225-60.

Langelüddecke, H., "I finde all men & my officers all soe unwilling": The Collection of Ship Money, 1635-1640', *The Journal of British Studies*, 46 (2007), pp. 509-42.

Lloyd Kenyon, R., 'History of the Shrewsbury Mint', *TSANHS*, 2nd Series, X (1898), pp. 251-272.

Morrill, J., 'Mutiny and Discontent in English Provincial Armies, *Past and Present*, 56 (1972), pp. 49-74.

Osborne, S., 'The War, The People and the absence of Clubmen in the Midlands, 1642-1646' in *The English Civil War: The Essential Readings*, (ed.) P. Gaunt (Oxford, 2000), pp. 226-48.

Parker, G., "The Military Revolution", 1560-1660 – a Myth?', *The Journal of Modern History*, 48 (1976), pp. 195-214.

Pennington, D., 'The War and the People' in *Reactions to the English Civil War, 1632-1649*, (ed.) J. Morrill (1982), pp. 115-35.

Roberts, M., 'The Military Revolution, 1560-1660' in M. Roberts, *Essays in Swedish History*, (Minneapolis, 1967), pp. 195-225.

Sandford, G. (ed.), 'Incidents in Montgomeryshire during, and also before and after, the Civil War in the time of Charles I, and during the Commonwealth', *Collections Historical and Archaeological relating to Montgomeryshire and its Borders*, XIV (1881), pp. 293-330.

Underdown, D., 'The Chalk and the Cheese: Contrasts among the English Clubmen', *Past and Present*, 85 (1979), pp. 25-48.

Watson, M.D., 'Gazetteer of Moated Sites in Shropshire', *Transactions of the Shropshire Archaeological and Historical Society*, LXV (1987), pp. 1-11.

Willan, T.S., 'The River Navigation and Trade of the Severn Valley, 1600-1750', *The Economic History Review*, 8 (1937), pp. 68-79.

Worton, J., 'Beautifying Shropshire's Churches', *The Salopian Recorder*, 74 (2012), pp. 2-4.

Worton, J., 'Ludlow's Trained Band: A Study of Militiamen in Early Stuart England', *Journal of the Society for Army Historical Research*, 99 (2013), pp. 4-23.

Worton, J., '"The Strongest Works in England"? The Defences of Shrewsbury During the Civil Wars, 1642-1651', *Transactions of the Shropshire Archaeological and Historical Society*, LXXXVII (2012, issued in 2014), pp. 95-112.

Theses

Hayman, R., 'The Shropshire Wrought-Iron Industry, c. 1600-1900' (PhD, University of Birmingham, 2003).

Wanklyn, M., 'Landed Society & Allegiance in Cheshire and Shropshire in the First Civil War' (PhD, University of Manchester, 1976).

Index

Index of Persons

Index of General Subjects

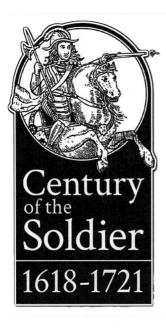

The Century of the Soldier series – Warfare c 1618-1721

www.helion.co.uk/centuryofthesoldier
https://www.facebook.com/pages/Century-of-the-
      Soldier-1618-1721/1537642189825966

'This is the Century of the Soldier', Falvio Testir, Poet, 1641

The 'Century of the Soldier' series will cover the period of military history c. 1618–1721, the 'golden era' of Pike and Shot warfare. This time frame has been seen by many historians as a period of not only great social change, but of fundamental developments within military matters. This is the period of the 'military revolution', the development of standing armies, the widespread introduction of black powder weapons and a greater professionalism within the culture of military personnel.

The series will examine the period in a greater degree of detail than has hitherto been attempted, and has a very wide brief, with the intention of covering all aspects of the period from the battles, campaigns, logistics and tactics, to the personalities, armies, uniforms and equipment.

Submissions

The publishers would be pleased to receive submissions for this series. Please contact us via email (info@helion.co.uk), or in writing to Helion & Company Limited, 26 Willow Road, Solihull, West Midlands, B91 1UE.

Titles

No 1   *'Famous by my Sword'. The Army of Montrose and the Military Revolution*
        Charles Singleton (ISBN 978-1-909384-97-2)*

No 2   *Marlborough's Other Army. The British Army and the Campaigns of the First Peninsular War,*
        1702–1712 Nick Dorrell (ISBN 978-1-910294-63-5)

No 3   *Cavalier Capital. Oxford in the English Civil War 1642–1646*
        John Barratt (ISBN 978-1-910294-58-1)

No 4   *Reconstructing the New Model Army Volume 1: Regimental Lists April 1645 to May 1649*
        Malcolm Wanklyn (ISBN 978-1-910777-10-7)*

No 5   *To Settle the Crown. Waging Civil War in Shropshire 1642-1648*
        Jonathan Worton (ISBN 978-1-910777-98-5)

Books within the series are published in two formats: 'Falconets' are paperbacks, page size 248mm x 180mm, with high visual content including colour plates; 'Culverins' are hardback monographs, page size 234mm x 156mm. Books marked with * in the list above are Falconets, all others are Culverins